In the Shade of Spring Leaves

Portrait of Ichiyō by Kaburagi Kiyokata

IN THE SHADE
OF SPRING LEAVES

The Life and Writings of Higuchi Ichiyō,
A Woman of Letters in Meiji Japan

Robert Lyons Danly

NEW HAVEN AND LONDON
YALE UNIVERSITY PRESS

For Edwin and Rachel McClellan

The ornament used throughout this book
is a variation of the quince pattern
adopted as the Higuchi family crest.

Published with assistance from the foundation
established in memory of Philip Hamilton McMillan
of the Class of 1894, Yale College.

Designed by Nancy Ovedovitz and set in Zapf International type.

Printed in the United States of America by The Vail-Ballou Press, Binghamton, N.Y.

Library of Congress Cataloging in Publication Data

Danly, Robert Lyons, 1947–
   In the shade of spring leaves.

   Bibliography: p.
   Includes index.
   1. Higuchi, Ichiyō, 1872–1896. 2. Authors,
Japanese—Biography. 3. Higuchi, Ichiyō, 1872–1896
—Translations, English. I. Higuchi, Ichiyō, 1872–
1896. Selections. English. 1981. II. Title.
PL808.I4Z63   895.6′34 [B]   81-50434
ISBN 0-300-02614-5   AACR2

10   9   8   7   6   5   4   3   2   1

Contents

Illustrations

Preface

The literary histories inevitably describe her as a shooting star who appeared out of nowhere and in four short years left behind a trail of works bordering on genius. This is Higuchi Ichiyō's story: where she came from, where she went in her brief life. It is a life that in its vicissitudes has become something of a symbol to the Japanese—of the old Buddhist belief in the vanity of all things, of the precariousness involved in passing from one age into another.

Ichiyō joined that wistful pantheon of heroes who do not wear their honors out. As if according to some uncanny presentiment, she documented her short, bittersweet life in an exquisite diary, and then at just the right moment died a death befitting one of the melancholy heroines she herself created, thereby gaining a hold on the popular Japanese imagination for almost one hundred years now. In Tokyo in the mid-1970s, her diary was read aloud every morning on the radio. All of her best-known short stories have been made into successful motion pictures. In Higuchi Ichiyō, then, people have found what they went looking for: until recently she was the last woman of the old Japan; now she is modern Japan's first women's liberationist.

What she has always been is one of the first writers of consequence to appear in the Meiji period (1868–1912) and, with no serious contenders, Japan's first woman writer of stature in modern days. During Ichiyō's brief life, she wrote nearly four thousand classical poems, numerous discursive essays, twenty-one short stories, and a multivolumed diary that is hailed as the equivalent of a great, rambling, impressionistic autobiographical novel. The sheer amount of her writing is extraordinary, the more so for one plagued almost every day of her adult life by poverty and disappointment. But Ichiyō was a formidable figure, desperate to achieve and blessed with a talent equal to the task. Largely self-taught, she made herself into an accomplished classicist and then into a profound writer, who in her final work never forgot the essential thing about fiction: that one imagines a yarn as much to tell the truth as to tell a story.

In her day, this was not as obvious as it might sound. For two hundred years, Japanese literature had been largely in the grip of writers who were entertainers. Ichiyō loved the entertaining side of literature but she was attracted by the serious side as well. She stood at a crossroads, like one of her own characters: behind her, the playful writers of the Edo period (1615–1868) and the elegant, if now mannered, sensibilities of Heian (794–1185); ahead, the new, sometimes all-too-serious novels of psychological vivisection.

Somehow she managed to resolve the conflict between the two—style and insight cohabit Higuchi Ichiyō's fiction—and this book is the story of that resolution.

I have concentrated on the short stories and the diary, for the most part ignoring the poetry, which Japanese scholars consider a notch below first-rate. I have also rejected the view that the personal life of an author is irrelevant to a study of his or her final work, as if writings necessarily form a closed system. It does not seem an ancillary undertaking to examine the experiences and preoccupations out of which great literature grows, especially when those experiences are themselves so literary. If any writer gave her life the shape and meaning of a work of art it was Ichiyō—this was a central purpose of the diaries. I have striven, then, for a literary biography, with due critical digression.

Ichiyō's life itself is a splendid story, richly documented in her diaries and the memoirs of her friends. To what degree these primary sources are stories themselves is another matter. I have relied on the painstaking research of Ichiyō experts in Japan as a corrective. The published sources are more than adequate in quantity and quality. The scholarship of Wada Yoshie and Shioda Ryōhei has been particularly helpful.

In a work like this every sentence could end with a footnote. I have tried to select the significant and telling details from a life that may have been short but was not uncomplicated; some five hundred people pass through the diaries, most without leaving a trace of an effect on Ichiyō's work. I have cited all direct quotations. Indirect quotations, attributed thoughts, facial quirks, turns in the weather, all come from reliable sources, and those that seemed to cry out loudly enough for annotation were given it. Inasmuch as the biography is narrated in a linear, organic fashion and relies so heavily on Ichiyō's journals, line-by-line attribution did not seem called for. All translated excerpts from the diary are cited, keyed to the latest edition of the complete works (referred to in the Notes as *Zenshū*, an abbreviation of the Japanese title), which, as of this writing, is in the final stages of publication by Chikuma Shobō, Tokyo.

In Part 2, I have chosen for translation nine of Ichiyō's most representative stories, all of which are discussed in the biography. Some of the early stories are included primarily to illustrate the first phases of Ichiyō's development; the later works speak for themselves. All are annotated, and, although the annotation required by Western readers is significantly different from that required by Japanese, I have relied a good deal on the spadework done by scholars in Japan, particularly Wada Yoshie. I have had to ferret out and explain things that Mr. Wada and others did not, and I have even uncovered an allusion or two that they missed, but my notes would be far scantier without the help of their meticulously annotated texts.

Several of these stories have been translated before, as noted in the Bibliography, but I have found only one distinguished version. Although it takes a few liberties, Edward Seidensticker's very moving translation of "Takekurabe" was my introduction to Ichiyō. After repeated readings, I can hardly claim that nothing of Mr. Seidensticker's language or conception of the work has crept into my own. Still, I wanted to attempt a new translation; without the keystone there was no reconstructing the literary house that Ichiyō built.

A few further preliminaries: Japanese names appear in the Japanese order, surname first. In the biography, ages are converted to the Western count. (According to Japanese reckoning, a person is one year old at birth and a year older every New Year.) In the stories, ages have been kept as in the originals. Japanese words are italicized only on their first appearance, where even those that are now common currency, like *samurai*, are explained in the text or in an endnote. Diacritical marks are used to indicate the long vowels in all words, proper names, and place-names except for Tokyo.

Finally, I owe special thanks to several people: to Edwin McClellan, Thomas J. Harper, and Hamako Itō Chaplin, my professors who helped and inspired me; to William White and Thomas McNamee, who read earlier drafts of my translations; to Anne Granger and Lillian Weitzler, who typed the first version of this book as a dissertation; to William F. Sibley and Robert Leutner, readers of the dissertation; and to Ellen Graham and Barbara Folsom, my editors at Yale University Press. Many people in Japan helped me obtain the illustrations for this book, and I would like to thank especially Ujitoko Mitsuko and the staff of the Museum of Modern Japanese Literature, Nakazato Mitsuo and the staff of the Higuchi Ichiyō Museum, Oketani Hideaki, Ōtori Shinkichi, Matsumoto Norihiko, Kimura Keiichi, Okamura Meikichi, Kadokawa Tsuguhiko, Sayama Tatsuo, Kimura Shigeru, Yamada Hajime, and Kudō Taeko. I would also like to thank the Graduate School of Yale University, whose generous support through Sumitomo and Yale Prize fellowships made my study of Higuchi Ichiyō possible, and the Center for Japanese Studies at the University of Michigan, whose grant underwrote the preparation of the index, which was compiled by Nancy Nakayama. In closing, for many happy and stimulating hours I would like to thank my colleagues and students in the Department of Far Eastern Languages and Literatures at the University of Michigan, most of all Robert H. Brower and Wayne P. Lammers.

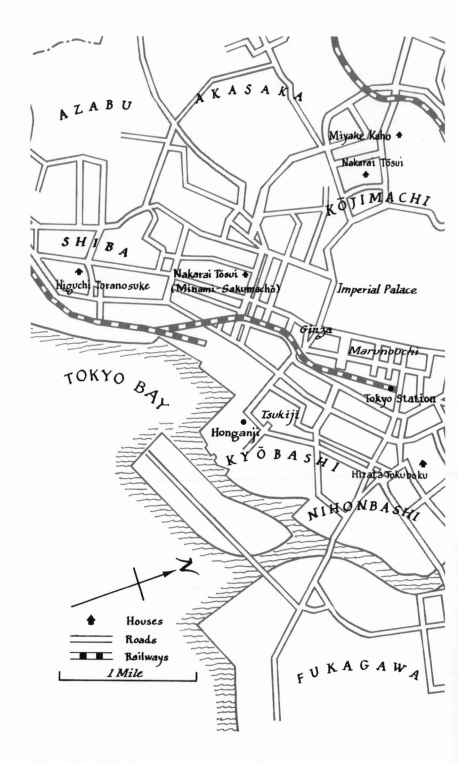

Tokyo in the 1890s. Ward names are in capital letters.

USHIGOME

KOISHIKAWA

Tanaka Minoko
Itō Natsuko
Haginoya
Nishimura Sennosuke
Denzūin
Tanaka Minoko
Nakarai Tōsui
Kudan
Ichiyō (Maruyama-Fukuyama)
Hitotsubashi
Kusaka Yoshitaka
Ichiyō (Kikuzaka)
Nakarai Tōsui's Tea Shop
HONGŌ
Ochanomizu
Mori Ōgai
Itō Natsuko
Tokyo University
KANDA
Surugadai
Shinobazu Pond
Tanaka Minoko
Ichiyō (Awajichō)
SHITAYA
Ueno Library

ASAKUSA

Mishima Shrine
Senzoku Shrine
Daion Temple
Ichiyō (Ryūsenji)
Yoshiwara

SUMIDA

RIVER

HONJO

See following page for enlargement of inset.

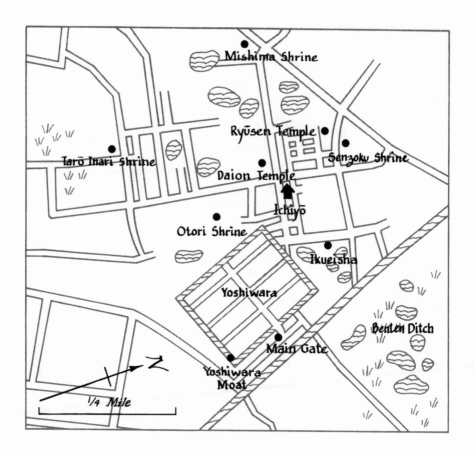

Ryūsenji and the Yoshiwara

PART ONE
A BRIEF LIFE

1
The Family

Higuchi Ichiyō was born in the spring of 1872 and she died in the autumn twenty-four years later. It was a world of impermanence she was entering, as she herself, in other contexts, had frequent occasion to say. Even the date of her birth would soon change. Within half a year's time the old lunar calendar derived from China was replaced by the Gregorian calendar as part of the Westernization movement that swept Japan in the early years of the Meiji Restoration. By the new European reckoning, the child had been born on the second of May 1872 at eight o'clock in the morning. Her name was different then too. Ichiyō was her pen name; she came into the world as Natsuko, the second daughter and fourth child of a minor official in the new Tokyo municipal government.

Her parents had come to the city from farming families in nearby Kai Province, or Yamanashi Prefecture, in 1857, ten years before the Restoration. Her father, Noriyoshi,[1] was the son of a moderately prosperous and scholarly peasant in the town of Nakahagiwara, Higuchi Hachizaemon,[2] who farmed in fair weather and studied in foul. Hachizaemon had managed to accumulate just under one hectare of land and to take a surname, Higuchi, although technically these were not privileges that the Tokugawa authorities accorded the peasantry. Through the local religious records of Nakahagiwara and documents concerning water rights, Hachizaemon's family can be traced back to 1707. It is thought that his ancestors may have been members of the military class who had fallen on hard times and moved into the area from neighboring Shinano Province, but this has not been substantiated. In any case, whether or not the family had slipped from the respectable ranks of the *samurai*, or the military gentry, by the time Hachizaemon's first son Noriyoshi was born in 1830, the Higuchi house enjoyed the modest comforts of a solid and educated rural life.

In fact, Hachizaemon's learning had elevated him to a position of some influence within the village, first as an amanuensis for the other farmers and later as their spokesman in disputes with the authorities. Hachizaemon was the kind of scholarly man of taste that one forgets it was possible to find beyond the circles of the samurai and the city-dwelling sophisticates of the merchant class. He was an adept composer of Chinese poetry and comic

3

linked verse, in addition to a type of popular song known as *chobokure*, and he was also respected for his attainments as a Sunday painter.

If Hachizaemon's seemed like the life of a gentleman farmer, the operative word was still *farmer* as far as young Noriyoshi was concerned. When the boy was only six, one of his father's closest friends, Mashimo Sennosuke, bought himself the rank of a samurai in Edo, the military capital that was to become Tokyo in 1868, and the event captured little Noriyoshi's imagination. In fact, Mashimo's success would long exert a powerful influence over Noriyoshi. After frequent trips back and forth between his hometown and the capital, Mashimo had settled in Edo in 1828 at the age of twenty-nine, by which time he had already turned away from farming and had failed in an effort to operate a pawnshop. In Edo he affiliated himself with a *hatamoto*[3] family by the name of Kohara, whom he served as an attendant. From there he worked his way up through a series of lowly posts within the bureaucracy, inching his way toward the day when his savings would enable him to obliterate the last line of demarcation between himself and the samurai status that he was already gradually attaining in all but name.

There were, in other words, certain clerkships within the government for which men of plebeian stock were eligible.[4] With the proper literacy, which Mashimo had acquired as a youth at his temple school, a man who was not of the samurai class could gain a toehold within the bureaucracy. And if he were willing to save assiduously and to bide his time, he could hope that the chance might come his way to purchase pro forma adoption into an impoverished samurai household. This is precisely what Mashimo Sennosuke did, and it was not unrealistic for young Noriyoshi, back in the provinces, to dream of following in the footsteps of his father's friend. He had the same background as Mashimo, including the same educational opportunities and even the same teacher. In later life Noriyoshi described his boyhood aspirations: "I did not want to be a farmer when I grew up. I poured my whole heart into reading the Chinese classics, and I studied with Zeshō [who had also taught his father Hachizaemon and the successful Mashimo Sennosuke] at the Hōshōji, the Jōdo Shinshū temple in my village."[5]

By the time he was twenty-one, Noriyoshi had convinced himself that he would have to seek his fortune in the capital. It was not simply a matter of aversion to his father's calling. Hachizaemon's efforts on behalf of his fellow farmers had finally brought him into conflict with the authorities. The future of the Higuchi family in the Nakahagiwara area seemed less than promising. In September 1853, speaking for twenty farming families from the neighborhood, Hachizaemon had petitioned the authorities in Edo concerning what he and the others regarded as an unfair ruling by the local courts in a dispute over water rights. He had first submitted his petition to the local authorities in August. For his insolence, Hachizaemon and his three companions were clapped in irons, but the experience failed to chasten them. Upon release they headed for Edo rather than home and presented their case to the domainal representatives on 7 September. They were again detained and questioned. But in the end they were not charged with any crime, which in itself was something of a victory for Hachizaemon, who appears to have become a local hero upon his return to the province. The authorities in Nakahagiwara, however, took a different view. By them he was considered a carper—or worse, an agitator—and they kept him at a distance. This was a blow to a man who had enjoyed considerable access to the local powers ever since the days, twenty years before, when his friend Mashimo Sennosuke had been on the scene as a clerk in the magistrate's office. Now Hachizaemon's position became more and more isolated. All he could hope to pass on to his ambitious eldest son were a few modest plots of land and the arduous life of a peasant.

Noriyoshi had his father's learning, but he also had a restlessness that would not permit him the solace in scholarship that his father had always found. He was a quiet enough young man, and yet he liked to take to the stage in the local productions—an enthusiasm, if not a talent, that won him the nickname of one of the characters in *Chūshingura*[6]—and he was popular with the girls of the village. It was on his way to school one day that he had met his future wife, whose bamboo grove served as a shortcut to the temple school, and whose pregnancy before they could marry hastened Noriyoshi's long-contemplated departure for the military capital. He was by this time twenty-six, and his bride-to-be, Furuya Ayame, was either twenty-one or twenty-three, depending on the document. Although she was from the same circumstances as Noriyoshi, it appears that Ayame's parents were opposed to the match; if this is true, it was probably the result of Hachizaemon's loss of influence following the Edo petition. Like thwarted lovers in fiction, on 6 April 1857 the two abandoned their birthplace for love and marriage and the dream of city lights.

Six days later, traveling slowly because of Ayame's condition, they arrived in the shōgun's capital. As they rested for a moment at the last stop on the post road, the Tōkaidō, where the suburb of Shinagawa merged into the city, already they could feel the presence of a great metropolis. Stalls of booksellers lined the streets and competed with tobacco shops and armorers and purveyors of ready-made clothes. Jugglers appeared, and sword-swallowing magicians. A storyteller attracted an audience in front of a shop advertising "long-life pills." Travelers from afar gathered in the row of teahouses perched above the bay. From there the roads were even more congested. Inside the city, pedestrians and porters, shoppers and merchants, palanquins and officers on horseback all jostled in contending currents.

When they came to higher ground, they could see beyond the low-lying commercial districts. Before them, Edo sprawled for twenty miles and gave ample suggestion of its several million inhabitants. The shōgun's castle, with its triple ring of moats, sat like a crown atop a range of hills in the center of the city. The mansions and barracks of the privileged military class girded the ramparts and broad moats of the castle and stretched over the wooded slopes to the south and the west. These residences of the feudal barons were themselves impressive establishments, with their massive, imposing gateways flanked by outbuildings for a quarter-mile on either side. Here and there was a tea-garden—a haze of pink, its cherry trees just now in full bloom—amid the dense mass of houses and the lush growth of cypress and cryptomeria that blanketed the hills around the fortress. Below, from the new batteries along the bay, came the frequent sound of gunfire, another round of artillery practice, for no one wanted any more surprises from the foreign powers. Below also, to the north and east of the castle, spilled the *shitamachi*, the commercial valleys that were known as "the downtown." These were the stamping grounds of the spirited, self-reliant sons of Edo, the *Edokko:* hard-working artisans and merchants, lively entertainers and bons vivants. Indifferent to the solemn, majestic air of the shōgun's retainers with their ceremonial costumes and their grand estates, downtown the Edokko set another tone for the city.

It was on the aristocratic highlands, however, that Noriyoshi fixed his gaze. Over there, on the hilltop, he would hitch his wagon to the falling star of shogunal fortunes. He had sold his beloved books, 150 of them, to finance the trip and to help tide them over the early days in Edo. Worried about money and the impending responsibilities of fatherhood, Noriyoshi lost no time in visiting the man who had inspired him. He found Mashimo Sennosuke basking in success near the height of his career. The previous year Mashimo had been appointed to an important post in the newly formed Bansho-shirabesho, "Office for Examining Barbarian Writings," a school and research bureau that the government had established in Ogawamachi in 1855, following the visitation of Commodore Perry, for the study and translation of diplomatic documents and other Western writings. At first the school was open only to the sons of hatamoto, but later sons of all retainers were eligible to apply. The Bansho-shirabesho offered courses in Dutch studies and commerce as well as in English, French, German, and Russian. (After the Meiji Restoration, it would undergo several transformations before becoming part of Tokyo University.) Mashimo was now a busy man. There were his administrative duties at school; there were his poetastering and calligraphy (for which he had taken the literary-sounding name of Bansū, "mustard plant at eventide"); and there were his gatherings with celebrated scholars of Chinese studies, with one of whom he was also coediting a book. He could always use an errand boy, and he took Noriyoshi on as his attendant and messenger. Noriyoshi and Ayame were to live in Mashimo's official residence in Kudan, there to work in exchange for room and board.

Through Mashimo's good offices, it was also arranged that Noriyoshi become apprenticed to a doctor by the name of Kitamura Yasumasa, who was publishing a series of medical books and found himself in need of assistance. It was soon agreed that Noriyoshi should find a house closer to the doctor's residence in Koishikawa; and so, only a few days after their arrival in the city, Noriyoshi and Ayame left Mashimo's establishment, although Noriyoshi continued to run errands for Mashimo in his spare time.

Mashimo was equally solicitous of Ayame. He saw to it that the young bride was properly established in her new home. He sent baby clothes when her daughter Fuji, named for Mashimo's wife, was born on 14 May. And he arranged for Ayame to serve as a wet nurse once she had recuperated from the birth. On 24 June, Ayame left Noriyoshi and the newborn Fuji in Koishikawa for the time being and went off to the Yushima estate of Inaba Daizen, a hatamoto whose daughter, Kō, Ayame was to nurse. It was while Ayame was living in the Inaba compound that she began to call herself Taki, the name that her own children were to know her by. And it was here, in the house of one of the shōgun's personal retainers (albeit a house with a modest 2,500 *koku*),[7] that Taki formulated her ideas about how the well-bred lived, and how, when her own family attained a certain respectability, they would comport themselves.

But there were hard years ahead of them before that respectability would come. For the moment the situation was far from ideal. Because she was living vicariously through her betters, like a Heian woman from the provinces who suddenly found herself in the world of the court, Taki was constantly reminded of her inferior position. When nursing the Inaba child, deference required her to place a piece of tissue over her mouth lest she breathe on "the little princess." She paid for the privilege of serving the exalted child by being forced to put her own baby out to nurse and to endure long absences from her new husband. Noriyoshi eventually closed up the house they had rented, their first house together, and returned to Mashimo's official residence in Kudan. In this way he could economize and commute to Dr. Kitamura's house in Koishikawa. It was a lonely life for him, but he kept busy doing odd jobs for Mashimo when he was free, and he knew that he had the future ahead of him.

As a result of his earnestness, Noriyoshi soon graduated from his position as Mashimo's personal porter to that of custodian at the Bansho-shirabesho. The atmosphere of the school exhilarated the young man. The halls bustled with instructors who knew foreign languages and read Western books and who could discourse on faraway lands. He was surrounded by a learning altogether unlike any he had hitherto known. Noriyoshi's enthusiasm must have appealed to the scholars; one man helped him learn a little Dutch and another gave him several books and a dictionary. And then there were strange novelties to intrigue him, devices locked away in the storehouse of the school: a steam engine and a gadget called a telegraph. These gifts from the United States had been turned over to the Bansho-shirabesho for examination and safekeeping; and now, with the imminent visit of Townsend Harris from Shimoda in December 1857, they were brought out and dusted off and stared at by one and all in a desperate attempt to figure out how the contraptions really worked, for the officials were determined not to let the United States consul think that these were objects of anything less than the utmost utility and veneration. From his descriptions of the telegraph in his diary, it is obvious that neither Noriyoshi nor his superiors had understood how the telegraph functioned. (This is curious on two counts: by this time the Dutch were teaching the Japanese how to operate a telegraph at Nagasaki; furthermore, in their misunderstanding of what the telegraph could do, Noriyoshi and the others had apparently anticipated the telephone, which was not invented for another decade.)

The coming visit of the American dignitary kept Noriyoshi busier than ever. The Bansho-shirabesho was to receive Harris when he arrived in Edo and to translate the treaty that he was bringing with him. The reception rooms had to be remodeled for the meeting. Something had to be done about cleaning and repairing the American gifts for proper display. And it fell to Noriyoshi, among all his other chores, to learn how to prepare soft-boiled eggs for the foreign visitor.

For all the excitement of the Bansho-shirabesho, Noriyoshi did not stay long at his post there. The following year, 1858, he formed the first of several affiliations with samurai employers that would take him to various parts of Japan. From the summer of 1858 to the summer of 1859, he accompanied Tanabe Tarō, an official of constabulary rank, on his tour of duty at Ōsaka Castle. After his return to Edo, Noriyoshi went to work for a man by the name of Kikuchi Daisuke, who was head of the shogunate's accounting bureau. He was employed by Kikuchi as a page of middle rank and earned the most money he had seen yet, four *ryō* per year.[8] Noriyoshi accompanied Kikuchi whenever he made one of his inspection tours for the accounting bureau—to Ise or Mino, for example—to review riparian and other public works on which the government was spending its money.

Not until 1863 were Noriyoshi and his wife Taki finally able to live together as a family. By this time Kikuchi Daisuke had been reassigned to a position in the Office of Foreign Affairs and Noriyoshi's life had become more sedentary. In April 1864 their second child and first son, Sentarō, was born. In March of the following year, Noriyoshi, never a malingerer, received yet another stimulus to hurry on his way to a rank that would count in society. His best friend and fellow *arriviste* from Kai Province, Ueno Heizō, had just purchased a place in the house of a samurai.

For the first time, one wonders if Noriyoshi's vision of himself as a dynamic man was entirely accurate. In less time than he had already spent in Edo, his friend had achieved the goal Noriyoshi was still dreaming of. It was to take him two more years to find the same opportunity. Noriyoshi's timing was emblematic of the haplessness that would plague the family throughout Higuchi Ichiyō's life. Having scrimped and saved for ten years, and having seen his wife farmed out as a wet nurse, Noriyoshi was finally able to purchase the rank of *jikisan*, or direct retainer of the shogunate, from a subordinate in the office of the Minami-machibugyō, the south magistracy. But the long-awaited day came in May 1867. He was buying into an order that had less than a year's life in it. No sooner were the convoluted maneuverings for the purchase finished than the rank was too.

Once more it was through the intercession of Mashimo Sennosuke, Noriyoshi's old patron and hero, that the dealings were consummated. Noriyoshi left the employ of the Kikuchi family in March 1867 in order to assume the position he was acquiring along with samurai status. For some reason, however, Noriyoshi's application for adoption into the family of Asai Takezō, a constable in Hatchōbori and a minor official in the Minami-machibugyō, was refused by the authorities on its first submission. They gave as their reason the fact that Noriyoshi was not himself of jikisan rank and therefore could not be adopted by the Asai family. Mashimo Sennosuke then came up with an ingenious stratagem. As it happened, Mashimo had previously had Noriyoshi pose as the brother of his friend Ueno Heizō when Ueno was applying for his adoption into a samurai family two years before. (It was thought that Noriyoshi's affiliation with the distinguished Kikuchi family might be helpful to his friend.) Now, according to Mashimo's plan, all Noriyoshi had to do was continue the pose. Being the brother of a samurai with the rank of direct retainer, Mashimo reasoned, was close enough to having the rank oneself. To sweeten the picture, the previous year, 1866, Ueno Heizō, who had no heir, had temporarily adopted Noriyoshi's son Sentarō before being sent on one of the shogunate's punitive expeditions against rebellious samurai in the southern domains. This made Noriyoshi's own son technically a samurai. Therefore, two members of the military aristocracy who were closely related to Noriyoshi, his putative brother Ueno Heizō and his "former" son Sentarō, could request to have Noriyoshi adopted into the Asai house. To complicate the situation further, for the moment Noriyoshi took the name of his son, whose own name had been changed to Tamenosuke, and Tamenosuke reverted to his original name, Sentarō.

Whether the authorities were by this time thoroughly confused or simply satisfied that the appropriate formalities had been observed, Mashimo's scheme worked, and the second petition for adoption was approved in May.

Noriyoshi had now to tender a hundred ryō in gold, half of which was payable to Asai in advance. He had also to agree to look after Asai's mother with due filial zeal and to assume Asai's debts of three hundred and eighty-odd ryō. It is likely, however, that these last two conditions were purely a matter of form. In return, the gates parted for Noriyoshi and, with a tidy stipend of fifteen koku, he left behind him—forever, he thought—the vicissitudes of life outside the system.

2
The Prodigy

In the early years of the Meiji Restoration, when the feudal order of the Tokugawa shogunate was overthrown and the young Emperor Meiji took up residence in Edo as the figurehead of "culture" and "enlightenment," Noriyoshi did not fare badly. He was able to convert his samurai status into a post in the newly formed Tokyo municipal government. Although he was only a junior official, the bureaucracy had yet to burgeon, and his position as a clerk in the department of records was rather enviable in a time of uncertainty. Noriyoshi had been low enough in the feudal scheme of things that it was a simple matter for him to transfer his loyalties. The new government proved to be satisfying his ambitions quite as well as its predecessor. He did not have the problem of samurai of greater stature—men like Mashimo Sennosuke, who himself had once been a parvenu but a much more successful one. As one of the heads of the Bansho-shirabesho and a loyal supporter of the shōgun, Mashimo saw his career brought up short by the Restoration. For him, life came full circle; he returned to the peasantry and resumed his original family name. Mashimo chose to live out his days in virtual seclusion in Yokohama, where he opened a small school to teach the Chinese classics and went by his literary sobriquet, Bansū. To his protégé, the old calligrapher was a man the times had passed by.

Noriyoshi, on the other hand, had plans for how to exploit the opportunities of the new age. All the while he was moving through a fairly rapid succession of assignments in the municipal bureaucracy, Noriyoshi was once again saving his money. In 1873 he began dabbling in real estate. This proved profitable, and he extended his activities to moneylending. This too proved profitable, and he began to dream of still wider horizons.

As fortune seemed to fill out nicely for Noriyoshi, so did his family. A second son, Toranosuke, had been born in 1866. A third was born in 1869 but died soon afterward. Then Natsuko was born in 1872, and the precociousness of this second daughter soon swept away the cloud of melancholy that had hung over the family since the death of the last baby. Two years later Kuniko, the third daughter and youngest child, was born.

Clearly it was Natsuko who was the apple of her father's eye. So much deference was paid to the child that visitors to the Higuchi house were a little startled. The indulgence of the eldest son, Sentarō, would not have been unusual. But in the Confucian order of things, Natsuko was a mere daughter, and the middle daughter at that. Nonetheless, she was swathed in the warmth of good clothes and paternal affection. Relatives remembered her as being better dressed and attended to than her younger sister. As might be expected, she grew into a haughty little girl, quick to learn and quick to recognize her own worth. Noriyoshi taught her his favorite poems from the classics and she would recite them, to lavish praise, whenever there was company. At age seven, when her father's eyes had begun to bother him, Natsuko was already proficient enough to read the newspaper aloud to him. The story is told by one of Ichiyō's students that by this age she was able in three days to polish off all of *Hakkenden*, 106 volumes that had taken Bakin twenty-seven years to write. The story is pure hagiography, but it contains an element of truth.[1] Natsuko was such an avid reader that she was often forced to sneak off to the family storehouse with her *kana zōshi*, her storybooks, in order to escape her mother's reproof. Unfortunately, the bad light in the storehouse did nothing to improve the child's poor eyesight. By the time she started school she wore reading glasses and still she had to hold her book close to her face. She could read amid any number of distractions (as long as her mother's nagging wasn't one of them), and she could read very fast. Once her cousin asked her if all the talking going on around her didn't bother her.

"Not at all," Natsuko replied, flipping the pages of her book and never looking up.

"But how do you read so fast?"

"I read three lines at a time."

Her other standard answer was that she had two eyes, so she could read two lines at once, naturally.[2]

In her diary, the adult Ichiyō recalls the bookworm years of her childhood. To some degree the artist's brush has done its retouching, but the self-portrait yields a believable picture of a child who early on developed a true devotion to the written word, a child more resolute than most:

> From the time that I was six, I used to love storybooks. Games of ball and shuttlecock didn't interest me. All I wanted was to read, and what I loved to read most were stories of the great and the valorous. Heroic exploits, full of honor and virtue, had quite an effect on me. I was spellbound by anything brave or spectacular. By the time I was eight, I knew that I couldn't bear to go through life being ordinary. It was all I thought about: somehow I had to stand out. In those days I had no eyes for the real world around me. I was walking on clouds, I was reaching for the stars. Everyone who saw me admired how well-behaved I was and how quick I was to learn things. My father was very proud of me. I was the teacher's pet. But in my childish mind, there was no self-reflection. The world, it seemed, was not such a frightening place. I was

sure I could accomplish anything I wanted to, although I had no idea yet
what that was. All I knew was that I hated the pursuit of wealth. What
fools people made of themselves over money! As far as I was concerned,
gold and silver were no different from debris.[3]

Needless to say, Noriyoshi saw in this gifted child his own aptitude and
steely ambition. Physically they were frail people, he and Natsuko, with their
spindly shoulders and their fine, almost birdlike heads. Even as a child,
Natsuko had her papa's sad face. Others in the family were more robust, but
father and daughter had a vulnerable air about them, a slightly misleading
look of acquiescence. She was in fact nearsighted, yet Natsuko's little eyes
seemed to see far into the distance.

Her father had great expectations of her. From his own experience, he
knew that she was not as meek as her physical appearance might suggest. He
hoped that she would continue the scholarly tradition of her grandfather, a
tradition that he himself had relinquished for worldly success. And so he
gave a great deal of thought to Natsuko's formal education. Noriyoshi was a
curious blend of modern flexibility and conservative reluctance (a mixture
that would eventually undo him). He had little faith in the new public school
system, which was based on Western pedagogical standards. For Natsuko, he
decided, a private and more old-fashioned school would provide the proper
education. She was therefore withdrawn from Hongō Shōgakkō, one of the
government's model public schools, which she attended briefly at the age of
five, and enrolled in Yoshikawa Gakkō not far from their home in the Bunkyō
district. Her new school was a private establishment run by a former Buddhist priest, Yoshikawa Fuji, and very much in the spirit of the old temple
schools from which it had evolved. The emphasis was on writing and arithmetic, the essential skills for children of merchants and artisans who made
up the majority of the enrollment. It offered a less rigid education than the
public schools; talented children were allowed to skip grades and were less
subject to the grand plans of the central government. As might be expected,
these little private schools tended to foster greater individuality.

When the Higuchi family moved from Hongō to Shitaya in the fall of 1881,
Natsuko was transferred to Seikai Gakkō, another private school from the
same mold, where classes were taught by the owner, Yamamoto Seigi, and
his wife and daughter. The curriculum was divided into upper and lower
levels, each lasting four years. The course of study for the lower four years
consisted of spelling, vocabulary, grammar, penmanship, letter-writing,
reading, arithmetic, anatomy, hygiene, and geography. Upper level courses
were offered in history, geometry, chemistry, physiology, drawing, and
natural history. Though not listed on the syllabus, poetry was part and parcel
of this traditional education. The head of the school was a poetry-loving man.
Every day Yamamoto would read to his students from the imperial poetic

anthologies. It was here, under his influence, that Natsuko wrote her first poem, on the power of the brush:

Hosokeredo	Slender, and yet
Hito no tsue to mo	To some they form a veritable staff,
Hashira to mo	A pillar of support:
Omowarenikeri	The bristles on the tip
Fude no inochige.	Of the writing brush.[4]

It was a prophetic piece, for writing was to become the solace and support of Natsuko's adult life.

Her mother Taki, unfortunately, had less foresight than Natsuko. For her own benighted reasons, she insisted that the book learning had gone too far. In December 1883, after only three years at Seikai Gakkō, and having just completed the first year of the upper level, Natsuko was withdrawn from school. She was eleven years old and she was heartbroken. Years later she recalled the event in her diary.

> When I was eleven, I stopped going to school. According to Mother's opinion, it did not do a girl's future any good to spend too long in the classroom. She wanted me to learn how to sew and how to run a household. Papa did not agree with her at all. "Let her study a little longer," he would say to Mother, and this would provoke an argument. Then they would ask me what *I* wanted to do. But I was born so timid and mealy-mouthed that I couldn't tell them. And so I stopped going to school. I would rather have died, of course. I felt so miserable. Things were the same until I was fourteen. I took sewing lessons and helped out around the house, and, somehow, the time went by. Every night, I worked at my desk. Papa bought me collections of poetry and some of the other classics, for he was determined to help me overcome these obstacles thrust in the way of my education.[5]

Taki had several motives for taking her daughter out of school. There were the obvious ones: she herself was unlettered and for her learning held no magic. She was a less complicated person than her husband. In Noriyoshi, the pull of the old and the new were frequently at war; in Taki there was no such tension. She adhered to beliefs dating from tenth-century Heian times (though by no means unusual in her day) that too much learning did not become a lady. She was a peasant woman whose limited experience with the upper class, as a nursemaid for the Inaba family, had reinforced her rigid and naive understanding of what was proper to one's station. For a woman, household affairs and the feminine accomplishments were what mattered. Like the tea ceremony or flower-arranging, the ability to write poetry was a mere accouterment, although perhaps a necessary one if a young woman wanted to marry well. But, then, Natsuko already knew her poetry, Taki reasoned.

There were other complicating factors. Whether from parental neglect in favor of the brightest child of the family or from some unfortunate karma, Natsuko's older siblings had not fared as well as she. Eldest daughter Fuji was on her second stormy marriage. And second son Toranosuke, a ne'er-do-well who ran with bad company, had taken to pawning the family possessions. It came to such a pass that he was finally apprenticed to a potter in Shiba and virtually disowned. In the meantime Sentarō, the eldest son, upon whom the future would depend, had developed consumption. As his condition deteriorated, it brought Natsuko's situation into sharper relief. When Sentarō was forced to withdraw from school in August 1883, Taki felt it was only right that the education of his younger sister should also be discontinued. She seemed to have all the arguments on her side. Sentarō's convalescence was beginning to put a strain on the family finances. This was no time to be raising a mannish daughter whose intellectual prowess would scare off future husbands. If Natsuko didn't get herself into the kitchen, not only would it be unseemly, it could prove improvident.

Finally, when Natsuko was fourteen, an *entente cordiale* was reached between her parents. Taki agreed with her husband that Natsuko should be allowed to engage in the formal study of poetry. Through friends, Noriyoshi found what was by consensus the best of the poetic conservatories, a school in Koishikawa run by the poetess Nakajima Utako. On 20 August 1886, Natsuko entered the Haginoya, the "Bush-Clover Cabin." The school soon became for her the nourishment she needed for her classical knowledge and her literary talents to grow, the nucleus around which the unstable elements of her later life would frequently regroup themselves.

Her new teacher, Nakajima Utako, belonged to the conservative traditions of the Keien school of court poetry, which was founded in the late Edo period by Kagawa Kageki (1768–1843) and invoked the Heian poet Ki no Tsurayuki as its ideal. Utako, who was considered one of the best women poets of the day,[6] offered her students an impressive grounding in the classics of Japanese literature. In addition to the weekly poetry lessons, which were held in groups of five or six students (and which were sometimes taught by one of Nakajima Utako's assistants), lectures were given on the *Kokinshū* (Collection of Ancient and Modern Times, ca. 905), *Ise Monogatari* (Tales of Ise, ca. 945), *Genji Monogatari* (The Tale of Genji, ca. 1000), and so forth. There was also a monthly meeting, the *tsukinamikai*, where various kinds of poetry competitions were held and to which all active and recent members were invited. One of these gatherings might number forty or fifty persons.

Predictably, for a milieu that looked back to the courtly past, with its elegant poetry fests and its outings to view the early blooms of the plum and the cherry, the Haginoya catered to the daughters of the upper class. Some, like the Ogasawaras, were members of old aristocratic or feudal families. Others were the daughters of successful businessmen or influential government officials. For most of them the Haginoya was a finishing school. They tended not to take their literature as seriously as Natsuko, but they had a polish that she lacked, and for the first time she felt poor.

Soon after entering Utako's circle, Natsuko began keeping the first of her diaries. In an entry the following February (1887), she describes her feelings of inferiority and apprehension as the first big poetry party at the Haginoya draws near.

The nineteenth of the month came. The poetry contest was now only a few days away, and everyone was excited. I was quite worried, though, as I did not know what to expect. I just listened to everyone else talking.

"So and so's going to wear long sleeves. She'd look good in a white collar and something with a wide hem."

"No, no," another girl said. "She ought to wear a white layered robe with patterned lining."

"And what colors for the linings?"

"A lavender and three beige I should think."

"No, not at all!" someone else interrupted. "A Korean pattern would be better—black figures on a white ground—and an underrobe of pink and plum. That's what would suit her."

On and on they went with their debates. It all depressed me, and I tried to think about the poems that I would write when the day of the party came.

"What about you?" someone was asking me.

I turned around. It was Sonoko.

"What are you going to wear?"

"I don't know," I mumbled. "When you're as clumsy as I am, even something bright looks dull. I guess I'll wear what I always do."

"Natsuko, if you wear a plain kimono, I will too."

I was so touched that I began to cry.

Pretty soon we did our poems for the day, and, surprisingly, I received a high mark. I left as soon as the poems were over.

I thought about it on the way home. It was all well and good to say that I would wear my everyday clothes, but everyone else would be in their finest kimonos, complete with family crests. I'd stick out like a sore thumb in front of all the fine ladies, and the thought of going to the party began to revolt me.

When I got home my parents were waiting for me and wanted to know how the lesson had gone.

"I've got something to show you," Mother said, taking a package out.

I stared at it. It was a sash of damask and a wilted-looking, hand-me-down silk kimono from Hachijōjima. Whose had these been, I wondered.

"Do you know what the other girls are going to wear?" Mother asked me.

I told her what everyone had said.

"Oh, that won't do! You'll be embarrassed, won't you? Going to a celebration like that in these things? You'd better give it up." There were tears in Mother's eyes.

"It's up to you, Natsu," Father said, but I could see the look of regret in his face at the thought that I might not be able to attend the party.

Conflicting thoughts ran through my head. How poor we were, how little I had to recommend me. And yet I owed it to my parents; they had placed their hopes in me. I made up my mind to go. I let down the hem of the kimono and ironed it and got things ready for the big day. All I could do was wait for it to come.

Then it was the twenty-first. Outwardly I looked composed, but inside I was trembling. I tried my best to calm myself as I dressed. At eleven, a rickshaw came from the neighborhood stand. The party was to be held at the Mankamerō Restaurant, at the top of the hill in Kudan. The others were already there when I arrived. "This way," someone said. I looked around at all of them. The patterns of their silk kimonos and the colors of their sashes were the most brilliant and exquisite that money could buy. But Sonoko was wearing a semiformal kimono of gray crepe with three crests, and with a pale lining, just as we had decided the other day.

I was so ashamed of how I looked, and yet I realized that I wouldn't have traded my hand-me-downs for all their damasks and brocades. In these old borrowed clothes of mine, suddenly I saw the very proof of how kind and generous my parents had been to me.

As soon as everyone was assembled, we went down the hill to the shop of a photographer by the name of Suzuki. Mrs. Nakajima went by rickshaw, as did Kameko, who had taken to wearing European clothes lately, along with shoes, which had hurt her feet. Passersby stopped and stared at the beautiful procession: Ayakōji Yaeko, Tanabe Tatsuko, Katayama Teruko, Arai Masako, the Ogasawaras, and the Nabeshima sisters. It was like a row of hothouse blooms moving down the hill.

Once the picture-taking was over, we walked back to the restaurant.

The guest who was to be the judge for the competition had already arrived and we were told that for the first round we would draw topics. We had what remained of the morning for making our selections. Some were unfortunate enough to draw from the miscellaneous category. There was much agonizing:

"I hope I draw the cherry trees."

"I want to write on plum blossoms."

"No, I want the willow trees."

I was the last to choose.

"What did you get?" someone asked me. "The moon? The cherry blossoms?"

All I could think of was what a hard time I was going to have writing a poem on any topic. "I don't know yet," I said as I opened the slip of paper: "the morning lark" it was to be.

There were quite a few, actually, who did not compose a poem. I, however, was runner-up for this first round.

In the next round, where we would vie for points, the topic for everyone was "willows in the moonlight." My hand was trembling as I put something down, but my parents must have been praying for me, the gods in heaven must have favored me, for the judge chose my poem over more than sixty others for the first prize![7] Yaeko was runner-up. Third place went to Miss Masanari, one of the instructors.

Tatsuko and Teruko poked me and grumbled, "How could we let a novice win?"

And Itō Natsuko chuckled, "Don't worry—when it's time for the clean copies to be made, mine will be the only poem that endures."

That afternoon I took my leave of the party before any of the others.[8]

When she was younger, Natsuko had struck people as no stranger to the art of putting on airs, even of downright impertinence. But the family fortunes, such as they were, had begun to slip just as adolescence took away some of her confidence. Nearsighted and unprepossessing, with her small stature, her plain clothes, and her thin hair, she knew that she could not compete with these coddled young ladies, except perhaps on literary turf.

From the very beginning Natsuko felt ambivalent about the Haginoya. She threw herself into her poetry lessons with the desperation of a reader too long deprived of her books. But each Saturday morning when she came to Koishikawa, she put her face up to a window onto another world. Despite her father's *shizoku*, or gentry, status as a former samurai and his new commercial aspirations, only in the most generous sense were the Higuchis even on the fringes of the upper class. Natsuko felt herself waver between pride in being the daughter of a samurai and envy of those who were really members of the aristocracy and the *haute bourgeoisie*. She yearned for the same elegance as her classmates, and yet it was not mere bravado on her part to write in her diary that, in the end, she wouldn't have traded her hand-me-downs for all their damasks and brocades.

In not very subtle ways Natsuko was reminded of her place. The other girls had the cheek to refer to her and two of her friends as "plebeians," the *heimin-gumi,* and to take it for granted that the three of them, who were too good-humored to complain, would serve the tea and cakes after the lessons. These spoiled rich girls must have struck Natsuko as unpleasant and conceited creatures, even as she wished she were one of them. It was not that she cared for their wealth. But they did represent a privileged situation and a grace, however insensitive, that was somehow identified with the classical tradition. What they lacked of Natsuko's literary talents they made up for with other trappings of the courtly esthetic, their fastidious emphasis on appearance and decorum, the wherewithal to indulge in brilliant costumes and elaborate ceremonials, and their sentimental stance, always susceptible to the pull of nostalgia and the beauty of the moment.

The Haginoya so emulated the gossamer world of the Heian romances, where breeding and taste and literary sense were all synonymous, that Natsuko soon imagined herself living in some latter-day court. Her girlish journal reads like a long-lost diary from the days of Prince Genji:

Last month, on the sixteenth of April, I believe it was, we were having our lesson; it was one of those spring days when the weather was perfect. After we had finished with two or three poems, Mrs. Nakajima suggested we go to see the cherries at the nearby Misono Garden. Who could tell when a storm would come up and scatter the blossoms in a single night? "Oh, yes, what a lovely idea," every one agreed, delighted, and off we went.

We decided to take a short cut through the temple grounds, thinking it would be quicker and more interesting. The path was very uncertain, however, and we made our way gingerly. So high was the grass that here and there we would come upon a gravestone hidden in the tangle: a most forlorn sight. All one saw was a thick growth of bamboo grass and small bamboo trees everywhere. It was nearly impossible to make one's way. Off in the distance, the haze of spring trailed lightly among the foothills. In the folds of the hills, in the fields closer by, children of the village gathered new greens. As we stood and watched, we had little hope of traversing the difficult terrain that barred us from this scene, a sight one could gaze at forever.

Mrs. Nakajima had gone on ahead, trying to find a path for us. I didn't want to be taken for a straggler, and I rushed after her. "What have we here?" she laughed as she saw me flying down the hill. "The Minamoto attacking at Ichinotani?"[9]

We came to a brook with a log bridge. I am not sure quite where we were, but it was all we could do to get across without falling. No doubt the ordinary person would have no trouble negotiating such obstacles. We cloistered maidens, however, were not as adept at these things.

When we finally reached the garden, I did not find it so extraordinary. Nor was our outing particularly elegant: everyone running about, picking a spray of blossoms here, breaking off a branch there, all rather disgusting. The garden was a planted park, after all, not a wood by the roadside. And it was women who were doing all this—not men, mind you. I stood to the side and did not enjoy watching.

"Let's be going now," Mrs. Nakajima said. "Which way shall we take this time?"

"Why don't we take the way we came?" I suggested. The others were of the same mind. Because we were used to it this time, I suppose, the path wasn't so perplexing. Along the way, the others compared their spoils. They were very pleased with these branches acquired so selfishly.

Then someone asked me why I hadn't taken any flowers. "Oh, I would feel too sorry for blossoms picked by the likes of me," I answered. And yet I did not want to be different from the others. I noticed a maple sprout growing inside a crevice in the rocks, where it would never get enough sunlight to survive. "This will be my souvenir," I told them as I picked it. "I'll take it home and plant it in my poor little garden."

"Well, the cherries weren't too bad today," Mrs. Nakajima commented, and then added, looking at everyone's trophies: "But my, how they do bring out the children in people."[10]

In the circle of the Haginoya, Natsuko may have fancied herself a cloistered maiden but she kept her wits about her. She knew she had one thing to recommend her: a control of the brush. She would be the learned and the literary one, the Sei Shōnagon to their Empress Sadakos.

There were, however, other talented girls, and many with better academic credentials. In the beginning some of them found Natsuko tedious. She would recite from memory long passages from the Chinese classics, quickly winning for herself a reputation as a show-off. In fact, she was merely trying to demonstrate to her classmates that she had the same ability as they. In her pride, for she never wanted to be ordinary, Natsuko may have gone too far; she was a young girl looking for acceptance. As she gained confidence, after the first major poetry competition, she began to wear her learning more lightly. She stopped vacillating between the two infuriating extremes of being painfully reticent one moment and an intellectual exhibitionist the next. She became more likable, and her fellow students began to appreciate her abilities and her wit. By this time her teachers clearly recognized her promise. Nakajima Utako encouraged her to be ambitious. Each week the students were assigned two topics on which to compose their poems for the next lesson; Natsuko was given three or four.

The year following Natsuko's enrollment in the Haginoya, 1887, saw the first signs that the secure little shell of prosperity Noriyoshi and Taki had struggled to provide for themselves might perhaps be all too porous. There had been earlier hints of this. The marriage of their eldest daughter Fuji had ended in failure; the oversexed appetite of her respectable husband, a doctor in the military, had driven her to seek a divorce. And their second son, Toranosuke, was a total disappointment. Before he was finally established in a cadet branch of the Higuchi house, the young man's peccadillos had carried with them into the family many a chilly current of discouragement. These were mere eddies in a stream, though, compared to the maelstroms of the next two and a half years.

In June 1887 the bureaucracy was reorganized, and Noriyoshi was "selected out," as they say, from his post in the Metropolitan Police Department. At fifty-seven, he had little hope of finding another position. His earnings plunged from a monthly salary of twenty-five yen, a height he had only recently attained, to a monthly stipend of eight yen thirty-three sen. As if by premonition, the previous year Noriyoshi had already divested himself of the last of his commercial real estate holdings, selling the houses that he rented out in Kyōbashi and Yushima. He now had the principal to live on, but little income.

The same month in which Noriyoshi was dismissed, Sentarō, the eldest son, entered the Ministry of Finance through the good offices of one of Noriyoshi's best friends from Edo days. Although Sentarō had been suffering from consumption for several years, he was enjoying a temporary remission. His new position in the prestigious ministry buoyed the family spirits. It proved only a brief respite, however, for by October Sentarō had entered his last decline. He took a leave of absence, but his condition continued to deteriorate so rapidly that he was forced to resign in November. By the end of December he was dead—twenty-three years old, a good son, a bright boy, the cornerstone of the family's future.

Disheartened, Noriyoshi sold the last bit of land he owned, with the family house in Shitaya, for a hundred and forty yen, and the following spring, in 1888, the Higuchis moved to Shiba, Toranosuke's part of Tokyo, where they rented a small house and attempted a reconciliation with their wayward and now sole-surviving son.

Noriyoshi never fully recovered from the blow of Sentarō's death. Overnight he began to age, and he became sickly. Living in an uneasy alliance with Toranosuke, and without a proper job to occupy his hours, Noriyoshi grew increasingly anxious and impatient. With his investments liquidated, his cash idle, and his hopes for his family's future dashed, Noriyoshi, restless as in youth but now a weaker man, was a ripe target for opportunists. Not long after the family moved to Shiba, certain men began to call on Natsuko's father. There was talk of starting a company. Noriyoshi seemed to rally. The old dreams returned, and one can hear him asking himself the same sorts of questions as the ambitious characters in his daughter's future fiction: "What kind of life was it, anyway, dangling like a gourd from a fence? Was he going to go through life afraid of getting scratched? What would he have to show for fifty years of that? Luck came when a person least expected it. One never knew when the gods would present one with an opportunity. Let the little sparrows squeak. . . . It was the eagle one admired, riding high on the wind, sweeping the clouds away."[11] He had overcome obstacles before, hadn't he? He had set himself a goal and he had achieved it. Why, even as a boy he had known that he was meant for bigger things than the rest of the village. He had pulled his family into the elite ranks of the military class. He had strad- dled two epochs. He was always in tune with the times, and the times called for daring: it was the age of the entrepreneur. Was one not forever hearing these days about the latest success in business? The Tokyo Electric Light Company, the Japan Railway Corporation, newfangled products like cement and glass and beer. The opportunities were there, waiting to be seized. It was only fitting that he try his hand at commerce. After all, everyone said the same thing now—in today's world, the way of the samurai was the way of the merchant. He owed it to his family, and to the nation.

Leaving the bureaucracy might yet prove to be a blessing in disguise. No more "being fettered by all kinds of regulations and restrictions . . . having one's life measured out, as if one lived within the boundaries of a map. Restricted by invisible lines. Following other people's orders. Always working according to instructions. Never achieving any success that might outlive one. When such a man died, who mourned him but a few acquaintances? Who observed the anniversary of his death but a few descendants? What was the difference between that and a dog's life? If one were going to dream, one ought to dream of paradise."[12]

The men who sought Noriyoshi out in Shiba came bearing, if not the plans for Elysium, a compelling idea for a new business venture. They proposed starting an intracity shipping agency consisting of several partners located in different sections of Tokyo. The catch was that they needed money. They supposedly had the know-how; Noriyoshi had the spare cash.

Through the summer of 1888 preparations for the founding of the Tokyo Cart Contracting Association lurched precipitously forward. By the end of June a license had been obtained for the new company and offices for its first headquarters had been located in Kanda. Not much is known about the partners in this undertaking. Tanabe Yūbei, who brought Noriyoshi into the group, is believed to have been from the vicinity of Noriyoshi's hometown in Kai Province, now Yamanashi Prefecture. The other two men, Yamamoto Kyūkichi and Takano Kenjirō, came from even more obscure backgrounds. One thing is certain, however. Their expertise could not have been as substantial as Noriyoshi was led to believe, for they were willing to begin operations with an initial capitalization of only four hundred yen.[13] One hundred yen of this amount was a loan from Noriyoshi, to be repaid in December, and it is quite possible that he provided much of the remaining three hundred yen, either in the form of loans or direct investment. How meager these resources were is demonstrated by the fact that around this same time the Central Overland Transport Company in Nihonbashi, restyling itself the Japan Transportation Company, Ltd., was recapitalized at five hundred thousand yen.[14]

Furthermore, the four would-be empire-builders did not bother to organize themselves along any of the rational Western lines that the government was promoting as the key to modern business success. (As with Noriyoshi's previous, and belated, great leap forward—from the peasantry into the lower levels of the rentier class—once again he had only partially grasped the essence of the age.) It is unlikely that any of the four gave serious attention to the literature available from the Ministry of Finance that was designed to encourage and to guide fledgling venture capitalists and to tout the advantages of the joint-stock principle of organization. Two of the ministry's pamphlets written by Shibusawa Eiichi, "A Description of Corporations" and "Rules for the Organization of Corporations," might have sobered Noriyoshi and his partners.

But they forged ahead, neither properly financed nor soundly managed, and opened their doors for business in late September. By this time, Noriyoshi had moved the family (minus Toranosuke) to Jinbōchō, in Kanda. It was only a short walk to the office, and he spent most of his time there, which is more than can be said for some of his partners. The burdens of the business seemed to grow exponentially, and to weigh unevenly on the four consciences. Noriyoshi's loan to the company fell due in December but went unpaid. Tanabe Yūbei was suddenly nowhere to be found. Worried and weak, Noriyoshi caught a chill as the year drew to a close. As he nursed his cold and tried to deflect his creditors, he began to suspect the worst, that all along perhaps some of the funds had been diverted.

"What fools people make of themselves over money!" Natsuko later railed in her diary.[15] Her lifelong contempt for the materialists she saw around her stemmed in part from the disgust she came to feel toward her father. In spite of her great affection for him, she could not help thinking that in his ambition and hastiness he had betrayed the family.

By March the situation seemed hopeless. "There were all kinds of incidents," younger sister Kuniko remarked cryptically in her diary. Noriyoshi's health had not mended; his cold looked, rather, like a case of consumption.

On the twelfth of March the family moved to Awajichō, a more remote part of the neighborhood, hoping to put some distance between their ailing father and the unrelenting pressures of the moribund business.

The misadventure finally foundered at some now unknown date in the late spring of 1889, making Noriyoshi one more statistic: another former samurai who had tried his hand at business and failed. The earnings from his commuted stipend, the proceeds from the sale of his real estate holdings, all of his savings were gone—along with his health. Looming before the sick old man was a specter that all but literally frightened him to death. The streets were full of once-proud men of the old military aristocracy who were peddlers now, or egg dealers, or paper-lantern makers. Why, even the "little princess" his wife had nursed at the grand Inaba estate thirty years before, the daughter of a personal retainer to the shōgun, was now the wife of a common laborer. Was this what he had to look forward to, after all his struggles? In the newspapers, one only read of the successful ones. But for every Iwasaki with his fleet of ships, or Shibusawa with his power-driven cotton mills, there was many a threadbare samurai trying to make a go of it with the less impressive fruits of modernization—the rickshaw or the bicycle or the rodent-proof warehouse.

Now Noriyoshi didn't even have the wherewithal for that. On 12 July 1889, at two o'clock in the afternoon, he died at the age of fifty-nine. His widow Taki was fifty-five. Natsuko was seventeen. Kuniko was fifteen. A passage from Ichiyō's later fiction describes the desolation that descended on the house:

> How fragile good fortune is! . . . Her father, all that she had left in life, had died. It would have been bad enough had he succumbed in due course to an illness, after nursing and medicine had done all they could and his allotted time was up. But such was not the case. The charges of speculation and shady business deals lingered long after they had prompted him to act. The young woman herself did not accept the accusations, and when she tried to reckon with whatever offense had led her father to his suicide, she found it hard to believe that heaven made no distinction between right and wrong. The one who had committed a crime was not her father, but the unctuous gentleman with his fancy clothes and his neat little beard. Her father had been only his assistant. Her father was the one who had had to run ahead and clear the path. He was the one to be sacrificed, like the taster swallowing the poison, while his master survived to sleep on soft pillows and dream of flowers on a spring night. At the very least, he might have felt compassion for the daughter of the man he was indebted to. But now when he passed her gate, he was loath to stop for fear of rumors. Disgusting, indeed, is the human heart.[16]

3
The Mentor

"The sun and moon shed their light impartially on all who dwell under heaven," Natsuko wrote in one of her first stories. "The flowers in spring bloom for everyone. Is it only in this treetop that storms rage?"[1] She felt forsaken by the one person who mattered most to her, and there were more betrayals on the way. A family friend, the illegitimate grandson of Noriyoshi's old protector, Mashimo Sennosuke, had given the dying Noriyoshi his word that he would marry Natsuko. Now the young man, Shibuya Saburō, was frightened off by the family's straitened circumstances. Both he and his promise suddenly evaporated—just so many words, Natsuko mused.

And Toranosuke was no more dependable than ever. In September, after the traditional mourning observances of the forty-ninth day, the three women sought shelter again in Shiba with the last son. One might have hoped that now he would come to his senses, but at twenty-three Toranosuke had not changed. He had the artistic temperament suited to the craft his father had chosen for him. He also had enough talent to paint acceptable porcelains for export; but it was a talent without discipline. If he possessed a rather clever, exuberant eye for color and line in his work, this was a modest endowment compared with his gift for indolence, a capacity that never failed to drive his mother and sisters to distraction.

Within a few months, Kuniko was looking for a situation with a family and Natsuko was discussing the possibility with her poetry teacher, Nakajima Utako, of working as a live-in assistant. The idea was Mrs. Nakajima's. Each week when she saw Natsuko come for her lessons, the girl looked more forlorn. Sometimes, after the others had left, the two of them would talk. Mrs. Nakajima learned how tight the Higuchis' finances really were, how difficult it was for them to live in the same household with Toranosuke, where mother and son were always at loggerheads. Natsuko was one of the best students at the Haginoya, and just then Mrs. Nakajima needed someone who would reside in the school and help her run it. She offered Natsuko a position akin to that of an apprentice. She promised, furthermore, to see if she couldn't find her a teaching position at one of the new girls' schools where she had acquaintances.

And so in May 1890, bubbling with enthusiasm, Natsuko took up residence at the Haginoya in Koishikawa, "the pebble brook," with its leafy hills on the northwest outskirts of the city. The peonies and azaleas were in bloom along the stone steps to the old, crumbling temple of Gokokuji and in the nearby grounds of the Kōrakuen, the gardens of the Edo mansion that until recently had housed the Mito branch of the Tokugawa family. The flowers, the lambent air of late spring, the refuge of the Haginoya, and her teacher's pledge of assistance all gave Natsuko reason for hope. She even half-believed that she might one day succeed to the headship of the school.

By the time the summer rains came, however, Natsuko was disillusioned. Assisting Mrs. Nakajima, it turned out, did not mean quite what she had expected. For every session with the students, or every hour with her brush producing fair copies of the day's poems, there were longer stints in the kitchen. Gradually the menial work seemed to increase; and Natsuko had never been one for housework. At home, only too happily had she palmed off such chores on good-natured Kuniko, who didn't seem to mind doing the woman's work while her scholarly sister enjoyed her books. Natsuko sorely resented being treated now as a scullery maid. She was the daughter of a samurai and an accomplished young lady. After a gathering, why should she be the one to arrange for the rickshaws? She saw a different side of the Haginoya from the kitchen, and a different side to her teacher. At forty-seven, Natsuko observed, the elegant Mrs. Nakajima knew how to apply her makeup. She had idolized the woman as the very paragon of female virtue, but now stories began to reach the back stairs. It appeared that the widow enjoyed the company of men. And worse, as far as Natsuko was concerned, Mrs. Nakajima did not keep her word. Perhaps she found Natsuko's services a little too convenient. No post at any of the girls' schools was forthcoming. Like all the other promises Natsuko had heard recently—from Shibuya Saburō's marriage "proposal" to her teacher's suggestion of succession—in the end, nothing came of this one either.

The girlish Natsuko became increasingly sullen. Mrs. Nakajima seemed to begrudge her any time now for literature. And when she did participate in a poetry fest, she felt as awkward and tongue-tied as on those first days at the school four years before. What progress was this, she asked herself. She could look around her and see other students already beginning to earn distinction. Tanabe Kaho, for one, had even published a novel. All of the others had families to foster their talents; with the death of her father, Natsuko had lost her only patron.

Other people who have studied with the same teacher I have go sailing right along. The months and years go by, and they just seem to hoist their sails and let the tail winds carry them further and further. Not me. I'm so sluggish. I'm like a cart huffing and puffing its way up the hill; even when I do make a little progress, I soon roll right back down again. I embarrass myself. My handwriting is terrible, I can't compose a decent poem to save my life. Why don't I ever show my poems to any of the others, Minoko asks me. I'm too sensitive, she says. "Miss Keep-to-Herself" she calls me. They all have a good laugh at that one. "That's right! Miss Keep-to-Herself!"

At one of the recent poetry gatherings, sometime in July, Itō Natsuko asked to see what I had written. I immediately hid my poem, the way I always do. She smiled and didn't press the matter. But then a little later she handed me a slip of paper. "To Miss Keep-to-Herself" it said. I opened it to find the following poem:

> No fold of sleeve,
> However artfully arranged,
> Will hide for long
> The luster
> Of true gems.

As I read, I could feel the beads of perspiration on my brow. I was mortified, my mind seemed to go blank. But somehow I managed to respond,

> If I had jewels to show,
> I'd let them shine—
> But what have I
> To hide, I ask,
> Behind these sleeves of mine?

"This flattery makes me uneasy," I said, almost tearfully, as I handed her my poem. "Here, this is the best I can do."

Then Minoko had a poem:

> You turn your back on me
> As if I were a proper stranger—
> Yet bluebells both are we,
> In bloom together
> Along a single fence.

I didn't know how I should reply, and finally submitted something I hoped would pass muster:

> Take pity
> On one who shrinks
> From other flowers
> With finer scents
> Than she.

This, however, only brought me cackles.[2]

In the early autumn, Natsuko moved out of the Haginoya. She gathered her mother and Kuniko, who never had found a domestic position for herself, and the three of them returned to Hongō, the section of the city where Natsuko had spent happier days in early childhood, and where they still had kinsmen. They took a house in Kikuzaka, "chrysanthemum hill," not far from elder sister Fuji and her second husband, Kuboki Chōjūrō, and close to the home of Inaba Kō, who regarded her former nursemaid Taki almost as a mother.

Hongō was just to the east of Koishikawa. It was a half-hour's walk from the new house to the Haginoya, where Natsuko went every Saturday morning to help Mrs. Nakajima with the lessons. She still hoped that the teaching post Mrs. Nakajima had promised to arrange for her might eventually materialize. In the meantime, the three women took in laundry and sewing to support themselves. There was an occasional gift of a bolt of crepe or a box of salmon or a few yen from Mrs. Nakajima to supplement their meager earnings, and Natsuko began to consider writing professionally as a source of extra income.

Her encouragement these days came from an unexpected quarter. Two years earlier, one of the older students at the Haginoya, a pampered young lady and a poetic rival of Natsuko's, had published a wildly successful novel, *A Songbird in the Grove* (*Yabu no Uguisu*). Miss Tanabe, who is better known by her later name, Miyake Kaho, was a disciple of the influential critic Tsubouchi Shōyō (1859–1935). His backing and her youthful abilities catapulted her overnight into the forefront of women writers. She was twenty years old at the time, and the handsome royalties from *Songbird*, thirty-three yen twenty sen, were only so much pocket money to the wealthy Kaho. Natsuko was acutely envious, for here was a young woman who enjoyed life's advantages. Her father was an elder statesman for whom an audience with the Emperor was an everyday affair. Kaho not only knew her Chinese and Japanese classics; she could hold forth on the traditions of Europe—such was her up-to-date education. Her sense of style was equally impressive, and in vogue. A broad-brimmed bonnet and a smart summer suit were only the beginning. She carried a European parasol, and she preferred French blouses with high lace collars. Rickshaws? She sometimes rode in a buggy.

Both her wardrobe and her humor were unconstrained by older conventions. Kaho was completely openhearted, even if her tongue was a little tart at times. In fact, she reminded Natsuko of a latter-day Sei Shōnagon. She was by far the best calligrapher at the Haginoya, and the instructors called her a genius when it came to poetry. It was almost infuriating, this embarrassment of riches, for her prose was flowing, too. Natsuko particularly esteemed the writing in *A Songbird in the Grove*: the way it combined elements of classical and modern style; the way it had a pleasant, lingering aftereffect. It was no wonder Miyake Kaho had many admirers.

In the Japanese reckoning, Natsuko turned twenty with the new year of 1891.[3] She was now the same age Kaho had been when she wrote her first novel, and the parallel was not lost on Natsuko. Like her father, she measured herself against the success of others. She was a mere junior to Kaho, who was seldom seen these days at the poetry circle; but when the older girl did appear, she had a word or two of encouragement for the aspiring writer. Perhaps when the time came, Natsuko could ask her for advice about publishing. In the meantime, she took up her diary again with a renewed sense of purpose. She was going to make herself into a novelist. Poetry wasn't such a problem now, but prose—that was what she needed to work on.

In April of the new year, Natsuko began to keep her diary in earnest. Hundreds of pages and some sixty volumes were to flow from her brush before she died in 1896, five years later. Her compulsion to put her thoughts and feelings down on paper resembled that of a pointillist, building up, night after night, a picture of life from the dots of quotidian detail. Before she completed her first short story, we see Natsuko emerging as a born writer. In writing she could assert herself. Recording the day's events was not only the exercise in style she oftentimes pretended; it was a necessary act and a source of strength. If it was good practice for a budding novelist, it was also a way to exorcize self-doubt—now to touch reality, to make some sense of this illusory world, and now to retouch it, to cast herself as the heroine of her own autobiographical tale. In her diary, life could be captured on her terms, not necessarily avoiding the unpleasantnesses, but not sacrificing any of the little elegancies of language and sensibility that offered consolation. In the early years, when she was especially concerned with proficiency, her diary was her copybook. The aroma of Heian hangs heavily over the page. Fine writing and a studied style, which even for Natsuko's day were beginning to smell musty, at times obscure the stories she had to tell, her disquisitions on human foibles.

"Stirred by the blossoms and yearning for the moon," she wrote in the preface to the first volume of her new diary,

> I am a creature at the mercy of my moods. They say that, unexpressed, the feelings in the heart will fester. And I have all too many; sadness and joy commingle. It is time to let them out. I know that there are things best kept from others' eyes, but I add no glaze to what I tell, no flowers to my prose. I set out merely to express the way I feel. There may be times, of necessity, when I seem to be boasting where I ought to be chagrined, times when others might laugh at me, or dismiss me for my breach of taste. The title I have chosen for the diary, "In the Shade of Spring Leaves," may perhaps seem pretentious, although I use it only for its air of elegance. I do not mean to suggest that the future days described herein will all be lush and green:

If only I could live
In the shade of spring leaves,
Instead of in a world
Of disillusion
And despair.[4]

No sooner did Natsuko begin to write "In the Shade of Spring Leaves," following in the tradition of Heian poetic diaries, than she came into her own with a subject worthy of poetry. On 15 April, four days after her first entry, she met her future mentor and the love of her life, the handsome and raffish writer of popular newspaper serials, Nakarai Tōsui.

Natsuko first laid eyes on the handsome Mr. Nakarai in her new capacity as, of all things, a washerwoman. Through the good offices of one of Kuniko's friends, the two sisters had contracted to do the laundry and sewing for the Nakarai family. Only a few trips delivering her handiwork were necessary to convince Natsuko of several things. She knew she must at all costs obtain an audience with the dashing young novelist. She longed to earn his respect as a writer, not as a seamstress. Miyake Kaho had for her mentor the distinguished critic Tsubouchi Shōyō; now Natsuko knew whom she wanted for hers.

The choice was hardly an informed one. She had read nothing of Nakarai Tōsui's work. She had caught only a glimpse of him. All she had to base her decision on were her brief impressions of his sunny household—already a widower, he lived with his two younger brothers and his sister and assorted friends and admirers—and the rapturous words of Nonomiya Kikuko, the friend who had introduced them. The Nonomiya girl was infatuated with Tōsui herself. As a classmate of his younger sister, she called him "elder brother" and lavished such panegyrics on him that by the time Natsuko met him, she was already half in love with the man. It seems never to have occurred to her that she might examine his work before requesting his tutelage. At her behest, a meeting was arranged by Nonomiya, who, as the affair unfolded, was to prove as much a mischief- as a matchmaker. Knowing nothing of Nakarai Tōsui's standing in the literary world, on an afternoon in mid-April, through a fine rain, Natsuko went seeking permission to enter his gate, as they say of one embarking on apprenticeship.

Today I went to see Mr. Nakarai for the first time. Nonomiya Kikuko had already arranged an introduction. I set out just after lunch. He lives near the water, in Shiba, in a section called Minami-Sakumachō. I had been there once before, when I took some things to a girl named Tsuruta who lives with them, so I didn't have any trouble finding the house. It's behind the music hall on the street that runs through Atagoshita. You go round behind the theater, and it's the last house on the left. As I opened the gate, Mr. Nakarai's younger sister came to greet me. She showed me down a corridor to the left of the front hall and into the sitting room and explained that her brother wasn't back yet. I was thinking to myself how busy he must be as a writer for the newspaper *Asahi* [The Morning Sun]— there were his novels to write for serialization, and the general news articles—when I heard the sound of a rickshaw stopping in front of the gate. It was Mr. Nakarai. Before he came into the sitting room, he went to change his clothes. Then he appeared and greeted me warmly. I was not used to these things. My ears felt flushed, my mouth was dry, the proper words wouldn't come. All I could do was bow my head. What a ninny I must have seemed! I was so embarrassed![5]

Indeed, the diminutive, stoop-shouldered figure did not immediately captivate thirty-one-year-old Mr. Nakarai.[6] Parted at twenty-four from an extraordinarily beautiful wife (who had died of consumption), and with his ensuing reputation as a ladies' man, at first glance he found the girl cringing before him rather lusterless. She managed, somehow, to suggest both a ninny and a granny: her drab kimono, years too old for her; her hair tied back in a businesslike bun, plain as could be. She looked like the pitiable wife of a shopkeeper—no color, no embellishment. Through her fear, she was obviously straining to be charming, but the overall effect was gray and sallow, enlivened only by an occasional blush. And that spare, almost inaudible voice, as she bowed and scraped like a young goose of a girl! What was he to make of this? Could *she* be the one who had importuned Nonomiya and his sister for an interview?

Natsuko's impressions of him, on the other hand, were altogether favorable:

> Mr. Nakarai would be around thirty, I suppose. I know it's rude of me to write about his appearance, but I'm going to go ahead and set down my impressions. He has a beautiful complexion and gentle features—the kind of smiling face that children take to immediately. He's a tall, strapping man. He really is someone to look up to.
>
> During the afternoon, he talked discursively about the novels that are popular now: how the kind of fiction he admires isn't appreciated, how infantile the audience for newspaper serializations has become, how you can't sell anything that isn't already a twice-told tale of traitorous samurai or oversexed women.
>
> "None of my stories now are the things I really want to write," he confided. "It embarrasses me to think what a critic or a scholar would make of them. But what can I do? I'm not writing these things to further my reputation. I have a mother and father and sister and brothers to

feed. I have no choice but to ignore the critics. If I had the freedom to write what I wanted," he laughed loudly, "it would put an end to the bad reviews."

I was sure that some day he would write something great.

"That's enough about me," he went on. "I hear from the Nonomiya girl that you want to be a writer. She's told me about your plans. It's not going to be easy, you know. But stick with it. I don't know that I'm qualified to teach anybody anything. You can think of me as someone to talk things over with though—whenever you feel like it. Really. Don't hesitate."

He was so kind to me that I don't think I have ever been as happy. I could feel the tears in my eyes.

I managed to talk about something or other for a few moments, and he told me I must stay for dinner. Dish after dish was being brought out. We had only met, however, and I didn't think I ought to presume upon them any further. I tried to take my leave, but he wouldn't hear of it.

"No, you must stay! We do things country-style here. A friend is a friend—no distinctions between old and new. There's not much to offer, but do stay. Please. If you're going to be visiting us, you might as well get used to staying for supper. We all eat together."

I could scarcely refuse.

During all of this, it had begun to rain harder, and as we ate it grew darker and darker.

Finally it was time for me to go. He insisted on calling me a rickshaw. Before I left I gave him a draft of the first part of a story I had written, and he loaned me several of his books.

I didn't get home until eight, and all the way I kept thinking how wonderful Mr. Nakarai had been to me.[7]

She was in love. And by the end of the conference he, too, was obviously smitten. The two-timing Shibuya Saburō, the callow youth who had promised her dying father he would marry her, and her father himself—these were earlier and tainted heroes. They were smaller, fallible men, for whom in her heart she had a soft spot, yes; but they were hardly the stuff of dreams. All the manly traits she had thrilled to as a child spellbound by storybooks seemed to coalesce in this one shining figure. He had the strength and the beauty that children look up to. His smile was dazzling and his features gentle. She remembered the old tales that had enthralled her from the age of six, "the stories of the great and the valorous, heroic exploits, full of honor and virtue."[8] Was not this a man who would save her? He would teach her what she needed to know in order to stand on her own in the world, to make her way as a professional writer—something no other woman, not even Kaho, had ever attempted. And his large and lively household, brimming with siblings and students and friends, would be a refuge from the sad shadow of the former glory and happiness of her own etiolated house.

The free-and-easy humor of her new preceptor, the piquancies of his conversation, his worldliness, his extraordinary good looks—everything about him instantly fascinated Natsuko. Small wonder that the precise nature of the man was at first lost on her. How was she to know of the scandal besmirching the Nakarai house? These things unfold slowly, and who had ears for them anyway? Life was about to flow smoothly again. She was, after all, in the heyday of youth. Her new acquaintance left her braced and ready to lay the proper groundwork for a career she was determined would be nothing short of brilliant. Questions of Mr. Nakarai's literary stature were matters that did not concern her. Nonomiya, her go-between, had provided Natsuko with only a modicum of information, all of it as pleasant as the man's countenance. Only gradually were more unsettling details imparted by Nonomiya. At this point, as she rushed to have more of her story ready for her new teacher, all Natsuko knew of him were the bare essentials.

His urbanity notwithstanding, Mr. Nakarai and his family hailed from the provinces. His father had been adopted into a samurai house of eighty koku in Hizen Province in the south and had moved the family to Edo when first-born Tōsui was eleven. In late youth, the eldest son had traveled through the Kyōto-Ōsaka area before joining the *Asahi*, where he started as a reporter; but, with his flair for storytelling, he was soon assigned to write novels for serialization in the newspaper. During the past two years that he had been toiling as one of the house novelists, he had turned out a half-dozen potboilers, none of which Natsuko had read until now. He was what they still called a "*gesaku* writer," and, if she had stopped to think about it, Natsuko would have realized that the expression was, in the new age, not a complimentary one.

The term "gesaku"—"playful compositions"—had been coined in the latter half of the Edo period to distinguish popular, commercial literature (in time, especially fiction) from more sober literary endeavors. What was playful about these best-sellers was not necessarily their subjects—impoverishment or love suicide were hardly laughing matters—but rather the writer's stance. The gesaku label was attached to novels as a caveat emptor: the reader was forewarned that the work was not a serious expression of the author's learning or abilities, lest the austere, neo-Confucian society of the military capital disapprove. Gesaku novelists fancied themselves true townsmen, dilettantes and connoisseurs, who took no more responsibility for their prose (they liked to think, at any rate) than they would for a dalliance with a courtesan. In its various forms, all plebeian and all written largely in glib, colloquial language, gesaku was the most popular literature of the late Edo period. However, it had fallen into disrepute with the coming of "culture" and "enlightenment." A literature on the one hand so avowedly amateur and on the other so professionally entertaining was considered too frivolous in the more serious, and ambitious, Meiji era. At a time when novelists were beginning to grapple with psychological realism and questions of sincerity and truthfulness, the "playful compositions" of the gesaku writers had degenerated into a mannered, irrelevant literature of the demimonde.

Little did Natsuko know how faithfully the dapper Mr. Nakarai embodied the essence of this old gesaku tradition: a writer of fripperies, a playboy, a romantic, a man of parts who could match wits with the best of them in the downtown world of entertainers or launch into yet another affair without quite surrendering his heart—in short, an epicure "living only for the moment," in the words of one of the first Edo storybooks, "enraptured by the pleasures of the moon and the snow, the cherry blossoms and the maple leaves; singing, drinking wine, making sport: floating and floating, like a gourd that bobs along with the current, not a gloomy thought in his head, not a care in the world for poverty."[9]

Well, perhaps this was a slight exaggeration. Life did bring its disappointments. Money was tight. And even if Mr. Nakarai did enjoy a visit to the pleasure quarter now and then, he still mourned for his beautiful wife, still vowed he would never remarry. But what was really troubling him these days was that the Tsuruta girl was pregnant with the child of his younger brother Hiroshi. She was a classmate of his own sister's, a mere schoolgirl, and their boarder to boot! Tongues wagged over this one. No sooner had he tucked her away in a little house in Kōjimachi than Higuchi Natsuko came knocking at the gate. Was it any wonder he was wary? In the end, he had agreed to see what he could do to help Natsuko, but this time he was going to observe the proprieties.

Natsuko was back again within a week, with the second installment of her story to show him and with enough confidence now to refer to him in her diary occasionally as "Tōsui" rather than "Mr. Nakarai." She might have waited a few days longer, until she had finished the story, but she was eager to hear Tōsui's appraisal of the first chapter, which she had left with him. The verdict was not what she had hoped for. Politely, ever so tactfully, Tōsui dealt with the problems in her writing. Anyone less adept at human relations would surely have incurred the full wrath of the determined Natsuko, who had assumed that a repetition of the sudden and spectacular entrance Miyake Kaho had made upon the literary stage three years earlier was hers—if not for the asking, then for the perseverance. In spite of her mother's strictures, the lamp had burned late during these nights, as slowly and painfully she crafted her prose. In a sense, her very lucubrations were the problem. How should he put it? The writing was too fine, too literary for a newspaper serial. The sentences had a way of running on, he ventured, and the allusions to the classics—might they not be too dense for popular fiction? Then, too, the plot was a little on the thin side. One had to entertain, after all. . . . It was positively odd: the girl wanted to write for the mass market in order to support her family, and yet when she took up her brush she couldn't help straining for the elegant effect. Clearly, Tōsui would have to introduce Miss Higuchi to the ways of more vulgar fiction.

Natsuko left that day with her ardor undiminished. Her teacher had told her what had to be done; and he had promised, in due course, to introduce her to other writers and to set up an appointment with a man named Komiyama Tenkō, his senior colleague at the newspaper. Obstacles did exist, but she was indubitably on her way, and with such a splendid guide to lead her! "There are some people you like when you first meet them," she confided to her diary, "but who seem less appealing the second time. With Mr. Nakarai, though, today I had an even greater feeling of rapport than I did on my first visit. How lucky I am to have met this marvelous man!"[10] She spent the next two days immersed in her writing, polishing the last installment of the story, with which she hoped to make a stronger showing. On Friday evening she completed her fair copy and sent the manuscript off to Tōsui by night mail. On Saturday, when she returned from the weekly poetry lessons at the Haginoya, a reply from Tōsui was waiting. She was to see him the next day, Sunday, at a boardinghouse in Jinbōchō run by a man named Tawara, where he would discuss the story with her and introduce her to Komiyama. To meet in a rented room seemed vaguely indecorous, but deliberations on the matter were held with her mother, and it was agreed that she should go. That night Natsuko had trouble sleeping.

The next morning I woke up early, and, when I looked outside, the sky was completely covered with black clouds. Today of all days it was surely going to rain, I pouted.

"In that case, maybe you'd better not go," suggested Mother.

"No. I can't break the appointment, when it was for my sake that the whole thing has been arranged," I protested. "Unless it rains hard, I *must* go."

As I was getting ready, the bank of clouds began to disperse. I set out delighted at this change in the weather. But near Tamachi, dark clusters reappeared everywhere. And all of a sudden it started to rain, as if a bowl of water had been overturned. What was the point in going back now? Either way, I was in for a soaking. I might as well go on then, I reasoned, and found myself a rickshaw.

The lodgings were in a newly cleared area in Ogawamachi, to the south of the Kōshūkan market. This was the first time in my life I had ever been to visit anyone at a rooming house. For a second I lost my nerve. But hovering about the door wouldn't accomplish anything, I told myself. So I took a deep breath and went in, asking for Mr. Nakarai.

A maid with a rather dour, suspicious-looking face inquired who I was. "This way," she said when I told her, leading me down a hall lined with countless cubicles. The room where Mr. Nakarai was, on the first

floor in the two-story wing, looked as if it could be made into an apart-
ment of two smaller rooms. A chest of drawers, a cabinet, and the like
lined the walls; it was well-furnished, I thought, as I took a seat.

Master Nakarai was in the midst of writing a letter. "Just let me finish
this," he said. Today he was dressed in European clothes rather than
Japanese-style.

After a moment he put the letter aside and spoke in his gentle way.
"The weather was so nice yesterday, I never imagined when I wrote you
it would be like *this* today! It wasn't very thoughtful of me. Actually,
Komiyama has already left. This morning, all of a sudden, he decided to
go to Kamakura for a rest—he's been having headaches. And here I've
put you to all this trouble . . ."

He was very apologetic and went on to talk to me kindly and at great
length about writing, with suggestions of what I should try next, ideas
that he had had for stories he wanted to write but hadn't had the time
to—how I ought to use them, and, if I did such and such, how interesting
it would be. Then he told me there was something else he had been
meaning to discuss, before any of the rest.

"Is something the matter?" I asked.

"No, no. But you know, I am not an old man yet." He seemed to find it
extremely difficult to speak. "And you—just at the age when a young
woman marries. What do you suppose people are going to think?"

I know, I wanted to say. These were things I had already thought
about. My face burned. I didn't know what to do with my hands. My
embarrassment was all too obvious.

"So I've thought of a solution. From now on when I see you, I'm going
to pretend that you're an old friend, one of the fellows I grew up with.
And you must do the same. Don't think of me as a man. Treat me as if I
were your girl friend," he smiled. "There are differences between us we
musn't think about."

Then he added that he understood my family's circumstances, and
told me to let him know when we were in a bad way. He said he would
do whatever he could to help; he described with complete candor his
own financial troubles. It made me stop and think. Again today he
served me lunch, and then I took my leave. After hearing about Master
Nakarai's money worries, I realized that my own family's problems are
nothing. The hardships that he must have seen make our difficulties
pale by comparison.[11]

April gave way to May, and cherries to tree peonies and wisteria. Every day
the spring greens grew more varied and more generous, climbed higher over

the stone and earthen walls of family gardens, reclaimed more ground along the wayside and the banks of the canals that Natsuko passed in transit to Mr. Nakarai's new house in Kōjimachi. And every day her spirits seemed to rise still higher, in step with the luxuriant foliage. There were outings with her poetry companions to see the shocking pink azaleas behind the Denzūin, the great mortuary temple where the mother of the first Tokugawa shōgun lay buried, not far from Mrs. Nakajima's garden. There were the pastimes and trifles of the Haginoya; an idle moment might find the young ladies and their women teachers pitted against the gentlemen instructors in a contest of "comparing ages," where the years of each side were tallied and, inevitably, the few but ancient men would win. And there were, above all, her visits to Mr. Nakarai—the anticipation of each encounter stretching to fill a good half-week before the visit, the memory lingering a half-week's time beyond, until it melted once more into anticipation.

And as if the sheer splendor of his presence were not enough to make her blood race, Tōsui was always producing surprises. One week it was news: sooner than expected Natsuko might see herself in print, for he had mentioned her to an Ōsaka man who was launching a magazine. The next week it was sorcery: imported crane from the mountains of Korea, most auspicious of birds and rare of delicacies, appeared on her dinner tray after the lesson. When he wasn't delighting her with these astonishments or captivating her with his theories of literature, such as they were, Tōsui was teasing her with a familiarity more like that of an older brother than of the school chum he had instructed her to consider him. Why did it always rain on the days when she came, he wondered. Natsuko found herself teasing him back. When he suggested that perhaps the rain was his fault—he had risen early today— Natsuko retorted that, for heaven's sake, the next time she came he was to sleep in, please. For a moment, the mere awareness that they could joke like this embarrassed her.

When the real rains came, with the summer season known as "plum showers" lasting from mid-June to mid-July, they also brought with them a sudden dampening in relations. The beginning of the rainy season and a slight indisposition had kept Natsuko away from the Nakarai house for longer than usual. On 16 June a letter arrived from Tōsui. She was invited to come the following day. He had something to tell her, he said. When she put the letter down, she felt her heart beat faster. No doubt he wanted to discuss her stories. That night, as had not happened for weeks now, she had trouble sleeping; but she doubted it was the rain that made her restless.

What transpired the next day in the course of their meeting is not entirely clear. There is a long entry in the diary for the seventeenth, but the essential information is exceedingly opaque. After a break in the clouds around noon, Natsuko set out on her visit. She walked partway with an old friend of the family, the widow Okuda, who frequently lent the Higuchis money after Noriyoshi's death, and who had come calling in the morning. They walked as far as Masagochō together. From there, without a companion, Natsuko began to notice how sultry the day was. As she approached Tōsui's neighborhood, the languor of the early afternoon seemed to express itself even in the limp paper lanterns hanging in bright holiday clusters underneath the eaves. It was festival time, no doubt, at nearby Hie Shrine, but at the moment everything was quiet. When she knocked at the gate, the family maid looked surprised to see her. Master Nakarai was not expected home until late today. His younger sister Kōko returned just then from her errands, and she and Natsuko chatted desultorily through the remainder of the afternoon. Natsuko ended up staying for supper—it is quite possible that these visits to her friends were the only time she got a square meal—and as they were finishing Tōsui finally arrived. He had many things to tell her, Natsuko later recorded in her diary, but at this point she becomes cryptic:

> He passed on some carefully considered suggestions from Mr. Komiyama [whom she had finally met], and, as usual, Master Nakarai had many kind and thoughtful things of his own to say. I was very grateful. And yet I cannot bring myself to write down what he said tonight. I just don't know if I am capable. Right now is too soon to decide. How I wish this were already some talk from the past! For the present I can't bear to write of it.[12]

What was it that it was too soon to decide about? What was it, precisely, that upset her? Perhaps Tōsui had been less tactful than usual. Perhaps he was more aloof that night: for all he cared for her and respected her determination, the memory of the scandal involving the Tsuruta girl still smarted. As head of the household, he was blamed for his brother's indiscretion. So soon again in the same family, another liaison with a younger women, or even the suggestion of it, was something to be avoided. So perhaps he seemed cold that night, too uncaring in his critique of her recent literary efforts. Sensitive Natsuko, born writer that she was, could be thin-skinned when it came to what she perceived as excessive or insincere criticism. In her eyes Tōsui was so much more than a teacher that perhaps she felt rebuffed and began to lose confidence in her talent. Or perhaps the explanation is simpler. Perhaps the new recommendations for a story or a style were finally too alien to her. Perhaps for the first time she understood fully the difference in their approaches to literature. Perhaps the additional advice from Komiyama, a fellow dime novelist at Tōsui's newspaper, drove home to Natsuko the gap between her literature—lofty and pure, even if it was meant to earn a living—and their "playful writing," so easy, so workaday.

Whatever the cause, and perhaps it consisted of threads of all of these distresses, Natsuko was profoundly disillusioned. On the long walk home she thought of suicide:

The evening breeze was almost chilly. In the moat, the surface of the
water looked dusky and somber. The branches of the pines seemed to
reach out toward it. Some of the trees were bent with age, some stood
tall, but they all looked as if they had seen service here as sentries for a
thousand years. So this is what it meant to improve with age, I thought,
looking back around me. The sun was down now behind the western
hills, and red wisps of cloud trailed in the sky like banners. For all the
passersby, the rest of the city seemed far away. I was overcome with a
feeling of loneliness.

As I walked along the bank I watched the willow branches sway, and I
thought to myself how like human beings they are: a breeze of fashion
blows this way, and a wind of convention blows that, and, every time,
everybody follows. How different are the pines. That slow drumming
sound they make, as they decide to permit the breeze to nudge them, it
echoed high up in the trees. It spoke with such integrity that it helped to
bring me back from my despair. It was not even autumn, and here I was
letting everything around me make me brood. I had even thought of
suicide. But now I remembered there were others I had to live for.
Mother and Kuniko were depending on me.

Before I noticed, I had reached the top of the hill in Kudan. The clatter
of carriages coming and going in all directions filled the night. I had to
watch my step now, and yet I was still distracted. How curious I must
have looked to others, trudging along with my head down. But I couldn't
bear the thought of anybody seeing me in this sorry state of mine. To put
a smile on my face would have been more than I could manage. By the
time I reached home, it was after dark.[13]

The rest of the summer was quiet. Natsuko saw Tōsui only once after the
seventeenth, at the end of June, and then no more until fall. The muggy days
passed by uneventfully. The three women tended the little kitchen garden
behind the house, putting in eggplant, picking plums. While Kuniko sewed
and laundered and fashioned bamboo sandal facings known as "locust tops"
and her mother ran the house, Natsuko was often freed from the piecework
and chores in order to make her rounds of the library in Ueno and the poetry
group in Koishikawa, whose ranks were depleted now for the summer. In
spite of her resounding will, a feeling of defeat now haunted her. Before they
parted, Tōsui had urged her to write another story without worrying about
publishing it for now, but Natsuko's confidence was shaken. She had more
studying to do first, and so she went as often as possible to the library.
Perhaps in an effort to become more like Tōsui, she reread her Edo fiction,

beginning with the novels of Ueda Akinari and Takizawa Bakin.[14] But even as she concentrated on Tōsui's literary forebears, the selections she made revealed the serious bent Tōsui himself would always lack. Along with Akinari and Bakin she read the essays of Matsudaira Sadanobu, the antithesis of gesaku. Not only did the straightlaced Matsudaira write in a learned, high-minded style; as the adviser of the eleventh shōgun and the instigator of the Kansei Reforms (1787–93) designed to sober up "decadent" Edo society, he had perhaps done more than any other man to cripple popular literature.

These trips to the Ueno Library in a sense replaced the weekly visits to Tōsui. On such days, removed from household drudgery and lost in her books, Natsuko found some measure of relief from her summer melancholy:

Not a cloud was in the sky. The sunlight baked everything within its reach, and the dust from the gravel in the road rose like smoke. I cut through the university and came out into Ikenohata, where the scent of lotuses carried over from Kayachō. It was such a fresh smell that I felt invigorated, and I pursued it. Willow branches rustled at the side of the pond. Sei Shōnagon had no use for them in full leaf, as I remember, but what cool shade they give on a summer's day.[15] The pond itself was a great respite from the heat. Water lilies all but covered the surface. A breeze played across the flowers, lifting now a pink petal, now a white, and revealing the underside of the lily pads. I could have done without the rowboats moored in a corner of the pond, however. No doubt they are for gathering lotus roots. What's more, at the edge of the garden was the back wall of a riding track that was crumbling and pathetic-looking, which did make it a little better, or is that just my own taste? As I climbed the steps to the Tōshōgū, the breeze and the dew beneath the cedars felt wonderful; here it didn't even seem like summer.

Crowded as it always is, the library I had expected would be unbearably hot today. But the ceilings were so high and the windows so wide that a pleasant breeze blew through the room. It was almost too cool, a welcome surprise. Whenever I come to the library, there are always lots of men but never any women. It was quite odd, I thought, going about my business as I always did, copying down the titles of books I wanted, putting down their call numbers, bringing them up to the counter along with all the men. "This one's not right. Please redo it," said the man behind the desk. I felt my face flush, and I was on the verge of trembling. I thought that if anyone looked at me, or spoke to me, I would disintegrate. I was bathed in sweat. For a moment I lost all desire to take the book.

The bar examinations would be held soon, and there were many people checking out law books. But for me, it was a matter of reading the things I wanted to. All afternoon I read, and then, before I realized

it, the long summer day was over. In the park outside, the locusts sang in
the trees. Somewhere a faint bell announced dusk. The light through the
window had faded.

Could it be that late already? Everyone was leaving. I rushed out of the
reading room and returned my books. As I went outside, a flock of crows
crossed the sky, headed home to their nests. And here Mother had made
a point of telling me to come home early today. She didn't want me to
tire myself. I hadn't slept well last night, et cetera, et cetera. I hadn't
forgotten, but now already it was late. Well, I'd hurry and take the short
cut through Yanaka.

All that remained of the sun was a disk of crimson. "Red sky at night!
Sailors' delight!" I heard the children chanting as I hastened by. Back
from the evening bath, people cooled themselves on benches in front of
their houses. Everyone seemed to sport a clean, crisp kimono and a fan
that fluttered back and forth, back and forth, across the chest.

Dashing by me went a little ten-year-old with white spots on her face.
She'd been into her mother's powder pot, apparently. On her back she
was carrying a baby. The child, about three I should think, seemed to be
suffering from a case of prickly heat. Only her face wasn't pink from the
rash, and the two sisters, with their white faces, presented an amusing
sight.

On the way, I saw some new sweet potatoes at a vegetable stand in
Katachō and stopped just long enough to buy Mother a few, and then I
hurried along. I walked as fast as I could and soon was perspiring. Beads
of sweat rolled into my eyes, into my mouth. I kept dabbing my face
with my handkerchief, until it began to smart. What a sight I must be, I
thought. The only solution was to put up my parasol, no matter how
dark it was by now.

As I crossed underneath one of those pedestrian bridges, I noticed a
group of students clustered around the railing, looking down at me. I
couldn't tell what they were saying, but they were muttering something
and chuckling to themselves. I pretended not to notice and walked even
faster. One of them pointed at me and called out, "Hey! Look here a
minute." Who knows what they were up to? It didn't seem like any way
for students to behave.

When I reached home, Mother was waiting outside for me. Kuniko
was busy getting dinner ready. "Here, take your things off and have a
bath. You must be hot and tired," Mother said. "The bathwater's ready."

How good it felt to get my dirty clothes off, how I appreciated my
mother's thoughtfulness! She put out clean clothes for me while I was in
the bath. "Wear these," she called. "I washed them while you were out."

And then Kuniko called me to the table. "Guess what's for dinner!
Something you like—fried rice and sweet potatoes." I was starved from

all my walking today and relaxed from the bath, and everything tasted delicious.[16]

There were, then, little pleasures, even as Natsuko withdrew into umbrage and gloom, even as penury and disappointment seemed to engulf her family. Occasionally her mother would get a little tipsy on some rice wine. A mid-summer gift of fabric would make Kuniko's face beam. Now, if only they knew how to get silk from the cocoons Kuniko had discovered on the tea plant. . . . Her mother took great pains with the plantings: the little garden provided one of the few delights the three women knew.

It provided occasional surprises too, for after living for thirty years in Tokyo, Taki had let her farming heritage slip through her fingers. Cucumber seeds, for instance, did not seem to yield the expected results. A friend with a green thumb was called in for consultation and pronounced the cucumbers moonflowers. Taki and her daughters were not disappointed in the least. They waited impatiently for the first flowers to bloom. Bloom they did, in due time, but not as moonflowers. What came up were funny little yellow buds. Taki's friend was brought back for further consultation. "Oh, it's cucumber after all," they were told, "but not the usual kind. It's sponge cucumber." This second turn of events brought its own excitement. If it was sponge cucumber, then they could count on sap for making face cream. They were all the more anxious for the mystery plant to ripen. Finally the seeds bore fruit, and the would-be cucumber turned out to be winter melon.

"Yes," Mrs. Nakajima nodded sagely when Natsuko told her how foolish they felt. "Isn't that the way the world is? You never know what you're getting. A person who towers head and shoulders over others, giraffelike, turns out to be as stupid as a packhorse." Indeed, Natsuko mused, an expert like Mrs. Nakajima had a theory for everything.[17]

Natsuko had by no means lost her sense of humor, her liveliness, her curiosity (and in fact, through all of her misfortunes ahead, she never did). She was an avid reader of the Meiji newspapers, windows on the world for the many inquisitive people like herself who would never travel beyond Japan. One day, for example, she noted in her diary "What Makes Londoners Different from Parisians":

Parisians walk on the right side of the street; Londoners, on the left. In Paris, several families live in one building, like a barracks; in London, they live one family to a house. Parisians gather in cafés, Londoners prefer private clubs. Parisians sleep along the wall; Londoners sleep in the middle of the room. Parisians eat twice a day; Londoners, three or four times. Parisians have long bread; Londoners, square. Parisians drink coffee; Londoners drink tea. In Paris, they talk incessantly during meals; in London, they don't talk at all.[18]

At sunset Natsuko liked to go for walks. Sometimes she and Kuniko went to shop for sewing materials over on the main street. Sometimes she would take her mother for an evening constitutional, and they would walk to the pond at Shinobazu to see the lotuses. In the summertime, the festivals were frequent and they would often find themselves in the midst of revelry. Whirling bands of supplicants to the seven gods of good fortune would sweep them up into their juggernaut and carry them past other bobbing heads, paper lanterns, a crush of pink and white valerians. Another night, they would take in the tinsel strung in honor of the Herdboy and the Weaver-Maiden, those sad, celestial lovers who yearned for each other from opposite sides of the Milky Way.

On one of these walks with Kuniko, they passed through their old neighborhood and the house where they had lived as children. "How things have changed!" Natsuko sighed.

It's been only eight years since we moved away, but at Shitadera, where the land rises to a plateau, they've built a railroad, and now the steam engines go whistling by. The place where the trains stop, the ward office, the post office—so many new buildings! Who could have imagined it? When we were little and just learning how to write, we used to pass by there every day on the way to our lessons. I can remember hearing people talk about how the area would soon develop. It had all sounded like a dream to us then; Kuniko and I had laughed at the idea. But, sure enough, things have happened just as people said they would. Projects had mushroomed overnight; industry was moving forward. And yet here we are, still the same. We haven't done anything with our lives. All we have gained are years. It's enough to make a person cry.[19]

That summer, two years had passed since Noriyoshi's death. For all Kuniko's handiwork and Natsuko's ambition, they could not make ends meet. Natsuko would watch her younger sister fondling a bolt of new material, alms from a more prosperous friend: time and again Kuniko unrolled the cloth and gazed at it lovingly, almost entranced, for such everyday items had become luxuries beyond their reach. Her sister's very happiness bespoke the unbearable thinness of their lives. Now, when locusts began to trill the announcement that summer was ending, it reminded Natsuko of all the other things that had ended. One by one the supports had fallen away, and the last vestiges of a time of stability had crumbled into dusty insignificance. Perhaps the most painful, irrevocable symbol of decline was the news that Inaba Kō's husband had decided to pull a rickshaw. "Inaba Kō!" Taki must have gasped—her "little princess" of Edo days, the baby she had nursed like a lady-in-waiting, the daughter of a military house once worth several thousand koku! The bare statement of fact recorded in Natsuko's diary needed no metaphor to heighten its impact. "After lunch Mr. Inaba came. Things have gotten worse and worse for them, and he talked of becoming a rickshawman. Life is full of sadness."[20]

If there was any succor to be derived from the sight of how others had fallen in the world from greater heights than they, it was surely ephemeral. The precariousness of their own position struck them anew whenever the money they had borrowed to keep going ran out again and it was time to seek another loan from their dwindling pool of friends with sufficient capital and patience. By September, the time had come once more. On the seventh, Taki set off on her unpleasant task of entreating help from Saegusa Shinzō, a nephew of Mashimo Sennosuke, Noriyoshi's old benefactor.

[Yesterday morning] Mother went to see Mr. Saegusa, in Asakusa. Our misfortunes keep piling up, nothing comes of any of our plans, all our hopes depend on the distant future. And there is nothing we can do to improve the situation. We get poorer all the time. Now Kuniko is sick; she's spent most of the last few days in bed. It's just one thing after another. What will we do when we can't borrow more money? Mother wasn't back by lunchtime; she still wasn't back by three. I wondered what had happened. After all, I thought, it's the flowers—the bright and the beautiful—that people are drawn to. Who wants to talk to someone down on his luck? Who wants to listen to our tiresome requests? Maybe she'd had trouble persuading Saegusa. Maybe she'd gone looking for someone else to ask. The thought of it made my head ache. Every time something like this happens, I can hardly live with my own fecklessness—what have I done to help? Even if I am a woman, I'm nineteen years old, for heaven's sake, and I can't even take care of my poor old mother. Don't think I don't know what a dolt I am! If I were alone, I would do whatever kind of loathsome work I had to in order to survive. But Mother is so conscious of the family name. She says she'd rather die than see a child of hers do something shameful. If it's to support her, she says, then please find a way that will not disgrace us. Of course, she's right. She and Papa came up to the capital when they were both so young and full of plans for the future. All they wanted was to make a name for themselves. But first Sentarō died, and then Papa died. Little by little, people have come to scorn us; now the world dismisses us as of no consequence. It's not easy to endure sometimes, and I sat lost in these sad thoughts when, at four, Mother returned.

"How did it go?" I asked.

"Cheer up! People are kinder than you think. Mr. Saegusa is so generous. He told me to tell him everything, not to apologize. When I asked him for more money, he lent us another thirty yen without blinking an eye. 'How thin you look, though, Auntie,' he said and ordered us some eel. 'Here now, eat up,' he said." Mother dabbed her eyes; she seemed almost overcome with gratitude. We were both profoundly thankful, and at the same time embarrassed at our own helplessness.

*

Today Mother went to visit the Mochizukis in Koyanagichō, to see how the baby is doing. She went to see them yesterday, too, but the baby is so sick that she wanted to go again today. "I feel so sorry for them," she said as she went off.

It was evening before she came home.

"Natsuko," she said, "I . . . uh . . . I'm afraid I've done something terrible."

"What?"

"I know you're going to be very angry with me."

"Well, what on earth did you do? You don't need to be afraid of telling *me*. What is it?"

"All right. Well, I went to the Mochizukis' house, and the baby is so frail, it doesn't look as if it will live. And they're in desperate straits. They didn't even know if they could scrape together enough money to feed themselves tonight. An old woman like me—I can't help it if I get emotional—I felt so sorry for them. I know I shouldn't have done it, but I loaned them some of the money Saegusa gave us. It was only a little. I hope you'll forgive me, Natsuko."

"What are you talking about? Of course I forgive you. You did the right thing," I said. "People say that charity begins at home, but in this house we should do all we can for others. It was a wonderful thing, what you did."

When she heard this, Mother smiled with a look as if the burdens had been lifted from her back.[21]

The long, hot summer was over, but Natsuko had nothing to show for it. She was no closer to a career as a writer than she had been the previous summer when she quit working as Mrs. Nakajima's live-in. In late September, as she cut through the park at Shinobazu on her way to the Ueno Library, she noticed the withered lotuses floating on the pond and the forlorn-looking duckweed. The autumnal scene only reminded her of time's passing. Soon it would be a year since her resolution to turn herself into a professional novelist, but she felt that she was actually losing ground. All the good days, it seemed, were in the past.

In this world, perseverance is more precious than treasure. . . . It is not that my mind is unaware of the fact. Why, then, do I have trouble persevering? In the winter it is bad enough, but in summer it is even worse: as I study by the lamp, I struggle to fight off drowsiness. I pour ice water over my face, and for a while this revives me. But in no time I am warm again, my arms and legs are overcome with the same old lethargy, and before I realize it I have put my head down on my books. I am always embarrassed when Mother finds me like this and wakes me up with her "What have we here?" just as I am starting to dream. I open my eyes and resolve to work harder. I take up my book and can remember reading two or three pages when the same thing happens again. No matter how many times I go through my resolutions, they don't seem to do any good. The sages said our bodies are gifts from our parents; in China when they felt drowsy they would prick their legs with an awl, and the pain, hard as it was to bear, would make them alert again. But when my mind isn't on my work, then even when my eyes are open, nothing from any book sinks in. This weakness of the flesh is certainly lamentable.

When my father was living, he used to tell me about his early days. He would go to bed at the hour of the rat [midnight] and rise at the hour of the tiger [4:00 A.M.]—in the old days two hours were the equivalent of four hours today—and he said if he slept this much it was enough for him. Why am I always so sleepy, then? I wonder if I have some disease. Until I was about thirteen, I don't remember ever getting sick. My parents, my brothers and sisters all suffered from headaches; I was the only one who never had them. Perhaps because I was so healthy, from the time I was very young I learned faster than the other children and forgot less. My teachers would often remark on this. Whenever I memorized something, I would tell myself that I must never forget it, no matter how many months and years went by. But gradually I grew up. I began to catch whatever sickness went around. Worst of all were the headaches I now began to get and the pain in my shoulders. My ability to remember things vanished. Today I have no perseverance. Things I hear one day I forget the next. That's bad enough. Things I hear in the morning I forget by night! Whatever I learn soon slips away. Nothing makes me worry more: what will I be like in the future? I mean to study and persevere as long as I live—but this is beginning to sound like the ambition of a fool who doesn't know his own limitations.[22]

Like the sleepy Chinese sage prodding himself with an awl, Natsuko decided that a resumption of her friendship with Tōsui might prove revivifying. By the end of September, unsettling rumors had reached her. Friends were telling Kuniko that Nakarai Tōsui was a womanizer. Kuniko passed on the information disapprovingly, as if to say Natsuko would be well rid of him.

"Touch red and you'll be stained," the saying went, Kuniko reminded her. The criticism seems only to have rekindled Natsuko's dedication to her mentor. Mr. Nakarai had been a good teacher and a close friend, she advised Kuniko, and he had promised to do still more for her in the future. She refused to believe he was immoral.

In the next few weeks, Tōsui was much on her mind, and so were his "palaces of clandestine pleasures." One of her nocturnal walks took her past a new teahouse in her old neighborhood, on the hill at Nakazaka. It was a somewhat odd-looking, lively establishment, a *machiai*. Natsuko wasn't sure exactly why, but of late she found herself intrigued by these houses of assignation. (Little did she dream at this point—as she was, in a way, still growing up—that the teahouses and the pleasure quarter would provide the setting for her most important fiction.) "What on earth is a machiai, anyway?" she wondered that night in her diary.

I don't really have much of an idea. From the way the word is written, it would appear to mean a meeting place. But—who would imagine it from such a name?—at these machiai, the lamps are lit and geisha are called; wine and sweet words flow, and men amuse themselves all through the night. The owner is invariably a woman. Two or three comely maidens serve the guests. The entrances to these establishments are always enticing, and from the rooms inside, fitted with their bamboo screens, floats the sound of soft, cool voices—the atmosphere is nothing if not elegant. Out in front the lanterns and signs are festooned with the names of the houses: Plum House, Bamboo House, Evergreen, Lake & Moon are all well-known spots in Karasumori, along with The Moon Blossom in the back streets of Shinbashi. These are the palaces of clandestine pleasures. In a back room at Igarashi's, or the annex of the Oboro, the great merchants and the gentlemen can scatter the flowers, as it were, and give themselves to excess, far, far away from the winds of the everyday world. No neighborhood, surely, is without at least one machiai—not to mention whole streets of them, lined up cheek by jowl, with delivery boys running back and forth bringing in refreshments. How the idle rich can wile away their days. . . . I would almost say it seems a little wasteful, but, without a proper education, I suppose I am in no position to understand these things.[23]

Natsuko wanted to see Tōsui again and judge his character for herself, but she did not want to go to Kōjimachi until she had a story to show him. It was as if the succession of brilliant October days with their blue skies and autumn bounty—chestnuts, persimmons, and grapes from relatives in Yamanashi— restored her energy of the previous spring. Though she worked furiously at her desk, the proper story would not come. Perseverance had become her new watchword. If she had convinced herself that her childhood powers of concentration were diminished and her literary gifts less imposing than everyone had prophesied, this made her all the more determined to cultivate what talent she did possess. Drafts were discarded, self-imposed deadlines passed, but she told herself that her "mediocre mind," "growing duller every day," would still, somehow, prevail. Part of the problem was that Natsuko had not yet reconciled two essentially conflicting goals; she wanted to write for money and she wanted to write art. The results were neither fish nor fowl, and each setback prompted her to self-abasement. But as she scrutinized her failures, she also revealed something of her pride and her understanding of how different she was from other young women. "If only I could take the same path that every other woman does, but it isn't meant to be. And yet I cannot live the kind of life a man does—I don't know enough about the world. . . . 'He who errs must start again,' they say. I am always thinking that tomorrow I'll begin anew. It's time I stopped having all my resolution on the night before."[24]

The sewing, the laundry, the housework, the seasonal observances—an offering of chestnuts to the Healing Buddha, a viewing of the first chrysanthemums, the harvest moon—all the everyday activities were subordinated to her one obsession. And when fiction failed her, these daily affairs themselves became the theme of her brushwork, for the diary continues unabated; this informal record of her frustrations with her formal writing bears witness to the prodigiousness of Natsuko's energies and her sheer need to write.

On Sunday, 18 October, Nonomiya Kikuko, Kuniko's friend who had first introduced Natsuko to Tōsui, came with a message from her mentor. Tōsui was anxious to see Natsuko again and worried about how she was faring. When she heard this, Natsuko decided she would go to him whether she had a story ready or not. She wrote to Tōsui on the twenty-second, proposing a visit for the twenty-third, but he wrote back that evening asking her to postpone her plans for a week, as his younger sister Kōko was to marry on the twenty-seventh.

Before they could meet, it appears that for the first time Natsuko heard of the Tsuruta girl's pregnancy. This bombshell was dropped by Nonomiya, either directly or through Kuniko, and the old adage about stories told at second hand proved all too true. About the crux of the matter Natsuko remained forever misinformed, for, as she understood it, the father of the child was Nakarai Tōsui, not his younger brother. Perhaps at first she had no inkling that either man was implicated, but in time the Tsuruta affair, and her misconstrued notion of Tōsui's role, would rankle until eventually it helped to destroy once and for all the intimacy that was about to renew itself between master and disciple.

They saw each other, briefly, when Natsuko brought a wedding gift for Kōko on the twenty-fifth, and then again on the thirtieth, when she returned for a longer visit. Face-to-face, Natsuko let her old shyness get the better of her. It had been months since they had talked, and in the interim she had learned some disconcerting things about her mentor. Only recently, on the twenty-sixth, she had heard from another of Kuniko's friends that Tōsui was near insolvency. This in itself would hardly have earned him her disapproval; who was she to criticize on that score? But if it were true—and it appeared to be true, for no sooner did she arrive than he had led her off to a "hidden house" he was keeping a block away, the better to avoid his creditors—then the mounting debts, the dissipation at the teahouses, the siring of bastards all added up to a considerable flaw in the man she had thought of as perfection incarnate.

Tōsui's retreat was a little four-room bungalow with books, papers, and writing brushes spread about haphazardly. Unbeknownst to Natsuko, it was the same house where he had sequestered Tsuruta Tamiko while she was pregnant. They sat down together by the brazier, but Natsuko felt uneasy: it was not entirely proper for the two of them to be alone like this, and what was Master Nakarai saying! He was talking about the Tsuruta affair! What grief it had brought him, how difficult the gossip had made it to marry off his sister. She didn't believe all the rumors she heard, did she? (Natsuko could feel the cold sweat beading up.) He himself was as pure as snow; no one knew how it hurt him to be mistrusted. She might think he was a crude person, but the last thing on earth he wanted was to bring harm to a refined young lady. (Natsuko groped for her handkerchief.) Was it her mother who had kept her from coming to see him all this time? He certainly hoped she wasn't going to let gossip affect their friendship.

Acutely uncomfortable and fumbling with the edges of her handkerchief, Natsuko reassured him. At last, mercifully, the conversation moved on to literature. He rather liked the story she had mailed him the other day and thought perhaps she ought to publish it. But this, too, embarrassed her. It was all she could do to mutter thank you, she would leave the matter up to him. Somehow she managed to parry the inevitable dinner invitation, borrowed several novels, and departed. The lovesick ninny of the spring had suddenly returned.

It took Natsuko what remained of the fall to regain her composure, but gradually the rapport that she and Tōsui had once enjoyed returned. "Relax," he would tell her, "you're too stiff." And she would reply, he ought to know by now that was the way she was. "All the more reason to try to relax," he would tease her.[25]

Before the year was out, two important events occurred. Tōsui made what amounted to something between a statement of fellow feeling and an oblique declaration of love, and Natsuko decided on the literary sobriquet "Ichiyō," by which the world would come to know her. A century later the details of both events seem almost as crabbed as a secret code.

First, to decipher the "declaration": it came during one of Natsuko's regular visits, near the end of November, as she described to Tōsui the outline for a story she was planning to write on the subject of unrequited love. After offering her some suggestions on the plot, Tōsui proceeded to discuss, with authority, the capriciousness of love—how women turn men's heads, how handsome youths deceive young ladies. "Clever young men trifle with the honor of girls of good family," he warned her. "They don't really love women, they do them harm." There were more important things than true love, he wanted her to know. "A woman should first think about finding a man who will make a reliable husband, who will offer her a lifetime of security. . . . *True* love is when a man worries, 'If I don't protect this woman, who will? Who will see that she lives a life of happiness and safety?'" Predictably, Natsuko began to fidget. Once more he told her to relax: "Let's not have any barriers between us." Somehow, Natsuko summoned her courage and made a nonconfession of her own. She confided to Tōsui that for a long time now she had regarded him as a teacher, an elder brother. Tōsui fell silent for a moment and then sighed, "Ah, what an unhappy man I am."[26]

The lament, apparently, was not in response to Natsuko's understatement so much as it was to the web of liaisons, reputed liaisons, and grief in love that had left him, at thirty-one, wary of any further entanglements. But at this point, the diary breaks off. Ichiyō scholars have suggested that the abrupt end, the kind of mystery that keeps annotators annotating, can be explained in several ways.[27] It is likely that by stopping here Natsuko purposely invites misunderstanding, that she wrote the entry as if it were a chapter in a novel and therefore intentionally omitted whatever reasons Tōsui went on to give for his unhappiness. By foreshortening her scene in this way, she intensifies its romantic implications. She intimates that what in fact may have been only a piece of avuncular advice on seeking a husband should be construed as a veiled declaration of love. She suggests the unfolding of an affair destined to remain unconsummated, the same threnody that runs through much of her later fiction.

Ironically, a second interpretation presents itself as equally compelling. From other available information, letters and later entries in the diary, we know that Natsuko was worried about her family's debts, which would all fall due at the end of the year, and that around this time (late November or early December 1891) she had requested financial assistance from Tōsui. The sigh he heaved may well have been for his own increasing indigence. Perhaps the diary breaks off here because Natsuko couldn't bring herself to record having asked Tōsui for a loan. She was not only proud, she was loath to let lucre tarnish the glow of their friendly relations, at least in print. Perhaps, in other words, Natsuko was already becoming more hard-boiled than she was willing to avow in her diary. Perhaps she had gone out that day looking not for love but for money.

The diary certainly yields ample evidence of Natsuko's growing concern for her finances. She still hoped that when her future readers gave their benediction, her efforts and her standards would be rewarded—nothing extravagant, just enough prosperity for the three of them to live on. She still believed that recognition would come, and in preparation for it she selected a pen name suitable to the occasion. The choice, a complicated, waggish one, was the last major event of her nineteenth year.

When, precisely, Natsuko settled on the name Ichiyō is uncertain, but it turns up in a short, undated collection of fugitive writings, the last volume of her diary for 1891. Why she picked the name is only slightly easier to explain. Its meaning for her—its literal meaning is "one leaf"—depends upon a rather esoteric conceit of the sort she was so fond of in her writing. "One leaf" referred to the legendary boat consisting of a single reed upon which Bodhidharma, the Zen patriarch, was said to have crossed the Yangtze River after a disastrous interview with Emperor Wu-ti (502–50). Tradition has it that he disembarked from his miraculous vessel and seated himself before a wall in the monastery of Shao-lin-ssŭ, where he remained without moving for nine years. This form of meditation, known as *pi-kuan*, or "wall-gazing," became a standard way to Zen enlightenment—not to mention loss of limb, for by the time the nine-year stint was up, both of Bodhidharma's legs had atrophied. (The tradition is still perpetuated in Japan, where little red, roly-poly "Daruma" dolls are ubiquitous; give them a push and immediately their legless, rounded bottoms right them.) It so happened that the expression "to have no legs" (*oashi ga nai*) also meant to have no money. Natsuko, in her own way proud of her hardships and wanting to distinguish herself from "lady writers," decided to flaunt her humble circumstances. Like Bodhidharma, then, in a manner of speaking she had no legs, and so she adopted his single-leaf skiff as her literary sobriquet:

It's been almost a year now since I began to work at writing fiction, and I've yet to come up with anything I can show the world. I haven't written a single story that I'm satisfied with. People like Mother and Kuniko say I'm too hesitant, always dwelling on the past, letting the days and months slip by. Even the greatest writers, they keep telling me, are not necessarily lionized from the beginning. At this stage, I ought to welcome criticism. I suppose what I write is no better than the most ephemeral popular literature, but, all the same, when I take up my brush I am trying for something higher. I intend to support myself by writing, but I'm not about to publish junk. Once I decided to become a writer, I made up my mind that I would never produce the kind of book that is all too popular today, read once and thrown into the wastebasket. People are frivolous, I know; what delights them one day is discarded the next. But even so, if I can appeal to the deepest emotions of the reader and portray what is true in men's hearts, then the fiction of Ichiyō, slight as it may be, will have some worth, will it not? I have no use for brocades, for stately mansions. A name that may last for a thousand years I am not about to sully for the advantage of the moment. I rework even the shortest pieces three times before I am ready to ask the world what it thinks of my writing. If all my efforts come to naught— brushes, paper wasted for nothing—I am prepared to accept it as the will of heaven.[28]

From now on, with a few exceptions, Natsuko would sign her stories "Higuchi Ichiyō,"[29] and hereafter we may appropriately refer to her as Ichiyō, according to the custom in Japan whereby the literary style replaces the given, or what we call the "first," name. All at once she seemed to sense that, at long last, her career was about to begin, for when the year turned Ichiyō left behind the things of childhood.

It was as though the moment she decided on a pen name the publishing seas parted for the solitary leaf. In February Tōsui told her of his plans to start a magazine and asked her to contribute a story to it. There were the usual delays in the launching of the new journal, which was designed to resuscitate Tōsui's flagging reputation, but after what seemed an interminable wait, *Musashino* (Musashi Plain)[30] made its debut on 23 March 1892, and in it, with a slender offering entitled "Yamizakura" (Flowers at Dusk) Higuchi Ichiyō was presented to the literary world.

Before discussing Ichiyō's maiden work, it is necessary to consider the nature of the new magazine, the literary roots from which it sprang, and the reasons it was doomed to fail. If *Musashino* was conceived by Tōsui partly to help establish his impressive pupil, it was created primarily as a rearguard action. He hoped that the new journal would shore up what, by now, had become the threadbare status of the gesaku tradition. Though men in the prime of their lives, Tōsui and his oterie were remnants of a bygone era. Dream they might of recapturing the former glory "playful writing" had enjoyed in the twilight of Edo, but the innovative light literature of a Tamenaga Shunsui or a Ryūtei Tanehiko[31] had long since degenerated past saving into a popular, facile kind of fiction that was the staple of the "little" illustrated newspapers (the *e-iri shinbun* and the *ko-shinbun*) catering to a semiliterate public that preferred gossip of the demimonde and cliffhanger romans à clef to hard news or political analysis, let alone true novels. What had once been a vigorous and fresh plebeian literature was now little more than mechanically produced ephemera and filler: souped-up novelizations of current events (a love suicide, perhaps, or a murder) or recent history (a sensational account of the Seinan Rebellion of 1877, for example). In other words, these stories consisting of "three parts fact and seven parts fiction," as they have been characterized by one scholar of the period,[32] were precisely those "twice-told tales of traitorous samurai and oversexed women" that, at their first meeting, Tōsui had complained to Ichiyō the public kept forcing him to write.[33]

The "little" newspapers (so-called in contradistinction to the "big" papers, which did run editorials and political coverage and articles that addressed the questions attending "culture" and "enlightenment") offered essentially three types of stories. All three were derived from later (1790-1860) gesaku-style fiction and were usually serialized and known as *tsuzukimono* or *shinbun-shōsetsu*. The solicitous, "serious" accounts closest to news stories suggested the didactic or homiletic vein of the *yomihon*, the self-proclaimed, serious "books-for-reading" category of gesaku, named to distinguish them from the supposedly more frivolous picture books. The amatory novels were in the tradition of the *ninjōbon*, "books of human sentiment," which provided their predominantly female audiences with endlessly complicated, vaguely erotic love stories. The satirical offerings were reminiscent of the *kokkeibon*, the colloquial "funny books" that mirrored and mocked the life of the Edo townsmen.

Kanagaki Robun (1829-94), who wrote, among other things, a fictional life of Napoleon, was perhaps the most prominent of the early newspaper novelists, followed in the mid-Meiji period by Aeba Kōson (1855-1922) and Murakami Namiroku (1865-1944). The weaknesses of these writers are the predictable flaws of popular fiction for the mass market. Their stories tend to concentrate entirely on action at the expense of characterization, although the dialogue is sometimes very vivid. The gesaku qualities in these works are usually pale reflections of the original strengths of the genre. The satire is thin and superficial, the humor is more often vulgar than acute, the love stories are feeble attempts to wring a tear from the trials and tribulations of a stale troupe of stock figures.

But even this abject end to the once-proud tradition of the yomihon, the ninjōbon, and the kokkeibon had already seen its heyday. The "little" newspapers had achieved the height of their prosperity in the previous decade, especially in the years 1885-87. Tōsui himself was employed by one of the "big" papers, where he wrote serial novels, to be sure, but where news coverage far outstripped fiction. By the 1890s escapist gesaku serializations had given way in popularity to "high collar" political novels, inspired in part by recent translations of Disraeli and other English political novelists. These new novels aspired to a greater distinction than the outmoded grab bag of whimsy and titillation. Riding the crest of enthusiasm for the popular rights movement of the 1880s and 1890s, the promulgation of the Meiji Constitution of 1889, and the convening of the Imperial Diet in 1890, the ever-timely political novel captured the imagination not only of the young intellectuals but of a wide segment of the populace. Bearing such rousing titles as *Before and After the Opening of the Diet*,[34] the resulting literature is in its way as jejune as the last gasp of gesaku, which exerted a considerable influence on the new genre.

The political serial was nonetheless one of the first steps toward the development of genuinely modern Japanese fiction. These novels, in which the heroes usually personified their authors' own political ideals, were often patently tendentious. And like gesaku, the characterization stopped at ill-defined stereotypes. But the most serious of the political novelists did at least address reality, did express a personally perceived truth—indignation toward the times and those in power—rather than a conventional, mannered view of life. And they responded to the vitality of the new age in a way that a writer like Tōsui could not. Whether they depicted the ancient government of Thebes[35] or "the equality of all four classes" in contemporary Japan, the political novels, written in an intoxicating, sinified prose well suited to their pedagogic purposes, were compelling reading to a public increasingly stirred by the promise of reform implicit in the Meiji Restoration.

The Meiji period, however, was a time of frenzied mutability, and no sooner did the gesaku newspaper serial give way to the political novel, than the political novel, having reached the apex of its ascendancy around 1890,[36] gave way to the novels of the Ken'yūsha. In 1885 a group of students in the preparatory course for Tokyo University, literary dilettantes with more than a slight resemblance to gesaku writers, styled themselves "the Friends of the Inkstone" (the Ken'yūsha); founded a journal, which they facetiously dubbed *A Library of Rubbish* (*Garakuta Bunko*); and proceeded to denounce the old-fashioned and blasé professionals like Tōsui who wrote for money rather than for art. (Lest they themselves be mistaken for frivolous writers, in 1889 they deleted any mention of rubbish from the title of their journal, which left them with the less cavalier but also less colorful *Library*.)

Although later disparaged by writers like Kunikida Doppo (1871–1908), who called Ken'yūsha fiction "Japanese literature in European garb,"[37] and the naturalist writer Tayama Katai (1871–1930), who belittled the attempt to reconcile realistic description with ornate style as nothing more than "gold-plated" writing,[38] the Ken'yūsha, led by Ozaki Kōyō (1868–1903), remained the only coherent, essentially modern literary movement active in the 1890s—modern in the sense that its members took a serious approach to fiction and strove for a realistic, objective depiction of life. Works such as Kōyō's *Ninin Bikuni Irozange* (The Amorous Confessions of Two Nuns, 1889) were so enormously popular that he and his fellow Friends of the Inkstone came to dominate both the literary scene and publishing decisions through the turn of the century. *Musashino* was Tōsui's attempt to capture some ground from them and the influential journal, *Miyako no Hana* (Flower of the Capital), edited by one of the leading lights of the movement, Yamada Bimyō (1868–1910). (Later, when he was unable to achieve this, Tōsui was to admit that he had been left behind in the literary evolution: he offered to arrange for Ichiyō a more rewarding affiliation with Ozaki Kōyō.)

But gesaku's coup de grace was dealt, ironically, not by the political novelists or the Ken'yūsha; the fatal thrust came from an admirer of the old, playful Edo compositions, Tsubouchi Shōyō (1859–1935). (Shōyō, it will be remembered, was the mentor of Ichiyō's fellow student at the Haginoya, Miyake Kaho, whose *A Songbird in the Grove* had inspired Ichiyō to set her sights on a novelist's career.) As a young man from the provinces, Shōyō had come to Tokyo with the hope of becoming a gesaku writer himself. Although he at one time considered apprenticing himself to Kanagaki Robun and maintained a lifelong respect for the epic romances of Bakin, his interest in English literature (he would eventually translate the complete Shakespeare) led him to write the first piece of modern literary criticism in Japan. When *Shōsetsu Shinzui* (The Essence of the Novel) appeared in 1885 and 1886— advocating the creation of a modern literary style somewhere between the classical and the colloquial and arguing that the novel is a serious form of art whose purpose is to portray the subtlest human feelings in ordinary, contemporary characters drawn from an objective and psychologically penetrating observation of real life—the theories put forth in his essay had a galvanizing effect on young writers.

The Essence of the Novel inspired men who would never before have considered the possibility that the novelist's profession could be anything other than disreputable. Confucianism had always looked askance at "frivolous writers," and in the early years of the Meiji era imported Victorian propriety did likewise. Suddenly literature was seen in a new light; it too could make a contribution to civilization. With the political novel, one saw the first inklings that the writing of fiction could be a serious business; for, as the 1884 translation of Disraeli's *Coningsby* had proven, even prime ministers wrote novels. It took Shōyō, however, to articulate the conviction that storytelling was not only inherently serious, it was art. For the first time in Japan since the Heian period, the novel was accepted as a legitimate form of literary expression (heretofore virtually the exclusive province of poetry), and the notion spelled the end for pulp gesaku.

Although Shōyō himself was unable to attain most of the stringent goals he set for the new novel, and his first attempt to do so, *Ichidoku Santan Tōsei Shosei Katagi* (Read Once and Groan Thrice: The Character of Today's Students, 1885–86), is usually viewed as a valiant but bungled tour de force, the mere definition of these new goals would, in time, sweep all before it. If a decade, and then some, was required for a new generation of writers to digest this manifesto fully, the delayed reaction only underscores how revolutionary—almost despite itself[39]—the 1885 essay was. "Looking back on it now," Kōda Rohan (1867–1947) would reminisce, "nothing has ever given me such a jolt. There have been various shocking things since then, but this was bigger by far than any of them. It was like tossing a rock into a quiet pond."[40]

No ripples, however, lapped at the shores of Nakarai Tōsui's circle. The political serials, the offerings of the Friends of the Inkstone, and the first scattered attempts at the new novel might as well have never existed. But while Tōsui lived the life of a *gokuraku tonbo*, "a dragonfly in paradise," making his rounds of the vaudeville theaters and the teahouses, fabricating his string of amorous tales about just such fey inebriates as he, more sober writers, like Futabatei Shimei (1864–1909) and Mori Ōgai (1862–1922), were taking the words of Tsubouchi Shōyō to heart.

Futabatei, a disciple of Shōyō who went on to become a distinguished translator of Russian literature, is credited with writing the first truly modern Japanese novel. It is entitled *Ukigumo* (Drifting Clouds); it was written over a three-year period beginning in 1886 (one year after the last installments of *The Essence of the Novel*); and this effort to bring the theories of his mentor to fruition proved so frustrating an experience that Futabatei did not attempt a second novel for another twenty years.

Futabatei was about as far removed from Nakarai Tōsui as a man could be. He was a ponderous person, an intellectual given to brooding and caustic remarks, a man with an intense devotion to literature. Like Shōyō, he believed that the novel was the highest form of art, and, like the Russian writers he read so avidly (Belinsky, Goncharov, and Turgenev in particular), he believed that the novelist had a duty to uncover the truths unique to his time. For Futabatei, this meant the writing of a realistic novel that would portray the society he saw collapsing around him in spasms of materialism and moral paralysis. Futabatei viewed his fellow countrymen in Meiji Japan as drifting clouds, buffeted by winds from the West: new ideas—democracy, romantic individualism, Christianity, progress—and new technology had cut them loose from the moorings of their own civilization.

Drifting Clouds was Futabatei's impressive attempt to describe, for the first time in a unified, colloquial literary language, this society that had lost its center. The protagonist is an introspective, intelligent, sensitive, sometimes neurotic young man outside the mainstream of modern life. He has come to Tokyo from the provinces, but his rigid adherence to the traditional values of honesty and sincerity and restraint in a time when everyone else has learned to compromise soon costs him his job, his girl friend, and all security.

He is not the least bit pragmatic, nor does he seem to have been graced with any instinct for self-preservation. In his integrity, his gentlemanliness, and his inability to yield to passing fashions, he is an admirable person, but he is feckless, and his unbending ways are sometimes stubborn and self-serving. The antagonist is a smart young man so in step with the times that his name, Noboru, literally means "rising." Unlike the country-bumpkin hero, he is city-born and street-wise. He is glib, superficial, and insensitive. He knows how to charm the ladies; he knows how to ingratiate himself with his superiors. He is shrewd, aggressive, and, when the occasion demands it, a sycophant. In short, he is an opportunist, and the very model of vulgar success, complete with his half-baked enthusiasm for democracy and his blind admiration of the West.

Futabatei's landmark novel has been so frequently and thoroughly discussed, even in English,[41] that it might be more instructive to turn here to another pioneering work of modern fiction that is sometimes overlooked. If it is neglected, it is because the career of its author, Mori Ōgai, is so illustrious, so diverse (literature, medicine, publishing, the military), that his early short stories, the so-called German trilogy—"Maihime" (The Dancing Girl, 1890), "Utakata no Ki" (A Tale of Impermanence, 1890), and "Fumizukai" (The Courier, 1891)—are overshadowed by the sheer number and more obvious brilliance of his later accomplishments.

Many of the great men of letters in the formative years of Meiji literature were deft translators of European fiction as well as writers of experimental novels, and in this respect Ōgai, prodigiously well-read in art, literature, philosophy, and esthetics, was no exception. As an accomplished translator, he introduced Japanese readers to a wide assortment of European writers: Goethe, Heine, Byron, Hoffmann, Rousseau, Daudet, and Hans Christian Andersen were a few. But Ōgai *was* an exception in being the only major figure of the early and middle decades of the Meiji epoch who knew Europe firsthand. For four years, from 1884 to 1888, the young Ōgai had lived as an army officer and medical student in the capitals of the German Empire. His days were spent observing war games with the Saxon army and studying with the most distinguished doctors of the day; his nights, reading the great German philosophers or the romantic poets, attending the musicales at the palace in Dresden or salons where the sofas were draped with tiger skins. He returned to Japan in 1888 a worldly and well-read young man, the likes of which the country had never seen, and proceeded to find time from his medical and military duties to establish what became one of the most influential literary magazines of the period, *Shigarami Zōshi* (The Floodgate Journal, 1889–94), and to write a story, "The Dancing Girl," that heralded the beginning of the romantic movement in Japanese literature. Like *The Essence of the Novel* and *Drifting Clouds*, "The Dancing Girl" influenced a whole generation of writers. Having tasted the sweets of European liberty, love, and intellectual ferment for himself, through his stories Ōgai enabled Japanese youth to experience these things vicariously.

For the first time, "The Dancing Girl" introduced the Japanese to some of the main ingredients of European romanticism, although the denouement, where the hero is cynical enough to opt for a successful career rather than a successful love affair, is a triumph of reason over emotion somewhat incompatible with the romantic spirit. In the end, the mood of nostalgia and regret evoked when the narrator-hero relives the events leading up to his decision outweighs whatever is inherently unromantic in the final choice.

Far from home, a diligent young Japanese lawyer in Berlin suddenly awakens to the possibilities of life. He is the kind of person who has always been at the head of the class, is always the boss's favorite. Then one day, released from the pressures of long years of study and his job, this exemplary grind is dazzled by the splendor and brilliance of Europe. The cosmopolitan, intellectual atmosphere turns his head. He realizes there is another side to himself that he has never explored, and he begins to appreciate ideas more than information. He's through with memorizing case books, since the spirit of the law, not the narrow interpretation of precedent, is what matters.

He is the romantic hero in more ways than one. Not only has he discovered his own self-worth; with the affirmation of his identity comes isolation, from his country and from his fellow foreign students. He shuns others and basks in splendid and fragile seclusion—like the silk tree, he says, whose branches shrivel when someone touches it. He compares himself to a virgin, awakening tremulously to love.

And that's just what happens. He meets a beautiful blond German girl crying in the churchyard and loans her money for her father's funeral. They fall in love and eventually set up housekeeping, or rather he moves in with the girl and her mother. But his transformation into a romantic hero, we shall see, has been less than complete. Even as he severs his ties with his post in Japan and becomes a free-lance journalist (an act of bohemian daring in those days), he can't quite rid himself of his preoccupation with what society will think of him. (Perhaps all romantic heroes are more self-conscious than they want to let on.)

In spite of their poverty, the couple's love is total and their days are blissful. The liaison is one of prince and showgirl: she is a dancer in a dance hall, though we are assured by the hero that his girl never sinks to the low things the other entertainers do. He has stepped down in the world to become her lover and her professor. She has native intelligence and has always liked to read, and now he schools her, taking her beyond the meager selection of the lending library.

One night the dancing girl faints on stage, and it is soon discovered that she is pregnant. Not long after, a letter comes from the hero's one friend in

Berlin who is secretary to the minister of the Japanese legation and who had earlier helped him find his present newspaper job. He offers the hero a chance to redeem himself by translating for the minister. As the dancing girl helps him dress for his appointment with the minister, she pleads with him not to abandon her if more prosperous days should ever come.

This, of course, is precisely what he does do. The minister offers him a way to return to Japan in good grace. By then he has had second thoughts about renouncing his past. As he has more contact with his successful friend and the minister of the legation, the hero realizes how far from the mainstream he has drifted. His ambitions revive. He agonizes over the minister's offer, and in the end he accepts it, leaving his pregnant dancing girl behind to suffer a nervous breakdown. He is torn by guilt and regret as he narrates his story on the ship back to Japan, remembering with irony the vow he had made never again to live the mechanical life of a drudge.

The romantic elements in Ōgai's story are apparent. The cult of feeling and individuality collides with the ambiguity of one's place in the world (to what does a man owe his allegiance?) and the larger question of what, in fact, the self really is—for the hero is obviously a man of contradictory parts: a student who shuns bourgeois virtues but yearns for respectability and success; a youth imbued with wanderlust who longs to return to his homeland; a man who awakens to his own subconscious, only to find that the "liberation" forecloses the possibility of any assurance or peace of mind; an innocent thrust into a world of such diversity and flux that he is forced to discover all the answers for himself, whereas those who came before him had the comfortable advantage of operating from a set of givens; a man who, in his anguish, turns to personal lyricism to find self-expression and self-understanding.

One can only wonder at how different the career of Higuchi Ichiyō might have been had she known of a story like "The Dancing Girl," had she kept herself abreast of the novel's development during her years of immersion in poetry. Shōyō, Futabatei, and Ōgai had impressive university educations and a wide knowledge of other literatures, and they had devoted much thought to the nature of the Japanese novel. Any one of them would have made a superb teacher for her. Though she lacked a command of other tongues and knowledge of other cultures, intellectually and temperamentally Ichiyō was closer to these men than she could ever be to Tōsui. Both by instinct and by her classical training, she held an almost reverential view of literature that had a closer affinity with Futabatei or Ōgai than with her own mentor. In her own words, Ichiyō "would never produce the kind of book that is all too popular today, read once and thrown into the wastebasket."[42] She had the same commitment to her writing as Futabatei Shimei. Without ever having exposed herself to modern theory, she believed intuitively in the integrity of the literary calling. And though she did indeed consider it a craft, from the beginning she was drawn to fiction as a means of expressing her disquietude, her private perception of the truth.

In other circumstances, Ichiyō might well have made her debut in Tsubouchi Shōyō's new journal, *Waseda Bungaku* (Waseda Literature, 1891–98), or Mori Ōgai's *Shigarami Zōshi* (1889–94), and she might have written a very different kind of first fiction. Instead she had chosen a mentor who was a full three steps behind the literary vanguard, and the loss was more than one of fashion. By any rational appraisal—although of course reason did not necessarily have the upper hand in Ichiyō's relations with Tōsui—the newly launched *Musashino* was a bulletin from the backwaters of literature.

Sales for the first issue of *Musashino* were disappointing. The magazine had to sell two thousand copies before it turned a profit, but this was a thoroughly unrealistic goal. Only at their peak did even the most successful literary journals enjoy a circulation of that magnitude. *Miyako no Hana* had a circulation of twenty-five hundred and *Shigarami Zōshi*, a circulation of two thousand. In fact, the Meiji literary magazines, which sold for a cover price of around seven sen, had a half-life so short that they were considered a success if all they did was avoid bankruptcy. Although *Musashino* was destined for a fate so common among new journals that there was a name for it—"three-issue magazines" (*sangō-zasshi*)—soon after the first number appeared on the stands, in late March 1892, Ichiyō received a favorable notice in the newspaper *Asahi*. The reviewer found the plot of "Flowers at Dusk" rather pedestrian but the prose style resplendent. (Curiously, even in her maiden work Ichiyō's language was already being compared to that of Saikaku, the great late seventeenth-century stylist, although Saikaku's true influence on Ichiyō would come in the second half of her career.)

The plot of "Flowers at Dusk" is indeed thin: a young beauty pines for the boy next door, who doesn't realize until too late that his childhood playmate is dying of unrequited love. And the language is indeed luxuriant: hardly a sentence goes by without the rhetorical plangencies of Ichiyō's beloved classics. In fact, "Flowers at Dusk" seems more like the prose equivalent of a Heian poem than a real short story, deferring as it does to so many of the conventions of classical poetry—allusions, language, and conceits—while neglecting such essential elements of storytelling as plot and characterization. (Ichiyō's overwhelming dependence on the devices of classical literature will be gleaned from the notes to the translation, pages 308–12 below, where the intricate web of wordplay, allusion, pun, and half-pun is unraveled thread by thread.)

In her first stories, Ichiyō was even more self-consciously Heian than in her early diaries. In her journal "In the Shade of Spring Leaves," for example, where courtly sentiments overspread the daily entries, but where Ichiyō wore her learning and her taste more lightly, she quite naturally described many of the events in her life in the manner of a Murasaki or a Sei Shōnagon. If she idealized things a bit and tended to see herself as the heroine of a great romance, the result was never pretentious or mechanical. In the early stories, however, where she writes for other eyes, Ichiyō feels compelled to demonstrate mastery of her literary heritage. This flexing of her classical muscles is some of Ichiyō's least satisfying work, a stage, like adolescence, through which the young writer must self-consciously pass before arriving at a more supple and luminous prose.

An excerpt from "In the Shade of Spring Leaves" will serve to illustrate how superior to the early fiction the early diaries are. In her journal, Heian sensibilities are part and parcel of the world Ichiyō describes, and the classical language—with the same honorific and inflected forms and the same indirection to be found in *The Tale of Genji*—is the natural medium of expression. Precisely because the diary was her escape, her one self-indulgence, wherein she forgot for the moment the shadows that had fallen over life and moved once more in a world of poetry and leisure, the entries have a spontaneity and naturalness that the belabored stories lack. The following scene, from the entry for 11 April 1891, is a party held to celebrate the flowering of the cherry trees. It takes place at the home of one of Ichiyō's classmates, near the banks of the Sumida River.

We were joking back and forth, as we always did, when someone remembered that today was the day of the university boat races. This caused great excitement. Everyone wanted a glimpse of the boats as they sped by the trees along the riverbank. We passed the binoculars round just as the boats were rowing by, and from the tall-storied house that Katoriko lived in we had an excellent view of all below: uniforms of red and white and blue and purple, sculls gliding through the water as easily as ducks. From the shore friends cheered them—"Go reds!" "Come on, whites!"—and some of the boys, completely caught up in the competition, darted off at full speed after their schools' entries in the race.

Minoko and I were all excited, eyes riveted on the scene below. "Oh, I hope they win! I hope they win!" she would shout gleefully, and then I would moan, "I can't bear it if they lose." Our zeal brought little chuckles from the rest of them.

Just then Mrs. Nakajima and the others arrived. Tatsuko and Shizuko came in only long enough to say hello. *They* had been invited to see the race, they said, and would join us later. Those of us remaining divided into two groups and held a little poetry match, debating back and forth the merits of each side's offerings. Somehow, though, I couldn't keep my mind on the contest. I kept dreaming of the cherry trees, when all at once fireworks began to go off outside. This inspired Mrs. Nakajima to recite:

> Not only do the cherries bloom,
> The sky has flowered into sparkles.

It was then Itō Natsuko's turn to compose opening lines to the refrain, which she dashed off effortlessly. The result was unextraordinary enough, and yet quite lovely all the same:

> In love we wander in tumult,
> But even in tumult
> Is joy:
> Not only do the cherries bloom,
> The sky has flowered into sparkles.

Minoko composed the next refrain:

> Today the frog's song, too,
> Is lazy and serene,

and I was startled to be called on for the verse! My mind had been wandering beneath the blossoms; brought back so suddenly, I was completely at a loss. All that went through my head was how long it was taking me to compose something. I don't even remember what I finally gave them, though this is perhaps close to it:

> Lovers think only of love
> And dream
> In the shade of cherry trees;
> Today the frog's song, too,
> Is lazy and serene.

Altogether, there were a number of good poems composed during the afternoon, but already I have forgotten them. Once we had finished with our poetry, Hisako played for us on the koto. She has great verve when she performs. Even I, who have no ear for such things, found her rendition of "Pine Wind" as beautiful and moving as the real sound.

"Goodness!" Mrs. Nakajima said. "It's getting dark. What a shame—before we've seen the cherry blossoms! Hisako's music has been too diverting."

Just as she spoke, Tatsuko and Shizuko finally came back from the boat race.

"Oh, don't go yet," Katoriko urged, but Mrs. Nakajima insisted.

Her menservants stayed behind for a moment to finish their wine, as the twelve or thirteen of us followed her down to the riverbank. To the west, the sun was sinking. In the evening breeze, here and there blossoms just beyond their prime fell from the trees like butterflies in dance. Young men who had had too much to drink began to pester us, and we were all very annoyed at their lack of manners. They drifted off, however, as the sun went down. What a relief to stroll under the trees without being bothered! As we laughed and joked among ourselves, the night grew darker. Across the river, a mist now spread like a white robe covering the water, and all that could be seen from the other side were the picnic bonfires glowing faintly through the fog.

"All we need to make tonight perfect is the moon," Mrs. Nakajima remarked. No sooner had she spoken than she seemed to regret her words, as well she might. We were all too young for anything so romantic. "I think we'd best be going," she added quickly.

"Not yet!" I felt like saying, but just then the men accompanying her appeared; now that they were ready to leave, they were in a hurry to be off.

It was sad to see the evening end. As we left the cherry arbor and boarded rickshaws to take us home, light rain began to fall. "Like tears of parting," everyone said. We went as far as Makurabashi together, and from there our rickshaws went their different ways.

A more ideal spring day would have been hard to imagine. Then again, I thought, if only the sky had stayed clear a little longer—but we're never satisfied, are we?[43]

Where in Ichiyō's early stories is the simple beauty of such a passage? Instead of enriching these first frail narrative attempts, the poet's impressive command of her classical heritage tended to overwhelm them. Not for nothing had Tōsui cautioned Ichiyō about her style. No doubt she could have written many a lyrical piece had she chosen to go on mining the classical vein as she did in her early diaries. But Tōsui was perfectly right when he told her that the Heian style was only so much dross as far as formula fiction was concerned. Perhaps if someone like Mori Ōgai had been guiding her, Ichiyō would have been able to fashion a story that took advantage of her classical inclinations, as "The Dancing Girl" made use of his. But the marriage of fine writing and pulp fiction was a misalliance from the start. As she slogged away trying to write something publishable—which, by Tōsui's definition, meant something entertaining—time after time in the first two and a half years of her career, the results were like bad *waka*, classical poetry at its most mannered: long on *kotoba* (diction) and short on *kokoro* (feeling), to borrow the standard terms from Japanese poetics. "Flowers at Dusk" and her other two stories that appeared in *Musashino* before the magazine folded that summer had all the aridity of literary exercises,[44] as if Mrs. Nakajima had just handed her pupils their topic for the next round in a poetry competition: love not returned, or love in conflict with duty, or the effect of the seasons on the heart. And so, because it is manipulated, the very beauty of the language and the classical motif seems faded and artificial.

Ichiyō felt constrained to begin her early stories from a lovesick and tearful stance not unknown to classical literature but greatly exaggerated by Tōsui's brand of fiction, which was in direct line of descent from the gesaku form known as ninjōbon, "books of human sentiment," or nakibon, "crying books," as they were sometimes disparagingly called, which told of unrequited love between beautiful young virgins and irresolute and irresistible "love-boys" (iro-otoko).[45] Waifs, bad debts, and thwarted feelings pepper the stories and, under Ichiyō's care, fine writing and literary allusion give a high finish to the entire empty project. Plot takes a back seat to impressionistic, emotional description. In the ninjōbon, the latent sexual attraction between the characters bubbles so close beneath the surface that the stories often border on the erotic. But in Ichiyō, the yearning is muted and melancholy and tempered by the sort of maidenly refinement that came with the pretensions of her class, or at any rate the class to which her parents had had pretensions. In both the ninjōbon and early Ichiyō, although the characters have tasted misfortune and have often come to know loneliness and poverty, they are so refined that all they seek from life is love and beauty. This heightened sensitivity to the promises of love and the beautiful is, of course, not incompatible with the sentiments of classical literature. Given her training, it was only natural that Ichiyō should strive to combine the ninjōbon with elements of traditional poetry and Heian romance.

And yet, surprisingly, in her hands the two strains separate like oil and water. This is partly because Ichiyō wasn't writing true ninjōbon. (Her early works lack any of the titillating elegance of the demimonde that gave the ninjōbon its flavor or any of the intricately plotted, convoluted love affairs that kept ninjōbon readers coming back for more.) And it was partly because, for the purposes of the novel, Ichiyō was too deeply read in the classics to write freely. To see how close the Heian legacy came to stymying Ichiyō's attempts at writing fiction, a few technical points and examples are in order.

Ichiyō's prose in the early stories is what Tsubouchi Shōyō, in his treatise The Essence of the Novel, had categorized as gazoku setchū buntai, a compromise between elegant (ga) and vulgar (zoku) styles; but it is vulgar only insofar as it permits an occasional colloquial utterance to find its way into the dialogue. In diction, rhythm, and overall mood the effect is considerably more ga than zoku. Most writers of this period were also still using some variation of Shōyō's compromise style rather than a true unification of the elegant and the vulgar, which only Futabatei Shimei and Yamada Bimyō had so far achieved. But unlike Ichiyō, other writers leaned more heavily toward the colloquial. The prose of Ichiyō's early fiction may be further classified as what Shōyō called kusa-zōshi style, referring to the illustrated storybooks of the Edo period which were written in a predominantly elegant style, often in the seven-five meter of classical poetry, but which did have passages of dialogue in a language approaching the colloquial. The main difference between the prose style of Ichiyō's early stories and her early diaries is that in the diaries the dialogue, too, is usually written in Heian-period, or "elegant," literary language—fluid but not even remotely colloquial. Ichiyō's style in this first phase, then, is what might be called extremely educated (in the classical sense) kusa-zōshi prose. Native Japanese words and classical inflections prevail (although Tōsui did succeed in adding some Chinese loanwords and modern vernacular forms). Rhythm and allusive variation carry all before them.

And that was precisely the problem: the story itself is dominated by the literary flourishes. Ichiyō is so intimidated by the great ladies of Heian that the classical inspiration behind her work exposes itself a little too blatantly. What remains when the quotations from *The Tale of Genji* have been stripped away? Not only were familiar ideas employed, sentences were borrowed lock, stock, and barrel.

While little more than a curiosity, the unfinished "Kare Obana" (Withered Grass) of the year before is a good example. The fragment of a story seems to be skimmed from the "Yugao" chapter in *Genji*. The story opens with a description of a lonely, isolated house in late fall. The garden is overgrown with mugwort. The geese call, and the scent of the last chrysanthemums and the mist of autumn rains envelop the house. Inside lives a sad young woman with her maid. The fragment breaks off before anything can happen. Ichiyō herself must have realized that here she was only offering warmed-over Murasaki. There is none of the special feeling that marks the personal experiences described in the diary, or the special melody, one might almost call it, that plays in her mature prose. On the contrary, nearly every sentence seems a reworking of Murasaki or the poets.[46] It would have been another thing if, in echoing the words or conceptions or situations of earlier works, Ichiyō had added new depth to them or had used them to add depth to her work; but neither was the case.

For the first two years of her career as a short-story writer, which is to say for half of her career, Ichiyō would continue to depend upon the classics in a way that nearly hobbled her. After "Withered Grass," if she did not always turn to Heian works as a source of inspiration for her plots, she nonetheless continued to invoke them, as if allusion could lend her work a certain legitimacy. One Japanese scholar has counted thirteen allusions to *The Pillow Book* (ca. 1002) alone in Ichiyō's twenty-one stories, and a total of fifty allusions if her diaries and discursive essays are included.[47] In one of the later stories, for example, "Yamiyo" (Encounters on a Dark Night, 1894), there are three allusions to *The Pillow Book*, three to *The Tale of Genji*, one to *The Tale of the Heike*, and three to poems in the imperial anthologies, as well as references to Chuang-tzu, Po Chü-i, and Lady Pan thrown in for good measure. This is actually a modest offering, as the allusions are spread throughout thirty-one pages. "Flowers at Dusk," which is only seven pages long in the recently published edition of the complete works, contains eleven allusions to poems in the imperial anthologies and a total of twenty clear cases of borrowings or allusive variation from sources that run the gamut of premodern literature.

Yet the imperfections of "Flowers at Dusk" and the other first fiction should not be exaggerated. If nothing else, Ichiyō's virtuosity in manipulating the Heian tradition, her enthusiasm and sincerity, and her desperate need to write something publishable—not only to make money but to assert herself as an individual—all inform an otherwise uninspired fiction. These qualities alone make her work fresher than the now decadent gesaku. And even if she appropriated only the most technical and sentimental aspects of court literature, the same tone and sensibility that give the early diaries their distinction can be detected in the early fiction: a fascination with the mutable, the ethereal; vague and contradictory moods of anticipation and yearning for the past. The rhythmic, the lyrical, and the associative had only to learn the art of modesty; they were not flaws in themselves.

By the time the March breeze ruffled the plum blossoms, it looked to Ichiyō as if everything she had ever wanted was within her reach. The gracious amenity of Nakarai Tōsui and his endeavor to transform the young poet into a money-making writer were promissory notes that any day now she could redeem for true and lasting love, and for fame from her own brush. There were some who lived in golden pavilions and wore brocades and sheer silks, she wrote in her diary, and then there were those who, like her mother and Kuniko and herself, wore the same cotton clothes for three years.[48] But who, she asked herself, could be happier than she when the harbinger light of early spring shone through the little grove in the garden and the scent of the first flowers filled her heart? She had published, she had been favorably reviewed, and she no longer felt beholden to her poetry friends, who were blessed with greater worldly endowments than she.

Ichiyō was not about to decorate her words or her feelings for the sake of her friends, she told Kuniko when her sister suggested that perhaps they ought to move to the bigger house next door, where she would have more room to entertain. No, a friend who dismissed her because of her small house or her old clothes was no friend, Ichiyō replied. Quite so, Kuniko agreed; all the same, she doubted that her elder sister would object to living in surroundings that were slightly more commodious. Kuniko's idea was prompted by Nakarai Tōsui's first visit to the Higuchi house on 18 March. As if to symbolize the restlessness of the times, people in the Meiji era seem to have been forever moving to new quarters, and Tōsui came that day to tell Ichiyō that he had found yet another new house in Hongō, Nishikatamachi, only a few minutes' walk from the Higuchis' place in Kikuzaka.

Ichiyō was delighted with the news, and her mother and sister were delighted finally to have set eyes on the man. Taki was quite taken with Mr. Nakarai, who was turned out in his usual style. He reminded her of her dead son Sentarō. She thought Mr. Nakarai was a gentleman no matter what others said. But Kuniko had her reservations. He looked to her a little too much like a gentleman, a little too handsome and polished to be trusted implicitly. Kuniko's opinion gave Taki pause. Living so close to them, Mr. Nakarai was certain to start dropping by in the evenings, and then what would the neighbors say?

Ichiyō did not fret about such things. Her enthusiasm for Tōsui remained as intemperate as his ebullient way of life: his late nights at the kabuki theater, and still later nights writing his daily installments for the newspaper, his tousled hair, his cluttered apartments. She loved it all, and, different as his life was from the upright ways of her departed father, Tōsui's very disarray seemed to her the true definition of manliness. When he overslept for one of their appointments and she arrived to find him bleary-eyed and in dishabille, the experience proved as erotic to maidenly Ichiyō as the innumerable scenes from the ninjōbon where the heroine calls on her unkempt, incorrigible love-boy.[49] In fact, one sometimes wonders if Ichiyō was not perhaps writing to type when she described Tōsui, this paradigm of the gesaku hero, in the pages of her diary.

Like Kuniko, however, Ichiyō's friends saw no such romantic aureole around the man; to them, his radiance was as artificial as the new incandescent lamps along the Ginza. The unfavorable reaction to Tōsui (whose name, one can imagine, was forever on Ichiyō's lips) continued to increase through the spring. It was as if within the next three months the unkind Fates withdrew their endorsement of the man. *Musashino* foundered; the rumors of his involvement with the Tsuruta girl persisted; he was racked with hemorrhoids and influenza, and as a result the word went out that he had syphilis. At first, the more in disgrace he was, the more Tōsui won Ichiyō's affections. For in this new set of circumstances a new aspect of Tōsui emerged to attract her. In place of the gallant hand held out to rescue her—through tutoring, introductions, and finally the publication of her work—was the fevered brow of an all too vulnerable man who needed her ministrations in order to recover from the fatigue of failure and the disreputabilities that dogged him. Never more than on his sickbed did the haggard but still handsome Tōsui so resemble the iro-otoko of the amatory novels.

Had Ichiyō stopped to reflect, she would have recognized that in Tōsui she had a hero right out of *A Plum Calendar for Spring Love,* the most renowned of the Edo "crying books." He had suffered the same melodramatic ups and downs as the famous Tanjirō. He, too, was out of favor with respectable society and had perennial reasons to seek shelter in the shadows. If his reputation as a man of dubious character was uncalled for, his debts he had earned with a spendthrift's industry.[50] But as money and physical strength slipped away, the love-boy only became more attractive. He was languid and passive and moody, even sickly, but he was still so gentle and so amorous that—in fiction, at least, for the scholars maintain that Ichiyō never did surrender—he could not help responding to the passions he inspired in the women who knew him. He was the soft, delicate male whom one finds all but indistinguishable from the women in the ukiyo-e prints, except for those illustrations in the pornographic tradition of the "spring pictures," where the love-boy's member belies his otherwise flaccid appearance.

This one remaining strength of his and a considerable, if somewhat wan, charm were, in the end, what would save the love-boy, for the women enamored of him—and in the ninjōbon they were always legion—would do anything to support their man and to prove that society had misjudged him. This combination of motherly love and desire for the hero inspired in women the loftiest ideals of self-sacrifice, purity, sincerity, and faithfulness. Although the iro-otoko always paid for the debauches of his youth, the very flaws in his character were of a noble strain. He may have been blasé, but he was never callous in his treatment of women. And for all his sensual enjoyment of luxury, at the root of his financial woes there was no taint of materialism; he was generous and without personal ambition, seeking neither money nor power for its own sake, although, in the storybooks, his underlying virtue would eventually bring him plenty of both. As could not have been lost on Ichiyō's courtly imagination, the love-boy was the last scion of a noble line of lovers extending back to Prince Genji, men whose only fealty was to love and to sentiment.

Not surprisingly, time and again traces of the love-boy, inspired by Tōsui, were to surface in Ichiyō's fiction. What is surprising is that in real life, finally, Ichiyō did not choose the ninjōbon role of the loyal heroine. Ochō in Plum Calendar is ready to sell herself into prostitution in order to protect Tanjirō, whereas Ichiyō ultimately decided to look out for herself. (She would never have admitted it, but this is of no consequence; in later life she was also reluctant to admit she had ever loved Tōsui.) By summertime rumors were swirling so persistently around the man's behavior that even Ichiyō was beginning to believe them. Compounded by the impending failure of Musashino and her fear for the future, the durable doubts were no longer little clouds on the distant horizon. On 12 June 1892, to be precise, they suddenly took on a new immediacy and a new menace.

Nakajima Utako's mother had died on the third of June; on the twelfth, Ichiyō and her friends gathered at the house in Koishikawa for the tenth-night observances. During the party, Ichiyō's best friend, Itō Natsuko, drew her aside. They went into a small adjoining room, where her friend inquired rather cryptically which she valued more—her duties to others or her family name?

"I take my responsibilities to others very seriously," Ichiyō responded, "and I've endured many hardships as a result. But of course I value my family name. I can't say which is more important—it's not only a matter of myself. I have a mother and brother and sisters."

"In that case, don't you think you ought to break with Mr. Nakarai?" Itō Natsuko asked point-blank.

"Why do you say such strange things? I've told you before—Mr. Nakarai is a handsome man, and so I *have* been careful about going to see him. I've thought many times about ending our friendship. But I can't turn my back on a man who's been so kind to me. I've done nothing to be ashamed of. *You* ought to know that. Why do you say such things—you of all people?"

The party in the next room grew increasingly festive, and Itō Natsuko suggested they continue the discussion later. As they walked back into the other room, she inserted the knife: "You tell me you can't break with Mr. Nakarai, so I suppose even *I* will have my doubts about you now."[51]

Knowing full well what kind of reputation Tōsui had, Ichiyō could not have been completely dumbfounded by the confrontation, as she pretends in her diary. What did shock her several days later was the suggestion that, far from being a question of whether she might at some future time be corrupted, she and Tōsui already knew each other as man and wife. On the fourteenth she asked Mrs. Nakajima for advice. She explained to her teacher that her relations with Tōsui had been perfectly aboveboard and without selfish motive, that her one goal was to support herself and her family through writing, and that Tōsui was helping her to achieve this.

Mrs. Nakajima asked Ichiyō if she and Tōsui had ever discussed marriage. Hearing this, Ichiyō was appalled. Even her own teacher, who had known her for seven years now, had apparently misunderstood her. It was all Ichiyō could do to keep from crying.

"Actually," Mrs. Nakajima said, "this man Nakarai is telling everyone that you're his wife, someone told me. If there *is* any bond or vow between you, then there's no need to pay attention to what other people say. But if there isn't—if it's not true—then I would advise you not to see him any more."[52]

All of a sudden Ichiyō found herself hating Tōsui from the bottom of her heart. He had sullied the name of an innocent and scrupulous young woman with boasts of his virility. If she could, she would have ripped open her own flesh and exposed her liver—the seat of courage and integrity—to all who doubted her. Now she understood what Itō Natsuko and the others had been hinting at. They were, after all, her loyal friends, who had no wish to see her throw her future away on a man of such small moral stature, and such slim talents into the bargain. Ichiyō blanched when the maids at the Haginoya added insult to injury by assuring her, as if it could possibly offer consolation, that there was no one who had not heard about Mr. Nakarai and poor Miss Higuchi! "How base! How despicable!" she scrawled in her diary. In a fit of anger and outrage, she finally went to bed that night, but how could she sleep?

In fact, Ichiyō, ever the novelist, was not entirely forthcoming in the account of the affair she recorded in her diary. For one thing, she herself was a source of the hateful rumors. And for another, the more she thought about the entire situation, the more it appeared to her that a break with her unpopular mentor was not without certain compensations. No matter what Tōsui may or may not have insinuated among the boys, the infatuated Ichiyō of the past two springs had dropped plenty of seeds on her own that now sprouted to her disadvantage. She herself had hinted to Miyake Kaho that Tōsui had proposed to her. There is no evidence of such a proposal. On the contrary, letters, memoirs, and Tōsui's statements after Ichiyō's death yield considerable circumstantial evidence that no proposal of marriage or liaison was ever proffered.[53] According to the reconstruction made by Japanese scholars, it is believed that in the very early stages of their friendship Tōsui may have suggested that Ichiyō become the Nakarai family housekeeper.[54] She had first met him as a seamstress and washerwoman, and, while she was anxious to trade this arrangement for a student-disciple relation, her fastidiousness may well have prompted Tōsui to propose that she live in, though not with him. In her lovelorn heart, where fact and fantasy were easily confused, Ichiyō may have ended up believing that the offer, if ever made, was a veiled proposition of another sort. She may have lied outright to Miyake Kaho, although it seems out of character. Or she may have intentionally misled Kaho by alluding to quite a different kind of proposal from Tōsui, duly declined, of course. Or she may have honestly believed that an offer of marriage had been made and rejected and that she had the upper hand. The only thing known for certain is her own culpability as a source of the rumor. It is a mark of her irrational love that she was sincerely shocked when confronted with the ensuing gossip.

The accumulated grievances, so slow in forming, finally left Ichiyō disenchanted. The collective ill-will Tōsui had earned, the affront to her pride at the thought that he could have trifled with her feelings, and his recent dismal showing in the literary world all robbed her of much to admire in her mentor. The more she heard about Tōsui's womanizing, and especially the story of the Tsuruta girl (for whom she herself had been asked to do sewing), the more Ichiyō's resentment grew. The idea that he could treat her in the same cavalier fashion as every other woman he had known and then boast of false conquests to his cronies was more than her self-esteem could endure. Those friends who did not urge her to abandon him on moral grounds (he was supposedly syphilitic, after all) argued from a more pragmatic position. These daughters of affluence sneered at the failed man of letters. Tanaka Minoko renewed her offer to arrange for Ichiyō to publish serial novels in one of the illustrated papers. Miyake Kaho, her old inspiration, was willing to introduce Ichiyō's work to the editors of the influential *Miyako no Hana*, provided she drop the execrable Tōsui.

It did not take long for her poetry friends to convince Ichiyō that Nakarai Tōsui had lost his utility. And yet, for all her resentment, she still had a residue of feeling for the man. Even if all the stories were true, the gentle Tōsui had shown her many kindnesses. He had showered her with more attention than she had received since the days of childhood. He had tried his best to teach her the tricks of the writer's trade. He had worked until he was sick and impoverished to keep *Musashino* afloat as their own private show-case. He had promised that as soon as the journal began to make money, she would be first to be paid. He worried about her family's finances. He said he would give her his share of the profits. And then, when everything ground to a halt, when the dream of a new literary voice was all but extinguished and he himself must have known that he had done all he could for her, he had made the ultimate confession of failure: he offered to arrange for her to study with a better teacher, Ozaki Kōyō.

On 15 June, with a lump in her throat, Ichiyō went to tell Tōsui that everything was over:

> This afternoon I went to see Mr. Nakarai. The endless summer rains are so dispiriting. His cousin and aunt were there, but Mr. Nakarai was napping in the next room, the one that looks like a study. All the shutters were closed tight for fear the heavy rain would come in, and the house was very dark. When she saw me, his cousin turned to her mother and said, "Look how nice Miss Higuchi looks today, with her pretty combs and her fancy hairdo."[55]
>
> "Yes, it certainly becomes you," her mother agreed. "Turn around and let me see the back. You look like one of those ancient ladies at court. It's a splendid hairdo! I can't abide the preference nowadays for wearing the knot low."
>
> Mr. Nakarai came in from the next room at this point. "Well, well! Look who's here! It's too dark with all these shutters closed—" he said, sliding several of them open, "I can't see how pretty you're looking."
>
> "Listen to him!" his aunt chuckled.
>
> I smiled, too. From that same glib mouth, I thought to myself, had come the lies that have brought all my unhappiness. I couldn't help glaring at him. But then I remembered what Mrs. Nakajima had counseled me, and I proceeded with the story we had agreed upon:
>
> "Mrs. Nakajima has asked me to come stay with her for a while.

There's no one to help her run things; she says she doesn't know what she'll do if I don't come and help her out. I didn't see how I could refuse her. She's done so much for me over the years. I suppose you've already made all the arrangements for me to meet Ozaki Kōyō, haven't you? And now I won't be able to go through with it—after putting you to all the trouble. But there's no point seeing him right now, when I'm not going to have time to do any writing. It's ungrateful of me. I'm sorry. I wanted to let you know right away; this was the first chance I had."

"That won't do! Everything is set with Ozaki. He's all ready to talk with you. He said anytime. I was planning to write you tomorrow. It's not going to be easy to decline now. Why don't you go ahead and meet him, whether you've got something to show him or not?"

"What would be the point of it, if we can't discuss my work? I have so many things weighing on my mind, it's hard for me to put them into words. I don't know—I feel as if I'm taken to task no matter which way I turn."

"Well, tell Mrs. Nakajima, then—if you're not happy with the arrangement. Nothing's going to be solved by keeping everything to yourself. You have to think clearly about things. You can't think only about the gratitude you owe to people. You have to think about supporting your family. Do you suppose anybody else is going to spend time worrying whether you can keep food on the table?"

Ordinarily, his words would have made me very happy. But today I could only listen halfheartedly. Master Nakarai kept on talking, trying to cheer me up; he told me something about a coal mine in Takashima; he tried to get me to laugh. But I couldn't bring myself to listen to what he was saying, and finally I left. I had a few things to do at home, so I went back to Kikuzaka for a moment, and then I returned to Koishikawa. I told Mrs. Nakajima the gist of what had happened, and she told me what she thought I ought to do next. I sent a letter off to Mr. Nakarai.[56]

One week later, on the twenty-second, she went back to see Tōsui again.

I came home, and here, too, there were many things to talk about.[57] Then I went to Mr. Nakarai's house to return his books. It was still morning and he was sound asleep inside his mosquito net. I was wondering if I should wake him, but before I was able to make up my mind just before noon he woke up.

"Natsuko! Why didn't you wake me? Instead of watching an old man snore." He quickly got up and dressed.

We sat down across from each other by the brazier and talked solemnly. I am a great one for getting sentimental. To think that this was the last time I would see him filled me with an unutterable wave of despondency.

Itō Natsuko and Mother and Kuniko and everyone kept telling me it was better not to break off relations with Mr. Nakarai too abruptly. I should explain everything to him first. It was important that he understood and agreed. I, too, was of the same mind. With no one around today, it seemed like the perfect time to unburden myself. As usual, though, at first I could only hem and haw and look at the floor. But this would accomplish nothing, and finally I forced myself to speak:

"I'm sorry I came early today, when I know perfectly well you like to sleep in. I've disturbed your dreams, thoughtlessly. Forgive me. It's because I had something important to tell you."

"What is it? Something happened to you?"

"Not just to me. I'm afraid your name has been tarnished too. I'm so sorry. It seems my visits here have become the subject of rumors. Friends of mine—even Mrs. Nakajima—have begun to hear things, and to have their doubts about me. Everyone thinks there's something between us. The more I try to explain the real situation, the more suspicious they become. I don't see any way to clear our names. Even though I tell myself that as long as *I* know I've done nothing wrong, I shouldn't worry what others think—and in fact I don't care about most people—Mrs. Nakajima is another matter. If she gets the wrong impression and loses faith in me, it could do me great harm. I've been so anxious about all of this, I haven't known what to do. One thing I do know: as long as I keep coming here to see you, the rumors are never going to go away. I don't think I'll be able to see you for a while, that's what I wanted to tell you. But I won't forget all you've done for me. You can't imagine how it hurts me to say this."

"So that's it. I misunderstood. You're always saying you don't like to meet men; I thought that was the reason you decided not to go through with seeing Ozaki Kōyō. I thought maybe Mrs. Nakajima had arranged for you to marry someone. That's what old Mrs. Kawamura said. Now I see. It's no good having people talk this way, is it? I don't much care—a man isn't really affected by this sort of gossip. But what a terrible thing for you! You know, I'm not surprised, actually. I almost expected something like this would happen. Put yourself in other people's shoes: the Higuchi girl comes to see Mr. Nakarai all the time—Mr. Nakarai, who's no wizened old man, mind you, and who's still single. There's bound to be talk. Since when does a young lady come to visit a man for no reason? The truth of the matter, that there's nothing between us," Tōsui chuckled offhandedly, "people find much harder to believe. Still . . . I wonder who started the rumors. I haven't told any of my friends about you. It just goes to show, the more you try to keep something quiet, the more it comes out. People know more about me than I do. You know, when I think about it, though, in the end, it may have been my own fault. The other day when I was talking to Miss Nonomiya I said some things I probably shouldn't have. I told her if you had trouble finding a proper husband, I'd like to help find someone for you. If I weren't the eldest son of the family, I told her, why, I'd marry you and carry on the Higuchi name myself, if I could persuade you to have me. She must have gone and told people. . . . I've only wanted what was best for you, Natsuko. I've always tried to do what I could to help you. I suppose you'd better not come to see me the way you have been. On the other hand, if you stop coming altogether, all of a sudden, people are going to wonder about that, too. Stop by once in a while. In any case, you *should* get married. You know that—I'm always telling you. I'm sure the rumors will die down. But, if we both remain single all our lives, then, no matter what they say, people will always suspect us. You don't think anyone is going to say you jilted me if you got married, do you?" he laughed. "Somehow I doubt they'll talk about me as the one who was always faithful."

We chatted for a while. There were many things to say, but finally I thought that I should go.

"No, no—give me a parting gift and stay a little longer. Who knows when we'll have another chance to have tea together like this? Don't go yet."

It was not that I didn't know by now what his feelings were. But as I thought of the reason we were forced to part I was filled with a profound hatred for the man. What kind of friend was it who would spread the rumors that he must have? I didn't know what to believe. What I did know was I was not going to let him overwhelm me with more lies. And yet, face-to-face with him, I felt my heart being pulled back again. His sad words made me cry. I was appalled at my own spinelessness.

Just then Kuniko came for me—even my own family doesn't trust me—and the two of us left for home.[58]

4
The Yoshiwara

Happiness may be good for the body, as Proust said, but it is grief that develops the powers of the mind. Grief was one thing Ichiyō now had in abundance. The family's financial worries only increased, while regrets for the stillborn affair with Tōsui, and perhaps a sense of guilt on her part, kept Ichiyō from enjoying any deliverance from the thralldom of first love. Once again she turned to literature as a means of escape. Hard work would help her forget her unhappiness and would, she hoped, bring in the money her family badly needed. In the summer of 1892 Ichiyō seemed to have put career before passion, but in fact she had merely traded one passion for another. As her enthusiasm for Tōsui waned—and she began to suspect that the emptiness of her desire for a personified ideal lay not in frustration but in fulfillment—literature became, incontrovertibly, the real love of her life.

She took her poetry friends up on their promises, wrote four more stories during 1892, and used their good offices to see her way into print. While they show little discernible advance in artistic merit over the *Musashino* stories, one of the pieces is worth mentioning. "Umoregi" (In Obscurity)[1] was one of her longest stories to date. Written in ten chapters, it was published in November and December in three installments in the prestigious *Miyako no Hana*, through the intercession of Miyake Kaho. The story was well received and brought Ichiyō favorable notices; in a year-end review of the literary scene in the magazine *Jogakusei* (Schoolgirl), Ichiyō was listed as a promising new author.[2] "In Obscurity" marked Ichiyō's arrival as a professional writer, a swift ascent, considering that her first story had appeared only nine months before. With publication in *Miyako no Hana*, one of the prime literary journals of the day, she had come a long way from the flimsy *Musashino*. Furthermore, she was now paid for her writing. Her fee was twenty-five sen per manuscript page, which amounted to a total of eleven yen seven sen. It was no fortune, but it was nonetheless payment for work rendered and was of incalculable worth to Ichiyō's self-esteem.[3] She and her mother could now tell their friends that she was a professional, breadwinning writer and that making a loan to the Higuchis was no longer by definition throwing good money after bad.

In addition to its modest success, "In Obscurity" is of interest as the first sustained attempt Ichiyō made after her break with Nakarai Tōsui to find a

new model for her fiction. Written in the same decorative style as the other
early works, the story is a poor imitation of the artisan novels of Kōda Rohan
(1867–1947), a major writer of the 1890s who, along with Ozaki Kōyō (of
the Ken'yūsha), is credited with introducing neoclassical elements and vigorous, rich, recondite prose into Meiji fiction. (He would later go on to enjoy a
distinguished career as an essayist, historian, and literary scholar.) Ichiyō
was especially influenced by Rohan's recently popular *Gojū no Tō* (The Five-
Storied Pagoda), which appeared as a serial in the newspaper *Kokkai* (National Assembly) from November 1891 to March 1892. Like the protagonist of
The Five-Storied Pagoda, the hero of "In Obscurity" is a man dedicated to the
solitary perfection of his craft, ready to sacrifice himself for his calling and to
forsake all corrupting influences in his single-minded revolt against the ram-
pant, crass materialism of his age. In Rohan's novel, the art is carpentry and
the obsession is the building of a perfect pagoda; in Ichiyō's story, the art is
the painting of porcelain and the hero, in an ironic twist, is her scapegrace
brother Toranosuke, metamorphosed into a man of integrity and artistic
passion. Deprived of her mentor and disappointed in her own kin, in fiction
Ichiyō gave herself the kind of brother she could admire.

The story opens with a lament for the decline of a great artistic tradition,
now that Satsuma porcelain was being mass-produced and artisans cared
only about money. Even in a story set in the modern, mechanized world of
1892, Ichiyō manages to impart her special sense of nostalgia. More unusual
in her work, since she herself was not particularly concerned with Westernization, are the occasional hints of Japan's preoccupation with its standing in
the eyes of other countries. Producing exquisite porcelains was one way to
win the foreigners' approbation. But, unfortunately, there were fewer and
fewer men with the talent or the dedication to show the world Japan's great
art. Nowadays "artists" all wore looks of self-satisfaction and defined excellence in terms of market price.

Though the genre of the artisan novel was not really her own, the sentiments were. This opening tirade against the lack of pride in one's work and
the easy materialism of the Meiji craftsman is a variation on a motif that
winds its way through Ichiyō's diary: her vows never to produce anything
ephemeral, never to pander to the public. The loss of an artistic ideal becomes her symbol for the moral deterioration of society. In its indirect way,
"In Obscurity" marks the first of Ichiyō's pleas to her countrymen. The time
had come, she warned them, to think about more than money and well-
being and material progress. In the gravel in front of hardware shops and
general stores, potters and painters bemoaned their fate and worked at
breakneck speed churning out their worthless wares. But what else could
they expect after ten years of acquiescing to the wholesalers? The fault lay
with themselves for not maintaining the standards that would have pre-

served their craft and given them a sense of accomplishment and a meaning to their lives.

The hero of "In Obscurity," the idealized version of Toranosuke, however, is different. He is not interested in amassing a fortune and he doesn't care if others consider him eccentric for his devotion to his work. Predictably, he is poor as a consequence. "In the Meiji era, when frivolity and insincerity are mistaken for talent," he asks, "what good is simple honesty? What good is earnestness? Where is dedication to a craft going to get you?"[4] He is an embittered man, and someone has nicknamed him "Mr. Righteous Indignation," but he goes on living in obscurity, obedient to his personal ideal: to create only works of which he can be proud, works that will endure in the history of porcelain. His sole companion is his sister Ochō, a beautiful young woman of seventeen who prays for her brother's eventual recognition and makes handkerchiefs to help support them.

One morning the hero, Irie Raizō, encounters a former friend from the days of his apprenticeship. The man, once their teacher's favorite and slated to become his adopted son, had absconded with an order and was never heard from again. He bows down before "Mr. Righteous Indignation" and begs forgiveness for having strayed from the path of humanity. In the intervening decade, he has become a wealthy and influential man, having married into a prosperous family from the provinces. Now a widower with a fortune that allows him a comfortable retirement, he is driven by remorse to spend his time doing good works for the sake of his country.

Hearing the man's story, Raizō begins to feel more charitable toward this former friend, Tatsuo, who has obviously been tormented by his youthful misconduct. Raizō sees that Tatsuo is fundamentally a good person and that he has atoned for his mistake, thereby attaining even greater grace than he enjoyed as the favored student, like a clouded gem that is polished to a new luster. Raizō sees in Tatsuo a kindred spirit, for like himself his friend has a dedication to something higher than the endless improvement of his own creature comforts. He is a man trying to improve, rather, the life of the masses in Meiji Japan.

But his very dedication contains the seeds of tragedy. His high-minded philanthropy never considers the toll it takes on other human beings, any more than Raizō's immersion in his art acknowledges the hardship his sister must suffer because of his refusal to compromise. Though the aspirations of both men are of the loftiest order, they are not without elements of the egomaniacal. Raizō is downright pigheaded. It is Ochō who pays the price. As Raizō and Tatsuo renew their friendship and Tatsuo becomes Raizō's liberating patron, Ochō falls in love with her brother's handsome and generous friend. She soon has her heart set on marriage, and Tatsuo appears to be of the same mind.

At the last moment, however, he lets her down. A colleague whose partici-
pation Tatsuo finds crucial for underwriting the construction of a new hospital, his latest pet project, becomes enamored of Ochō and requests Tatsuo's
assistance in arranging a marriage to her. Putting service to the state ahead
of personal feelings, Tatsuo agrees. Ochō's feelings are never considered, and,
when she hears of his plans, the crestfallen young woman commits suicide.

The loss of his sister finally opens Raizō's eyes: his idealism has been
warped by its failure to include the human dimension. He is no better than
his friend Tatsuo, sacrificing others for the sake of an unbending notion of
integrity. He tells himself that his obsession has killed Ochō. He blames
Tatsuo for deceiving him, but he blames himself for permitting him to do so.
Once again he is the embittered man he was at the start of the story, only
now he lacks an ideal to sustain him. He stares at the magnificent designs he
has painted on a pair of porcelain vases for the Columbian Exposition in
Chicago, executed for the glory of Japan. He hears his dead sister speak to
him, summoning him from the reds and yellows and greens of the glaze. He
decides to follow Ochō. "Let's go together!" he says, as he hurls one vase and
then the other against a stone in the garden. The midnight bell rings in the
distance and the story ends. All that remain are the broken fragments, bits of
a dream, glittering in the moonlight.

The story is long-winded, contrived, and almost infuriatingly elegant, but
it is not without power. For the first time the convictions of the author, so
frequently displayed in the diary, shine through a work of fiction. "In Obscurity" is both an appeal to man to live by some higher religion than the cult of
success and an affirmation of the direct and personal responsibilities every
man bears as his brother's keeper.

It will be revealing to look here at other stories written in the next two
years, which complete the first phase of Ichiyō's career, 1892–94. The protest against cynical ambition and conventional materialism continues, as
does her concern for the outcasts and those less favored by society. For every
polite young lady of the *Musashino* stories, a vein which persists in her
writing, Ichiyō also presents a waif, a misfit, or an innocent crushed by the
decadent times. As "In Obscurity" first demonstrated, Ichiyō's inherently
serious approach to fiction was struggling to shed the playful, mannered
chrysalis inherited from Nakarai Tōsui.

Interestingly, the last four stories of the first period appeared in a new
coterie journal that was to assume tremendous significance in the history of
the modern Japanese novel. The magazine was *Bungakkai* (The World of
Literature), founded by a group of recent graduates of Meiji Gakuin, a Christian university whose European atmosphere of chapel bells and stained glass
instilled in the young men a heady sense of emancipation, individualism, and
an almost naive sentimentality. The new journal came to function as a house
organ for the romantic movement during its heyday from 1893 to 1898.

Though Ichiyō cannot in any meaningful sense be considered a part of that movement, her connection with the magazine did provide her with a modest exposure to new currents in European literature—new to Japan at least. In Europe it had already been superseded by realism and naturalism, but romanticism was the first of the great nineteenth-century literary waves to hit Japan. The young *Bungakkai* writers were swept off their feet by the beauty and humanism of the English romantic poets. In essays and "new-style" verse, the Japanese romantics explored their awakening to the dignity of the individual, their burgeoning desire for self-assertion, their yearning for the true, the beautiful, and the unattainable, their mood of bittersweet re-membrance, and their Christian belief in the equality of all men. In time, Ichiyō was stimulated by this idealism of her fellow *Bungakkai* writers—Kitamura Tōkoku (1868–94), Shimazaki Tōson (1872–1943), Baba Kochō (1869–1940), Togawa Shūkotsu (1870–1939), Hirata Tokuboku (1873–1943). Over the next few years, their fervent pursuit of the literary calling was a great encouragement to Ichiyō to persevere despite adversity, and, although she did not in any conscious way take up their romantic banner, these insurgent men of letters had a salutary effect on her morale and on her work.

The first of the *Bungakkai* stories was begun at the end of 1892 and published in March 1893. It was entitled "Yuki no Hi" (A Snowy Day) and was inspired by the memory of an idyll with Tōsui the winter before. Little need be said of it here, as it continues in the mold of the lovesick, "classical" *Musashino* stories.

The next story, however, constitutes the first chapter in what might be called Ichiyō's waif literature. Although not completed until the end of 1893, "Koto no Ne" (The Sound of the Koto) is a slight offering of only five pages. The story is little more than an evocative set piece, but in its simple form it presents one of the purest examples of an important theme in both the early and mature phases of Ichiyō's fiction, what critics have called "the beauty in the valley" tradition in Ichiyō.[5] In general, the tradition comprises a lonely young woman of almost ethereal beauty, a waif who falls in love with her, and, offstage, a handsome man of the world who has forsaken her. Like the urchin who happens by and identifies with her loneliness, the heroine has also lost her parents. Although she is invariably of good family, without the backing of her father she is now neglected by the world—the fate of so many of the ladies in *The Tale of Genji*, who, shorn of parental assistance, are defenseless against the intrigues of love and court. Secluded in the darkness of her retreat, surrounded by thickets of mugwort so dense that only the light of the moon can penetrate the tangle, she mourns for the past, broods over the sweetheart who has discarded her, and finds her only solace in such classical attainments as the playing of the *koto*.

Along comes an adolescent waif who is so smitten by her beauty, or the beauty of her attainments—the mere sound of the koto in this story—that he reforms his delinquent ways and vows to consecrate his life to her. More often, in other stories, he finally meets her face-to-face. Her compassionate heart and her fragile, flawless beauty, "like a flower dwelling on a mountaintop,"[6] like another Ono no Komachi,[7] are enough to make him forget both his former violence and whatever wild ambitions he may have entertained, to become a doctor, to be elected to the Diet.[8] In sacrificing his own aspirations and even his former self for the sake of his passion, the budding love-boy stands at the antipode of existence from the man the heroine still pines for. Her handsome former love, a man now in the prime of his life, is the physical opposite of the immature, unprepossessing waif. Moreover, he has put success, not love, on the pedestal, and for that reason he has abandoned the beauty who can no longer further his interests. Together, the two male figures are not unlike the contradictory parts that Ichiyō perceived in the character of Nakarai Tōsui: weak, immature love-boy; strong, older man of the world. Just as the fainéant Tōsui could not, in the end, inspire Ichiyō's complete confidence, so the waif never quite captures the heroine's affections, since the one she yearns for is the man who will hold out a gallant hand of rescue.

There are certain ironies in Ichiyō's reworking of reality. The heroine proves to be as ambitious as the man who has jilted her. In spite of the romantic veneer of her yearning, she is not interested in calf love. What she wants is a way out of her predicament, and only the stronger, older man can offer it. In fiction, furthermore, it is always the man who does the abandoning.

Clearly, then, the sequestered and "willow-waisted"[9] maiden, too delicate to survive an encounter with the wind, was the culmination of Ichiyō's classical fantasies about herself. A keepsake from her family's more prosperous past, "the beauty in the valley" is always an adept at calligraphy and music and a connoisseur of the classics of Chinese and Japanese literature, though she is too well-bred, of course, to flaunt her talents.

Just as clearly, the waif is also *her* other self: violent emotion surging beneath the ladylike calm. Ichiyō identified with the discarded souls who live on the fringes of society, who lose their humanity through loneliness and desperation. The story of the savage orphan boy who is saved by the sound of beautiful music—by art—is her story:

> For fourteen cruel years the child, an innocent, had seen his family dispersed like the leaves that scatter from the autumn tree. Battered by the wind and rain, he was the last leaf clinging to the branch. But in fact he had nothing to hold on to; he was adrift in a world of uncertainty. . . . Nowhere was there anyone to take the boy in, to care for him and see him to adulthood. And the boy himself had no hopes for his future. At first he ached with envy for those who had their parents. He knew his mother [who had abandoned husband and child] was, no doubt, still

living, but her whereabouts and her life were to him a mystery. In spite of everything he still felt love for her. But then, with his father's death and the shock of knowing that he was now the last of his entire family, he grew to hate his mother for a deed as evil as the devil's own. . . . His beady eyes seemed to pierce whatever he looked at through his mop of tangled hair, . . . and everyone mistrusted him. They were sure the urchin never missed a chance to do some harm. He was glared at even by the police. At festivals and holidays, wherever people gathered, he was always the object of suspicion. How he hated them, with their shouts and accusations, "Pickpocket!" "Thief!" . . . He couldn't bear the bitterness in his heart; he wished that he could die. He stared into the river and wondered if he should jump, but death does not come easily. Alone and without hope, the boy found it increasingly difficult to sustain himself. He wandered here and there and sometimes managed to find work. At night, he stopped wherever he could. Life was like an unending nightmare. He drifted from day to day. The longer he lived, the taller he grew, but as his height increased his heart became more twisted.

Then one night he stumbles upon the lonely mansion of "the beauty in the valley":

> That night the sound of the woman's playing helped another to be reborn. Through fourteen springs and fourteen autumns, the boy had been buffeted by the rains. His heart had gradually toughened until it had become as hard as stone. . . . But now, at once, the tenderness it held buried within it was freed by the midnight strains of the koto. For the first time in many years he felt tears come to his eyes. . . . On this night of an ever-brighter moon, the scent of chrysanthemums along the hedge caressed his sleeve. How could a stormy wind blow now? The clouds in his heart had disappeared. Once more the woman began to play. The sound of the koto would be his friend for a hundred years, the seed for a hundred years of yearning. He had entered a world where a hundred different flowers were in bloom.[10]

The next installment in Ichiyō's waif literature, equally sentimental, does not end so fortunately. In the ambitious "Yamiyo" (Encounters on a Dark Night), an involuted and extremely *literary* work that borders on a self-parody of Ichiyō's allusive, circuitous style, the heroine persuades the waif to murder the man who has spurned her. The lengthy story, which was serialized from July to November 1894, has a gothic flavor to it. On a dark night, outside the gate of a dilapidated mansion, a passing rickshaw hits a boy. The caretaker of the estate discovers the victim and brings him in. When the boy comes to, there are balmy scents in the air and beside his pillow is a goddess such as he has never seen. For a moment the waif thinks he has been reborn in paradise. In fact, the woman is the usual "beauty in the valley." Her father has committed suicide after involvement in a questionable business venture with her erstwhile fiancé. She is now alone in the world, except for the couple who look after her; for, true to type, the man to whom she was engaged has abandoned her once her father's death renders her useless. While she withers away in the ruins of her estate, her former love has gone on to fame and fortune and is now a successful politician. The lonely beauty is the first person to show the waif a moment's kindness, and as he recuperates he falls in love with her. Once she has him under her sway, she persuades him to avenge her.

In "Encounters on a Dark Night" Ichiyō explores her own rancor toward the business partners who swindled her father and, in effect, killed him. She saw the glib and the unctuous for the predatory posturers they were. Succeeding in the new society at the expense of the honest and the innocent, always pragmatic and always unencumbered by ethical baggage, they were the strutting, sweet-talking politicians who never delivered on their promises. It is a mark of her mettle that she could dream of such a vendetta and a mark of her talent that, badly flawed though the story is, Ichiyō succeeds in describing her desire for revenge so dramatically.

Of course, if all she had done were to write stories that illuminated her own life, Ichiyō would hardly be remembered. But even in the early fiction, as we have already seen with "In Obscurity," Ichiyō casts an austere eye on her society. The stories of the first three years are written—frequently overwritten—in labyrinthine, almost self-indulgent prose, her development of character is shaky, the narrative is bereft of action, the sentiment is too treacly, and the gauzy and remote tone deliberately lacks verisimilitude, but these early offerings nonetheless speak to us with some urgency.

One of the last stories of the first period offers a particularly strong dissenting opinion on the new age. In "Hanagomori" (Clouds in Springtime), published in two parts in February and April of 1894, Ichiyō sizes up the ambition and cruelty of the Meiji middle class. She takes a hard look at the shrews of the bourgeoisie who stage-manage their children's success; in the process she achieves her most vivid characterization and lifelike dialogue to date. The plot is simple: pretentious, hot-tempered Ochika, whose "aspirations rose higher than Mount Fuji, though her station in life kept her back among the foothills,"[11] engineers an advantageous marriage for her only son, Yonosuke. As a result, the budding love between the acquiescent young man and his cousin Oshin is thwarted, and Oshin, too docile to protest, is cast aside and forced into exile. Though in Yonosuke Ochika has a handsome, scholarly, filial son whose recent graduation from law school destines him to rise in the world, Ochika can never be satisfied and so brings unhappiness to everyone. In her lectures to Yonosuke she unwittingly exposes the callousness behind her social climbing. She starts out solicitously and then, when it appears that she may not get her way, she slowly stirs herself up into such a froth that her full ire comes cascading down on poor Yonosuke. The passage is one of the most masterful in early Ichiyō:

Ochika puffed rings of smoke, her mind absorbed in gloomy thoughts, as she walked from the sitting room into the study. One of Yonosuke's books lay open on the desk; her son gazed out the window at the fragrant blossoms, his mind far from his reading. Ochika stirred the fire in the brazier next to him and quietly sat down on the cushion she had carried along into the room. It seemed that she had something to say—on her usual topic, no doubt. Even without speaking, her manner was harassing.

"Yonosuke, if you're not still a child!" his mother laughed. "Haven't you made up your mind yet? It's entirely up to you, you know. Yes or no, that's all you have to say. Why don't you decide one way or the other and put my mind at ease? I certainly won't try to force you—this isn't something a parent can demand. If you don't want to do it, don't do it. But there's no need to hesitate. You're better off speaking your mind. Don't worry about what I want. And remember, there's never been any promise of an engagement to Oshin, even if she has been with us all these years. There's no reason to feel sorry for her.

"But don't get the idea I'm promoting the Tawara girl," she added, "I've never even met her. I have to admit, though, day and night I worry about you and what the future will bring. Ever since your father died so young, as you well know, we've had no one to depend on. Quite the contrary, everyone in the family comes to *us* for help! Like flies attracted to anything that smells. I've always held high hopes for you, but a widow in my position—how was I to help you become the scholar you could have been? Not to mention the debts we have! When I think what lies ahead for you, it's no wonder my dreams are seldom sweet.

"It's hard on an old woman, Yonosuke: to lie awake night after night. I know, I'm just unburdening all my clumsy thoughts, but this talk of marriage coming out of the blue as it does—and, heaven knows, I've never been partial to Otatsu, who brought the matter up—I just wonder if it isn't a good omen, if it wasn't meant to be. Luck comes when we least expect it. You never know when the gods are going to give you an opportunity. Don't think it's impossible. Of course, I'm only interested in what's good for *you*. If it's not what you want, that's all right, too. Everyone has his own mind. . . ."

She spoke softly, yet her words had an undercurrent to them. Gradually, it began to irritate her son. "I'm not sure I know what you're talking about," he said. "You know I've never forgotten what I owe you for having raised me single-handedly. I always tell myself I should be a better son. But I'm not going to hide under a father-in-law's sleeves in order to get ahead. You may think it sounds naive—it doesn't matter—I want to stand or fall on my own. You don't need to worry. Success doesn't always hang from another's rope."

"Yes, that's what I thought you would say," his mother stared at him and sighed. "That's really what you believe, isn't it? Well, I'm afraid it's a child's notion. That's precisely why a mother has to worry so about her children's future. I'll go to my grave worrying. The trouble with you scholars is, you live in your fantasies. You sit at your desk and the whole world looks like a dream. You've never had to lift anything heavier than a pen. You've read too many books. You can't think for yourself. A fine future it'll bring! They say life is like a long journey with a heavy load, but you'll never make it more than halfway.

"Oh, sure, it's fine to say you'll succeed on your own, but listen, Yonosuke, the woods are full of people like you: smart young men who wind up kicking around a corner of the garbage heap. They all had their dreams of success, too. Their backgrounds vary, but they all have the same thing in mind. To make a name for themselves, to become rich. For people with ordinary goals, ordinary means may suffice. The world's a nest of mediocrity. Do you want to be contaminated by it? Nine out of ten people end up worthless, but someone with a little cunning can occupy the profitable position of that last one-tenth. If you knew how to think big, you wouldn't see anything embarrassing about becoming Tawara's son-in-law. It's a mistake to consider going under Tawara's wings the same as being manipulated. You can use *him*. What's so shameful about letting him be your stepping stone? On the contrary, it's a fine idea. Who cares what others say? After all, criticism is the other side of envy. Let the little sparrows squeak. All their ruckus in the bushes will never reach the heavens. It's the eagle one admires, riding high on the wind, sweeping the clouds away.

"I'll give you a more concrete example, Yonosuke. Look at Tawara's wife. She used to be a geisha in the Gion. Her family was nothing special. But she wasn't any ordinary girl, I can assure you, or today she'd have her apron on and her sleeves rolled up. She'd be cooking rice or running to the well or standing in the kitchen dicing vegetables. Instead, she's risen far above such mundane things. She has a high official in the palm of her hand, and the serene indifference of a married woman of leisure. You can be sure any criticism of her is whispered in the shadows. As Tawara's wife, now she's somebody. No fancy aristocrat has anything on her. Charity balls and concerts—things we've only heard of—why, she's chairman, or something, of them. And that's nothing. Sometimes she appears before the Emperor! We don't count next to her. It's the difference between the Milky Way and the gutter. The nice, obedient virgin is never appreciated, Yonosuke. Those who make their influence felt are people like the Tawara woman.

"I know I probably shouldn't criticize the dead, but your father was the same way you are. He always thought he could do everything for himself. And that's fine, but without a certain daring to go out into the world, how can life be anything but small-scale? . . .

"The day will come when you see your wife and children freezing in their threadbare clothes, with the wind whistling through your house on a frosty night, and you won't feel any peace of mind then. By avoiding all the ambitions you consider beneath you, there's no guarantee you won't find yourself working for someone else who's worse. The only difference is the amount of money you'll make. Your monthly salary won't be any better than the daily wages other people earn for doing piecework. Surely even you know of people like that, who live out their short lives without a single moment of beauty or glory.

"I hear other people praise you to the skies for being so noble and honorable and handsome, but you're really just a repetition of your father. You'll end up like him, too—a laughable little man everyone likes but nobody remembers. I suppose you'll be angry with me for saying this, but it's your interests I'm thinking of, Yonosuke. . . . Even if you pass the bar exam and get your appointment as a magistrate, you could end up spending years somewhere out in the sticks. And, you know, you'll be hampered by all kinds of regulations and restrictions. I'd put my seal to it—no one will know your name in the capital. Your life will be measured out. It will be like living within the boundaries of a map. Bound by lines you can't even see. Following orders other people give you. Always working according to instructions. Never achieving any success that might outlive you. And when you die, who will mourn for you but a few acquaintances? Who will celebrate the anniversary of your death but a few descendants? I don't see much difference between that and a dog's life. Your dreams and your life will all go up in smoke. Is that what you want? If you're going to dream, dream of paradise! Drink a little of life. Truth and lies, beauty and ugliness—taste it all, why don't you? Surely *sometimes* you must feel like taking flight.

"What do you say, Yonosuke? When you keep quiet like this, I think you still don't understand half of what I'm talking about. I feel sorry for you if you're still moonstruck over Oshin. Maybe it's *my* mistake, fretting over anyone as slow as you. If you're not going to answer me, you can go ahead and do what you want. But don't tell me your cold feet aren't on account of Oshin. Because if you weren't in love with her, you'd see how important this match is to you. Certainly you're not going to tell me the Tawaras aren't good enough for you—"

"I'm not interested," Yonosuke said. "I'm not interested in the Tawara

girl, and I'm not interested in Oshin. I'm not interested in a single thing
you have to say."
   What obstinacy! It was a hopeless struggle, just like the old days with
her husband. Ochika's case, which she had tried to build so carefully,
had collapsed into raw vituperation.[12]

Unfortunately, "Clouds in Springtime" suffers from the same uneven
execution as the other early stories. It remains a string of soliloquies that only
come to life when the virago Ochika is speaking. It has the same flaws as
"Encounters on a Dark Night" with none of the dramatic tension. But after
these two stories (written in reverse of the order in which they have been
discussed here) a new phase of Ichiyō's career was about to commence. A
new phase of life had already begun.

On 20 July 1893 the Higuchi women gave up any pretense of belonging to
the gentle class. The furnishings that Noriyoshi and Taki had accumulated
over thirty years of marriage were sorted, packed, and carted off by a friend
who had agreed to sell them on consignment. The remains of their formal
wardrobes were redeemed from the local pawnshop. As useless keepsakes of
the world of poetry Ichiyō was renouncing, the satin sashes and crepe
kimonos were dusted off and sold for fifteen yen, cash on the barrelhead.
Then, when still more money was needed to embark on the new life they
were planning, Noriyoshi's ten prized scrolls of landscapes and calligraphy,
the last relics from the salad days, were unrolled for a farewell look, put
away into their boxes, and deposited at the shop of an antiquarian friend. On
a cloudy morning in July the three women closed up the house in Kikuzaka.
In one cartload—*load* is almost too generous a word—they moved their
paltry belongings to the lowlands on the outskirts of the city. Here they would
open the tiny equivalent of a five-and-ten-cent store and hope that none of
their former friends from the aristocratic hills would amble down to find
them.
   The move was not an easy one. But abhorrent as the idea of toadying to
customers struck the proud Ichiyō, she had decided to take a leaf from
Nakarai Tōsui's book. When *Musashino* failed, her former mentor (whom
she saw now and then, and of whom she was still half enamored) had
opened a little tea shop in Kanda to supplement his newspaper earnings. In
spite of her break into print, the finances of the Higuchi family had continued
to slide until by mid-1893 they were hugging a precipice. Her writing would
not keep food on the table, and it had occurred to Ichiyō that only the drastic
step of becoming shopkeepers could save them from tumbling over the brink

into starvation and despair. The income from a shop would have the added advantage of freeing her to write only the kinds of stories she wanted to, not the inanities publishers were soliciting: love suicides, historical pieces, detective novels, elegant tales about devotees of poetry (her specialty in the eyes of her editors). In fleeing to the far reaches of the city, she was running from the temptation to become a hack.

She was also retreating from the mock courtiers, "who do nothing but hold their hands to their hearts and dream of the blossoms and the moon."[13] For more than a year she had resented having to waste time on the poetry crowd. She was tired of laughing at their jokes, which were not funny, and pretending to share their delights, which no longer beguiled her. She was tired of the outings to see the flowering plums and the spring cherries, tired of the parties at chic restaurants following the excursions, where she could scarcely enjoy herself for knowing that her mother and Kuniko were at home without a morsel of food in the cupboard. Not only did the amusements fail to amuse her; by calling to mind her own precarious position, they often brought her to tears.

Moreover, the world of poetry itself was in a state of disorder, as one faction contended with another and Nakajima Utako, basking in prominence, allowed the Haginoya to stagnate. The contests and poetic debates were shallow, inconsequential affairs. Ichiyō told herself she was only too happy to exchange a life of obscurity on the dusty side streets for the empty hours of social and artistic pretension. The money her robes would fetch was worth more to her than all the fine silks in brilliant cherry and maple patterns, bright costumes for a false role. The move to the commercial quarter would put a final barrier between Ichiyō and the daughters of privilege. No longer would she have to pray for rain or snow to force the cancellation of an outing.

Nonetheless, Ichiyō, her mother, and her sister agonized over the thought of driving a trade. The bold pronouncements in the diary sometimes sound as if they were designed to convince their author. Ichiyō was trying to persuade herself that she felt no regret at forsaking Mrs. Nakajima's little court of precious exiles from a more elegant literary era. She put up a game front, but the confidences to her diary were actually an uneasy mixture of optimism and prickly dread. Her mother found the prospective transition even more wrenching. Taki had spent too many years courting respectability to abandon cheerfully even the mere vestige of her hard-won status, and a vestige was all they had left. The old Confucian order of the universe was still too fresh in Taki's mind. In her Edo cosmology merchants stood even lower on the scale than peasants, whose ranks she had toiled through the best years of her life to escape. To enter trade at this late date would be tantamount to a betrayal of her husband. It was no wonder she sometimes wished she had died five years ago, before Noriyoshi. If only her two girls would get married, she often lamented. Even if they did open a store, what could three women do? It wasn't right to part with all their possessions for such a harebrained idea. She didn't like it, she kept telling them, she didn't like the whole business.

In the end, Taki's daughters prevailed upon her, but Ichiyō herself was not without trepidation. Tōsui's example had given her the idea of going into business; it had also served as a specter of ultimate humiliation. She had seen her former teacher lower his head before every customer who wandered into his shop. She knew that she would have to do the same, and she wondered if she was up to it. "In my twenty years, I have never been on friendly terms with any of my neighbors," she worried in her diary. "I have never been any good at exchanging pleasantries at the public bath. How, then, am I going to go around saying 'Hot today isn't it?' or 'A little on the cool side,' how am I going to dicker with a customer? How will I get on with suppliers? How will I attract any patrons? None of this is going to be easy."[14]

The financial aspects of the move were as troubling as the mental anguish. One reason the Higuchis decided to locate the shop in the shitamachi, the "downtown," away from the neighborhoods they had always known, was that only in a less expensive section of the city could they afford to open. More than pride drove them from the polite part of Tokyo. Not only were rents too expensive in the hilly, upper-class areas; they could not afford to stock the kind of merchandise befitting a store in a good location. The three women estimated that they would need fifty yen to open a modest paper shop selling inexpensive writing goods and children's sundries: balloons, cutouts, cheap candy. But they were destined to make the same mistake Noriyoshi had, for they would launch their enterprise without the proper capital. After all the family furnishings and clothing had been sold, the rent and the deposit on the new place had been paid, and they had borrowed all the money they could borrow, their coffers contained only five yen with which to stock the new store. This was one-tenth of the sum they had planned to invest, and even this was not hard cash but a mere promissory note from one of their most long-suffering financial backers, a friend by the name of Nishimura Sennosuke.

The preliminary arrangements for the move were fraught with shocks for Ichiyō. Amazingly, only now, four years after her father's death, did she comprehend how poor they were, how many tokens of middle-class life had slipped irrevocably beyond their grasp:

> From the fifteenth [of July] we started looking for a new house. Before the sun was even up, Kuniko and I set out for Izumichō and Nitchō-machi and then on to Asakusa. From Torigoe we went to Yanagihara and from there to Kuramae. Needless to say, our plans don't call for anything fancy—we are under no illusions about opening a smart little shop in a first-class location. All we want is a place as inexpensive as possible, where nobody we know will see us.

With these modest requirements in mind, we went looking at only the smallest houses in the shabbiest sections. It's been several years since we first fell on hard times, but until now we've always managed to live in a house, albeit a tiny one, that had a proper gate and a front door with a lattice, at least. We've had a garden with trees in it and a sitting room with an alcove. In the houses downtown that we've seen so far, however, the ceilings are covered with so much soot that it's depressing to look up at them, the pillars are bent, the floors are sinking, the eaves touch the next house, the back doors are lined up one after another. As if all this isn't bad enough, most of the places don't even have matting on the floor, or any sliding doors to separate the rooms. They are houses in name only.

In the beginning we were so appalled we didn't bother going inside any of the buildings. But I knew we'd never find anything that way, and at one place I made myself go next door to inquire. The first people kindly told me all about the house and the neighborhood. The others couldn't be bothered and directed us curtly to the real estate agent. The agent was a balding man in his forties sitting at a counter balancing his books. Behind him were displayed what looked to be the gifts he had received at midsummer: a puny little bag of sugar, some noodles, et cetera, all lined up as if oblations to a man of consequence. His patronizing air disgusted me.

We did at last find a place, however, that wasn't too bad: a little house on a lane running between Mikurabashi and Izumibashi. It had a four-and-a-half-mat room and a two-mat room for living quarters, with a three-mat space for a shop at the front. The shop had a wooden floor, and the other rooms were fitted with matting and the proper fixtures. It was a tenement, again, but not as dirty as the other ones we had seen. They were asking one yen eighty sen a month and a deposit of three yen. Everything seemed very nice, except that the place had no garden whatsoever. The back of the house was right up against the tenement that fronted on the next street. There would be no seeing any trees *here* even in our dreams. That was the only drawback, though, and so we thought we'd show Mother, and, if she liked it, then we would take it. By this time Kuniko was getting tired. I felt too sorry for her to drag her any farther and decided we should quit for now. It was not yet noon when we returned home. The three of us talked everything over again. No matter how many times we thought about it, none of us was looking forward to moving downtown. Maybe this afternoon we should look once more in the nicer neighborhoods we were accustomed to. We really did have to have a garden.

After lunch, we walked through Komagome, Sugamo, and Koishikawa. They are all lovely, quiet areas dotted with handsome estates. If we were to open our two-bit emporium in any of these neighborhoods, however, we would never draw a single customer. We have no choice, then, but to find something downtown. Ushigome would be a possibility, in which case the area around Kagurazaka looks promising. But there are people nearby that I know, and the thought of having them see us is too discouraging. We started for home without having settled anything.

As we strolled from Iidabashi to Ochanomizu we saw the river festival in progress. Little boats filled with passengers plied the waters of the canal. On the shore, horse-drawn carriages raced by and sightseers promenaded, preening themselves in their holiday finery. When I looked to see how Kuniko was doing, she had fallen behind, feet dragging, forehead dripping beads of sweat. Poor thing, she looked worn out. Sometimes I feel so sorry for Kuniko. She was still a little girl when Papa died, when we lost Sentarō. She never had a chance to enjoy the things other children do. She's spent these years with nothing to depend on, nothing to look forward to. I don't think Kuniko is capable of much joy any more. The quiet beauty of the spring cherries is not going to make up for the years of hardship. What will become of her? When I think of her lot in life, and of poor Mother, it makes me heartsick. I don't know how things are going to work out; I don't know what I should do. All I do know is that there's no going back. It's times like this a person learns what despair is.[15]

Two days later the Higuchis found what they wanted. Taki and Ichiyō went looking in Shitaya, part of present-day Asakusa, while Kuniko, tired from all the walking of the last few days, stayed home to rest. Mother and daughter came to an area called Ryūsenji, where they found a dwelling twelve feet by thirty-six that was part of a "long house," a block of row houses. It was tiny and lacked fittings and furnishings, but it had a northern and southern exposure, it was clean, and, most important, it had the requisite garden. Not only did it have a yard in the back; beyond that stretched a leafy thicket, which belonged, as it turned out, to a dormitory for prostitutes who worked in the nearby quarter. Inside, the house had a five-mat room and a three-mat room, with a six-mat room at the front for a shop. With a deposit of three yen and a monthly rent of one yen fifty sen, it came to a bit more than they wanted to spend, but the garden so impressed them that they decided to talk the matter over with Kuniko. They told the man who ran the saké shop next door they were interested, and that evening Ichiyō returned with her sister in tow. Kuniko was amenable, but there seemed to have been a slip-up during the afternoon. It looked as if the house might go to someone else. Disappointed and weary of house-hunting, they quickly enlisted a cousin, Hirose Isaburō, who lived in nearby Asakusa, to negotiate for them. By the following evening, 18 July, the dispute was settled in their favor and the three women prepared to move.

The next day, their last in Kikuzaka, they took what remained of the family furniture to their friend Nishimura, who had agreed to sell everything in order to supply them with capital for starting the store. In between the packing and cleaning, Ichiyō went to call on a select few who would have to be informed about the move. She visited one of her editors, Fujimoto Tōin, at *Miyako no Hana*; she stopped to tell her best friend, Itō Natsuko; she went to the Haginoya to tell Mrs. Nakajima. That night, as she lay in bed, all the arrangements for the move completed, she felt her heart palpitating. It was one of those rare and frightening occasions when the end of things is transparent to the mind's eye but the beginning of whatever supersedes is still coalescing in the nebulous half-light. The hour was late before she finally fell asleep.

Ryūsenji, the area they had finally settled on, was in the heart of the downtown district. It was only three miles from the Haginoya, but it might as well have been in a remote province. Not only was their new neighborhood located in the flat crescent of the rough-and-tumble wards south and east of the respectable parts of the city, in Ryūsenji they had chosen a spot in the very shadow of the notorious pleasure quarter. The walls of the Yoshiwara were a five-minute walk away. "The bawdyhouse lights flickered in the moat . . . and the noise from the rooms way up on the third floor—it was all near enough to touch."[16] Strains of the samisen and the laughter of courtesans carried from the teahouses, but this was all of the rococo splendor that penetrated to the back street. The tenements of Ryūsenji did not share in the prosperity of the quarter. The Higuchis' new neighbors were rickshawmen and waitresses and bouncers for the famous brothels. Almost everyone was involved, in one way or another, in the business of the houses, but they were the little people on the periphery of the booming red-light industry. They sent their daughters, who never quite had the makings of remunerative cocottes, to be serving girls in the great establishments. The brawnier sons of Ryūsenji wound up as "horses," enforcing goons, in the stable of bill collectors who shadowed defaulting customers, nagging, threatening, getting tough if that was the only way to persuade a visitor to make good on his debts to the house. In a neighborhood where money was tight and children were saucy, the little dime store Ichiyō had in mind looked made to order:

The new house is on the only road leading directly from Shitaya to the Yoshiwara. After dusk the rickshaws come thundering by, lanterns swinging. The noise and the lights beggar description.The last stragglers to the quarter don't arrive until after 1:00 A.M. Then, at 3:00, starts the clatter of rickshaws heading home. The first night here, after the peace and quiet of Hongō, is certainly an experience!

Living in a row house, we have only one wall between us and our neighbors, a rickshawman and his family, I hear. These are the kind of people who will be our customers; I hope we won't rub any of them the wrong way. Everyone says people near the quarter are barbarians. Without a man in the house, I'm afraid we're in for some rough treatment. For myself, I don't particularly care. But Mother is old and Kuniko defenseless. I don't want to see them treated unkindly. Then there's the question of how we should go about opening the shop—a thousand and one questions to worry about. I must say, this place is swarming with mosquitoes. Big "bush mosquitoes," awesome things. They buzz from sundown and don't stop breeding, someone told me, until winter comes and it's time to put on padded clothing. How on earth are we going to stand it?

The well has good water, but it's deep and bringing the bucket up takes some doing. I suppose once we get used to everything the place won't seem so bad. Once we make some friends and the shop starts to turn a profit, it won't be long before we feel at home. All our old friends will forget us, I suppose, now that we have fallen in the world and drifted here to rot in these stagnant waters. I wonder if I will ever see Mr. Nakarai again. I'll be forgotten, completely forgotten. Love will vanish like a floating cloud, disappearing from the empty sky. Until yesterday he used to call on us. If just once in a while he would think of the old house and remember me, that would be reason enough for living. But he has no idea of our whereabouts, and now that I have slipped into the dust and consort with the dregs of society, even if he did for some reason chance to think of me, it would not be with pity or compassion, but with contempt for one who could not lead a noble existence, who ended her days in the dirt; he would never bother calling me to mind again. With these thoughts going round and round in my head, I am too disconsolate to sleep. It is already getting light outside, and I can hear the birds beginning to stir. During the night there was dreadful thunder and lightning. It gave me a good scare.[17]

After making the momentous move and preparing themselves psychologically to become tradesfolk, there remained one problem for the Higuchis. They had to collect the five yen from Nishimura Sennosuke before they could lay in a supply of balloons. Nishimura's dillydallying provoked Ichiyō to show her fighting colors:

> Until bedtime Kuniko and I discussed what steps we might take to remedy our situation. The old adage is true: a person doesn't know who his friends are until he's in trouble. When we didn't need anything, then everyone was kind to us. I used to think that people never change. But they do, and that's what makes life difficult. People are only sympathetic on a full stomach. It's disgusting. Old friends may not look any different from the days when we still had Papa and Sentarō, but peer into their hearts—now that we're having our problems—and one finds they've

changed along with everything else in this fickle world. Small wonder there are few heroes or true gentlemen, that a faithful wife and a dutiful son are both curiosities. People live their entire lives governed by the emotions of the moment. It's a vain, inconstant world we live in, and a sad day when one has to admit it.

That Sennosuke is a perfect example. In the past, he always behaved in good faith toward our family, but his cruel conduct of late shows how thoroughly the human heart alters. Even now, if we told him he could marry Kuniko, he'd change his tune faster than he could turn his palms up. It's fascinating, all the different types there are. Here's a man who supposedly loves Kuniko, and look how he treats us. In the old days our house was high, his was low; being ambitious, he wanted to marry into the family. Gradually our positions have changed. He is now prosperous, we are now poor. So he expects us to do obeisance before him out of gratitude for his little favors. Maybe he's acting this way because he doesn't think we've been sufficiently appreciative. This is his chance to teach us a lesson; he's going to sit back and watch us stew for a while.

Or am I letting my imagination run away with me? Surely Sennosuke isn't that sort of person. On the other hand, a house like his shouldn't have any trouble coming up with five yen, or ten yen for that matter. Even if he doesn't have the money, he has friends, he has acquaintances. He's a man, he can do anything he sets his mind to. Especially after Mother went begging with her head down!

The more I think about the way he's behaved, the more convinced I am he *meant* to hurt us, as if we were his enemies. If that's what he wants, he'll get himself an enemy, all right! Does he think the last two daughters of the Higuchi house were born without guts, without backbone? To sound reason we will yield as pliantly as sheep; but we are not about to let an enemy stab us in the back. In this world of emptiness, I am perfectly willing to meet a good death. Why should we submit to the likes of Sennosuke? For Mother's sake, I'll try to settle things quietly—this time. I'll send him a polite letter. I'll decide what to do next after I see what his answer is.[18]

The next morning, 26 July, she sent off a missive, as dulcet and deferential as could be. While they waited and fretted, they took in the sights of the quarter:

It rained off and on all afternoon. In the evening Kuniko and I went to see the lanterns. We wanted to see the festival dolls on display, too. On the way home it started to rain again.

The dolls were the work of Yasumoto Kamehachi and one of his apprentices, I believe. Yasumoto is one of the masters of the art of doll-making in Tokyo.

Every night there is a lady minstrel who plays songs of love suicide on her samisen. She must be well into her thirties, I suppose. She wears a scallop-patterned summer kimono of pale yellow and a sash of black satin. She ties a scarf around her hair, Yoshiwara-style. Her little lantern has a long handle that she can stick inside her collar. Quite lively and impressive. I wonder what she used to be. A geisha, it would seem. A heartbreaker, no doubt. "She must have made the thrushes cry," as the saying goes. She has not completely lost her beauty. She half suggests someone who's given up the demimonde, someone who's experienced enlightenment. And yet she looks as if she thinks rather highly of herself, knows how coquettish her songs can sound. The woman bears paying attention to.

One wonders if some of these loud-mouthed playboys who haggle out in front of the houses (will they come upstairs or won't they?), puffing away on the pipes the ladies proffer as bait to lure them in—do such gentlemen feel anything when they hear these songs of tragic love? The truly elegant, rather, are open to destruction. A man falls in love with a woman; a beauty and her patron cannot bear to be apart. Long after he is forbidden access to her chamber, he still steals upstairs to his darling. No tangle of ivy on the side gate where he enters is more hopelessly twisted and entwined than these two lovers are. They whisper and plot. When the bell tolls four o'clock and the quarter closes for the night, they will give up this unhappy life together: no waiting for the dawn, for the frost to settle on the rooftop ducks of porcelain.[19]

Through the main streets and the byways, the minstrel plays her music. Her repertoire is deeply moving. The fine clear voice, the sound of the samisen have a melancholy ring. Is it the songs that are sad, or the woman who sings them?

Two nights ago, I counted seventy-five rickshaws going down the road before our house within the space of ten minutes. That would make five hundred in an hour. What booming days, one would think, for the quarter! And yet, during the festival, I hear, many of the visitors are women and sightseers—no profits there for the great establishments. They say that even the Isekyū has nights without a customer, and perhaps it's true. Tonight we walked around till nine o'clock, and not a man did we see being escorted to the brothels. The Kadoebi, however, looked as prosperous as always.

As we were strolling in Edochō, we happened upon a lost child, a little four-year-old boy. There didn't seem to be much we could do; he couldn't tell us anything. We soon found out, though, that he had come with his parents and two or three others. The crowds were not really so bad where we were; it must have taken his parents some doing to lose him. They finally ran into us, but they did not even bother to thank us.

They picked up the boy and hurried off down a side street. There are certainly some odd people in this world.[20]

Up and down the street, their new neighbors were engrossed in a peculiar pastime. Whenever they could spare a moment from their duties in the quarter, they would fashion good-luck charms to sell at the coming autumn festivals in the Yoshiwara.

Outside the tumble-down houses everyone works madly: cutting up paper into queer little pieces, slopping them with paint, spearing them on funny-looking spits. Whole families, the whole neighborhood is wrapped up in the production of these strange, bright paper skewers. They dry the painted scraps in the morning and assemble them at night. And what are these things that have everyone so preoccupied? "You don't know?" a merchant will reply in astonishment. "*Kumade* charms! On Otori day, you ought to see the big-wishers buy them up."

Year in, year out, the minute the New Year pine bough comes down from the front gate, every self-respecting businessman takes up the same sideline, and by summer hands and feet are splattered with paint. They count on the earnings to buy new clothes for the holidays. If the gods grant prosperity to mere purchasers of these charms, the men who make them figure they stand to reap a windfall. Funny thing, no one hears of any rich men dwelling in these parts.[21]

Ichiyō, Taki, and Kuniko were to stay here only nine months. Before long, however, they themselves were infected with their neighbors' optimism. They did not expect to get rich selling paper charms, but like their fellow citizens of the shitamachi they did a lot of waiting. They waited for the money to order their stock. When the money came—three yen from Nishimura, seven from cousin Hirose Isaburō—they waited for the supplier to deliver their goods. When the merchandise was finally in place and the still half-empty-looking store was decorated for the grand opening, they toasted each other with saké and waited for customers. When the customers began to trickle in, they waited for business to improve. When the shop began to earn a feeble profit, they waited for it to become lucrative enough to make the whole backbreaking endeavor worth their efforts. It never did.

Their profit margin was reasonable enough, approximately 30 percent. Yet the unit prices and the volume were so low that they were making 30 percent of a pittance. It was not unusual for them to have a hundred customers in a day, but the average customer spent only five or six *rin*.[22] With sales averaging forty to sixty sen a day, their gross income was fifteen yen a month, and their average profit a mere four and a half yen. Their basic trouble was that they had started undercapitalized and they remained so. Lacking adequate stock when they opened, they found themselves with a self-perpetuating handicap. The turnover was too slight to generate the extra funds they needed to increase their supplies, and without greater bulk and variety the shop would barely sustain them.

As a result, Ichiyō had to make almost daily excursions to the wholesalers, one morning to the toy dealer, one morning to the bakery. She began to exhaust herself lugging bundles of paper, candles, and crackers home in the hot afternoons of August. There was almost no time for writing; she published only two stories in the nine months in Ryūsenji, "The Sound of the Koto" and "Clouds in Springtime." When she did find a spare moment, she preferred to lie down. Far from freeing her to become a more independent and original writer, the shop actually hobbled her. The idea was that Kuniko would run the shop, Taki would manage the house, and Ichiyō would visit suppliers once or twice a week and spend the remaining time writing and studying. It is clear that she did not know what she was getting into. In the first days of the business, in spite of its uncertain prospects commerce may have been something of a game to Ichiyō, just as the move to the downtown was her variation on the classical theme of retreating from the world—or at least from the only world she had known.

The difference, of course, was that, instead of fleeing the mundane for the contemplative quiet of the mountains or the sea, Ichiyō had chosen the capital of worldliness to escape to. By the time she had had a taste of trade, she could no longer delude herself that Ryūsenji equaled aristocratic retreat. The vulgar necessity of making money was too pervasive. If she could laugh now and then at her family's ineptitude as businesswomen, the things she observed increasingly filled her with dread. The dawn visits to the rambunctious wholesalers frightened her. Storms, word of a natural disaster sent chills up and down her spine. The squalid conditions of the back street, accentuated by the brittle, artificial beauty of the quarter, profoundly disturbed her. The corruption that she read of in the paper left her appalled. The news that two of their competitors had folded gave her mixed feelings. Buddha had forsaken her, she wrote in her diary, she would never reach the Pure Land. She began to get headaches. Sometimes they would last for half a week. On the bad days they immobilized her, and she could barely stand up.

On the good days, while she spent her waking hours running back and forth to the suppliers, Kuniko minded the store and Taki went out soliciting needlework from the demimondaines behind the walls of the Yoshiwara. One can only wonder what indignant thoughts raced through the mind of this woman who had once suckled the scions of the feudal peerage. One imagines from the tone of resignation in Ichiyō's diary and from Taki's very willingness to go knocking at the back gates of the quarter—which would drop down over the moat, now more a ditch, like medieval drawbridges admitting her to the ramparts of the unholy citadel, thereby saving her the longer trip around to the front gate, where the gentlemen callers entered— that even Taki was by now quite beyond considerations of pride.

To take her mind off these woes, Ichiyō read the daily newspaper and recorded current events in her diary. This intrusion of a world beyond the confines of their prosaic life as struggling shopkeepers gives the Ryūsenji journals a surreal quality: Ichiyō goes to purchase some string, the Crown Prince of Austria arrives at Shinbashi Station; Kuniko accidentally undercharges a customer by half a sen, Prime Minister Itō's son is critically injured in a fall at Hakodate; the holiday market at Senzoku Shrine deprives them of business, Japanese goods win public favor at the Columbian Exposition in Chicago. In fact, the entries in the diary begin to taper off. A month goes by between volumes, weeks between major entries. She had no more time for her journals than she did for her fiction; there simply weren't enough hours in the day to describe the flood of new experiences, the conflicting emotions. She chides herself in the diary, but the time passes.

Suddenly it was late autumn. The first frost lacquered the ground and the bothersome "bush mosquitoes" finally disappeared. Four months had elapsed since their coming to Ryūsenji. She could no longer pretend that the move had been anything other than a mistake. Her thoughts drifted back to the Haginoya; her resolve to renounce her former life began to waver. On 15 November 1893 she went to see Mrs. Nakajima. It was her first visit to Koishikawa since attempting to sink herself into plebeian obscurity.

Today I went to Koishikawa to call on Mrs. Nakajima. I had not seen her since the nineteenth of July. There were many things we both wanted to say, but the memories overwhelmed me; I had to fight back the tears in order to speak. Almost half a year has gone by, and in that time there have been many changes. The vines around the spindle tree have spread in different ways: Mizuno Senko has married the Marquis of Aizu. Miyake Kaho has had her baby; she gave birth to a big, healthy baby girl. Nakamura Reiko got married, but has already separated from her husband. Mrs. Nakajima has adopted a son to succeed her. Ōno Sadako died. Katō's wife has had some trouble with her leg. The number of new students at the Haginoya has increased this year and there have been many new developments, but some things haven't changed. The lessons are still held on Saturday; there are still two topics assigned for each lesson, and two poems on each topic. The students are still writing about the moon and the cherries. The waves that break in the real world and the winds that blow do not concern them. They cultivate elegance through poetic diction; they invoke nature's most beautiful settings to prop up their drooping literary style. They live in a world of tranquility like hermits totally removed from the here and now. The other thing that hasn't changed are the rumors of unusual rapport between the Plum Arbor and the Jasmine Garden.[23]

I noticed that Mrs. Nakajima has had more rooms built onto her house, which was never small to begin with. She had some additions built last year and some more this year, so that now there must be close to ten new rooms. The garden is carefully manicured. No expense has been spared in furnishing the house. So perfectly appointed are all the rooms that they could want for nothing.

Of course, Mrs. Nakajima is a well-known, respected woman. The light seems to shimmer even on the old, weather-beaten nameplate on her front gate. She rides about in her own private black rickshaw, lest the round of social obligations tire her. Her storehouse is filled with exquisite damasks and brocades. Today she had a party to attend at the home of Marquis Nabeshima, Lord Chamberlain of the Imperial Household. She devoted herself to her dress for the occasion with only slightly less intensity than the light shines forth from the winter moon. Two maidservants stood at her side to help her with her toilette—altogether a stately ceremony to behold. What a contented life Mrs. Nakajima must lead: revered by her students, honored by society. Now even the question of her legal heir has been settled. One would not imagine there is much left to trouble her.

But no sooner did such thoughts pass through my mind than Mrs. Nakajima started to complain. With a sigh, she told me that what she would really like is to get her hands on a diamond, one foot across, that would see her through her old age. "If I had a treasure like that, I wouldn't have to worry about money. I could turn a deaf ear to public opinion. I could live in peace. As long as one has anything to do with other people, one is forced to say things one doesn't mean, to do things one doesn't like. If I were twenty years younger, I would use all the energy I had; I would enjoy myself to the utmost, but I would also see to it that I was able to enjoy my last years. At this age, much as I want to live out a quiet life, I don't have the wherewithal to guarantee it. That's why I want my big diamond. It isn't from greed, you see."

Mrs. Nakajima is never at a loss for words when it comes to criticizing other people, but she doesn't like it when they criticize her. She discarded the diamond in her own heart, and then hankers for a jewel unearthed from some plain, some mountain. Doesn't she know that if we polish the gem in our hearts, it will make a poor man wealthy, it will cleanse a sullied soul? For mankind, dwelling in the dust, is the world not a pair of rotting sandals? Whether we choose to wear them or not is up to us. Whether or not we have riches is hardly the main question. What is ineluctable, however, is the fact of our flesh, whence issue all the dilemmas of duty and love and desire and illusion. For fifty years we roam along forked roads, taking now a path of pleasure, now a path of pain.

And yet life on earth does have its beauty. When I stood on the veranda of Mrs. Nakajima's house, the delicate scent of the gold and white chrysanthemums and the sight of the dew-drenched gardens made me wish for the days of the past. I used to spend morning and night at the Haginoya. For one brief moment I was treated like Mrs. Nakajima's daughter. The gardens, the bamboo gates—it was as if everything had been roped off as my exclusive inheritance. And now I live in a shantytown. I have beggars for acquaintances. I have to fight over every rin and haggle for one hair of profit. I am living a life without purpose. When I'm at home, I don't think about these things. Perhaps it was seeing the luxury of the Haginoya again that brought them to mind. I don't know why, precisely, but I started to cry.

Why *was* I crying? If I had wanted to spend my life swathed in fine fabrics, I suppose I could have—but what am I doing, having such smug thoughts after I have fallen so low in the world? I must be tetched. Sometimes it's as if I have two different hearts. Or are the true and the false mixed in this heart of mine? Every time one half tells the truth, is the other half lying? No, of course not, the heart doesn't lie. Nor does the heart change. What changes are our feelings. Laughter and tears do not come from the bottom of the heart; they are only the outward form our feelings take at any given moment.

Mrs. Nakajima seemed glad to see me. She lingered to talk when she should have been going off to her party. On and on we chattered, oblivious of the time. I didn't even think of leaving. We spoke without any barriers between us, a compassionate teacher and her adoring pupil. Where had the teacher gone that I used to criticize for her frivolity and hyprocrisy? And where, the selfish, unfaithful disciple who turned her back on her teacher and scoffed at her? Today we were like two fish swimming in the same pool, buoyantly passing a delightful morning. It reminded me of my old visits to Master Nakarai. . . .[24]

The chat only convinced Ichiyō that she could never be happy as a shopkeeper. She tried to console herself with the thought that there was more to life than the splendor of the Haginoya. She repeated a halfhearted litany of ascetic old saws from the classics: one does not admire the cherry blossoms only in full bloom; love is more than the moments when a man and a woman are in each other's arms; deep in the valley, beautiful streams flow. Are we satisfied, then, only when we attain everything we have wanted from life? No, her austere side answered, we must resign ourselves to the times when clouds will obscure the full moon.[25]

Despite these hortatory efforts, the luxury of Mrs. Nakajima's life intoxicated Ichiyō. She did not even seem to resent her teacher's incredible callousness, her hungering for diamonds while Ichiyō starved. Ichiyō was never naive enough to assume that wealth would bring happiness, but she was too imbued with courtly esthetics not to admire the inevitably expensive display of good taste. She felt worn out and fed up with her life downtown. Privation had done nothing so far to liberate her talent.

Once again Ichiyō entertained thoughts of a career in poetry. It was in the ten days after seeing the opulence of the Haginoya that she wrote "The Sound of the Koto," her paean to the saving powers of the classical arts. Her next visit to Mrs. Nakajima gave her the idea of starting a poetry school of her own. When she called with New Year's greetings on 2 February 1894, dressed in an old kimono that Kuniko had patched for the occasion, she found Mrs. Nakajima much vexed by the news that Miyake Kaho was planning to open a competing conservatory. Mrs. Nakajima was miffed that Kaho had failed to ask her permission; and, perhaps worse to someone as fond of money as she, Kaho had neglected to pay her a "shingle fee," the customary honorarium a disciple was supposed to tender before setting out to practice a profession on one's own. (In 1894 the going rate for shingle fees was around twenty yen.)

The double affront had Mrs. Nakajima so angry that she tried to persuade Ichiyō to start a school as well. She offered to wave the shingle fee in Ichiyō's case and, furthermore, to underwrite the start-up costs, including the expensive opening party. The thought of vying with her old literary rival, not to mention being head of her own school, must have sorely tempted Ichiyō. Mrs. Nakajima urged her not to let opportunity pass her by. Now was the time for her to put her name before the world as a poet and a teacher. Honor and wealth were sure to follow. The argument was compelling, but Ichiyō had heard Mrs. Nakajima's promises before. She declined the offer.

The idea stayed with her, however. Ichiyō saw two possibilities: she could join forces with her classmate, Tanaka Minoko, who had started her own school, the Umenoya (Plum Arbor), several years earlier, or she could strike out on her own, provided someone would give her the money. In either case, by late February she had decided to close the shop. In January a new store had opened across the street, and business, which had been slowly improving, inevitably suffered. This was the excuse Taki had been waiting for. In her heart of hearts she still longed for a house with a front gate. While she went to see if they couldn't collect an old debt from Noriyoshi's days as a moneylender, a sum that might enable them to leave the tenement, Ichiyō sounded out Tanaka Minoko. Minoko, who was not one of Mrs. Nakajima's favorites, was delighted at the idea of having Ichiyō for a partner. And Ichiyō had always felt a rapport with her sensitive and graceful older friend. Minoko was the widow of a contractor; like Ichiyō, she had been called a "plebeian" by the other members of the Haginoya. Like Ichiyō, she was something of an outcast. She didn't quite fit into polite society; there were tales of a demimonde past, and, more recently, rumors of an affair with the poet Koide Tsubara. But Ichiyō commiserated with her friend. Together they spent a heady afternoon planning their reform of poetry.

Nothing would come of the talk, though, without capital. The Umenoya was not yet lucrative enough to support the two women, plus Ichiyō's mother and sister. She would have to raise some extra money to live on in the first few months, until they attracted more students. The Higuchis could not even leave Ryūsenji without the money to make a deposit on a new house. Where that money was going to come from Ichiyō had no idea. The shop had not generated any savings. Their credit with friends was at an all-time low. The chances seemed slight of ever collecting any of the debts still owed them from their father's aborted business forays. Trusting in such means was as silly as the faith their neighbors placed in the potential earning power of *kumade* charms.

But one day Ichiyō had an inspiration. She concocted a plot so implausible it was worthy of her most preposterous fiction. She would throw herself at the mercy of a wealthy fortuneteller by the name of Kusaka. He would fall in love with her, or at the very least feel so sorry for her that he would part with some of his endless cash. She knew from his advertisements in the newspapers that the money flooded in to him. It was said he had a wide-eyed following numbered in the thousands, many of them speculators. A few yen could hardly matter to someone like him. Nor did it matter that they had never met, or that she had no introduction when she went to see him on 23 February 1894.

It would have been just after noon, I suppose. Hearing the bean-curd man as I walked along reminded me of when we still lived in Kikuzaka and I would rush out to buy something from him. The house I was looking for was supposed to be in a quiet area at the top of Abumi Hill. Someone had given me the address—number 32, Masagochō—and I followed the instructions and turned when I came to a boarding house. It was just above where we used to live. Set back, on a side road, was a wood of oak trees surrounded by a black wall. A sign pointed to a footpath leading in, but it had been exposed to the rain and the dew for so long that it was barely legible. "Headquarters of Divine Revelations" read the lettering. This was the place, then. My heart thundered.

"Excuse me," I called out as I entered the building.

"Yeah?" someone replied abruptly, pulling back the sliding door at the other side of the front hall. It was a student, I should think, seventeen or eighteen.

"Hello. I've come from over in Shitaya. I was wondering if I might talk with Mr. Kusaka. It will take a little while, I'm afraid, but if you would tell me a time when he isn't too busy with other people—"

"Is it for a general consultation?"

"No, no."

"Oh. An emergency, then. Your name?"

"Well, I've never been here before, so my name won't mean anything to him, but it's Akizuki."

The student disappeared for a minute and returned. "Whatever the problem is, he'll see you right now."

I was relieved that it should all be so simple. "Thank you," I said, following him in.

Just on the other side of the door was what must have been the consultation room. As one might expect, it was handsomely furnished. The cushions in the ten-mat room were exquisite; the book shelves and cabinets looked like the sort of things wealthy patrons would donate. Everything was dazzling. There were two pictures, one of something called the Seishinkan, I believe, and the other, I have no idea. In the alcove hung a pair of silk scrolls, and in front of the alcove at a large desk sat a small man, who I assumed was Mr. Kusaka, stirring ashes in the brazier. He had a low voice and was soft-spoken. He was a man of about forty. In front of the desk was a large round brazier and in front of that, a cushion. "Sit down, sit down," he said, motioning me to the cushion.

For a few moments neither of us said anything. Then he spoke: "Well, let's hear what's on your mind."

I was reminded of the saying from *Essays in Idleness:* "When we hear a name, we picture a face; but when we meet the person, he never looks the same."[26] It certainly is true. In the same way, before coming, I had planned what I would say. Now that I was there, some of what I had meant to tell him no longer seemed appropriate, and I disclosed other things I had never intended.

"First of all," I began, "I must apologize for barging in on you without an introduction. And second, I'm afraid what I want to say may sound improper from a young woman. I hope it won't offend you. I know that you're a man with a big heart, accustomed to dealing with the most difficult matters. Please don't be impatient with me if my words sound foolish, or crude. You see, I am one of those people living in the dust of the back street. But I've come here in good faith, and I hope you will listen—I'd be much obliged if you would give me your advice. Sometimes I feel like a wounded bird searching for a breast to nestle in. I go on and on, wandering and wandering. Ah, but Mr. Kusaka! Yours is a breast for sheltering—a good, strong breast—a tree of refuge for a lost bird. So I wondered, would you listen to my story?"

"Yes, of course. Go on," he said, leaning forward. "It sounds interesting."

"I lost my father six years ago. Since then I have been drifting on the rough waves of uncertainty. One day I am swept to the east; another day, tossed to the west. Yesterday I lived above the clouds, aloft from the worries of the world in a realm of moonbeams and flowering cherries. Today I live in the dirt, with an aging mother and a helpless younger sister to support. Until last year, at any rate, I lived like any other woman.

"Please listen carefully, Mr. Kusaka: in this floating world of ours, no one cares about anybody else. I used to believe in other people. I actually thought it was possible to improve the world. But I was too naive, I deceived myself. Time and again those I trusted disappointed me, and now I don't have much faith in anything. One morning I had my eyes opened; I started to wander like a lost bird, to know hardships most people never experience. I learned how uncertain life is. I gave up on the world. Now I live in a corner of Shitaya. I opened a little shop—you can hardly call it a business—and I put all my hopes in it. But why is it nothing ever works out? It's all I can do to provide my poor old mother with a daily scrap of food; you don't know how this upsets my sister and me.

"After a while, one simply gives up. I really don't know what is to become of us. I feel so sorry for my mother! Myself, I don't mind suffering for a moment. I'm ready to start taking risks. I thought I would try speculating. But I don't have the means to go about it. When you're as poor as I am, there's not one sen to spare. Then I hit upon the idea of discussing it with you. After all, they say even a hunter doesn't kill a wounded bird that flies to him for refuge. And you, with your wisdom, and your great charity, helping so many people overcome their suffering—I thought I would come to you for advice. How about it, Mr. Kusaka? Please tell me if you have any ideas. You *do* understand my desperate situation?"

Kusaka looked at me sympathetically several times and asked me how old I was, when was I born.

"Twenty-three," I answered. "I was born in the year of the monkey, on the twenty-fifth day of the third month."[27]

"Well, that's an auspicious date. On the positive side, you've been endowed with some fine traits: talent, intelligence, ingenuity. You have a natural insight into the meaning of life. Unfortunately, you set your hopes too high. You're inviting disappointment. Everything will crumble. But you've been blessed with good fortune, whether you know it or not: instead of wealth you have ability, and you should use it. All I have to do is hear that you're engaged in business to know it's a mistake. And to start speculating is the last thing you should do! I wish I could convince you of that. You must rid yourself of these extravagant expectations and make your life's goal attaining enlightenment, resigning yourself to fate. This is what heaven has ordained for you."

"That's odd. I wouldn't have said that resigning myself to fate was one of my problems. And what do you mean, my hopes are too high, everything will crumble? Everything *does* crumble. The five facets of human life all turn to air when we are dead, anyway. Who among us dies without crumbling once more into the four elements?[28] So much for our hopes and aspirations. I just wish my life *would* crumble into nothingness. I'd be happy to reach the last stage of my decline, to be a beggar lying at the roadside, knowing the end was near. Are these hopes too high for you? I'm just suffering until that day finally comes. I wish I had spent this fleeting life as the moon, shining brightly before it wanes, or as a cherry tree, in blossom for its short season. . . . All I really want is a nice, quiet place to die. Perhaps, Mr. Kusaka, you could tell me of such a place. I'm tired of dealing with the world," I said. And then, after a moment, I began to laugh: "Can't you at least suggest some line of work more pleasant than what I'm doing now, something a little more cheerful?"

"Now you're on the right track," Kusaka said and clapped his hands repeatedly. "Everyone wants some satisfaction out of life. It's my job to help them find it. This crumbling and destruction business is not something we ought to be discussing. Tell me, what is it you enjoy most?"

"Well, I'll tell you one thing: it isn't wearing layers of brocades. Nature makes me happy. There's a truth, or an honesty, to nature that makes me feel sometimes as if I'm communing with the silent flowers or with the still moon. I forget everything about the floating world. It's as if I have danced into the center of a great, specially created bloom. These are my moments of happiness."

"Then you should think of people that way, too. Remember that everyone is born with a different nature. Like flowers, there are irises and baby's breath and so forth, each with its own scent and its own character. So it is with all things. When we know there is a time for planting, isn't it foolish of us to forget there are seasons for everything in life? Of course there is no such thing as simple cause and effect. If we could understand what lies at the root of our suffering, we would not have to suffer in vain. When a person is prosperous, the powers of heaven cannot affect him. Nor can I do anything for such a man. I am a hospital for the sick in spirit, someone who comforts the distressed. I am like a ragman, sorting rags, scraps of paper, old copybooks; I gather everything together and sort it out and put it all to a new use. You might say I take a tatter of a discarded old *kosode* robe[29] and turn it into a costume presentable before the best company. That's my profession: some men fix up old clothes or repair broken objects; I do the same with people, I help them figure out how to make the best use of what they have.

"I completely agree with what you said a moment ago, by the way. You don't know how happy it makes me to meet someone like you. For a person who feels the way you do about the truth and beauty of nature, everything else in life will fall into place. Don't let little troubles weigh you down. . . . Once you understand the essence of life, then the question of how you should live will settle itself. I meet many people who understand their neighbor but don't understand themselves, who grasp the essentials, but get bogged down in details. Don't let this happen to you. I have thirty thousand followers throughout Japan, you know, and no two are alike. Depending on the matter, some are my superiors by far, some I look up to as my teachers. All I do is help them align the present with the future."

Kusaka rambled on and on, talking about his followers, about various other masters of divination, warming to each subject. It was as if we were already old friends. We talked for four hours. Near the end, one of his followers came with a problem, and then there was a telephone call regarding fluctuations in the Ōsaka rice market. Seeing that he was busy now and it was near dusk, I thanked him for giving me things to think about and took my leave. In the course of the afternoon, we had touched on many different topics—the enormous esteem in which he is held by Cabinet Minister Gotō and his wife, the industrialist Takajima Kaemon's new interest in divination, the philosophy of Inoue Enryō, and so on.[30]

It was a sad day for Ichiyō. The years of want had finally made her mean. She schemed behind her teacher's back to join a rival poetry school. She toyed with the idea of becoming a kept woman. The metaphoric language in the above entry—at a time in life when Ichiyō had jettisoned much of the flowery and figurative from her journal—softens the rough edges of her first encounter with Kusaka, and of course her account of the whole event may be half fiction. Even so, the implications of her little-bird imagery are unmistakable: the wounded bird was in fact a predator. She intended to lead the pompous, nouveau riche diviner down the primrose path. ("I know that you're a man with a big heart, accustomed to dealing with the most difficult matters.") Sometimes she sounds like one of the cynical characters she deprecated in her fiction, for example, Ochika in "Clouds in Springtime." ("Please listen carefully, Mr. Kusaka: in this floating world of ours, no one cares about anybody else.") She certainly did not care about him. She was still the proud Natsuko; she could only proposition a man she held beneath contempt, and even then she had to use an alias. Bursting in on the no-account stranger, she behaved altogether differently than she had during her tremulous and very respectful first petitioning of Nakarai Tōsui. There was no blushing this time, although the purpose of the visit should have occasioned far more embarrassment. Penury had slightly coarsened her. ("How about it, Mr. Kusaka? . . . You *do* understand my desperate situation?") Not only did she talk down to him and belabor the obvious, she described him in her diary in a manner extremely bald for a young woman of her genteel upbringing. No polite "Mister" or deferential "Doctor" garnished the man's name, only a bare, almost raw, and all too dismissible "Kusaka," rather as if the appellation were a kind of curse.

The man was oily, to be sure. His facile advice was nine parts formula (she should resign herself to fate and seek enlightenment) and one part perception (at a glance he could tell she was not cut out for business). He sat on the edge of his seat the minute she mentioned snuggling up to him. He gave her his undivided attention, until the daily quotations on the commodities exchange reminded him of his priorities. Her suggestive visit whetted his appetite, and five days later he wrote her reiterating his pleasure at meeting a woman of her refined sensibilities. Might she care to join him for a viewing of the flowering plums? It was his heartfelt wish that they get to know each other better. Unfortunately, he made the mistake of capping his missive with a poem—fatal, since the boor didn't know any better than to mix his metaphors: he had autumn twilight descending on a verse ostensibly about the spring buds! Ichiyō declined the invitation.

She was coy about it, all the same. She had had second thoughts, but now that she interested Kusaka she wanted to string him along for the time being until she decided what to do. A few favors exchanged, a little money from the vulgar man, and she and Tanaka Minoko would be in business, with a new, expanded "Plum Arbor" to teach the true way of poetry to all comers. Could she really bear to associate with a creature as uncouth as Kusaka, though? That was the question. The only alternative seemed to be a retreat to her old post as Nakajima Utako's two-yen assistant, not a very attractive prospect now that Mrs. Nakajima had settled on an heir to the fortunes of the Haginoya. So Ichiyō flirted with Kusaka even as she refused his invitation, all the while laughing up her sleeve. (Did he really think she would jump into the palm of his hand at the first opportunity?) She begged his pardon; a poor woman like her didn't have time to go enjoying flowers. But she did want him to know that the very invitation afforded almost as much pleasure as seeing the blossoms. She definitely planned to seek his advice again in the near future. She closed with a poem alluding to the bit of unintended doggerel with which he had ended his letter: many are those who say they wait for another, but few who really mean it. In other words, Kusaka, how about you?

To Ichiyō's chagrin, he meant it. But for several months she managed to manipulate the charismatic, if pathetic, little master of divining. That she could do so was one of the unexpected dividends from her wealth of bitter experiences. The daily bargaining with wholesalers had given Ichiyō a confidence that Natsuko never possessed. Her superior mind, her iron will, and her sheer desperation were rapidly transforming Higuchi Ichiyō, at the age of twenty-two, into a formidable woman. It would have taken a greater man than Kusaka to avoid being led by the nose. He was not clever enough by half to see through Ichiyō's quiet and ladylike demeanor. Though she never received any windfall, visions of which had prompted her first visit to him (Kusaka was too shrewd a businessman for handouts), she did succeed in keeping their relations just promising enough for him to constitute a possible avenue of escape should the hateful drudgery she now endured become too much for her. Unfortunately the more she saw of her elected redeemer, the more she despised him.

Kusaka became just one more disappointment in Ichiyō's life. Here he was—the head of an organization with thirty thousand followers, an eminent figure known for his compassion—and he was really as shallow and selfish as everyone else. She found talking to him tedious. He had a small mind and small aspirations. It was rather like discoursing with a child about the finer points of heaven.

By the end of the year, when Kusaka finally called her bluff and offered her fifteen yen a month to become his mistress, Ichiyō was too contemptuous of the man and too much her mother's daughter to go through with it. She was acutely aware of her parents' uphill climb, clinging to the lower ledges of gentility. She fumed at Kusaka for his indecent proposal and conveniently forgot that the whole idea was originally hers.

For once Ichiyō's sardonic sense of humor failed her. If the poor man thought she was a loose woman, he was quite mistaken, she wrote in refusal. In her diary she suddenly reviled him as a swindler, an adventurer. She neglected to mention that she had played the adventuress in their little farce. When the laughable fellow repeated his proposal, she did not deign to answer. She crumpled his letter, full of "leave-everything-to-me's," as if the sheet of rice paper were evidence beyond gainsaying that the world had entered its last decline.

She had ample reasons for thinking so. In Ryūsenji she was living on the edge of an open wound. Just up the street, in a painted fortress circled by a sad, turbid ditch of a moat—"dark as the dye that blackens the smiles of the Yoshiwara beauties"[31]—three thousand women were the prisoners of sexual commerce. Ichiyō well knew what these ladies looked like once they had faded from their prime. She had delivered sewing for her mother and had seen the beauties in the morning. She had seen the cages where they sat every night like trapped animals on display in front of the lower-class houses. She had passed the "inspection stations" where many a daughter indentured into the profession met her clap-ridden end. She had heard the haunting tunes that wafted from the quarter on late autumn nights, and the tin, tatty laughter.

It was spring now, and she longed for renewal. Incredibly, her fate seemed to hang on the stamina of this year's cherry blossoms. The three women were planning to close the shop, finally, and leave the hated back street with money that one of Noriyoshi's old debtors had at last promised to repay. There was one problem. The man was a *kamaboko*—a fish-cake—dealer, and his re-payment depended on the weather. The delightful week or so in early April when the cherries bloomed was his best season. In a good year, thousands of fish cakes would be washed down with barrels of saké by the happy throngs communing with nature in the clogged cherry pleasances throughout the city. In a bad year, when rain tore the tender blossoms from the trees prema-turely, less saké was sold and still fewer kamaboko. As luck would have it, 1894 was a bad year. Only little bands of ardent cherry fans attempted to negotiate the fitful rains. One can picture Ichiyō standing in the doorway of the shop on a chilly April morning, watching the rain wash her hopes away.

Across town, her first cousin was dying of leprosy. In the Diet, the politi-cians fiddled self-indulgently. With Kuniko on the verge of collapse, her mother grumbling, and the nightly sound of the rickshaws bound for de-bauchery nibbling away at Ichiyō's nerves, she saw everything, including her homeland, going to ruin. She felt like a horrified bystander watching helplessly as a fire raged out of control on the other side of the river:

Bedlam reigns in the National Assembly. Selfish schemes are uncov-ered, secret deals are exposed. Our leaders are not what one would call great men.

In the middle of the night, when I lie awake and think about the times, I wonder what is to become of the world. I am only a woman, of course. I can just hear what others would say: "Who is she to worry about these large matters? Like an ant or a worm holding forth? The wretch doesn't even understand herself—how can she expound on the state of the nation?"

Nevertheless, we are all born under one heaven. When storms brew, I am hardly immune. I was born and raised in a corner of Japan. I, too, have enjoyed the Emperor's blessing. I share in his bounty with the ministers and generals. Day by day catastrophe is approaching our coun-try. Because I'm a woman, am I to loll on the riverbank while shooting fires ravage the other shore?

As soon as they are comfortable, people get finicky. They only have eyes for the glitter of the West. They despise the time-honored customs of their own fatherland. Their fickle hearts follow fashion the way gar-bage floats downstream: their clothes, their houses, their poetry, their government, everything is flotsam. Where will it end?

In the world outside, the Korean question will not be easily re-solved.[32] The sinking of the *Chishima* reflects our dilemma: Japan is entirely in the right, and still we cannot win—not while the foreign powers hold us cheap.[33] It is high time the unequal treaties were re-vised.

At home, too, the situation is discouraging. Our "statesmen" indulge in sibling scraps. Their party squabbles are desecrating the halls of the National Assembly. Every man is out for himself, and the public interest is forgotten. I haven't the fingers for totting up all that ails this society.

A muddy stream is not purified overnight. Where will these reckless currents carry Japan? On foreign shores the eagles have sharp claws, the lions sharp teeth. Just hearing what happened to Egypt and India makes me shiver. Let people say I'm imagining things, let later generations laugh at me if they want. When I was born into these troubled times, am I to make no attempt to correct them? If we search hard enough for the way we shall find it. I only regret I had to enter this world as a woman. Still,

> When strong winds blow
> Across the autumn plain,
> Even the valerians
> Are not safe
> From the tempest.[34]

Ichiyō had never imagined that her troubles were also her opportunities in disguise. Her unhappy year in the shadow of the quarter was about to afford the inspiration for her greatest work. When she moved to Ryūsenji, she inadvertently discovered in the downtown and the demimonde a whole new source of material for her stories. Not long afterward, she took up the novels of a writer who proved irrefutably that low-lifes—characters she had always relegated to the domain of gesaku—were indeed as acceptable and worthwhile a literary subject as the well-bred sons and daughters of high station.

The writer was Ihara Saikaku (1642–93), and the occasion of Ichiyō's rediscovery of the Edo storyteller was the Saikaku boom that followed publication of the first complete edition of his work in 1894. Some of the leading lights of Meiji literature inaugurated the Saikaku revival: Kōda Rohan, Ozaki Kōyō, and Mori Ōgai among them. Though more meticulous scholarly examination of Saikaku dates only from the 1920s, the first blush of renewed interest at the turn of the century stemmed from the efforts of these popular novelists, who invoked the Edo master as a kind of antidote to the preoccupation of their fellow writers with the European origins of the modern novel. In Saikaku they saw not only a literary stylist of major consequence but the founding father of a realism native to Japan. They, in turn, had been introduced to Saikaku by the enthusiastic Awashima Kangetsu (1859–1926), writer and devotee of Genroku culture,[35] and the dramatist Yoda Gakkai (1833–1909). Awashima exerted a particularly strong influence on the young writers, urging Kōda Rohan and Ozaki Kōyō and his Friends of the Inkstone to emulate Saikaku's baroque and long-forgotten plebeian tales. In the end, however, neither Rohan nor Kōyō nor Ōgai succeeded in wedding Saikaku's pyrotechnics to the needs of modern realism.[36] It remained for Higuchi Ichiyō to master the dazzlingly playful style and make of it a serious medium of her very own.

Though separated by two centuries, Saikaku and Ichiyō shared remarkable affinities. Their bonds ranged from those of subject matter and style to sense of place and a realism infused with irony and contradiction. "Humor and pathos" is the catch phrase Japanese critics frequently apply to denote what Saikaku and Ichiyō held in common. In fact, the facile label cannot do justice to the resonance of Saikaku in the last works of Higuchi Ichiyō two hundred years later.

Saikaku's prose works, all written within a decade (1682–93), may be classified into four general categories. The *kōshoku bon*, or love books, included Saikaku's first novel, *Kōshoku Ichidai Otoko* (The Life of an Amorous Man, 1682), which explored the love life of a well-heeled townsman disporting in the licensed quarters.[37] Several of Saikaku's next kōshoku bon (*Shoen Ōkagami*, The Great Mirror of Beauties, 1684; *Kōshoku Ichidai Onna*, The Life of an Amorous Woman, 1686) dealt with love and pleasure from the courtesan's point of view. In *Kōshoku Gonin Onna* (Five Women Who Loved Love, 1686), however, Saikaku shifted his attention to the passions of young women who were not professional entertainers but ordinary members of the petite bourgeoisie. A second category of prose consisted of miscellaneous pieces, including travel sketches, tales, and adaptations. A third group of works was concerned with the various bonds between men: homosexual love between samurai and between young kabuki actors and their *chōnin*[38] patrons (*Nanshoku Ōkagami*, The Great Mirror of Manly Love, 1687) and also the place of the vendetta and the code of honor in the world of the samurai (*Budō Denraiki*, Traditions of the Martial Arts, 1687; *Buke Giri Monogatari*, Tales of Samurai Honor, 1688). A fourth category was composed of works dealing with the financial life of middle-class chōnin, the trials and tribulations of making money or simply avoiding debt (*Nippon Eitaigura*, The Japanese Family Storehouse, 1688; *Seken Munesan'yō*, Worldly Reckonings, 1692).

It was primarily the first and fourth categories of Saikaku's work that influenced Ichiyō. Reference here will be made especially to *Kōshoku Gonin Onna* among the love novels and *Nippon Eitaigura* and *Seken Munesan'yō* among the collections of chōnin stories. (The three books, along with *Kōshoku Ichidai Otoko* and *Kōshoku Ichidai Onna*, are generally considered Saikaku's classics.)

When Ichiyō happened on these works in the second half of her career, Saikaku's earthy approach to fiction liberated her from her classical prejudices, and in fact made it possible for her to return to the classical tradition and draw from it what had made the poets and the Heian women writers truly great: passion and frankness and honesty.

Although Saikaku never crops up in the diary, letters and memoirs attest to Ichiyō's fascination, in the second half of 1894, with the Edo novelist of downtown manners.[39] This was the year when the collected works of Saikaku were published for the first time, in Hakubunkan's Teikoku Bunko series. Ichiyō may have read her Saikaku earlier, since a surprising number of first editions had survived earthquake, fire, and the Meiji Restoration. The original editions, or later Edo reprints, may have found their way to Ichiyō either through her friends at the journal *Bungakkai* or from the extensive collection in the Ueno Library.[40] In any case, publication of the complete works in 1894 antedates by only a few months some striking echoes of Saikaku in Ichiyō's writing, including "Ōtsugomori" (On the Last Day of the Year, 1894) and the full flowering of Ichiyō's talents, "Takekurabe" (Child's Play, 1895–96). Not long after its publication, Ichiyō borrowed the two-volume complete edition from a member of the *Bungakkai* group and was soon remarking how a study of Saikaku encouraged her to persevere, no slight remark given her circumstances.

Indeed, the date of publication of the collected works was opportune. Since the previous summer, Ichiyō had lived on the fringes of the very heart of Saikaku's world—the famed licensed quarter of the Yoshiwara, that realm of extravagance and ostentation, of indulgence in the pleasures of the flesh, where wit and style were prized as highly as good looks or accomplishments, and connoisseurship, even among the youngest members of the back street, was as important as any concern for the pocketbook. It was a part of town where luxury, sophistication, and joie de vivre coexisted with sham, naiveté, and the starkest struggle just to keep on going hand-to-mouth. In short, Ichiyō found herself living in the world of the chōnin as it was exemplified by the originator of chōnin fiction. This category of Saikaku's writings now inspired her to take the shitamachi townsfolk into her purview.

The transitional work heralding the mature phase of Ichiyō's career was a short story published on 30 December 1894 in *Bungakkai* and titled, appropriately, "On the Last Day of the Year." Though it grew out of her own bitter experiences in trying to make ends meet as bill collectors pressed in on her family at the year-end closing of accounts, the story also tipped its hat in homage to Saikaku. The very title, "Ōtsugomori," came from her newfound Edo mentor. One of Saikaku's most famous collections of stories on the plight of the impoverished chōnin, *Seken Munesan'yō* (Worldly Reckonings, 1692), bore the subtitle "Ōtsugomori wa Ichinichi Senkin": "The Last Day of the Year is Worth a Thousand Coins of Gold." Ichiyō's "Ōtsugomori" recounts the financial desperation that a young girl and her family face as the year ends and their debts fall due. She has been hired out as a maid in order to help the family finances. When she returns home for a visit in December, her ailing uncle (who has raised her) begs her to ask her employer for a loan. The reasons he lists echo Saikaku's familiar catalog of year-end woes: no money to repay his creditors or to put up even simple decorations (important as a means of placating the gods) or to buy his little boy the proper New Year's fare (zōni, the rice-cake soup for the holidays, which seems to appear in every story in Saikaku's *Worldly Reckonings*). The girl obediently requests a loan from her employer, but the shrew won't part with any of her ample cash. In the end, the girl is forced to steal two yen from the woman's writing chest.

Although topically "On the Last Day of the Year" could fit with ease among the stories in *Worldly Reckonings*—one more tale about the desperate contrivances of men unable to pay their bills when the year draws to its unfortunate close—Ichiyō's story is rather too grim to be mistaken for vintage Saikaku. The bleak tone marked an advance for Ichiyō. It was a sign of a new realism totally lacking in many of the first stories; but the piece wants for that balancing of light and dark which distinguishes not only Saikaku but the best parts of Ichiyō's own diary and her stories still to come. Ichiyō enthusiasts, in their admiration for the riches that "On the Last Day of the Year" anticipates, have tended to overrate the work. She had, after all, criticized the nouveaux riches and the comfortable before, in "Clouds in Springtime." She had even peeked into the downtown, with "In Obscurity." But "On the Last Day of the Year" is narrated more succinctly and dramatically than the earlier stories, and the choice of a destitute heroine was indeed a departure for Ichiyō. The milieu is both so patently Saikaku's world and, perhaps more impressive, the realm of the naturalists who came a decade after Ichiyō, that her partisans may be forgiven their undue zeal.

More interesting and complex than the similarity of setting and subject in Saikaku's chōnin works and Ichiyō's last stories are correspondences in style, structure, and the author's stance. Underlying all three of these elements were principles of *haikai* poetry, or comic linked verse, that had carried over when Saikaku began to write his novels. A brief outline of Saikaku's career as a poet, therefore, will place Ichiyō's borrowings from the Edo stylist in perspective.

When students of Japanese literature hear Saikaku's name, no doubt the first attributes that come to mind are the comedy, or irony, of his prose and its unrelenting vigor. They are qualities that can not be divorced from their origins in haikai poetry. Before he turned to fiction in 1682, creating the genre that would be known as *ukiyo zōshi*, stories of the floating world, Saikaku was already the leading haikai poet of his day, the de facto successor to Nishiyama Sōin (1605–82), who had founded the Danrin school of comic linked verse (*haikai no renga*). Among men of letters, Saikaku was already renowned—one would almost say notorious—for his free-wheeling style of haikai composition. His irreverence toward the more formalistic poetics of Matsunaga Teitoku (1571–1653) and his followers had earned Saikaku the sobriquet *"Oranda,"* or "Dutch," Saikaku: a poet as wild and iconoclastic as the strange foreigners at Nagasaki. The exuberance and exhibitionism of his *yakazu* (arrow-counting) haikai[41] marathons of solo versification, another genre he invented, culminated in the dazzling tour de force of 23,500 verses composed in a single day's sitting.[42] Though this third and final yakazu blockbuster came in 1684, two years after Saikaku's first novel (*Kōshoku Ichidai Otoko*), two earlier feats of poetic prowess were sufficiently astonishing that one imagines Saikaku had attained legendary stature even before he published any fiction.

The success of the poet is everywhere apparent in the birth of the novelist. Scholars generally agree that Saikaku had taken his brand of haikai about as far as it could go. He was stymied. In 1682, with his master Sōin dead and the Danrin school in factional disarray, Saikaku must have needed new channels for his energies. There is a kind of pleasing inevitability to the turn his career now took, for in spite of the rigid rules of haikai composition,[43] in Saikaku's hands, especially with the development of yakazu haikai, poetry already verged on prose composition. Perhaps most important, the yakazu were essentially solo ventures,[44] unlike earlier haikai, where the ideal was a subtle blending of the voices of several poets, usually three. Traditional haikai consisted of one hundred verses. Saikaku's yakazu links stretched into the thousands. Spontaneity, therefore, became all-important, and scholars have likened these new sessions to an exercise in stream of consciousness.[45] The yakazu, like all haikai, were considered sustained compositions. Although each link consisted of a mere fourteen or seventeen syllables, and *tsukeku* (the appended, or second, verse that capped the preceding link) were frequently excerpted in anthologies, a sequence of linked verse was always conceived of as an integrated whole. Even Saikaku's yakazu sessions (the first two) were recorded and published as such.[46]

So described, these elements of yakazu haikai seem to determine the kind of fiction Saikaku would soon write: extended, light-hearted sequences of episodes or separate stories, often short on plot and long on what smacks of free association, bound by a common theme and written in a highly elliptical and punning style by one man, who nevertheless drew inspiration for his material from earlier literary works, the theater, and newsworthy events of the day—much as the haikai master had others suggest topics and opening images that he could use, asking fellow poets to contribute the beginning verses for each set of poems in one of his yakazu series.[47] As scholars have remarked, the increased speed of versifying was in itself almost enough to bridge the gap between poetry and prose.[48] (Saikaku's first two yakazu went from 1,600 verses in twenty-four hours, in 1677, to 4,000 verses, in 1680.) Moreover, the subject matter of these poetry marathons foreshadows the novels to come. By his second yakazu, Saikaku had fashioned a kaleidoscopic genre for depicting an endless series of vignettes from everyday life. In the afterword to the text of his second performance, published one year before his first novel, Saikaku hailed the value of impromptu, colloquial literature. There was no need, he said, for the poet to spend months polishing a sequence of his verse. Wit and speed were the ideals, replacing the pedantic wordplay and labored allusions to classical literature that had previously characterized haikai. Gone was the expectation that a work would necessarily endure. It was a playful composition, intended to give delight beyond literary circles, a popular entertainment of the moment.

The same could be said of the fiction that Saikaku went on to create. Many of his stories depend so heavily on haikai principles of organization and style that some scholars have christened Saikaku's new genre "the haikai short story."[49] Indeed, it seems that the haikai tradition in Saikaku's, and Ichiyō's, prose is what makes it so difficult and unpalatable to some readers today. Translators, for example, have tended to look for stories that are carefully plotted and concise,[50] but that was seldom what Saikaku aimed for. He was less interested in a neat beginning, middle, and end than he was in the cumulative effect that a progression of images, however tenuously related, could induce. A cluster of these images becomes a story (sometimes remaining an incoalescent array of subplots and digressions), and a cluster of stories becomes a book, or a "novel."

One story in *Worldly Reckonings*,[51] for example, opens with the tale of Hachisuke, an octopus vendor in Nara who removes a leg from each octopus he sells and supplies these to a restaurant for extra money. Greed gets the better of poor Hachisuke, and he starts chopping off *two* legs, until the fraud is detected by a customer, who notices how shriveled the octopuses have begun to look "around the cuff." Hachisuke is exposed as a cheat. People call him Ashikiri—or "Leg-cutting"—Hachisuke, and he loses his livelihood. Ostensibly this is the main story, but it takes up a little less than the first half of the entire piece, which then becomes an essay on the easy-going, convivial ways of Nara townsmen at New Year's, in contrast to the atmosphere in Kyōto and Ōsaka. From there the focus shifts abruptly to a description of the poor who hawk various charms during the holiday season. This is followed by an account of how Nara clothiers send bill collectors to gather payments in Kyōto on New Year's Eve. The collectors' return to Nara laden with gold and silver leads into the fifth and final section of the story, a vignette about a band of impoverished *rōnin*, disfranchised samurai, who decide to turn highwaymen but find to their chagrin that everyone is carrying vast sums of silver when all the rōnin want is a little pocket money. The episode ends as the men spot a traveler who looks somewhat less well-heeled. They rob him, only to discover that their take consists of a package of herring roe.

This story is representative of *Worldly Reckonings*. The seemingly random segments have little in common but a general setting in time and place, Nara at New Year's. At first glance, the modern reader finds that the diffuseness runs contrary to his taste for unity. He finds the story amusing in a quaint way, but deficient. According to one translator, *Worldly Reckonings* is not a coherent piece of work, "for the theme of money and its effect on the human mind, focused on happenings at the end of the year, constitute [*sic*] the only link that brings the stories together. In some cases, year-end events are merely appended to stories which otherwise have nothing to do with that season. Its weakness, then, lies in the manner in which the theme of the year-end struggle is applied to the stories."[52]

It is true enough that, with the exception of *Five Women Who Loved Love*, Saikaku's fiction is supported by a very spindly narrative framework. In fact, this nascent novel form, which we see in *Five Women* or in *The Life of an Amorous Man*, Saikaku largely abandoned in his later works, the chōnin pieces. Although often called a novelist, even "the father of the modern Japanese novel," he was essentially a short-story writer, as was Ichiyō. The important chōnin books are all collections of stories, sometimes only vaguely related to a general theme. The stories themselves often seem less important for whatever tale they tell than for the opportunity they afford the writer to digress and to display his virtuosity. Nothing is sustained for long, including character development, and yet for that very reason the stories seem to burst with possibilities. Everything is so compressed that Saikaku's stories seem too short for the wealth of material they contain.

This is not to say that Saikaku, and Ichiyō, did not appreciate some of the storyteller's most valuable techniques (matters of pace, suspense, or comic relief, for example), but rather that the writer of what was fundamentally a haikai short story was adhering to other standards. What is lost in unity, characterization, or architectonics is offset by other qualities freshly introduced into fiction. As one scholar has said, "A haikai short story is less closely knit, less compelling to the reader, than one constructed on dramatic principles. It is basically a succession of related digressions; but the fact that its principles admit the introduction of a broader variety of material is not entirely to its disadvantage as a literary form."[53]

What, then, were these principles that opened up the short story to other possibilities? Perhaps most basic was the haikai notion of how the parts of a composition are related to the whole, what might be termed the concept of unity and progression. Haikai sequences were a mix of mood and voice, whether the poets were one, as in Saikaku's yakazu sessions, or several, as was commonly the case. Each verse was savored in its own right as well as for the degree of mastery it displayed in capping the previous verse. In other words, each verse was read twice, first as a complementary, or capping, verse and then in turn as the foundation to be capped by the next verse. The original nuances of a verse would change, sometimes radically, as the second poet used his partner's lines for the beginning of his own poem. Each new link in the "narrative" chain had only to follow from the one immediately before it, and not necessarily according to logic. *Yoriai* (association) is one of the key terms of haikai poetics. The hallmark of the art was the smooth, quicksilvern flow of ideas by association, through punning, allusion, or a kind of mental quantum leap.

In haikai, as in all *renga*, or linked verse, it was not dramatic unity—or unity in any conventional Western sense—that was the ideal. Instead of a tightly controlled, purposeful building of images toward a climax, what was desired was a harmonious balance of images: some links that were closely associated to each other (through a fairly straightforward continuation of the same line of thought, which might be likened to narrative progression) and some links that were only remotely related to each other (through daring wordplay or by catching and amplifying implications, however faint, in the preceding verse). In place of unity was flux. No sooner would a theme emerge than the next poet would veer off on a very different trajectory. In fact, to some poets' minds, the more remote the linkage—the more spectacular the leap—the more it was esteemed.[54]

The most important verse in a sequence was the opening one, the *hokku*. The senior poet present at a gathering, frequently a haikai master, had the honor of composing the initial verse. It set the tone for the first group of poems in the series and defined the setting of the sequence. Saikaku continued the tradition of the hokku flourish in his prose. Invariably his stories open with heraldic messages in a style elaborate even by his own standards. A certain rhythm picks up straightaway as a swift succession of allusions to proverbs, classical literature, or popular songs flows by; all the while, Saikaku locates the setting and suggests the theme of the story. Moreover, especially in the shorter pieces, the hokku-introduction may be longer and more conspicuous than the story itself, which sometimes seems tacked on, as though Saikaku suddenly remembered he had a narrative requirement to fulfill. The essential distinction to be made between the hokku in linked verse and the opening of a haikai short story is the obvious one: the poet could not govern the drift of a sequence; the storyteller had full discretion. If anything, the hokku-introduction in Saikaku's prose takes on even greater significance than it enjoyed in haikai poetry. If he so chooses, the writer can quite consciously set the stage for his story. (Whether he remains on that stage or wanders off down a runway, like a kabuki actor, is another matter.)

Here is a typical hokku to a piece in *The Japanese Family Storehouse*, written four years before *Worldly Reckonings*, and entitled "Old-Fashioned Credit Accounts, Modern Cash on the Line":[55]

In ancient times men respected simplicity, but today extravagance rules. People crave splendor out of all proportion to their place in the world. Just look at the get-up wives and daughters wear. You'd be hard put to see how they could go any further—God only help them when they forget their station in life! Why, even the grandest aristocrats make do, after all, with Kyōto silk for their wardrobes. And from the daimyō to the lowest foot soldier, all members of the military look perfectly handsome in their black coats with the five crests. But in recent years, those cunning merchants in the capital have come up with all kinds of ways to make people spend their money. They outdo each other in purveying every luxury in men's and women's fashions. The tailor's sample book has every color in the rainbow. Fine-patterned designs of the latest style, imperial prints of a hundred different hues, random dyes of graded tints[56]—you will have to search in other worlds for greater novelty than this. A woman's closet, a girl's trousseau deplete the family coffers. Who knows how many merchants have had their wings clipped from overdoing things? The display of silks and brocades by the courtesan comes with her line of work. Let the lovely wives of laymen learn to do without. No need to impress us, ladies, with layer after layer of your fancy dress, except on the occasion of your wedding and a trip now and then, in spring and fall, to view the cherry blossoms and the autumn leaves.

The opening seems only tangentially related to the heart of the story that follows. But it sets the tone admirably. The real story in "Old-Fashioned Credit Accounts, Modern Cash on the Line" is that of Mitsui Kurōemon (in true life, Hachirōemon), who builds a fortune on the simple principle of accepting only cash for sales at his new Edo shop, the Echigoya, which he organizes into efficient sections like the modern department store. Saikaku's introduction is discursive but not irrelevant thematically. It establishes the general background of bourgeois vanity and exhibitionism against which the Mitsui family will rise. It posits the situation that they will come along to exploit. The courtesan's daily parade of silks and brocades, the motifs available in the draper's sample book, form a kind of panning shot of the atmosphere before Saikaku pulls back in stages to reveal his close-up of Mitsui at the end of the story, which occupies only the last third of the piece. In effect, the first two-thirds of "Old-Fashioned Credit Accounts" is introductory material. After the initial prelude quoted above, Saikaku makes additional remarks about the ingenuity of Kyōto tailors and the desirability of the recent government clothing edicts, and then he sweeps from the Kyōto-Ōsaka area to Edo, where many of the drapers had established branch shops in an environment of severe competition. At length, this leads him into a discussion of the Edo merchants' bane: the policy of credit sales, and from this topic he pivots into the Mitsui story he has been gradually approaching.

It is hardly wise, then, to adopt traditional assumptions in the case of the haikai short story. Is the fictional element (here closer to reportage) really any more important than the story's flamboyant beginning—with its impressive hokku flourish and the train of transitional associations?

The same question arises with Ichiyō's next work, the masterly "Takekurabe" (Child's Play, 1895–96). Because the novella was written over a year's time and shows Ichiyō's thorough maturation, other aspects of "Child's Play" not related to the Saikaku influence will be discussed in chapter 5. Suffice it to say here that the story, which made Ichiyō's reputation, depicts a feisty band of shitamachi, or "downtown," children, who seem to exist independent of their parents. They were the very types she saw every day in her shop. Living in a halfway house between the poverty of the back street and the luxury of the quarter, and between the innocence of childhood and the uncomfortable awakening of adolescence, they are all in a sense forgotten, and therefore free to play and make mischief. But the difficulties the children experience are as important and moving to Ichiyō as any adult anxieties, and they include the suffering of those without the means—whether financial or temperamental—to compete in life, and the loneliness and self-doubt that dog them even in a world of gaiety.

The opening chapter of "Child's Play" is almost all hokku, no story. At the very end, one character is finally introduced, but the rest of the first chapter consists of the same kind of stage-setting to be found in Saikaku. It is in these passages, before the writer gets down to the narrative business at hand, that Saikaku and Ichiyō are free to regale their audiences with the poet's bag of tricks. The brilliant command of rhythm and wordplay and the vivid feel for place are reason enough for many readers to appreciate Saikaku and Ichiyō. The Edo storyteller's baroque language and learned allusions naturally appealed to the classical bent in Ichiyō. Seeing what he did with these devices helped her learn how to control her appetite for literary ostentation and how to play with the rigid components of classical convention. (Saikaku's poetic tradition, comic and cheeky, was worlds apart, of course, from Nakajima Utako's mannered reverence for the dictates of the ancients.) As she was wont to do in stories from "Flowers at Dusk" to "Encounters on a Dark Night," Ichiyō studded the opening of "Child's Play" with kakekotoba, or pivot words, and puns in flowing cadences. But now she used these techniques with a purpose. They are no longer elegant digressions for whose sake alone the story seems to exist. Like Saikaku, from the very start she evokes the mood and ambience that will permeate her story. What she gives us is a character sketch of the shitamachi quarter. The opening is heraldic in the same way that Saikaku's introduction to the Mitsui story was. It takes the long view of a scene and marshals forth the themes that will be important to the story: the contradictory existence of luxury and poverty in the back reaches of the demimonde, the irrepressibility of the impoverished townsfolk, and the world of the children who grow up in this milieu. All this, f not the poetry, remains when Ichiyō's hokku-introduction is rendered into English:

> It's a long way round to the front of the quarter, where the trailing branches of the willow tree bid farewell to the nighttime revellers and the bawdyhouse lights flicker in the moat, dark as the dye that blackens the smiles of the Yoshiwara beauties. From the third-floor rooms of the lofty houses the all but palpable music and laughter spill down into the side street. Who knows how these great establishments prosper? The rickshaws pull up night and day.
>
> They call this part of town beyond the quarter "in front of Daion Temple." The name may sound a little saintly, but those who live in the area will tell you it's a lively place. Turn the corner at Mishima Shrine and you don't find any mansions, just tenements of ten or twenty houses, where eaves have long begun to sag and shutters only close halfway. It is not a spot for trade to flourish.

She then launches into a description of the townsmen's obsession with kumade charms, and from there goes on to explain the connection that people from the neighborhood "in front of Daion Temple" have with the nearby Yoshiwara:

> The menfolk do odd jobs at the less dignified houses. You can hear them in the evenings jiggling their shoe-check tags before they leave for work, and you'll see them putting on their jackets when most men take them off. Wives rub good-luck flints behind them to protect their men from harm. Could this be the final parting? It's a dangerous business. Innocent bystanders get killed when there's a brawl in one of the houses. And look out if you ever foil the double suicide of a courtesan and her lover!

Not unlike Saikaku's note of disapproval of downtown pretensions in "Old-Fashioned Credit Accounts," Ichiyō keeps her ironic distance from the atmosphere she describes, which adds to the reader's sense that he is looking at a panorama:

> Customs here are indeed a little different. You won't find many women who tie their sashes neatly behind their waists. It's one thing to see a woman of a certain age who favors gaudy patterns, or a sash cut immoderately wide. It's quite another to see these barefaced girls of fifteen or sixteen, all decked out in flashy clothes and blowing on bladder cherries, which everybody knows are used as contraceptives. But that's what kind of neighborhood it is. A trollop who yesterday went by the name of some heroine in *The Tale of Genji* at one of the third-rate houses along the ditch today runs off with a thug. They open a lean-to

bar, though neither of them knows the first thing about running a business. They soon go broke. The beauty begins to miss her former calling. Her assets are gone with the chopped-up chicken bones left from last night's hors d'oeuvres. Unlike the chicken, however, our charmer can still return to her old nest. People around here, for some reason, find this kind of woman more alluring than your ordinary one.

Finally, misdoubts about shitamachi life give rise to a new line of thought—the effect such a world has on the children—and this leads to the introduction of Ichiyō's characters, beginning with Nobu, the son of the neighborhood priest, at the end of the first chapter.

Like haikai poets, Saikaku and Ichiyō were less concerned with the continuity of a steady focus on one subject, one hero, than they were in creating a shifting tableau. The short story as Saikaku developed it and Ichiyō refined it gave them the freedom to range over a wide area in the relatively narrow space of a few pages. They swing from topic to topic by compressing narrative time, telescoping the point of view, and taking full advantage of elliptical constructions, so that a panoply of personages, scenes, and events, with appropriate asides from the author and generous use of ornamentation, can all be presented in a way that amounts to trompe l'oeil: everything seems to happen at the same instant. Questions of how one matter relates to another become irrelevant. We are carried along without time to ponder. Here are the speed and lightness of touch of the arrowlike poetry sessions. The syntax of this impatient prose is pruned to the bare essentials. Yet it is streamlined in only one sense. Particles and other elements of grammatical logic and whole clauses that would explain the relation between two thoughts are all cavalierly abandoned. Counteracting this abbreviation are elaborate wordplay and decorative filigree more commonly found in poetry. The following translation of excerpts from one of the stories in Saikaku's *Worldly Reckonings*[57] will illustrate these points. The story is titled "Some Sound Advice on Economizing" and subtitled "Early-to-Bed Kyūza Learns to Work at Night—The Art of Peddling Pepper on New Year's Eve":

> The Great Law on the Division of Estates has it that when a man's property is valued at a thousand *kanme*,[58] he should leave four hundred kanme and his house to his eldest son and heir. To the second son, he should bequeath three hundred kanme, together with a house. The third son is entitled to a hundred kanme and should be sent away as a bridegroom adopted into his bride's family.
>
> If the man has a daughter, he will provide her with a dowry of thirty kanme and another twenty for her trousseau; he would also do well to see her married off a little beneath herself. In the old days, forty kanme were spent on a girl's trousseau, and the dowry amounted to only ten kanme. But these days, men marry for the money,[59] so a father had

better fill his daughter's bridal chests with plenty of copper and silver coins.

When a girl's face is not much to look at under the candles on the wedding night, an extra thirty kanme makes the flowers bloom. Everyone is sure to praise the budding bride. "After all, she *is* the daughter of a wealthy house. Nothing but the finest delicacies have ever touched her lips. On her, the round face and the bulging cheeks look good. The way her forehead juts out, she'll wear her cloak nicely. With those big nostrils, she'll never run short of breath. She'll be cool in summer, too, with that thin hair of hers. Her hips are mighty ample, but don't worry, an outer robe will cover everything, even if it looks a little formal for around the house. And those strong arms will get a good grip on the midwife's neck when she's in labor." One by one, her flaws are made advantages.

"This just goes to show you the importance of careful reckoning," says one wise businessman. "If a man deposits his wife's dowry of thirty kanme at a guaranteed interest rate of six rin per month, every month he'll make a hundred and eighty monme—enough for four people to live on. In effect, his wife is supporting herself, as well as her maid, her attendant, and her seamstress, and at the same time she is catering to her husband. She'll tend the house conscientiously while you're away, innocent of selfish thoughts. If it's beauty you're after, the pleasure quarter is full of it. 'Welcome here! Come in, come in!' the ladies call from evening through the middle of the night. 'Well, well,' you think, 'isn't this appealing!' But pretty soon it's time to go. The bell tolls the dawn, the girls demand their seventy-one monme, and now it's 'Well, well,' you sigh, 'wasn't that a fleecing!'"

The wise businessman urges his young friends to tally up how much they waste on one night on the town and to consider the alternatives:

"With all this in mind, you ought to stay home at night, even if it is a little dull. Relax in your own house. For dinner you can have cold rice and boiled bean curd, or dried fish, or whatever is on hand. Let the old man who's your tenant tell you about Lord Itakura's handling of the gourd case.[60] Stretch out as you please with a nice, plump pillow. Let your attendants pull your toes.[61] Let your wife bring you tea while you rest. She'll serve it to you so you don't even have to lift a finger. In all things, you are the ruler of the house. Among the employees not one has the temerity to compete with you, and no one will offer you reproach. What more could you ask for?

"And when they know the master is home, the young men in the shop at the front will give up their folly of visiting the teahouses over by Yasaka Shrine. Their secret trips to the servants' lodgings in Oike will cease. They'll find it impossible to remain idle and will reread the correspondence from Edo, discovering things that they have overlooked. As a result, their master profits. The apprentices will save scraps of paper and twist them into bits of string. They'll practice their penmanship and read from their copybooks in a voice loud enough for you to hear them in your rooms at the back of the house. They, too, are profiting. Even Early-to-Bed Kyūshichi[62] stays up unraveling the reed wrappers from the yellowtail, making cords for stringing copper coins. Také works late getting the turnips ready, so they won't hold up her chores in the morning. The seamstress completes close to a full day's work in one evening, removing the knots from some Hino silk. Even the cat remains alert— with eyes that could pierce a three-inch cutting board—and lets out a ferocious snarl if anyone goes for the fish rack.[63]

"All this benefit accrues from the master's staying home one evening. Think what profits you could reap in a year if you made a habit of it! Even if your wife doesn't always suit your fancy, learn to make the best of things. Once it dawns on you that the quarters of the night are built on nothing but a pack of lies, you young men will understand how to manage your affairs."

At this point Saikaku drops his wise businessman, who "has gone on too long, considering what a busy time the year-end is," and the narrator proceeds to lampoon women for *their* extravagances:

In passing, it might be added that nowadays women imitate everything they see. They have taken up the manners and morals of the demimonde. In the capital, the most successful drapers' wives doll themselves up to look like courtesans. Wives of former shop clerks who have made it in the world are invariably, every one of them, the spitting image of a bathhouse whore. Women whose husbands run tailor or embroidery shops along the side streets ape the manners of the wenches at a teahouse. Droll, isn't it, the way they choose for their model the kind of woman appropriate to their husbands' incomes!

Reflect for a moment and you'll see: even if there seems no distinction anymore between the housewife and the courtesan, in fact a world of difference does remain. Why, just to begin with, the amateur is slow, tedious, and rather vulgar. In the art of letter-writing she cannot compete. She is without finesse when it comes to drinking. She cannot carry a tune. She does not wear her clothes well. Her step is uncertain. She sashays around the place with her hips swinging. Her pillow talk revolves around bean paste and salt and other matters of the kitchen. She's so cheap that in bed she hoards the tissues. She thinks aloes are a tonic instead of a perfume. Oh, she's a bore in everything! Yes, in her hairdo she may resemble her cousin of the quarter, but only a fool would think the two women could be equals.

Having said all this, Saikaku finally gets around to telling his "story":

On Karasumaru Street, in the best neighborhood of the capital, there once lived a man of consequence who bequeathed to both his sons the sum of five hundred kanme. The younger son steadily increased his capital through sound business ventures. Soon he was worth two thousand kanme—the pride of the family. But within four years the elder son had frittered his money away. On New Year's Eve, with his paper hood pulled low, he peddled pepper and lamented to himself, "They say that heaven never lets a man down. If the moon were out tonight—I'd start to think about the old days, and then how could I go on selling pepper? If it weren't dark, I couldn't do this." And so he greeted another new year of distress. His mind wandered and his feet strayed toward the entrance of the pleasure quarter. As the sun rose, he recalled the morning visits[64] he had made in better days. Now he could only turn around and head for home.

Once again it is apparent that the organizing principle of the Saikaku story is the looseness of association between the parts. The six-line "story" at the end merely caps the previous fifty-three-line discursive essay: a coda to an introductory flourish that has taken on a life of its own. There is a general consistency of theme—the proper management of money—but these are wide margins Saikaku sets himself. Within them, he sashays around almost as much as the bourgeois would-be courtesan. He moves from a discussion of inheritance to an aside on how to dispose of an ugly daughter, and thence into the financial opportunity she presents to her new husband. Once the point of view has shifted from the girl's father to her spouse, Saikaku slides easily into a whole new topic: the tendency of young men to squander money in the pleasure quarter, and the ways they ought to be economizing, which, in turn, leads to a new aside regarding the young man's employees. Everything up to this point has been the words or thoughts of the wise businessman. But the story now shifts abruptly, with no more than a *saruhodo ni* ("in passing [it might be said that]") to link it to the preceding topic. All at once we are given a diatribe on the encroachment of demimonde fashions. Just as the reader starts to discern a continuity of sorts, or at least a parallelism (for here we are given the ways that women, too, squander money), the emphasis on the demimonde theme shifts, to consider the infinite superiority of the professional woman. This new thrust then turns back, into a reprise of an earlier motif: the spendthrift tendencies of men visiting the quarter. This, finally, reiterates the central theme of the book, that the townsmen's day of reckoning comes at New Year's. All told, it is a most circuitous route to the actual "story," which picks up the original subject, the division and inheritance of estates, and thus brings the tale full circle.

Saikaku has no compunction about sacrificing continuity for the chance to hold forth on the human comedy (people will bend over backwards to ignore the coarseness in a rich girl) or the opportunity for a little wordplay ("An extra thirty kanme makes the flowers bloom, [and] everyone is sure to praise the budding bride").[65] The exuberance of the writer is there for all to see. He's ready to dance a jig when the rhythm suits his fancy ("Sore wa sore wa omoshirōte . . . kore wa kore wa omoshirokarazu").[66] The author's tone is everything. Without the irony, "Some Sound Advice on Economizing" would be a dreary and didactic piece. Too much can be made of Saikaku's "humanity" and his "spirit of egalitarianism,"[67] but it's a wide world we live in, as he is always saying, and he loves it for its richness and its contradictions. Nobody is fooling "Dutch" Saikaku, who seems to have seen it all. Still, the cynicism of the elder's worldly wisdom is laced with affection for man's endless potential for shenanigans. "These days men marry for the money" sounds purely cynical, but in Japanese the phrase is a clever pun on the expression "to take a wife" (*yome o yobu*). There's a smile of resignation behind Saikaku's twist on a familiar saying: "Tōdai wa kane o yobu." These days men summon the money. The practical and the ridiculous are juxtaposed; the prosaic and the elegant collide. One minute Saikaku is lecturing on sound money management, and the next a tightwad housewife is carrying his homily to extremes. Even in bed, she has the price of bean paste on her brain. In another story in *Worldly Reckonings* a son accused of stealing a packet of silver from his mother quotes loftily from the *Nihon Shoki* (Chronicles of Japan, 720) to prove that rats were the ones who carried the money off. Solemn religious incantations are intoned by con men who rook old ladies. The earthy jargon of the pleasure quarter and the business world is mixed with lines from the classics. A pompous Confucianist tries to discourse with the street-wise.

It is this tableau in lively and playful language that influenced Higuchi Ichiyō. In her earlier stories, Ichiyō had always had a tendency toward digression, but prior to "Child's Play" she generally focused on one topic and restricted her cast of characters. Then Ichiyō read *Worldly Reckonings* and saw Saikaku parade through one story alone nō troupes, kabuki actors, theater managers, understudies, physicians, drapers, Confucian scholars, import dealers, haikai masters, brothel owners, jesters, big spenders, artisans, and dandies. In fact, the list is even more varied. It turns out that none of the young boulevardiers is what he pretends to be. Before the tapestry is finished, Saikaku has embroidered a detail that depicts them, rather, as a lascivious little band of liars and extortionists—a glue dealer, an adventurer, a beggar, and a debtor—in a setting that shifts from the theater to the teahouse to the jail cell.

In "Child's Play" an inspired Ichiyō puts on her own parade. In place of the lachrymose couples in her earlier stories—irresolute love-boys and jilted young ladies with backbone—Ichiyō offers up a whole crowd this time. With the exception of Nobu, the gentle and scholarly son of a ribald priest, they are a rougher lot than Ichiyō's early characters. The precocious younger sister of a famous courtesan, the heir to a prospering pawnshop, the village bully, and the neighborhood buffoon are only some of the main characters who appear. And they are children, who move in and out of the licensed quarter and display more life and individuality than the stereotypes she had written about heretofore. Stylistically, too, Ichiyō benefitted from her study of Saikaku. She was always an elegant writer who soon found her own ironic voice, but at this point everything comes together. The literary allusions that encumber the earlier stories are reduced to more effective proportions. The decorative epithets (*makurakotoba*), and the pivot words (*kakekotoba*), the snippets of popular songs and proverbial sayings, and the strong sense of rhythm are all integrated now. She is not showing off her learning. She is showing us what she can do, and the haikai short story reaches its apogee.

Ichiyō has Saikaku's sense of comedy, but she also has a heightened sensitivity to suffering and vulnerability. In her hands, Saikaku's broadsides are balanced with a new and deft understatement. Here is the haikai juxtaposition, the blend of humor and pathos the critics talk about. Lines of thought shoot out like arrows. Some suddenly converge and others evaporate. As with Saikaku, we don't bother asking where Ichiyō is taking us. We sit back and enjoy the ride. Consider a typical jaunt from chapter 8 of "Child's Play":

In evening they rush into the quarter, at dawn they leave less cheer-fully. It's a lonely ride home, with only dreams of the night before to keep a man company. Getaways are under cover. A hat pulled low, a towel around the face. More than one of these gentlemen would rather that you didn't look. To watch will only make you feel uneasy. That smirk of theirs—not half-pleased with themselves as the sting of their lady's farewell slap sinks in. After all, she wouldn't want him to forget her. Careful when you get to Sakamoto. The vegetable carts come barrel-ing back from the early morning market. Watch out when you hit Crazy Street. Until Mishima Shrine, you won't be safe from those who wander home all gaga and enraptured from the night before. Their faces never look so resolute the morning after. It's rude to say it, but don't they all suggest love's fools? The fishwives seldom hesitate to sum them up. Look, there goes a man with money. But that one over there, he couldn't have a penny to his name.

One need hardly cite the Chinese "Song of Everlasting Sorrow" and the heights to which Yang's daughter rose to see that there are times when daughters are more valuable than sons. Many a princess comes into the world among the shanties of the back street. Today she calls herself "Snow" in one of those swank geisha houses over in Tsukiji, a celebrated beauty whose accomplishments in dance have entertained a nobleman or two. But yesterday she was a mere delinquent and she earned her spending money making playing cards, you know. "What kind of tree does rice grow on?" she asks, as if she'd grown up in the lap of luxury. Around here, of course, she is not the celebrity she used to be. Once they leave, they're soon forgotten. Already she has been eclipsed by the dye-maker's second daughter, Kokichi, a home-grown flower of a girl, whose name you'll hear throughout the park. The lanterns are up these days at The New Ivy, in Senzoku, where that one works.

Night and day, it's the daughters that you hear of. A boy is about as useful as a mutt sniffing round the rubbish. Every shopkeeper's son is a wastrel. At seventeen, the age of insolence, the young men band together. Before they go completely gallant—you don't see any flutes tucked into sashes yet—they join up with a leader whose alias is invariably a solemn, grandiose affair. They deck themselves out with matching scarves and matching paper lanterns. It won't be long now before they learn to gamble and to window-shop the quarter. Bantering with the courtesans will begin to come more easily. Even with the serious ones, the family business is only something for the day. Back from the evening bath they come in kimonos of a rakish cut, sandals dragging. "Hey, did you see the new one? At What's-Its-Name? She looks like the girl at the sewing shop, over in Kanasugi. But, with that funny little nose of hers, she's even uglier." It's the only thing remotely on their minds. They bum tobacco, a piece of tissue at every house. The pats and pinches they exchange with each beauty along the way: *these* are the things that bring a lifetime of renown. Even the sons of perfectly upstanding families decide to style themselves as local toughs. They are forever picking fights around the Gate.

Ah, the power of women. One need hardly say more. In the quarter, prosperity makes no distinctions between the autumn and the spring. Escort lanterns are not in vogue these days, and still the men are carried away. All it takes is the echo of a pair of sandals. Here she comes! The little girl from the teahouse who will take them to their ladies. Clip-clop, clip-clop. The sound mingles with the music of the theater. They hear it and they stream into the quarter. If you ask them what they're after, it's a flowing robe, a scarlet collar, a baroque coiffure, a pair of sparkling eyes and lips with painted smiles. The beauties may in fact have little of the beautiful about them. The minute they are courtesans, they climb the pedestal. Those of you from other parts may find it all a little hard to understand.

Ichiyō then cuts to her main character, Midori, the younger sister of the belle of the Yoshiwara, who will herself grow up to be a courtesan. Though she is still a child, we are told that Midori has already "taken on the color of the quarter." "It was all a little sad," the narrator remarks. "She was fourteen. When she caressed her dolls, she could have been a prince's child." From here, Ichiyō pivots back into the daily pageantry of the downtown:

Crazy Street, Sleepy Street. The half-witted, groggy gentlemen all pass this way as they head home. At the gate to this village of late risers, the sweepers and the sprinklers have already cleaned the streets. But look down main street. They have roosted for the night among the slums of Mannenchō or Yamabushichō, or perhaps Shintanimachi, and now here they come: what for want of any other word one might as well call "entertainers." The singing candy man. The two-bit player. The puppeteers. The jugglers and the acrobats. The dancers with their parasols. The clowns who do the lion dance. Their dress is as varied as their arts, a gauze of silk, a sash of satin. The clowns prefer the cotton prints from Satsuma, with black bands round the waist. Men, pretty women, troupes of five, seven, even ten, and a lonely old man, all skin and bones, who totters as he clutches his battered samisen. And, look, there's a little girl of five or so they've got to do the Kinokuni dance. Over there, with the red ribbons on her sleeves. But none of them stop here. They know where the business is, and they hurry to the quarter. The guest who has lingered at the teahouse, the beauty in a melancholy mood—these are the ones it pays to entertain. The profits are too good to give it up, or to waste time with benefit performances along the way. Not even the most tattered and suspicious-looking beggar would bother to loiter around here.

A lady minstrel passed before the paper shop. Her hat all but concealed her striking face, yet she sang and played with the bearing of a star. "It's a shame we never get to hear the end of her song," the shopkeeper's wife complained. Midori, bright from her morning bath, was lounging on the shop's front step, watching the parade pass by. She pushed her hair up with her boxwood comb. "Wait here. I'll bring her back!"

The child never mentioned slipping something in the lady's sleeve to coax her to perform but, sure enough, back in tow she came to sing the requested song of thwarted love. "Thank you very much for your patronage," she concluded in her honeyed tone, and even as it echoed they knew that they were not about to hear its likes again.

"To think—a mere child could have arranged it!" bystanders marveled, more impressed with Midori than with the minstrel.

"Wouldn't it be fun to have them all perform?" Midori whispered to Shōta. "The samisen and the flute and the drums! The singers and the dancers! Everything we never get more than just a glimpse of!"

Even for Midori, the proposal was ambitious. "Don't overdo it, girl," Shōta muttered.

Ichiyō's sense of locale in such a passage is overwhelming. This, too, seems partly the result of Saikaku's influence. Earlier stories are never the character sketches of a place that "Child's Play" becomes. They are usually set in the genteel sections of the city where Ichiyō had always lived until now, and which she therefore took for granted. But when she moved to Ryūsenji, the spectacle of the shitamachi, with the lights and the noise of the licensed quarter "near enough to touch"—as she says in the story—it all made a lasting impression.

Her stay in these spirited surroundings quite happily coincided with her discovery of Saikaku, the local colorist. In works like *The Japanese Family Storehouse* and *Worldly Reckonings*, Saikaku sometimes concerned himself less with storytelling than with portraying the fundamental qualities of a region—the frugal ways of Sakai,[68] the jaded, otiose life in Nagasaki.[69] Saikaku traveled widely and was keenly aware of regional variations. Each story in *Five Women Who Loved Love*, for example, is set in a different city, and his *Hitome Tamaboko* (The Open Road at a Glance, 1689) was the first comprehensive guidebook to Japan. Saikaku was fascinated by the question of why the characteristics of men of essentially the same class and calling differ so markedly from place to place. Why is it that Edo townsmen tend either to improvidence or ambition worthy of a feudal baron, while their counterparts in Kyōto and Ōsaka are more tight-fisted and less willing to take a chance?[70] Why is it that Nara families enjoy New Year's customs far merrier than those of the capital?[71] The atmosphere of a locality, with its power to mold men's characters, is the thing that often interests him. In some stories men are significant not as individuals but as features of their environment, shaped by it and in turn confirming the nature of the place in which they dwell.

Naturally, then, Saikaku excelled at limning out a setting. He paints some very vivid scenes that are rich in detail: the seven mysterious things in the Tenma district of Ōsaka;[72] the stormy night at the temple when young Oshichi steals into the acolyte's bed, with the crashing of thunder outside loud enough to drive the worms from the ground;[73] the pickpockets mingling among the handsome housewives at the autumn market in Tsuruga.[74] In the closing story of *Worldly Reckonings*, the year-end bustle along the To-richō, as merchants rush to get things ready for the holiday, calls to mind Ichiyō's opening description of the neighborhood around Daion Temple, where the subject matter is the setting.

This strong sense of place, and the precise detail and enumeration of phenomena that accompany it, are one reason Saikaku is always labeled a realist, even though his is by no means an illusionistic realism of the nineteenth-century European variety. By the standards of Flaubert or Zola, Saikaku would seem a very strange realist indeed. Like the Europeans two hundred years later, Saikaku attempted to reproduce normal, everyday life as lived by the ordinary person, thereby portraying universal truth. And like them, his technique was the exact observation of human behavior set against the physical backgrounds of contemporary life. One can even go so far as to say that he shared with Flaubert a passion for the mot juste—though surely it must have come more readily to Saikaku—and for the single, telling detail that was emblematic of a wider truth. What he did not share with the Europeans was the same rigorous code of objectivity. And yet even in the breach, Saikaku remains a realist. He was not one to eschew exaggeration or a fancy style, but in the overdrawn and decorative he still managed to capture aspects of human nature that ring true.

Although Saikaku never hesitates to comment on his characters, the voice of the author is still detached—sober and practical. In one sense, it seems almost too objective, standing so very aloof from an intimately familiar world that he cannot but see the contradictions in the broad picture. When he then focuses on one detail, it is so true and aptly chosen (even if it seems picked at random) that it constitutes a form of caricature, whether or not there is conscious exaggeration.

It is the realism, the specificity, in Saikaku's stories that makes them comic. When he tells us how chōnin would insult each other, the particulars of the insults give us a perfect picture of every aspect of town life. ("Your older sister went shopping for bean paste without any underwear and she slipped in the middle of the road!" "You're the kind to get a piece of rice cake stuck in your throat on the holidays—they'll bury you in Toribeno, mark my word.")[75]

The upshot is more comic still when Saikaku applies his practical, detached approach to the absurd, a method reminiscent of the way the haikai poet would juxtapose two jarring elements. In one story in *Worldly Reckonings*, in order to prove that rats could have carried off his mother's money, which he himself has actually stolen, a character recounts the various household effects that a pack of rats was supposed to have trundled with it when the imperial court moved from Asuka to Nara. The list is typical Saikaku whimsy: old wads of cotton to camouflage the entrance to the rats' nests, charms to protect them from neighborhood cats, bags of rice to take with them on their pilgrimages to Kumano Shrine, and so forth.[76]

But this ironic detachment of Saikaku's too often leads to the creation of stereotypes. Ichiyō has more claim to the title of "realist." The characters in "Child's Play" are fully wrought. People in Saikaku, on the other hand, stand up for only a minute on the stage and reveal only one side of their natures. Even in the longer stories, like *Five Women Who Loved Love* and *The Life of an Amorous Man*, although the characters spend more time before us, they still fail to become people with multifaceted personalities and real depth.

Ichiyō, too, had a detached and ironical attitude toward the folly and weakness of her characters, but she sustains her examination of them in a way Saikaku does not. He peeps at his characters through a spyglass and then trains the lens elsewhere. Ichiyō may leave a character in order to cut to another scene, but she returns later and watches him reveal another aspect of his identity. She does cast types in "Child's Play," but they are never the dominant characters. Shōta's skinflint grandmother, for example, fits several of Saikaku's favorite categories: the miser, the pawnbroker, and the selfish old lady. Nobu's father is another Saikaku type: the hypocritical priest, far too attached to eating eels and making money. But the major figures in "Child's Play" are never delineated in the exaggerated and ultimately unbelievable strokes that Saikaku would sometimes use. Character, motivation, and the situations themselves all tend to be oversimplified by Saikaku. A lump of lacquer floats down the river and a man makes a fortune by selling it in small pieces.[77] A woman is unjustly suspected by a jealous neighbor of having an affair with her husband; but why not? she asks herself, oddly untroubled at the prospect of forfeiting her life, the standard penalty for adultery in Edo.[78] Another character in Five Women is about to expire on the roadside when her companion urges her not to give up; if they go a little farther, they can make love again. She is on her feet in no time.[79] These women who love love are not the only ones in Saikaku who are slapstick and one-dimensional.

In any case, his comic insight was only part of Saikaku's realism. He is invariably remembered for his humor. One forgets that Saikaku was not impervious to the darker side of life. In one of the earliest and most important historical sources on Saikaku, Kenmon Dansō (A Miscellany of Things Seen and Heard, ca. 1738), Itō Baiu (1683–1745) accurately appraises Saikaku's realism: "He understood well from his own experience the lights and shadows, the remorse, the hardships, the joys and disappointments of this world. He was a man who, by nature, understood the human heart."[80] The storybooks before Saikaku, even those by chōnin, were fantastic and melodramatic. Saikaku was the first townsman to write from the standpoint of a townsman. He sympathized with the ideals, attitudes, and dilemmas of his class. Saikaku does owe something to Asai Ryōi (d. 1691), whose Ukiyo Monogatari (Tales of the Floating World, ca. 1661) articulated the philosophy of the new age of pleasure. Others before him pioneered the buoyant plebeian literature, but Saikaku was the first to look at life through the eyes of the lowly and the forgotten, and in this he and Ichiyō are kindred spirits. There is dignity even in the suffering of women and the poor. "I was born with the rights of a human being," one of Saikaku's women declares, asserting her freedom of choice in love.[81] "Money is our real enemy," a distressed employment agent sighs.[82] The desperately poor are ready to strike Faustian bargains, and they never get the better end of the stick. Penniless husbands are forced to offer their wives as security on loans[83] or send them into service as wet nurses in the homes of lecherous widowers, while their own babies starve on a rice-syrup concoction in place of mother's milk.[84] And Saikaku saw the tawdry aspect of the entertainer's life for what it was. With the greasepaint and fame came a salary that could never cover an actor's expenses and the resultant need to find a pederast for a patron. (Most likely the boy had been sold into the profession by financially pressed parents to begin with.) "Truly," Saikaku writes, "nothing is more painful in this world than the necessity of making a living under such circumstances. . . . All too closely do the actor and the courtesan resemble each other in their hopeless fates."[85]

This same attitude is a powerful undercurrent in "Child's Play." Carefree little Midori doesn't catch on to what is in store for her when she grows up. Only at the end does she begin to sense where the physical changes she is undergoing will finally lead her. The froth begins to evaporate from life as she grasps what little freedom she really has, as she understands that she is destined to become a courtesan. She would have agreed with Saikaku's heroine who demanded her rights. Midori desires the right to be left alone, to define what is causing her uneasiness, and to remain a child a little while longer.

For every joke, then, in this playful writing there resounds a discordant note of disillusion, of downright cynicism. Unlike gesaku writers, Saikaku and Ichiyō knew that the glamorous demimonde was not what it appeared. The loveliest of courtesans looked less fair when she doffed her clothes to play games like "naked islanders."[86] Even Midori's beautiful sister, the toast of the Yoshiwara, did not reign without paying for her brief supremacy. The dumb poor were miserable and the smart poor were scoundrels. Needy pilgrims offered lead "pigeon eyes" instead of real coins.[87] The rich were, if anything, worse. "All men are thieves,"[88] Saikaku says, but some are more successful than others. "For sheer duplicity, you needn't look beyond Japan."[89] And don't think that men of the cloth are any better. They, too, have feet of clay. The randy monk was a standing joke in Saikaku. ("Never show your sword to a drunkard and never show your daughter to a priest.")[90] Nobu's father in "Child's Play," a boozing cleric who fingers his abacus along with his rosary, comes of a venerable tradition. As Ichiyō said of Midori's fondness for the sweet life, it is all a little sad.

A literature that mixes the humorous and the sorrowful probably has as much claim as any formal school to the mantle of realism. With Saikaku, one tends to remember the brilliance of the wit and the fun that he had with language. Yet when the body of his work is taken together (or even just the collections of the chōnin stories), for all that each individual who appears is a type or a caricature, the variety of their number and situations succeeds in presenting a well-rounded picture of man. Saikaku embraced the contradictions in life and, in his mature works, shunned idealization.[91] These attitudes are marks of realism by any standard. Both in subject and stance,

Saikaku's work offers a host of contradictions. Despite a cool and detached point of view, we still hear the author's voice. He was aloof as an ironist, but close enough to his material to sympathize with the suffering of his characters. The occasionally bitter tone of the cynic is nonetheless decked out in a mischievous prose. Just when it seems that style is about to overtake substance, one senses the underlying gravity of the author. Irony, no matter how elegantly worded, is after all a criticism of life.

Ichiyō shared these traits with Saikaku. She wrote at the beginning of Japan's modern age, and there is much in her work that is modern. But "Child's Play" is also homage to Edo, and to the world her family came from before they put on airs, before they fell into the back street. Sitting in the dust of the downtown, Ichiyō discovered her own province and her true mentor. Within a few years of the story's publication in 1895, writers like Shimazaki Tōson and the naturalists would clamor for a higher kind of fiction, one that emulated the European novel. The things that they would soon admire in fiction were a rational approach, a serious tone, an element of self-consciousness, a claim to purity and sincerity of purpose, with psychological realism as the objective and a spare and concise prose style as their means.

Ichiyō, one last time, had summoned other standards: a literature that was unself-conscious, intuitive, and subjective. Here there was room for hyperbole and for writers who saw themselves as part of the entertaining tradition. Whimsy and digression were not out of place. The idea that because one was serious one had to be plain would never have occurred to Ichiyō, steeped as she was in the classics. In a way, the old "novel" was freer—to ramble and follow a looser form inspired by linked comic verse, and to indulge in a few flights of fancy. It was, in short, a more poetic genre. Never, Ichiyō might have said, undervalue harmony and rhythm in the narrative. It is important to have an interesting story to tell and a commitment to what one is telling but, in the words of Flaubert, who also celebrated the poetry in prose, "Quel que soit le sujet d'un livre, il est bon s'il permet de parler une belle langue."[92]

5
The Bundan

It is easy to recognize the old in Ichiyō but harder, today, to see the new. The deliberately vague and allusive courtly language, which prefers to suggest rather than define, to create a mood as well as a story; the ethereal, emotional tone; and the near obsession with the mutability of human bonds were all relics from the Heian past. The free-form, fluid sentences, drifting from descriptive passages to indirect dialogue to direct dialogue to narrator's asides to poetic allusion or punning or other literary prestidigitation, were the descendants of the playful early Edo storybooks. The drive to entertain, exalting performance and sheer technique—suspect qualities to Meiji writers more ponderous than Ichiyō—bespoke the frivolity of gesaku, that last holdover from feudal days.

Yet in Ichiyō's hands, supposedly "premodern" traits have something fresh about them. It is one of the ironies of literary history that Ichiyō's stories in the stamp of Saikaku's seventeenth-century fiction have more in common with the modern novel (Proust or Joyce, for example) than many of the self-consciously "modern" works of the early Meiji period. Freed from the exigencies of plot, Ichiyō could delve into seemingly extraneous things, like character.

The more ancient Heian legacy also took on a new pertinence. Part of the hold that Ichiyō still exerts over Japanese readers comes from her lyrical expression of a certain kind of longing. At first glance, it may seem little different from Heian melancholy, but a second look at "Child's Play" reveals an atmosphere altogether characteristic of Meiji and modern man: a yearning for freedom from the constraints of conformity, a sad, slowly crystallizing sense that one's dreams—whether of independence or of true rapport with another human being—are all beyond consummation. There were many promises in the air in the Meiji period, and many hopes that went unfulfilled. Ichiyō's generation grew up in the heady days of the 1870s and 1880s, when Japan was giddy with Western liberalism and Christian brotherly love, only to discover in the reactionary 1890s that many of the enlightened notions to which they had been exposed—popular rights, intellectual freedom, feminism, the sanctity of the private self—were in point of fact unattainable. When the bubble burst for the Higuchi family with Noriyoshi's death in 1889, Ichiyō was not alone. Poverty, broken promises, and the weight of convention crushed people as clearly as Midori's awakening to her inevitable fate in "Child's Play" crushed her. The story is Ichiyō's metaphor for this afflicted society. Like Midori, reluctantly leaving childhood behind, people in the Meiji period did not have the predictable certainties of Edo, a less capricious age, to depend upon any more.

It was as if in "Child's Play" Ichiyō rehearsed her foreboding that the last years of the nineteenth century would close the door on the youthful hopes of a generation, on all that was expansive and noble in the Meiji experiment. When the Imperial Rescript on Education trumpeted the preservation of "national virtues" in 1890, it ushered in an era of authoritarian retreat, a nationalistic denial of the exuberant, slightly juvenile infatuation with the wonders of the West. Egalitarian ideals and the spirit of freedom, still so new and enticing, gave way too soon to the stodgy and familiar old precepts of official Confucianism and service to the state. The false patriots, the blind accepters, the worthless idols returned to power. With the onset of the 1894 imbroglio with China, Japan became a graveyard of the young. The words were Shimazaki Tōson's: those he mourned were the casualties of more than war.[1] In its indirect way, "Child's Play," an elegy on lost opportunities, articulated the yearning of Ichiyō's generation for an age of innocence and optimism too quickly snatched from them. A decade later Tōson and others would make the same lament in the romantic pronouncements of their first novels.

"Child's Play" owes part of its popularity to this adolescent longing for the unattained, for the half-remembered sweeter days of youth. The very title— "Takekurabe," literally "Comparing Heights"—evokes the process of growing up and wistful regret for what might have been. It alludes to an incident in the tenth-century *Ise Monogatari* (Tales of Ise):

> A boy and a girl, the children of two men who traveled over the countryside, once used to play together beside a well. As they grew up they both felt rather self-conscious about continuing the old relationship, but the boy had set his heart on marrying the girl, and she too was determined that she would be his wife, and refused to agree when her father tried to betroth her to someone else. The boy sent the girl this poem:

Tsutsui tsu no	My height that we measured
Izutsu ni kakeshi	At the well curb
Maro ga *take**	Has, it seems,
Suginikerashi na	Passed the old mark
Imo mizaru ma ni.	Since last I saw you.

*The words forming Ichiyō's title are italicized.

She replied,

Kurabekoshi	The hair parted in the middle
Furiwakegami mo	That I measured against yours
Kata suginu	Now hangs below my shoulders.
Kimi narazu shite	For whom shall it be put up,
Tare ka agubeki.	If not for you?

After many such poems had passed between them, their wishes came true and they became man and wife.[2]

"Child's Play" likewise tells the story of adolescent love: between Midori, the spirited younger sister of a celebrated courtesan, and shy, bookish Nobu, the perpetually embarrassed son of a worldly priest. Like the boy and girl in Tales of Ise, they are neighbors, but here in the side street behind the quarter. In the forty-five-page novella serialized in Bungakkai over a year's time, Ichiyō depicts the sudden, painful passage from adolescent to adult. The two children are old friends, but when the story opens in late summer they are on the brink of self-awakenings that will forever change both them and their idyllic relations. By the time summer has given way to fall, Nobu is so uneasy about his new affection for Midori that he can no longer speak to her; by the time the sunny holidays of early autumn have yielded in turn to the chilly end of the season, tongue-tied, friendless Nobu has gone off to the seminary and Midori has begun to understand, at least subconsciously, that like her older sister she is destined for the life of a prostitute. The story is told with such restraint that any summary threatens to belie its subtlety. Midori's uncertain steps into young womanhood, like Nobu's unfolding awkwardness in first love, are beautifully and delicately rendered. "Child's Play" gives us the sentiment of earlier Ichiyō without the treacle. Never before had she described emotion so artfully, or succeeded so completely in creating the illusion of life in characters cut from whole cloth. This time they speak for themselves, they are not swallowed up in the lyricism. A masterful brush paints Midori's transformation from a childish spitfire with too much pocket money, thanks to her sister's success in the Yoshiwara, into a gawky and subdued, though beautiful, young lady.

True to the time-honored penchant in Japanese letters for surrendering to unbridled lyrical impulse, heretofore Ichiyō had allowed poetic gush to become the literary equivalent of boiler plate. Febrile depiction of setting replaced attention to plot or rigorous character delineation. The moon, the blossoms, the hero's mind, all became one when the author's emotions swept away disciplined narration in the besotted act of writing. "Child's Play" was an extraordinary achievement for Ichiyō: she now perfected a controlled lyricism that tolerated no waste, no irrelevant effusion. For all the surface brilliance of the style, the evocation of season and place is close to the narrative bone. It is a tighter, and thus more moving, lyricism than anything before (except the diary)—as here, where autumn's passing carries with it the last of childhood:

In spring the cherry trees blossom in profusion. In summer the lanterns twinkle in memory of the late Tamagiku. In fall the festival streets overflow with rickshaws. Count them: seventy-five down the road within the space of ten minutes. Then the autumn holidays are over. Here and there a red dragonfly bobs above the rice fields. Before long, quail will be calling out along the moat. Mornings and evenings, the breeze blows cold. At the sundries shop, pocket warmers now take the place of mosquito incense. It's sad, somehow, that faint sound of the mortar grinding flour at Tamura's, over by the bridge. The clock at Kadoebi's has a melancholy ring. Fires glow through all four seasons from the direction of Nippori. It's in autumn that one begins to notice them. Smoke rises each time one more soul embarks on the journey to the other shore.

Deftly, a geisha plays on the samisen. The refrain reaches the path along the bank behind the teahouses. A passerby looks up and listens. Not much of a song, really, but moving all the same. "Together we shall spend our night of love." Women who have done time in the quarter will tell you—it's the men who begin visiting in fall who prove to be the truly faithful ones.

Talk, talk: in this neighborhood, there is always grist for gossip. The details are tedious, but the stories make the rounds. A blind masseuse, she was only twenty, killed herself. With a handicap like hers, love was out of the question. Well, she couldn't stand it any more. Drowned herself in Mizunoya Pond. Then there are the incidents too commonplace to rate a rumor. Missing persons: Kichigorō, the greengrocer, and Takichi, the carpenter. How come? "They picked them up for this," a fellow whispers, and pantomimes a gambler dealing out the cards.

A moment ago there were children there, down the street. "Ring-a-ring-a-rosy, pocket full of posies." Suddenly it's quiet now, before you notice. Only the sound of rickshaws, loud as ever.[3]

If "Child's Play" is wistful and elegiac, it is also filled with playfulness. Sentiment and irony operate in tandem. Ichiyō's humanity prevented her indignation and her sarcasm—"like a sneer after crying," in the words of a contemporary admirer[4]—from turning caricature of Meiji crassness into unrelieved vitriol. Her barbs were always dipped in regret and delivered with humor. Nevertheless, they show Ichiyō's profound disdain for the materialism of her age, and do so more subtly and eloquently than earlier attempts like "Clouds in Springtime." The adults in "Child's Play" are not memorable worthies. Sangorō's father, "Groveling Tetsu," toadies to everyone in sight, including the landlord's roughneck son who terrorizes poor, bumbling Sangorō. Shōta's skinflint grandmother, whose heart is as cold as the metal locks she keeps on all her cabinets, only cares about collecting the daily interest on her loans. Midori's parents pamper their future courtesan as though she were a Strasbourg goose being fattened for pâté. Worst of all are the hypocrites. Nobu's father is an amalgam of every wily bureaucrat, vulgar priest, and smug citizen that Ichiyō detested, but she doesn't let her anger get the better of her art:

"Thus have I heard it spoken," the reverend priest intoned the sutra. As the holy words were carried from the temple by the soft breeze through the pines, they should have blown away all dust within the heart.

But smoke rose from fish broiling in the kitchen. In the cemetery diapers had been seen drying over tombstones. Nothing wrong here in the eyes of the Order, perhaps; those who fancied their clerics above worldly desires, though, found the doings at Ryūge Temple rather too earthly for their tastes.

Here the fortunes of the head priest were as handsome as his stomach. Both had rounded out nicely through the years. The man's glow of well-being beggared description: not the sunny pink of the cherries, not the deep pink of the peach; from the top of his freshly shaven pate to the bottom of his neck, he shone like burnished copper. When he whooped with laughter—bushy, salt-and-pepper eyebrows floating heavenward— the noise of the old man's excess could have toppled Buddha from the altar.

This all too corporeal priest has taken a wife and fathered two children: a son, the sensitive Nobu, and a lively daughter, Ohana, whose beauty and exuberance inspire the priest to install her in a little tea shop "where she could vend her charm." Money is always on his mind: "It seemed a shame to waste such a girl, for she might have been a geisha." And so he sees to it that Ohana does not go to waste. Her little shop is always crowded with young men who have "no idea in their heads how tea is weighed and measured," and seldom is the store empty before midnight. "But his holiness," Ichiyō observes, "was the busy one":

Loans to collect, the shop to oversee, funerals to arrange, not to mention all the sermons every month. When he wasn't flipping through accounts, he was going through the sutras. If things didn't let up, he'd wear himself out, he would sigh as he dragged his flowered cushion onto the veranda, where he fanned himself, half-naked, and enjoyed his nightly hooch. He was a fish-eater, and Nobu was the one he sent over to the main street for the broiled eels that he liked. "The big oily ones, if

you please." It galled Nobu. His eyes never left his feet as he trudged over
to the Musashiya. If he heard voices at the paper shop across the street,
he would keep on going. Then, when the coast was clear, he'd dart into
the eel shop. The shame he felt! He would never eat the smelly things.

The reverend was nothing if not practical. There were some who
might call him greedy, but that never bothered him a whit. He was
neither a timid soul nor an idler: give him a spare moment and he'd set
about fashioning kumade charms. On Otori day he would have his wife
out peddling them. Whatever doubts she may have had about the venture, they were short-lived once his holiness started to bemoan the killing everybody else made, rank amateurs up and down the street. He
soon persuaded his reluctant wife, set up a booth not a stone's throw
from the temple gate, and installed her there to sell his charms and
good-luck hairpins. She tied her hair back with a headband, just like the
vendors and all the young men. In the daytime, she knew enough to stay
out of sight and mingle with the crowd, leaving the florist's wife to
manage things. But when the sun went down—who would have guessed
it?—the woman had a field day. At dusk she took over for herself, quite
forgetting what a spectacle she made with her sudden itch for profit.
"Everything marked down! Prices slashed!" she barked after a customer
who backed away. Buffeted and dizzy from the throngs, the victim soon
lost his powers of appraisal. They had fled along with memory: two days
earlier he had come to this very temple as a pilgrim. "Three for only
seventy-five sen." But her price left room to negotiate. "How about five
for seventy-three?" "Sold!"

There were, of course, all kinds of sharp practices. Even if no one from
the congregation heard, Nobu wondered, what would the neighbors
think? And his friends? He could just hear them. Ryūge Temple is selling
hairpins now. Nobu's mother is out huckstering like a lunatic. Really,
didn't they think they ought to stop?

The reverend priest would hear nothing of it. "Knock it off. You don't
know what you're talking about." The mere idea sent the man into
paroxysms.

Prayers in the morning, accounts at night. His father's face beamed
whenever his fingers touched the abacus. It was enough to turn the boy's
stomach. Why on earth had the man become a priest?

There was nothing in his upbringing to make Nobu such a gloomy
child. He had the same parents as Ohana. They were part of the same
cozy, self-contained family. Yet he was the quiet one. Even when he did
speak, his opinions were never taken seriously. His father's schemes, his
mother's conduct, his sister's education—to Nobu everything they did
was a travesty. He had resigned himself to knowing they would never
listen. How unfair it was. His friends found him contrary and perverse,
but in fact he was a weakling. If anyone maligned him in the slightest,

he would run for the shelter of his room. He was a coward utterly
lacking in the courage to defend himself. At school they called him a
brain; his family's station was not lowly. No one knew how weak he
really was. More than one of his friends considered Nobu something of a
cold fish.[5]

They are alone, these children. *Tales of Ise* notwithstanding, Ichiyō was the
first to see the poignancy in their isolation. Like the adults in the story
oblivious to the pain of growing up, other writers had never bothered with
the subject. In Ichiyō's hands, however, a character like Nobu becomes as
emblematic of his time as any grown-up personage in Meiji fiction. He is an
outsider, another uprooted Bunzō in *Drifting Clouds*, cut off from his coarse
surroundings by moral scruples, denied the possibility of friendship by a
noble reticence, a timorous nature. His parents have no time to understand
him. Even Midori eventually misreads his signals; and that is the tragedy. For
the most part, these children of the side street can manage quite nicely
without the attention of adults. The real tragedy in growing up is that they
also lose each other. By the end they are all as isolated as Nobu. At the first
symptoms of puberty, Midori shuts herself up inside her room. Once Shōta is
old enough to collect the interest for his grandmother, he stops singing as he
makes his solitary rounds. On the verge of adulthood, they all retreat into
their private crannies. Their old haunts—the paper shop, the main street—
fall quiet, "as if a light had gone out."[6]

"Child's Play" raised Ichiyō's waif literature to a higher plane, beyond
stylization. The children in the neighborhood around Ryūge Temple are
livelier, and more complicated, than the earlier youngsters. Any fool can
sympathize with an orphan; it takes perception and resource to portray the
vulnerabilities of a bully or a coddled rich boy. Even cocky Chōkichi has his
tender moments. If he could beat up Sangorō for deserting his gang, he could
also stop in the rain to succor hapless Nobu:

"Nobu, what's the matter? Break your [sandal] strap? What a sight
you are!"

Nobu turned around to see who owned the unexpected voice. It was
obnoxious Chōkichi, decked out like a young gallant. He had on his
best-dress kimono, and he wore his orange sash profligately low on the
hips. His new jacket had a fancy black collar, and the umbrella he
carried was festooned with the trademark of one of the houses in the
quarter. His high clogs were sporting lacquered rain covers—this was
something new. What pride there was in the young man's swagger.

"The strap broke, and I was wondering what to do," Nobu answered
helplessly. "I'm not very good at these things."

"No, you wouldn't be. It's all right, wear mine. The straps won't give
out."

"But what will you do?"

"Don't worry. I'm used to it. I'll just go like this," he said, tucking up the bottom of his kimono. "Feels much better than wearing sandals, anyway." He kicked off his rain clogs.

"You're going to go barefoot? That won't be fair."

"I don't mind. I'm used to going barefoot. Someone like you has soft feet. You could never walk barefoot on the gravel. Come on, wear these," he urged, arranging his sandals obligingly. What a spectacle: Chōkichi was more detested than the plague god himself, and here he was with soft words on his tongue and bushy eyebrows moving solicitously. "I'll take your sandals and toss them in at the back door. Here, let's switch."[7]

Ichiyō labored for a year on this novella of the downtown, and when she was finished she had created one of the comeliest and most robust works of Japanese fiction. A less adroit writer could never have orchestrated so rambunctious a gang of characters—teasing and pouting and fighting with each other all at once, not in timid little twosomes. "Balls of fire in the Edo twilight," one critic has called them, and compared their tale very favorably to more tepid studies of adolescence and summers past spawned by the celebrated story.[8]

One might ask whether it was easier for Ichiyō to shed her authorial hesitancies when she wrote about children. Hauteur may have emboldened her to go slumming with Kusaka the diviner, but it was not what motivated Ichiyō to study the cock-a-hoop young ladies on the outskirts of the demimonde. She saw in obstreperous adolescents the lonely drama of self-discovery, and, paradoxically, the loss, not the gain, of autonomy that came with incipient adulthood. As she reached the end of her tether, the loss of any possibility of freedom overwhelmed Ichiyō. She studied those who were driven outside of the world of bourgeois convention, or were broken by it. She had no time anymore for the pallid couples of polite society. She preferred to examine the people life had ambushed. She looked increasingly at women: prostitutes, concubines, women who had affairs with their boarders. Her final parcel of stories addressed society's relegation of half its members to an oppressed, cipherlike existence.

Several regressive works did emerge from Ichiyō's last year of writing,[9] but the major stories, told in a controlled, increasingly spare style, dramatically condemned the plight of modern women. "Nigorie" (Troubled Waters, September 1895) might be considered the companion piece to "Child's Play." The reader who wants to know what will become of Midori finds his answer in this portrait of faded courtesans. One can imagine an older Midori, beyond the bloom of her Yoshiwara season, packing up for a second start in the tawdrier, nouveau quarter where "Troubled Waters" is set. Here Ichiyō plumps for a more straightforward approach than she did in "Child's Play." This time the story unfolds completely inside the pleasure zone. And an inelegant, inferior district it was, the Higuchis' new neighborhood of Maruyama-Fukuyama, where the "white demons" applied their lipstick liberally and resembled "man-eating dogs more than courtesans."[10]

The three Higuchi women had finally managed to fold up the sundries shop in mid-1894, but when they left Ryūsenji they exchanged one patch of the shitamachi for another. Because of lack of funds, Ichiyō had abandoned her plans to join forces with Tanaka Minoko. Since the shopkeeper's regimen did not suit them, the three women were forced to fall back upon their old way of life. Ichiyō ate humble pie and returned to her unprofitable position as Nakajima Utako's assistant. Without trade to worry about, she at least had more time for writing, and the result was her final cascade: prickly commentaries on woman's lot. Kuniko and Taki meanwhile redoubled their efforts as seamstresses. In prostitutes they had discovered their best customers, and it was for this reason that they decided to remain within the crescent of the downtown. No walls or moats separated them from the second-class courtesans of Maruyama-Fukuyama; the beauties came to Ichiyō when they needed a love letter drafted, and the former Miss-Keep-to-Herself became an expert on the inner workings of the demimonde. "Troubled Waters" is narrated with the authority of an insider, and with the sympathy for its ill-starred heroine of someone who could see herself slipping one day into the same muddy stream.

Oriki, the main attraction of a mediocre house, has been driven into the profession by her family's poverty and has learned to deaden the sting of life by consuming unladylike quantities of alcohol. Although the plot is slender, the lively dialogue and Ichiyō's sense of place make for a vivid rendering of these frayed edges of the night world. The ladies lament their wilting appearances, drag "pasty melons" (unwitting shop clerks) in by the sleeve, and dream of finding the man who will buy them a one-way ticket out of the district. "Troubled Waters" is another tale of thwarted love, but the least successful thing about it is the "story." The two main characters never meet on stage. What we have instead are scenes that evoke a world of defeat. One chapter finds Oriki moping in her cups for her beloved Genshichi, who has gone to seed after squandering his modest income as her number-one patron. The next chapter shows poor, listless Genshichi subjected to yet another diatribe from his wife, who is justly exasperated with her derelict husband. The milieu is reminiscent of Chikamatsu's love suicides of vulnerable courtesans and desperate chōnin—whose fates always seem controlled by money, or the lack of it—and the story resolves itself in the same way, almost. One day the dead bodies of Oriki and Genshichi are discovered in the temple grounds above the quarter; the mutilation which Oriki has sustained, however, suggests that she did not enter their lovers' pact willingly.

Despite her relative youth and outward nonchalance, and the great ease with which she draws men to her, Oriki's last days are not happy ones. "I am a human being, you know," she has to remind a customer. "There are things that weigh on my mind, too."[11] With one of her favorites, she is finally more candid:

> "First of all, there's no point in beating around the bush. I'm nothing but a slut. You know that. I'm not some innocent young maiden. To put it politely, if a woman like me *weren't* tainted by these surroundings—like a lotus flower flourishing in the middle of a swamp—do you really think I would have any callers? Do you think this place would be in business? You're different from most of the men who come here. Imagine what the others are like. Sometimes I wonder how it would be to live a normal life, and then I start to feel bitter and ashamed. I think to myself maybe I too could get married and settle down in a little house somewhere. But it will never happen.
>
> "As long as I'm here, I can't be rude to the men who come to see me. I have to think of something nice to say to all of them—how cute this one is, how sweet that one is, how I've never seen anyone so handsome. Some even take me seriously. Do you know, some of them ask a good-for-nothing like me to marry them? I wonder, would I be happy if I accepted one of their proposals? Would that be the answer to my prayers? You, I've liked from the very start. When I don't see you for a day, I miss you. But if you asked me to be your wife, I don't know . . . I doubt it would work, and yet, when we're not together . . . In a word, I guess you could say I'm fickle. And what do you think made me this way? Three generations of failure, that's what."[12]

Impoverishment and degradation have turned Oriki into a desperate character. Although Genshichi bludgeons her to death at the end of the story, her own self-destructiveness may have invited it:

> Oriki ran from the house as fast as she could. If only it were possible, she would keep on going, to China, to India. How she hated her life! She never wanted to hear another human voice, or any sound at all. She needed a quiet place, where her mind could relax, where there were no worries. How long would she be stuck in this hopeless situation, where everything was absurd and worthless and cruel? Was this what life was supposed to be? She hated it! She hated it! She felt almost delirious and leaned against a tree at the side of the road. "I'm afraid to cross to the other side; I'm afraid to stay where I am." It was her song and her voice, but where was it coming from?
>
> "I have no choice," she whispered. "I will have to cross the bridge by myself. My father fell treading it. They say my grandfather stumbled, too. I was born with the curse of many generations, and there are things I have to undergo before I die. No one's going to feel sorry for me, that

much I know. If I complain about how sad I am, 'What's wrong?' people say, 'Don't you like your work?' Oh, it doesn't matter any more what happens—I haven't the slightest idea what will become of me. I might as well go on as Oriki of the Kikunoi. . . ."

Oriki left the darkness of the alley and walked along a street lined with shops. They were all doing a lively business. If only some of the gaiety would rub off, she mused. As she trudged along, the faces of passersby seemed tiny to her. Even those of people who walked directly in front of her seemed somehow very distant. She felt as if she were hovering ten feet above the ground. She could hear the din of voices, but it sounded more like the echo of someone falling to the bottom of a well.[13]

In one way or another, Ichiyō's last heroines are all tumbling to the bottom of some well. Her next story, "Jūsan'ya" (The Thirteenth Night, December 1895), treats the effects that a loveless marriage has on a decent, sensitive young woman. The story takes place in one evening: Oseki, who to all appearances has made a brilliant match for herself, arrives unexpectedly at the humble house of her lower-class parents. After hemming and hawing and listening to her father hold forth on how lucky they have all been, Oseki confesses that this very night she has left her husband and that she wants a divorce.

The man, Harada Isamu, is a well-to-do, rising politician, but he is also a sadist. He has subjected Oseki to such psychological abuse that she is finally willing to pay the ultimate price for her freedom: estrangement from her cherished son. Between tears, she recounts the hair-raising gamut of indignities she has suffered at the hands of her statesman-husband. The once-affectionate Harada has spurned his wife ever since the birth of their child. When he isn't totally indifferent to her, he is hostile. He criticizes Oseki in front of the servants and makes fun of her lack of education. He bullies her, and the harder she tries to please him, the bigger the tantrum he throws. He has become more like an ogre than a husband.

Oseki's mother is horrified and utterly sympathetic, remembering that it was Harada, not they, who insisted on the marriage in the first place. But her father is the typical Meiji pragmatist who crops up in all Ichiyō's best fiction. "Women are always complaining," he says when Oseki first hints at her problem. "Your mother is the same way. What a nuisance it is. She's been irritable all day, just because she couldn't give you any of her dumplings."[14] It is not that he feels no sympathy for his daughter, but other concerns take precedence:

"Oseki, you may think I'm heartless, that I don't understand your situation. But I'm not saying any of this to scold you: when people come from different backgrounds, it's only natural their ways of thinking aren't always going to be the same. I'm sure you're doing your best to please Isamu. But that doesn't mean everything is fine and dandy—not in his eyes, anyway. Isamu is a smart man. He knows what's what. I don't think he means to be unreasonable with you. It's often the case, though: men who are hard-working and admired by the world can sometimes be very selfish. Away from home they hide their swollen heads. With their families they let their hair down; they take out all the discontent they bring home from the office. It must be terribly hard on you to be the target of all Isamu's grievances.

"On the other hand, your responsibilities as the wife of a man like Isamu are of another kind altogether. You're not married to someone in the ward office, you know—some fellow who lights the fire underneath the kettle for you and goes off to work every day with lunch box tied to his waist. You can't compare Isamu's place in society with an ordinary office worker's. Even if he is fussy and a little difficult sometimes, it's still a wife's duty to humor her husband. You can never tell, but I'd be surprised if there are many wives who enjoy completely happy relations with their husbands. If you think you're the only one in a bind like this, Oseki, it'll only embitter you. Fact is, it's a burden many people have to bear. What with the difference in your backgrounds, it's natural you'd meet with more suffering than a wife whose husband comes from the same class.

"Your mother talks big, but remember: the fine salary your brother is making is all thanks to Isamu. They say the light a parent sheds on his child is sevenfold. In that case, the benefits we've received from Isamu must be tenfold! His way of helping out is to do things behind the scenes, but we're indebted to him nonetheless. It's trying for you, Oseki, I know. Think what your marriage means to us, though, and to [your brother] Inosuke, and to Tarō. If you've been able to put up with things this long, surely you can continue. And how do you know a divorce is the answer? Isamu would have custody of Tarō, and you'd be my daughter again. Once the bonds are cut, there's no going back—even for a glimpse of little Tarō. If you're going to cry over spilt milk, you might as well do your crying as the wife of Harada. All right? Wouldn't that be better, Oseki? Get hold of yourself and go home tonight as if nothing had happened. Go on being just as careful as you have been. Even if you don't tell us anything more after this, we'll know now, we'll all understand how you feel. We'll share your tears with you." As he urged his daughter to bow to the inevitable, he too wiped a tear from his eyes.[15]

A subtle and mature accomplishment, this sketch: it shows all the self-interest of an Ochika in "Clouds in Springtime" with none of the stridence. Here is a man who loves his daughter; unfortunately he loves security more.

Ichiyō has shown both sides of him deftly, and through dialogue. Such scenes suggest the makings of a playwright. Ichiyō's sense of drama is certainly sure—almost too sure, for the story turns on dramatic contrivances. The conversation between mother, father, and daughter is too stagey. Though Ichiyō has a good ear, the three characters don't converse so much as deliver soliloquies. The alternating monologues appear a bit too arranged when Ichiyō begins inserting background material: what the family's social status is, how Oseki met Harada, how Harada courted her. The reader needs the information, but Ichiyō manages to supply it so facilely that the effect is unexpectedly wooden.

Then there are the equally smooth coincidences at the opening and close of the story, again good theater but not quite worthy of the shrewd narrator of "Child's Play." It is a little too tidy to have Oseki arrive with bad news just as her father congratulates himself on the family's good fortune. On the other hand, coincidence gives "The Thirteenth Night" its dramatic force: at the end, Oseki's chance meeting with her old love on the sad ride home to her husband is what makes the story. When she leaves her parents' house, after her father has persuaded her to remain married to Harada for the sake of her brother's success, Oseki boards a rickshaw, only to discover halfway home that it is being pulled by her childhood sweetheart. She climbs down from the seat, and the two of them walk together under the moonlight, talking about old times. The rickshawman is another love-boy; his obsession with Oseki has long since been the ruin of his little tobacco shop. Even in his reduced circumstances he still attracts Oseki, and as they stroll down a quiet lane she recalls her adolescent hope that he would someday take her for his wife. They part when they come to the main road, and the story ends—one more tale of longing in Ichiyō's storehouse of unconsummated dreams.

The last completed story, "Wakare-Michi" (Separate Ways), which appeared in January 1896 as Ichiyō was polishing the final installment of "Child's Play," is bereft of the sort of contrivance that marred "The Thirteenth Night."[16] In its simplicity and restraint, the slight ten-page story is Ichiyō's best work. Virtually all unnecessary ornament has been drained from the style. Ichiyō's tendency to court the twin dangers of over-reliance on sentiment and chance has completely evaporated, and "Separate Ways" emerges as a flintier, more nimble work than even the magisterial "Child's Play."

Many strains came together in this last piece, the story of a fleeting friendship between an unruly sixteen-year-old misfit and a seamstress who resolves to exchange her daily drudgery for the life of a kept woman. Okyō is the ragged end of a long line of heroines in Ichiyō's beauty-in-the-valley tradition, and the wild Kichizō, the last of Ichiyō's waifs. The story of these two improbable cohorts restates the essential themes of all Ichiyō's writing: the fundamental loneliness of modern man, the illusory nature of friendship, society's oppression of those who do not dwell within the mainstream, the inevitable disappointment that life brings, the generational sense of abandonment and yearning.

Unlike the earlier, quixotic plots of stories like "The Sound of the Koto" or "Encounters on a Dark Night," the plan for "Separate Ways" grew directly from a kernel of experience. Ichiyō had toyed with the idea of becoming Kusaka's mistress, and this story is a projection of how Higuchi Natsuko might have felt on the eve of losing her innocence. It is also a description of a boy's loneliness, the need to be loved, and his feeling of betrayal when his only friend, Okyō, decides to go away.

What gives "Separate Ways" its distinction is the author's quiet control. Ichiyō is usually considered unparalleled as a flamboyant stylist, but the soft-spoken precision of this story is also unlike anything achieved by her contemporaries: compact, understated, told largely in staccato salvos of dialogue, artistic in its apparent absence of art, a flawless blend of economy and drama. Ichiyō had by now learned to narrate with remarkable restraint. In her new asperity, no exhibitionism intrudes upon the action. Nor does excessive sentiment. Irony curbs lyrical instinct; dialogue replaces description. Although Ichiyō would forever lack the capacity to be explicit in the way that writers like Futabatei Shimei or Mori Ōgai could, her very indirection bespoke a subtlety and nuance of feeling at the heart of the modern psychological novel. Some of her reticence she had managed to overcome. "Separate Ways" is the shaped and tightened work of a writer who knew what she was up to and didn't beat around the bush. We have only to look at the dialogue—controlled, vigorous, direct—to see how completely it carries the narration, and what a well-wrought, quietly powerful accomplishment "Separate Ways" is:

Over her usual jacket Okyō was wearing a hood that came down almost to her eyes. She looked smart tonight, Kichizō thought as he surveyed her appearance. "Where've you been? I thought you told me you were too busy even to eat the next few days." The boy did not hide his suspicion. "Were you taking something to a customer?"

"I went to make some of my New Year's calls early," she said innocently.

"You're lying. No one receives greetings on the thirtieth. Where did you go? To your relatives?"

"As a matter of fact, I *am* going to a relative's—to live with a relative I hardly know. Tomorrow I'll be moving. It's so sudden, it probably surprises you. It *is* unexpected, even I feel a little startled. Anyway, you should be happy for me. It's not a bad thing that's happened."

"Really? You're not teasing, are you? You shouldn't scare me like this. If you went away, what would I do for fun? Don't ever joke about such things. You and your nonsense!" He shook his head at her.

"I'm not joking. It's just as you said once—good luck has come riding in a fancy carriage. So I can't very well stay on in a back tenement, can I? Now I'll be able to sew you that kimono, Kichizō."

"I don't want it. When you say 'Good luck has come,' you mean you're going off some place worthless. That's what Hanji said the other day. 'You know Okyō the seamstress?' he said. 'Her uncle—the one who gives rubdowns over by the vegetable market—he's helped her find a new position. She's going into service with some rich family. Or so they say. But it sounds fishy to me—she's too old to learn sewing from some housewife. Somebody's going to set her up. I'm sure of it. She'll be wearing tassled coats the next time we see her, la-de-da, and her hair all done up in ringlets, like a kept woman. You wait. With a face like hers, you don't think she's about to spend her whole life sewing, do you?' That's what he said. I told him he was full of it, and we had a big fight. But you *are* going to do it, aren't you? You're going off to be someone's mistress!"

"It's not that I want to. I don't have much choice. I suppose I won't be able to see you any more, Kichizō, will I?"

With these few words, Kichizō withered. "I don't know, maybe it's a step up for you, but don't do it. It's not as if you can't make a living with your sewing. The only one you have to feed is yourself. When you're good at your work, why give it up for something so stupid? It's disgusting of you. Don't go through with it. It's not too late to change your mind." The boy was unyielding in his notion of integrity.

"Oh, dear," Okyō sighed. She stopped walking. "Kichizō, I'm sick of all this washing and sewing. Anything would be better. I'm tired of these drab clothes. I'd like to wear a crepe kimono, too, for a change—even if it is tainted."

They were bold words, and yet it didn't sound as if she herself fully comprehended them. "Anyway," she laughed, "come home with me. Hurry up now."

"What! I'm too disgusted. You go ahead," he said, but his long, sad shadow followed after her.

Soon they came to their street. Okyō stopped beneath the window where Kichizō always tapped for her. "Every night you come and knock at this window. After tomorrow night," she sighed, "I won't be able to hear your voice calling any more. How terrible the world is."

"It's not the world. It's you."[17]

Where Ichiyō sat to write her final stories—miniatures of women and children in despair—she looked out on a scene of incongruous serenity. Carp danced in the pond in the garden, frogs croaked, and the floppy leaves of a squat banana tree fanned each other lazily in the summer afternoon. In a sense, Ichiyō had come home. The new house, once more in the Hongō district, was a stone's throw from her old neighborhood of Kikuzaka. In no time at all she could walk to the Haginoya in Koishikawa. But in another sense, the Higuchis had never left the downtown. Tucked beneath the bluff of the Abé estate, their rented cottage turned its back on gentility and peered down a narrow alleyway—it would not accommodate more than two abreast—to a ramshackle shop fronting the main street where their new landlord did a brisk trade in broiled eel. Next door to the tiny restaurant, and stretching back to the Higuchi garden, sprawled one of those ubiquitous gin mills that lined the streets of Maruyama-Fukuyama, thrown up overnight on former paddy fields in the boom years of the mid-Meiji.

Money worries dogged the Higuchis as always, but somehow it was a happy time for the three women. At last Taki had her front gate, or at least a bamboo wicket. Among the bar-girls of the neighborhood Kuniko found plenty of customers for her sewing services. And with no shop to manage any more, Ichiyō now had time and a backlog of ideas for a spate of new stories. Tumbling out they came: nine in one year, two novellas, four masterpieces, a burst of pent-up energy that hurled Ichiyō high and bright into the literary firmament.

"On the Last Day of the Year," "Troubled Waters," "The Thirteenth Night," "Child's Play," "Separate Ways"—the stories appeared month after month in 1895 and early 1896. Each brought Ichiyō new followers and new garlands from the *bundan*, the overheated Tokyo literary scene. She was acclaimed as a new Murasaki, a female Saikaku. When "Child's Play" was first published in its entirety, in April 1896, on the heels of year-long serialization in *Bungakkai*, it elicited encomiums from some of the biggest names in the bundan. Mori Ōgai pronounced Ichiyō "a true poet" who could teach the literal-minded new naturalists a thing or two about the art of writing realistic fiction: "What is extraordinary about 'Child's Play' is that the characters are not those beastlike creatures one so often encounters in Ibsen or Zola, whose techniques the so-called naturalists have tried imitating to the utmost. They are real, human individuals that we laugh and cry with ... [and] I do not hesitate to confer on Ichiyō the title of a true poet."[18] Kōda Rohan would have the dazzling style of "Child's Play" distilled into a magic potion, "that it might fortify the flagging talents of our critics and novelists who think writing great literature means applying the knife to a story's characters and gouging out their insides."[19]

To the gate at the end of the alley came all manner of admirers. Some brought gifts, some left fan letters. They asked for her autograph, for a scrap of calligraphy. Others simply stole what they wanted. One intrepid follower made off with the Higuchi nameplate, a souvenir in Ichiyō's own hand.

Original manuscripts seemed to disappear. New students sought her out to teach them poetry, to hear her lecture on *The Tale of Genji*. A merchant prince offered her as much money as she wanted every month. Another, more humble, man proposed that the two of them write a textbook together—a suggestion based, presumably, on the interest in children that "Child's Play" had shown—and then he broke down and made a proposal of another sort, confessing that he was hopelessly in love with her. A pilgrim came all the way from Ōsaka on behalf of the local Higuchi Ichiyō Fan Club, hand-carrying an invitation to address the faithful. Small wonder that magazines she appeared in now became collectors' items. *Bungei Kurabu* (The Literature Club) printed thirty thousand copies of its special issue on women writers and had to go to press a second time to meet the unprecedented demand.

Literary sophisticates within the bundan were as enthusiastic as the general public. She was asked to review the stories of Mori Ōgai. Publishers offered her exclusive contracts, generous advances. She received, and declined, invitations to all the right parties in the literary world. The list of writers who made their way to the house of this curious young authoress—as fresh as she was unschooled in the latest European currents or the new movements in Japan that were hurtling the novel toward modernity—the roster, which included the occasional condescending male, reads like a *Who's Who* of Meiji belles-lettres: Murakami Namiroku, Togawa Zanka, Baba Kochō, Hirata Tokuboku, Ōhashi Otowa, Togawa Shūkotsu, Ueda Bin, Kawakami Bizan, Saitō Ryokuu, Kunikida Doppo, Hoshino Tenchi, Kōda Rohan, Izumi Kyōka, Shimazaki Tōson.

The new friends, the loopy admirers, the good talk, the slight easing of her penury made much of 1895 and early 1896 a period of frenetic gaiety. Steadfast Nishimura Sennosuke urged the Higuchis not to worry so much about their finances, as he would tide them over any tight month, and it appears that sometimes Ichiyō actually took his advice. She went out and had a good time. In the morning they didn't always know where their next meal was coming from, but somehow the money turned up—a few yen from Mrs. Nakajima, another subsidy from Nishimura—and by evening the two sisters were off to hear Kuniko's favorite storyteller at the music hall. Tears one minute, laughter the next: life was unreal in its vagaries. A hint of courtly leisure returns to the journal. There are concerts attended at the Y.M.C.A. in Kanda, where Ichiyō heard her first European melodies, and sunny imperial pageants celebrating Japan's recent victory over China:

1 June [1895]. Went to Koishikawa for lessons. A big hubbub: everyone talked about the imperial procession the day before yesterday—who went, what they saw, what they thought of everything. Indeed, I realized the only ones who had missed the festivities were Mrs. Nakajima, Miss

Tanaka, and I. The arch of triumph was to be dismantled today, some-one said. It seemed a shame. An event like this happens once in a thousand years, and we weren't even going to get to see the great gate. Perhaps we could hurry over after the lessons, we decided, arranging for rickshaws to fetch us.

The students left at four o'clock, and the three of us, Mrs. Nakajima in the lead and Miss Tanaka and I in a rickshaw behind her, hastened to the palace. As we came through Wadakura Gate and up to the gate at Sakashita, we saw guards lining the street and we were ordered to stop. The Emperor was returning home from Aoyama. We could see the procession, we were told, if we left our rickshaws and stood along the way. We did so at once, delighted with our unexpected treat.

I didn't see any outriders yet and, thinking it would be a while before they appeared, I surveyed the other spectators. It seemed that everyone had come for the same reason we had: for a glimpse of the triumphal arch. There were old gentlemen whose wives had brought them from the country and young students with elderly mothers in tow. Four or five rickshaws were ranged at the side of the road, and nearby stood people in beautiful clothes. They had all alighted from their vehicles to pay homage to the Emperor's cortege.

The handsome, empty rickshaws bespoke a world of taste and re-finement. It brought to mind the Kamo Festival, when the imperial messengers ride in procession, ancient ox-carts clog the streets, and the cuffs on the sleeves of maidenly sightseers are cut to classic fashion. One tends to admire the things of the past, but the scene that moment was a spectacle I wished I could have captured on a picture scroll: gold crests on black-lacquered rickshaws, the spines of the folding hoods in hues of cinnabar and shrimp, velvet lap blankets of russet and black trim, rickshawmen in their immaculate white liveries resting on the lawn beneath the baby pines, and ebullient townsmen, in keeping with the solemnity of the setting, speaking in soft tones for once as they put their bundles down and milled about waiting for His Majesty.

"What would people think," I wondered to Miss Tanaka, "if they could see this scene a hundred years from now? 'How quaint and elegant the world of Meiji must have been!' Don't you suppose that's what they would say?"

"Exactly. Now, if only we had a few beauties from court competing in their carriages," she chuckled, "so the crowd weren't quite so plebeian.[20] If this were a scene in *Genji*, I'm afraid everyone here would be wearing those clumsy 'pot-clothes.'"[21]

"Yes," I agreed, laughing. "And the parasols would have to do for the sunshades on the ox-carts."

Just then the first of the outriders came into view. The crowd fell silent
as the imperial entourage approached. There were only two carriages in
the procession, however, and fewer escorts than one might have expected. Quietly, without a fuss, they passed beneath Sakashita Gate, the
Emperor's carriage remaining so far from the roadside that I was unable
to get a good look. Then, as the imperial guard disbanded, everyone
summoned his rickshaw.

We soon made our way to the arch of triumph, but it was already
being torn down. Here and there lay mounds of cedar boughs. How
could they dismantle the enormous thing so quickly? The side of the arch
facing Sakurada Gate was already shorn of its greens and the tall frame
stood exposed as we looked up at it. We climbed down from our
rickshaws and walked beneath the archway, the heels of our clogs sinking into the sand. A wind came up and blew forlornly through the great
structure, where the inside was still dressed in branches of cedar and
oak, as if in green brocade. At the front and back of the arch tiny red and
white carnations had been inserted to spell out "The merchants of Tokyo
hail His Imperial Highness," a lovely gesture. But many of the flowers
had wilted in the sun, and the effect was now rather wistful.

What kitchen fires would these discarded wreaths soon kindle? Mrs.
Nakajima and Miss Tanaka each broke off a sprig or two of cedar and a
spray of flowers by which to remember the auspicious afternoon. By
now the sun was sinking, and we acknowledged, reluctantly, that we
must go. This time we went by way of Kasumigaseki, up behind the
Foreign Office. As we rode toward Kudan, I looked out at the moat and
its green waters, at the silhouette of the overhanging pines, at the dusky
grass on the side of the embankment. At such moments I feel myself
transported by how beautiful the city is.

Before long we neared Ushigafuchi, and there the three of us parted
for the night.[22]

Returning home, Ichiyō would often find one of her new literary friends
waiting. The *Bungakkai* writers brought their classmates at the university to
meet the author of "Child's Play" and "Troubled Waters." They came to talk
of art and literature and love, and to forget about qualifying exams. They
presented her with flowers and writing brushes, and they sent out for sushi,
which they munched on till all hours as they debated the character of the
hero in *The Tale of Genji*. Ichiyō argued that she had her difficulties in
sympathizing with a man like Genji, who chased women night and day and
then complained that he never had any time to himself. It was not as if he
were busy studying, she pointed out, or translating, or looking something up
in foreign books. "Yes, but. . . ." The ruddy young romantics leapt to defend

love, tried to make a dent in her cynic's carapace. They delighted in Ichiyō's irony without realizing just how naughty it could be—compelling them to explain to her how a person falls in love, indeed.

But the more they tried to elucidate the mysteries of love's grip, the more several of them found themselves caught in it. Many a member of Ichiyō's burgeoning salon came away with a schoolboy's crush on his formidable hostess. She was one of them: young, playful, tenaciously literary. But she was also different: they were still struggling, she had succeeded; they could rail and theorize about injustice all they wanted to, but she had experienced it firsthand. One might say that as a result she was more "interesting." Her strong sense of self, her calling, her wit, her femininity captivated these literary youths.

Baba Kochō (1869–1940) and Hirata Tokuboku (1873–1943) were particularly ardent admirers. The one had been a classmate of Shimazaki Tōson's at Meiji Gakuin; the other, a convert to Christianity baptized alongside Hoshino Tenchi, the editor-in-chief of *Bungakkai*. Both were charter members of Tōson's and Kitamura Tōkoku's romantic circle.

Baba was a rosy-cheeked, aristocratic-looking young man: sensitive, excitable, and devoted to literature. He was so fond of Ichiyō that he called at Maruyama-Fukuyama several times a week, where he poured out all his troubles—would he get a teaching post? should he quit *Bungakkai?*—and announced proprietarily that the Higuchis' house had become his home away from home: "I'm like Ichiyō's spoiled son."[23]

Hirata was equally exuberant. The scholarly scion of an old merchant family in Nihonbashi, he would drop by in his cups after a high school reunion or a night on the town, and he and Baba and Ichiyō would sit in the lamplight sipping tea, laughing, arguing, gossiping about the bundan. He never wanted to go home. "You should be a little more polite," Baba told him. "But it's such a lovely night!" he protested. "Just a while longer."[24]

The moon always seemed bright on these evenings, and the conversation always brilliant. They brought young Ueda Bin, Kawakami Bizan, and others with them, and, like all members of a talented, witty coterie, Ichiyō wondered to herself if such a splendid group would ever form again. She only hoped it would last. She didn't think that anything could be more enjoyable. Modest to the end, she felt inferior to her male friends—without formal education, without wealth.

The men knew better. Both Baba and Hirata went on to careers as accomplished translators of European literature—Baba translating *War and Peace* and *The Scarlet Letter*, Hirata rendering *David Copperfield* and *Vanity Fair*. But their stabs at writing fiction and verse for *Bungakkai* were adolescent efforts in comparison to Ichiyō's. They must have known even then that they were not original writers, an admission that could only have fueled their high esteem for Ichiyō. They would have given their eyeteeth to write a work like

"Child's Play," and when the Mori Ōgai review came out, Hirata and another *Bungakkai* colleague, Togawa Shūkotsu, said as much:

The evening of 2 May [1896] Tokuboku and Shūkotsu came over.
"You ought to treat us to something special tonight," they said, and looked at each other, smiling. "And we won't accept anything ordinary."
"What's going on?" I asked.
Shūkotsu took a magazine out of the folds of his kimono and looked at Hirata. "Shall I read it to her?"
It was the new *Mezamashigusa* [The Eye-Opener], number four. I had seen an advertisement for it in the paper the day before yesterday. Apparently the new issue had a long review of "Child's Play," which came out last month in *Bungei Kurabu*. I wasn't about to jump up and down and ask them what it said. I just smiled.
"Well—aren't you going to celebrate? You should *see* this! Ueda Bin brought it to class today and couldn't wait to show us. 'Read this!' he said—he had it folded open to the very spot—and we grabbed it away from him and he pointed to where to start, and it goes on and on about you! It's by Ōgai and Rohan! 'A miraculous achievement'—that's what they call 'Child's Play'! 'The last word in fiction'! We were so excited, we read it out loud to everyone in the lecture hall. The minute class was over we ran to the newsstand. Then we ran to Hirata's room and pored over it again, repeating all the good parts. Poor Hirata started to cry, he felt so happy for you." Shūkotsu's excited words came flooding out, and his face overflowed with joy. "We couldn't wait to show you. Don't you know how envious we are? Come on, read it! Or shall I? Do you want Hirata to?"
"Ōgai—the god of the literary world—calls you a true poet. He doesn't hesitate," Hirata said. "And that's not all. It goes on to say that the rest of us should imbibe your words as if they were a magic potion. Why, as men of letters, Shūkotsu and I'd be happy to die if someone would only say such things about our work!"
"How happy you must be!"
"How we envy you!"
When they left a little while later, the two were still in a state of delirium.[25]

Literary schoolboys—*bungaku seinen*—were not the only members of Ichiyō's salon. The professionals also attended. Saitō Ryokuu (1867–1904), who with Ōgai and Rohan had penned the column in *Mezamashigusa* that had everyone excited, now became a regular, and a favorite of Ichiyō's. Ryokuu, a sickly young curmudgeon with a swift mind and an acerbic sense of humor—it was he who described Ichiyō's style as being "like a sneer after crying"—had one foot in the Ōgai camp and one in gesaku. Like Nakarai

Tōsui, he had received his start as a lowly newspaper serialist; but, unlike
Tōsui, he had risen above his roundly panned romances to the heights of
influential criticism. In the spring of 1896 he came often to the Higuchi
house, having taken it upon himself to steer "Miss One-Leaf" through the
uncharted, sometimes treacherous, shoals of the literary scene. He shared
Ichiyō's interest in Edo and the shitamachi. He knew hardship, and so he
admired her pertinacity. He saw in the young woman a person with whom
he could indulge in caustic banter, a fellow traveler through regions of irony
and the austere. Most of all, he appreciated the bundan's newest find for her
intelligence and her preternatural literary gifts.

He dashed off epistles in his knotted hand, evaluating Ichiyō's latest output. He warned her not to let her press clippings go to her head, for what
were the people who produced these puffs but lettered thugs? While he was
at it, she would do well to avoid the hangers-on: all those literary cockroaches
who came to see her; if she didn't send them away, they would end up
poisoning her work. He had a morbid fear of gossip—one would call it
pathological if the Tokyo publishing world had been any less ingrown—and
insisted that his letters be returned to him as soon as she had read them.

Ichiyō found Ryokuu a thoroughly odd and fascinating character: gaunt,
intense, intimidating. His mouth was friendly-looking, but he had a slightly
twisted face and a glint in his eyes as if he were always laughing up his sleeve.
He was twenty-eight, older than the *Bungakkai* crowd, more professional—
and more jaundiced. He lacked their merriment, but they lacked his mettle.
Ichiyō had to admit that he was far superior to Hirata Tokuboku or
Kawakami Bizan, who was always asking for her photograph and flattering
her that she should write her memoirs. She appreciated backbone when she
saw it, and she must also have appreciated eccentricity: Saitō Ryokuu didn't
like to be seen. If he heard the voices of other visitors he never came farther
than her front gate.

Ichiyō appreciated Ryokuu as one of the few critics who didn't treat her like
a "woman writer." He didn't handle her with kid gloves; he let her know
when her writing was disorderly; he said in print that she had as much talent
as any man, and that it was therefore pointless to treat her gingerly or
pigeonhole her as a lady author. Ichiyō hated being regarded as a curiosity.
She immediately sensed a certain condescension in some of the people who
came to see her. It infuriated her when a reviewer repeated received opinion:
"Ichiyō is the foremost woman writer," "Ichiyō is better than many men."
Why make the distinction? What difference was there, really, between
women and men? We are all born with the same hearts, she declared in her
diary, we all want the same things. Had she read her English literature, she
might have felt like Samuel Johnson's woman preacher: the critics were
treating her like a dog that could walk on its hind legs—who asks if the feat is
well done?

Ichiyō was by no means ashamed of her femininity. But, if the truth be told, she found her women friends rather shallow. She had no woman to whom she could confide her deepest secrets, or turn for consolation, or unveil any of her larger concerns. If only she had such a friend! One needed a woman friend, but most of the young ladies she knew kept their distance now. The uproar in the bundan had managed to antagonize everyone. The poetry-girls at the Haginoya were jealous of her; even Mrs. Nakajima seemed out of sorts. When she did meet an old acquaintance, the talk was never allowed to go beyond superficialities. Bourgeois gentlewomen didn't like to hear about the hard luck of prostitutes or the plight of the poor. For the moment it was easier to talk about the important things with men.

And with men there was always shop talk. How had she conceived of her last story? Who were the models for the children in "Child's Play"? Would she care to produce some vignettes for a manual on the art of letter-writing? What would she think of joining Mori Ōgai, Kōda Rohan, and Saitō Ryokuu in their monthly column for *Mezamashigusa*? Ōgai sent his younger brother Tokujirō to inquire. Ichiyō was hesitant. Ryokuu advised her not to join the magazine. But Tokujirō, in turn, advised her not to trust Ryokuu. Ichiyō was all the more confused. Ryokuu finally warned her that the Ōgai circle would collapse and the magazine would fold; she was better off above the fray. He himself was fed up with the fools of the bundan. He was tempted to throw it all over and become a bath-boy in the Yoshiwara, get a job at the post office, anything. The vanities, the intrigues, the endless maneuverings—it was all too oppressive.

Mori Ōgai sent his brother back again. They were waiting for a definite answer. It was time to start work on the next issue. He and Rohan gave her a choice of two dates for their first meeting. "Either one is all right," Ichiyō said noncommittally. But after Tokujirō left, she sent off a letter: she could not join them after all, she was too timid for such august company.

Now Kōda Rohan came to persuade her. He tried a slightly different tack:

In the midst of a great gale this afternoon, around two o'clock, Mori Tokujirō came unexpectedly, bringing Kōda Rohan. It was the first time I had met Mr. Kōda. As he introduced himself, I quickly scrutinized his appearance. He has a clear, pale complexion, a ruddy neck. He is short and quite on the plump side. His low voice has a weightiness to it; he speaks quietly, and deliberately. He wanted to know if I wouldn't write something for *Mezamashigusa*. It didn't have to be a story, necessarily.

We talked about different things: writing, the future, the public's love of gossip—a variety of trifles. Mr. Kōda said it's not easy being young; I'll be better off when I put on a few years. Then again, he chuckled, I probably didn't look forward to getting older, did I?

For a long time now, he said, he had wanted to find people to collaborate on a novel with him. Wouldn't I like to participate? "I thought if you were interested, today we could decide on your part. The plan is to get the general plot down; the details will be left up to the individual writers. You'll have complete freedom. That way we'll preserve the different styles and moods of each author. I think it should be interesting! We'll avoid a patchwork effect by telling the story in the form of letters—so the narrative voice doesn't seem to keep fluctuating. Anything a character couldn't express in a letter we can do as a diary. First of all, then, we have to decide on whom we want for the writers. Could we borrow your brush and ink for a minute?"

I nodded, and Mori Tokujirō took the writing things from the desk. "I certainly think Miss Higuchi should do the part of someone like Oriki in 'Troubled Waters.'"

At this point Kōda Rohan retreated: "Remember, of course, Miss Higuchi hasn't written anything long before—"

"What about an adaptation of *The Love Suicides at Amijima?* She could write the part of Koharu."[26] Clearly Mr. Mori wanted something dramatic.

"Hold on. We have to settle on what kind of character Miss Higuchi wants to write about before we can start getting specific. We need some sort of plot outline. Of course we would like you to do a woman, Miss Higuchi. Do you have any preferences? Middle class? Upper class? A woman of samurai blood? A shopwoman? The wife of an official?"

"I suppose they'd all be difficult," I said. "I wouldn't want to be choosy, but I don't know anything about horse-drawn carriages and that world. I'd better do someone of samurai birth—of middle rank, say."

"In that case, the daughter of a samurai," Mr. Mori said. "That's one thing decided." He bit on the end of the writing brush and spoke excitedly: "Here's what I think. We don't want a bashful heroine; it's never interesting. We should make her the kind of woman who goes to extremes—someone with a little of the wild animal, who gets hold of a man and won't let go. Someone large and florid."

"And that's Miss Higuchi?" Rohan grimaced.

"No. I'm thinking of the kind of woman Kikugorō would play.[27] Let's give it to Saitō Ryokuu. Wait a minute! I've got an idea for a story: about a civil servant, let's say, who's scholarly and doesn't know too much about the world—we can have my brother Ōgai do that part—and Miss Higuchi can be his younger sister. His superiors are jealous of him and block his promotion. He throws himself into his studies to make up for his disappointment. His sister is devoted to him and despairs over her brother's misfortune. (This could be a splendid part, Miss Higuchi!) Now, she has a boyfriend—perfect for you, Kōda-san—who likes to drink, a dissolute playboy type. But he's also involved with a temptress—Saitō Ryokuu—who tries to blackmail him. Well?" he said, intent on fanning our enthusiasm. "Don't you think that would make a terrific story?"

"I'm the boyfriend?" Rohan asked, rubbing his head and smiling. "I don't know if I'm suited to that part. I'd be better doing some impatient firebrand."

"Actually, you'll each have to take more than one role, or we won't have much of a drama. Miss Higuchi, how would you like to do an old lady? The mother, say, who meddles in her children's affairs?"

"No," Rohan said, "that's definitely a part for Ryokuu."

"Maybe—in any case, you and Miss Higuchi should have the leads, if we want our little play to get off the ground.[28] You've got to be the boyfriend. And, you know, we need a child in the story—that's the other part you should take. How about her younger brother? To make things interesting?"

"I don't know. Something's missing. We need a third party, a friend of one of the characters. Let's say it were a friend of the older brother . . . make him a narrow-minded official. In which case, Ōgai should do it."

"He certainly knows those people," Mr. Mori said. "One more thing: to add some color, how about a pair of illicit lovers? Perhaps I could do them. I'll tell you another idea I had, too: when I read 'Child's Play,' it occurred to me that we might expand it. Kōda-san, you could take the part of Nobu, the priest's boy, and my brother could be Shōta. Ryokuu would make a good Chōkichi. I'd do the part of bumbling Sangorō, and Miss Higuchi could be Midori of the Daikokuya. We'd have an all-star cast: Ōgai, a sort of Ichikawa Danjūrō; Ryokuu, a Kikugorō; Rohan, a Sawamura Shūjūrō; and Miss Higuchi, another Aratakoma—bringing the house down![29] In fact, we ought to write it as a play. Let's forget about a novel. The stage would be so much more interesting!"

I had listened with great amusement to Mr. Mori's powers of persuasion. Now, after a pause, Rohan began to speak in his leisurely way: "As far as things like setting go, you know that we must write about what we're familiar with. Ōgai could write about Europe, for instance, I could write about the countryside, and we'd have a story that was very realistic. Whatever we do, it's going to have to be a project that everyone finds satisfying. If we just do something for a lark, we'll get bored and throw our brushes down in the middle of the effort. None of us would feel any stake in it."

Then he turned to me: "I suppose you may think, Miss Higuchi, that we've been pestering you a lot lately, trying to force you to write something for *Mezamashigusa*. But that really hasn't been our intention at all. As fellow writers, we simply thought you might enjoy collaborating.

We thought it would be fun to share literary pleasures, learn from each other, and all become better writers in the process. Like Edo artisans. You've heard about Yokotani Shūmin and Ryōkan, who worked together happily on each sword they were commissioned to engrave.[30] Of course everyone has his own talent: when two people paint one picture the styles may not always mesh. But is that something to laugh at? He who says he has nothing to learn from working with others is blocking his own advance. [A barb aimed at refractory Saitō Ryokuu.] If we all join forces, think what we could show the world! We could disabuse the public of its misconceptions about the bundan; we could show them what a society of writers *is!* Since when does a true writer build bulwarks to protect his feelings? An association like this will only liberate us!"

He went on to say that he understood my reservations and to explain why I should get over them, but I told him I couldn't help feeling that my work was still immature, and I didn't see how I could join the ranks of such distinguished writers yet.

"Don't feel that way!" he said. "Do you think Ōgai and I have completed our education? We're still novices, the same as you. Why not learn together? Whether we succeed or not remains to be seen, but we can at least try. Why be timid when you're young and have everything before you? Over a lifetime, if you produced a hundred books, two hundred books, and they were all flawed, you'd still have time to revise the best of them. All you have to do is leave one good work behind you. Don't be so diffident.

"There's one thing I must ask you, though, and that's that we keep quiet about the project until it's completed. You know how rumors fly. When the novel's finished we can publish it in a special issue of *Mezamashigusa*, or give it to a book publisher, depending. Or we don't have to release it at all, if we decide we don't want to. It's up to us. The important thing is to relax and have fun doing it. Well, I've talked too long," he said, standing. "I'll come again when we have a definite story."

Altogether, we had talked for more than three hours. They were on their way to Ōgai's house now, they said, but I doubt they could have gone more than a hundred feet before it started to rain cats and dogs.[31]

Ichiyō's old friends, in the end, may have counted for more than the new. Nakarai Tōsui was still a touchstone. She had never actually severed their connection, although the scandal of 1892 made her visits more furtive and desultory, and the accretion of the years and new, unshared experiences had reduced the electric charge that the rendezvous had once had for an impressionable young virgin. Work, fame, and trouble had carried Ichiyō along.

Everything had changed—and then it seemed as if nothing had changed. She had never quite forgotten her first love and mentor.

This afternoon I went to Misakichō to see Mr. Nakarai. They told me I could find him at his parents' house in Iidamachi, number twenty-one in the fourth block, which, as it turns out, is only one street over from Tanaka Minoko's. The Nakarai garden has weeping willow trees and a fence with a coat of black paint. The house is far from sumptuous, but it's a nice, large place.

I saw Kōko [Tōsui's sister] for the first time in five years, and I told her how sorry I was about the death of her husband.[32] I felt so sad for her that I started to cry.

The child of the Tsuruta woman is living with the Nakarais. Her name is Chiyo—she's four years old already. She made herself quite at home with me, wouldn't leave my side: it was as if she thought I was her mother, and my heart went out to the poor thing.

"Chiyo, you haven't forgotten me?"

"No!" she insisted, shaking her bushy head. "I haven't forgotten you."

She followed me when I went upstairs and clung to my hand to negotiate the steps. She's so cute. She wanted to carry the tea things by herself and refused any cautionings or offers of assistance. "*I* want to serve the guest," she said, working assiduously.

Kōko's baby woke up while we were having tea and she brought him in to show me. He is only ten months old, and he's just like a plump little doll: tiny eyes, tiny nose, adorable. Kōko said he doesn't cry very much, fortunately. She let me hold him; then I put him down and dangled a toy drum and a papier-mâché dog in front of him and he came crawling right back into my lap again, not the least bit afraid of me. Kōko was surprised. He's a good baby, she said, but he's usually peevish with strangers, he won't let anyone touch him. The other day, apparently, he made a terrible fuss when Nonomiya and her friend, the Ōkubo girl, tried to cradle him—so Kōko found it very odd today the way he took to me.

Master Nakarai smiled and said the baby and I must have some bond between us. He ordered sushi and brought out fruit and entertained me royally. It was the first time I had seen him really laugh in four years, and I felt very happy, as if the gloomy clouds in my heart had all lifted. But where had his looks gone? When I first met him, he had skin like snow. Now a grayness had settled over his features. Only that distinguished nose of his was still the same. His broad shoulders, his sturdy legs—everything about him seemed diminished. At a glance, one might think that Mr. Nakarai was forty. When he smiled as he reminisced, though, something of his youth came back. Now truly he seemed like an older brother to me, or an uncle.

"How old are you now, Natsuko?" he asked. "Twenty-three? You know, you don't look any different from when you first came to see me five years ago."

He spoke without reticence. It was like old times. He still had no idea what agonies I had suffered because of him, what tears I had swallowed. To him, we were just ordinary friends, I suppose.

Thank goodness I have rid myself of my desires. I don't have the slightest wish any more to share my life with him, not even for a moment. But I don't hold a grudge against him, either. Ordinary friends— yes, that's fine with me. If we can just be good friends, that's enough. As I looked at him, feeling the way I do now, it was as if I had finally understood something: the Buddha and the Devil are two sides of the same thing. I felt as if I were in the presence of the true Holy One. I felt bliss of a sort I cannot express.

Near dusk I said good-by to him.

"You'll come again soon, won't you? And I'll visit you—on a day when there's no thunder.[33] We could go to the vaudeville sometime."

I went downstairs to say good-night to the family.

"Higuchi-san," called out Mr. Nakarai's father, "you're not leaving, are you? I wanted to visit with you. Come again now, you hear? I want a chance to visit with you too!"

It was all just the way it used to be, and I wished for a moment I could go back again in time. As I closed the door behind me, the happy afternoon already seemed a dream.

When I got home, I hurried over to the public bath. On the way, it started to rain, and it's been raining hard all night.[34]

Then one Saturday evening in midsummer Tōsui rushed up to the Higuchis' front gate. He had heard talk about Ichiyō's new affiliations. "Be careful," he warned her. "If I were you, I wouldn't trust Saitō Ryokuu. He's been snooping around for information about us, you know. He's a cunning one. Don't trust him."[35] Tōsui hurried off as urgently as he had come, and Saitō Ryokuu appeared. *He* had her best interests at heart. At all costs, she must avoid getting entangled with Rohan and Ōgai. Was it true she had agreed to write a novel with them? She told him she hadn't decided. Well, remember one thing, he warned her: Rohan and Ōgai did not really care about her work; they simply wanted to claim her on their side. The three of them had started *Mezamashigusa* together, but they no longer saw eye to eye. The magazine could not last much longer.

In fact, the literary world was on the brink of great change. Upheavals were coming, many new developments. It was all confidential: Rohan would

leave *Mezamashigusa* and become editor of *Shin Shōsetsu* (The New Novel),
which the firm Shun'yōdō was reviving to compete with its rival, Hakubunkan, which published *Taiyō* (The Sun) and *Bungei Kurabu*, which were the
magazines where Ichiyō's work appeared. And so it went. Ryokuu would also
leave *Mezamashigusa* and start his own magazine. Ōgai would have to
recruit an entirely new crop of writers. The candidates were all lackluster.
Did she want to cast her lot with them? The magazine was beyond salvaging.
Then, too, Friend of the Inkstone Ozaki Kōyō would almost certainly launch a
new journal. With so many possibilities in the offing, why should she tie her
hands?

Why, indeed, Ichiyō must have wondered. Her headaches kept bothering
her, and she had not been feeling well since April. As the literary world
played its game of survival-of-the-fittest, no one noticed that Ichiyō, underfed
and long unfit, was not surviving. By summer she had stopped writing. She
ended one story summarily and left another unfinished. Coughing and
feverish, she took to her bed. It is testimony to the tangled egos and youthful
ambitions of the bundan that no one seems to have recognized the obvious:
the young woman they all wanted to enlist was dying of consumption.

In early August Kuniko wrapped her sister in a padded winter jacket and a
blanket and took her to a clinic in Ochanomizu. The doctors told her it was
hopeless. Mori Ōgai heard about Ichiyō's condition from Saitō Ryokuu and
dispatched one of his colleagues, Dr. Aoyama Tanemitsu, but he could only
confirm the verdict: acute pulmonary tuberculosis, beyond remedy. On
19 August the newspaper *Yomiuri* reported Ichiyō's condition to the public.
Her best friend from the Haginoya, Itō Natsuko, rushed back from the family's
summer place in Kamakura to find Ichiyō sinking fast. Her eyes were milky,
her face had begun to take on the specter of a skull. Ichiyō insisted on bathing
and donning a proper kimono before she would see her old poetry friend, but
that was the extent of the energy that she could muster. Her work in this
world was accomplished. The stories had all been published, she had laid her
diary aside, and when she took up her brush it was only to scribble a message
of despair: "Even when you're sick, the summer is so hot!" "I have never
known anything as terrible as this."[36]

She would have had the disease for years by now, unaware of the first faint
symptoms—a languor, a vague feeling of malaise, nothing in her book that
perseverance couldn't overcome. Sentarō had died of consumption in 1887,
not quite ten years before, and her father, who died in 1889, was most likely a
consumptive as well. So the family must have known both a hereditary
susceptibility to the disease and a long, ample exposure to infection. Hers was
in fact a classic case, once it was far enough advanced to be diagnosed.
Everything in life—except Ichiyō's final success—had conspired to make sure
that once she had inhaled the tubercle bacilli, *they* would prevail: the long
hours of hard work, the years of anxiety over money, the most meager of

diets. The doctors did not even rule out the role of melancholy. Modern medicine had detected a link between consumptives and nostalgia. Case after case told of the tubercular fates of those who failed to forget unhappy love affairs, to surmount their disappointments. In more ways than one the very disease seemed somehow modern. It ravaged those who were self-centered enough to give themselves to their emotions—the new romantics. It was also the disease of "civilization" and "enlightenment." As in Europe, when industrialization came to Japan the incidence of tuberculosis tripled.[37] To the end Ichiyō was a product of her advancing times.

In September she rallied briefly. On a sunny, Indian-summer sort of afternoon, her *Bungakkai* friends came to see her. They sat on the veranda, by the pond and the swaying leaves of the banana tree, and she consoled them: "Don't worry. I'll be a butterfly in the next life, and I'll come back and tickle you on the sleeve."[38]

But it was only a temporary remission. In October the hectic fever, the incessant cough, the night sweats returned. She grew daily more emaciated, her eyes sank deeper, her breathing became increasingly labored as her body turned slowly to phlegm. Baba Kochō, who had called himself "Ichiyō's spoiled son" and who was the most devoted of her *Bungakkai* following, hurried home from his new teaching post near Lake Biwa when he heard that the end was now near. Ichiyō was asleep, but Kuniko asked him to go in and see her. He sat down beside her pillow and watched his friend—her hair disheveled, her cheeks flushed a vivid crimson—and perhaps it is not too much to imagine him recalling all the things that she had meant to their generation, and would mean to those to come.

This frail young woman had cut a wide swath though Meiji letters. Her grasp of high Heian, her love of low Edo were almost legendary, but she was still sui generis. In her bold and idiosyncratic style, she had rediscovered a way to be serious in fiction, something nearly two hundred years'-worth of writers had forgotten. She returned the novel to the province of the heart— not the wit or the intellect, though she had both, but those gray, elusive intermittences of feeling that only reveal themselves when a writer approaches them by way of indirect sally. In plumbing the depths of the beauty and sadness of life, her themes were as old as those of the ancient poets; yet her work was as fresh as anything the innovative Europeans were exporting. In speaking to her times, Ichiyō spoke for all times. The realism of her best stories was so grounded in her sense of place—Tokyo at the turn of the century—that it was hard to imagine "Child's Play" without the Yoshiwara or "Separate Ways" without the back street. But she distilled from her localities something that was universal, that captured a generation at the very moment of its rueful disillusionment: the perishability of friendship, the victimization of women, the profound disequilibrium between individual and society, the poetry and melancholy of memory, the road not taken.

In subject, setting, and theme Ichiyō had limited herself, but there were no shackles on the emotional range or literary effect of her stories. It was revolutionary of Ichiyō to see dignity and pathos in the unhappiness of children, and to make of this apparent trivia a metaphor for the drama, so new to Japan, of the sudden, confused attaining of selfhood. Baba and the other *Bungakkai* writers, and then Ōgai and the general public, found in Ichiyō's treatment of these adolescent rites of passage a metaphor for modern Japan's own precarious, deracinating journey. Some would call Ichiyō sentimental, perhaps. But after the stern and mannered years of Edo—when a thing was either serious or playful—the blending of humanity and splendor in Ichiyō's prose seemed both. As for the heart-rending mood of reminiscence—how it fit their own feeling of loss, of disappointment! If there was a risk that so much sensibility might end up disembodied and attenuated, Ichiyō avoided it. She endowed her characters with truly human lineaments, creating figures as vivid and identifiable as Midori, Nobu, Sangorō, Kichizō. The mature artist's sense of balance, her moral and ironic severity tempered sentiment. In the 1890s the entire effect was a new form of fictional honesty. Ichiyō spoke to her fellow youth with such beauty and intensity that Baba and company had no trouble responding to her message: cut loose from family and friends and the signposts of the past—in the "real" world of ambition and moral shoddiness, where modern man somehow loses touch with the deepest and truest parts of himself—we are all, in one way or another, foundlings.

Ichiyō awoke before too long and she and Baba chatted for a while. Despite her deteriorating appearance, she had her usual ladylike bearing, and a quiet resignation. Baba told her he would see her again. She died three weeks later, on 23 November 1896, twenty-four years old.

In after years, Kuniko maintained that her sister had departed, in the chilly hour of the dawn, with a full panoply of friends to salute her. As if the curtain were going down on a stage play, all the actors have assembled: Baba Kochō, Nakarai Tōsui, and so forth; only Nakajima Utako is missing, but she was long out of favor. In her distress poor Kuniko had picked up her sister's flair for fiction. Scholars aver that Ichiyō died alone, while Kuniko and Taki were still sleeping.[39] Like so much else in her life, the hour of death became, even after the fact, another uncertainty, fickle and subject to change: in the papers it was reported variously as 5:00, 7:00, 10:00, 11:00 A.M.

The family poverty remained the one immutable. In order to keep the funeral as simple and inexpensive as possible, the Higuchis declined Mori Ōgai's kind offer to accompany the coffin on horseback. From the Haginoya only Itō Natsuko and Tanaka Minoko attended. All told, there were ten who gathered in the rain at Maruyama-Fukuyama early on the morning of the twenty-fifth. It struck Itō Natsuko as a very lonely end: incense was offered, a slapdash priest read from the sutras, and the procession started out on foot for the cemetery. They went by way of Suidōbashi, to Sarugakuchō and Hitotsubashi, over to Marunouchi and Yūrakuchō, up the main street of the Ginza and toward Tsukiji, into the grounds of the great Buddhist temple, Honganji, where father and brothers lay already buried. Ichiyō's publisher, Hakubunkan, had sent flowers and votive lanterns, and this smattering of color and light offered some sign of warmth in the steady drizzle.

Taki died fourteen months later. And then, finally, luck turned for the Higuchi house. Kuniko married a man who worked hard and took the family surname. The two toiled long hours for Nishimura Sennosuke. As a result of Kuniko's charm and her husband's diligence, Nishimura's little stationery shop prospered as never before. Kuniko and her husband Masaji gathered a large brood around them: eleven children, each rising to a position in the world that Noriyoshi himself would have approved of.

Across town, Nakarai Tōsui, a bachelor-widower through all the years Ichiyō had known him, suddenly remarried. He had moved more and more into the demimonde, writing lyrics for kabuki and the vaudeville, and so he took for his new wife a young musician. She was a beauty, naturally, and it was said she was so adept on the samisen that when she played one of her refrains a man forgot every care he had ever had.

Model of the street in Ryūsenji where Ichiyō lived

Model of Ichiyō's last house, in Maruyama-Fukuyama

Higuchi Ichiyō, circa 1895

The three Higuchi women. From left to right: Kuniko, Taki, Ichiyō

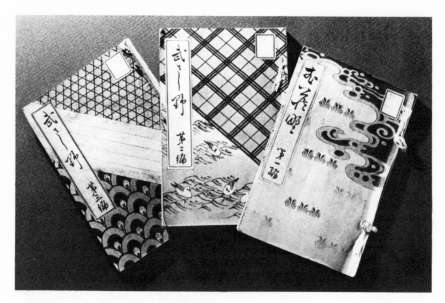

The three issues of Nakarai Tōsui's journal *Musashino*, where Ichiyō's first stories appeared

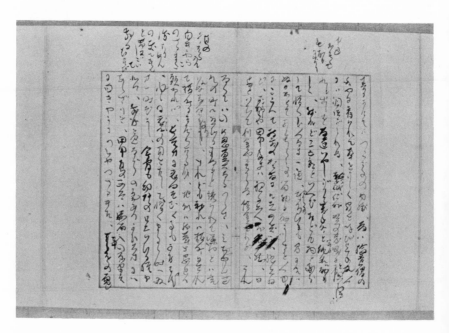

The first draft of "Child's Play"

Ichiyō's grave

One of the many canals in Tokyo during the Meiji period

Shinobazu Pond, mentioned frequently in Ichiyō's diary

April cherry blossoms

The wisteria gardens at Kameido in early May

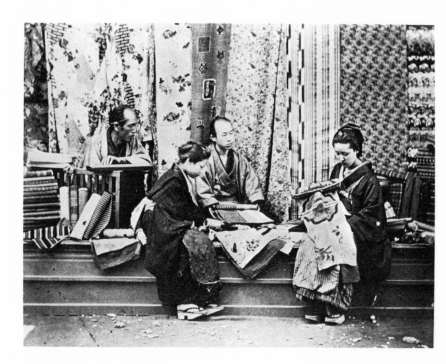

A kimono shop in the 1890s

Brothels in the pleasure quarter

Geisha in the Yoshiwara

Courtesans of the Yoshiwara

Children of the downtown

A Buddhist priest and acolyte, reminiscent of Nobu and his father in "Child's Play"

A rickshawman and young matron, reminiscent of characters in "The Thirteenth Night"

A woman in winter dress, reminiscent of Okyō in "Separate Ways"

A samurai. Ichiyō's father may have looked like this in the early years of the Meiji.

The pleasure quarter

Members of the Haginoya, 1887. First row, from left: third, Tanaka Minoko. Second row, from left: fourth, Miyake Kaho; fifth, Nakajima Utako. Third row, from left: second, Itō Natsuko; third, Ichiyō

Members of the journal *Bungakkai*. First row, from left: Ueda Bin, Hoshino Tenchi, Togawa Shūkotsu, Hoshino Yūkage. Second row, from left: Shimazaki Tōson, Baba Kochō, Hirata Tokuboku

Miyake Kaho

Oriki and Yūki Tomonosuke in "Troubled Waters," as painted by Kaburagi Kiyokata

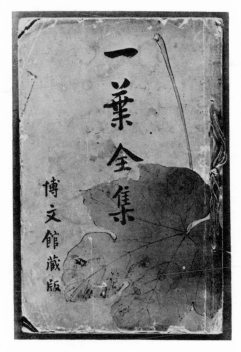

Cover of the first edition of Ichiyō's collected
stories, 1897

Nakarai Tōsui

Mori Ōgai

Kōda Rohan

Saitō Ryokuu

PART TWO
NINE STORIES

Flowers at Dusk
(Yamizakura, 1892)

Only a bamboo fence separated the two houses. They shared the same well, whose waters ran deep and pure, untroubled as the concord between the neighbors. The flowering plum beneath the eaves of one home brought spring to the other. Together they enjoyed the fragrant blossoms.[1]

The Sonoda family had lost the head of its household the year before last. The heir, Ryōnosuke, was twenty-two[2] and a student at the university.

The Nakamura family had only one child now. There had been a son, but he met an early death, and so their daughter they treasured as a priceless jewel. No wind was permitted to disturb the flowered ornaments that graced her hair. The hopes her parents placed in her were apparent from her name, Chiyo. It meant a thousand years, the life span of the crane.[3]

The chinaberry tree sends out its first leaves and already one catches its aroma. She was only two or three when others first began predicting what a future she would have. In her beauty she surpassed the buds unfolding in the rainy hills of early spring. But when would it come, her full flowering? She seemed to hesitate, the way the moon peeks through the branches of the pine.

And then one day she was sixteen[4]—a captivating sight, her hair done in the grown-up fashion and tied with a ribbon patterned in colored arabesques. She stood out like the safflower in the garden. "Have you seen her? The Nakamura girl!" Even strangers would go on and on. (How bothersome to be a beauty!) "She used to do the most amusing things," people said. "When she flew a kite, it would whistle with the northern wind. The telegraph poles were always in her way."

But that was long ago. She was grown up now, she told herself. If Ryōnosuke still wanted to play dolls with her, if he hadn't noticed that she'd changed, well, she wasn't going to fret about it. One minute they would chat with their usual familiarity. Neither had eyes for anyone else. But the next minute things would erupt into a fight.

"You needn't bother coming any more."

"Come here? Don't worry."

A mere two days would pass, and then the apologies would begin.

"I'm sorry, Ryōnosuke. It wasn't very nice of me. I won't be so selfish any more. Please forgive me."

Spring ice always thaws.[5] After all, he realized, she was still a little girl, an innocent. "No, it was my fault," Ryōnosuke protested. He had no sisters and could hardly imagine what they were like. Could a sister be as lovable as Chiyo?

She smiled and tugged his sleeve. "I had a wonderful dream last night. You had graduated and had gotten a position. You were wearing a top hat, Ryōnosuke, and riding in a *carriage!* Then you went into some fancy, European-style building."

"Are you sure it wasn't the other way around?" he chuckled. "Sure I wasn't hit by someone riding in a carriage?"

Chiyo was not amused. "You shouldn't say such terrible things. Something might happen. You'd better not go out today." Her superstitions did not become a girl with a modern education, but she meant exactly what she said.

Friends that they were, they did not stand on ceremony. There was no reticence, no wall between them. Sadness was something they never knew;[6] they spent their days in laughter.

Only February, and the winds were still cold, but the night before they had made plans to see the plum blossoms. It was the Day of the Martial Guardian.[7] Chiyo clung to Ryōnosuke's arm as they strolled along.

"You haven't forgotten last night's promise, have you? It's unforgivable."

"I haven't forgotten anything," he assured her. "Wait a minute. What was it now . . ."

"After we'd decided on it! I thought we were on our way."

"Oh, yes, I remember. You said you wanted to see the magic lantern show, didn't you? The story about Oshichi, the greengrocer's daughter?"[8]

"Oh, how hideous you are. Nothing but lies."

"—Or was it the wild bear from Tamba?[9] Was that what you wanted to see?"

"It doesn't matter. Make it whatever you want. I'm going home."

"Oh, come on—I was only kidding."

"You're always kidding."

"It was a joke. Of course, I should have known: Miss Nakamura isn't interested in anything so silly. What Mr. Sonoda thought he heard her say she wanted was—"

"Forget it. I don't want to see anything."

"You don't have to get angry about it. You want everyone to laugh at us? Let's not make a spectacle—walking along fighting."

"All you ever do is tease me. What do you expect?"

"I said I was sorry." They had already passed the notions shop. "Well, what are we going to do, then?"

"I wonder if it isn't up ahead, perhaps. Oh, dear, I'm not really sure."

"What happened to the girl who wasn't interested?"

"Let's not talk about that any more." Already the dispute had lost significance.

They turned into a side street, where the plum trees were in full bloom.

"Over here," someone beckoned. They heard the clatter of a pair of lacquered sandals. It was a blind woman playing the koto, a modern-day Asagao.[10] "Before the dew forsakes the morning-glory—how sad, how moving," she strummed the famous refrain.[11]

"Have a sweet! Delicious sweets!" called out a vendor.[12]

Vying with the one who praised the soft and sweet, a competitor extolled the crispness of his salted crackers.

"Chiyo, look over there. The second tree from the right."

"Mmm, aren't the blossoms lovely? Such a deep pink." She was completely engrossed, when suddenly someone tapped her on the back.

"Chiyo."

She turned around to see a group of her girl friends with their hair done up in the European manner.

"You two certainly look friendly!" The pert words escaped from the flower-like lips of one of them, and they all burst into laughter. "What are you up to?" They were gone as quickly as they had appeared. Only the evening breeze remained.

"Who were they, Chiyo? School friends? How rude they are!" If Ryōnosuke was taken aback as he watched the girls scurry off, Chiyo, her face lowered, was the embarrassed one.

Where had they come from, these new feelings of hers? Yesterday she hadn't noticed them. Now she was so unsure of herself. The world around her had turned pitch-dark. The sound of his voice seemed to penetrate her very being. All she had to do was think of him and she would tremble.[13]

She was in love. But she was frightened, and she felt utterly confused. If she said one thing, he would laugh at her; if she did another, he would hold her in contempt. She could not even answer a simple question. She would cringe and begin to pull dust balls from the matting on the floor—piling them up, piling them up, like the mountain of thoughts weighing on her mind. How she longed to see him! Yesterday she would have said it openly. She blamed herself for her predicament: she would not speak his name or mention his family, and it only made things worse. Clearly something must be done— even tears would have cooled the fire in her heart.[14]

She couldn't sleep at night. Finally, exhausted from her yearning, she would doze off. In her dreams, he would come to her.[15] His gentle hand would tap her on the back. "What are you thinking about?"

"You," she could not bring herself to say. She looked down at the floor. Even when she dreamt, her actions were the same, though she knew that hiding her thoughts might well throw up a barrier between them.

One glance, and he no doubt knew her mind. And yet he pretended to have no inkling that *he* was the cause of all her worries. "Whoever the lucky man is, I envy him."

"Do you think I'd waste away like this for some stranger? Look how thin I am."

Gently he took her slender arm and beamed, "Well, who is it then?"

She was about to answer when the temple bell tolled the break of day. It echoed at her pillow. All had been a dream. How hateful the cock's crow is to those in love, she thought, remembering the poem.[16] The sun was rising, but she was loath to put her dreams aside. What a strange mood she was in.

"What's ailing you?" her mother asked. "You look a little feverish."

Of course, her mother could not begin to guess the reason, but Chiyo felt her face flush anyway.

All morning she was at her sewing, though it failed to distract her. She knew she must drive these thoughts from her mind. What could possibly come of this languishing? If she revealed her feelings to him, he would spurn her. And wouldn't that be mortifying! No, she mustn't even see him again. That she had been like a sister to him, that they had never had any distance between them—all this only fueled her affection for him.

But soon he would be taking a wife. What kind of woman would he choose? She would have to be a beauty, that was certain. He could have the most attractive woman under heaven. Someone who could play the koto and flute, someone with a literary sense. Even she could predict that much. He had every reason to maintain the highest standards, and she knew that she fell hopelessly short of them. What if she admitted it openly? What would become of their friendship of all these years? How could things help but cool?

The more she contemplated her predicament, the more it distressed her. If only she could forget things, she told herself. They were still close, weren't they? He was like her brother. How could there be another girl for him? Surely he could never turn against her.

Yet the slightest word of friendliness from him was enough to set her off again. One minute she had made up her mind to pretend she didn't hear him, to take solace in her tears. The next minute, all her resolutions unraveled like a spool of thread.

For all that, she could not abide his tenderness. She would have preferred her beloved to be heartless—that would have put an end to things.

But in fact she no longer knew who was to blame. Was it her fault, this lovesickness? Or was he the one who was really in the wrong? He was the one! She hated him. She didn't want to hear his voice again. She didn't want to see him any more. The sight of him, the sound of his voice would only fan the fire in her heart.

Regrettable, perhaps, but if he never set foot in her house again she certainly wouldn't go to him. It was a sorry thing to wish for, and yet she knew that she would feel rather easier if their relations went sour. Fire and water, that was what they were. All right, then, from today she would not see him. If he took it amiss, well—this was the way she wanted things.

Just then she heard the voice next door. Her sewing slipped through her fingers; her determination wavered. What on earth had she been thinking of? She had to see him!

In his heart of hearts, Ryōnosuke had no other friend but her. Still, it was not love that sparkled in his eyes. There was no taint to his affections; they were offered to a little girl he considered charming. The thought had never crossed his mind that someone in this world might fall in love with him. Unaware of how she felt, how could he share her suffering?

Indeed, it was something to ponder. What is one to say when face-to-face with a man as appealing and indifferent as Ryōnosuke?

What future did she have to look forward to? When could she hope to find spring? The blossoms were beyond her reach. In poetry the new grass might proclaim the season, but in life the young shoot could not announce her love.[17]

"Chiyo, do you feel any better today?" Ryōnosuke pushed back the folding screen round her bed and knelt at her pillow.

How she hated to have him see her with her hair tangled! She tried to sit up. Her arms were painfully thin.

"No, lie down. Don't worry about being polite at a time like this; you've got to get your rest. If you want to sit, put your head against my shoulder. There, how's that?"

"Ryōnosuke, aren't you taking your examinations?"

"Yes, we're in the middle of them."

"Is it all right for you to spend so much time here?"

"You're not to worry about such things. It's not good for you when you're sick."

"But I don't want to take time from your studies. I worry about how you'll do."

"Instead of worrying, just get better."

"You're always so nice to me. But I don't know if I will get better."

"There you go again! Don't be silly. You'll never get better if you don't have more will than that. Stop being so pessimistic. Think what it does to your parents. It isn't like you not to see how this worries them."

"Yes, I know." Her voice was weak. "But I'm not sure this is something one recovers from." Her eyes brimmed with tears.

"Don't be a fool!" And yet he knew there was no denying the gravity of her condition. Anyone could see it. It was horrid to watch her decline day by day. Her lovely, dimpled cheeks were gaunt now. Her face was white, almost transparent. She had begun to lose her hair. It was still deep black, so deep one could almost see a tinge of green in it, but the sheen was gone.

Others, too, would be devastated at the girl's condition. The turmoil he experienced in his heart was surely what the poets had written of.[18] How many more days would he be able to see her, even in her present state? Her robe looked as withered as the grasses that had yielded the dyes to color it. Her pale pink sash was tied loosely in front.

All these years they had known each other. They had seldom been apart. They had always been close. Why, then, hadn't he perceived her true emotions? What yearning there must have been in that young girl's heart!

Yesterday evening Ofuku had come running over with tears in her eyes: Chiyo had a fever, she kept calling out his name. It was only natural, Ofuku sobbed, that she should want him there.

He blamed himself for not understanding sooner how she really felt. He blamed her for keeping everything a secret.

This morning when he went to see her, she had given him her ring. It had all but fallen from her emaciated finger. "Here, Ryōnosuke, I'd like you to have this as a keepsake." A forlorn smile was all she could muster. If only he had known sooner—he would not have let her condition deteriorate so far. Everything was his fault.

"Ryōnosuke? Are you wearing the ring I gave you this morning?"

He was too choked to answer. Instead, he held out his hand. She pulled it toward her, staring at it. Remember me, she wanted to tell him. Her tears fell, and she buried her face in her pillow.

"Chiyo, are you feeling worse? Ofuku! Get her medicine. She's very pale. Mrs. Nakamura, you'd better come here a minute."

Her mother, at her prayers in the next room, and the maid Ofuku, at the family altar, came running to the girl's bedside.

Chiyo opened her eyes. "Ryōnosuke."

"He's right here, beside your pillow," Ofuku explained.

"Mother—ask him to go."

"Why?" Ryōnosuke was startled. "Does it bother you to have me here?"

"Why do you want him to go?"

"Ofuku, you ask him to leave," Chiyo persisted.

"What are you saying?" her mother asked. "How can you talk that way, when he's been so nice to you?"

"Yes," Ofuku added. "Here, take your medicine and you'll feel better."

"Mother?"

"I'm right here, Chiyo. Here I am."

"How is she?" her father asked as he came rushing in.

Chiyo braced herself and took her medicine. "Oh, it hurts." She held her hand to her chest.

"There, there. Ofuku, get the doctor. She's feverish. Father, don't just stand there—do something. Ryōnosuke, hand me that towel."

"Oh, Mother, *please* ask him to leave."

"Ryōnosuke, you hear her," the woman said, beside herself. "It's rude, I know . . ."

With every word, Chiyo's breathing became more labored. Her face turned still whiter as they watched.

Life is as fleeting as a beaded strand of dew, Ryōnosuke remembered,[19] but, even so, he refused to believe that tonight might be the end. He knew she wanted him to go, but only with the greatest difficulty could he bring himself to leave her.

Chiyo, for her part, could not bear to see him worry as the end drew near.

He had only gone two steps beyond the folding screen round her pillow when her voice, thin and weak as a solitary thread, called after him. "Ryōnosuke."

He turned around. "Yes?"

"Tomorrow—I'll make up for chasing you away."

There was no wind in the air, but the cherry blossoms fell beneath the shadows of the eaves. In the evening sky, the temple bell resounded.[20]

A Snowy Day
(Yuki no Hi, 1893)

A day like this inspires poetry and song. How I envy those who see the snow spread out before them and fashion their metaphors. Silver sprinkles the earth. Softly, snowflakes fall like dancing butterflies; wings flutter but there is no sound. Six-petaled crystals come to rest on withered trees, spring's first flowering.[1]

But for me, the snow invites fresh pain, summoning as it falls and falls a past beyond forgetting. Eight thousand regrets I have[2]—what little good they do me. What waste—I've thrown away a lifetime, a family heritage. I've turned my back on the graves of my ancestors and walked away from an aunt who gave me everything. My parents named me Tama—Jewel—as if I would remain some precious, flawless gem. What ignominy I have brought upon my name! How could they have guessed that I would end up as worthless as a shard of tile? I have fallen like rubbish into the stream and have drifted into tainted waters. I was too young to know better. Love was my mistake, and the go-between, a snowy day.

My home was in a mountain village where the grass grew deep. My people, named Usui, were prosperous and respected, but my parents both died young. I was the last of a line. My aunt, a widow who had moved away on marrying, returned to our village to care for me. From the time that I was three, she devoted herself to my upbringing as if I were her own child. The love showered on me was as great as any parent's. When I reached the age of seven, she saw to it that my lessons in penmanship commenced under proper tutelage. Music lessons she herself provided with utter earnestness.

But no border guard can stop the years from passing by. The little girl's folds in my skirts were lowered, and I began to pluck my eyebrows. What delight I experienced when I could wear a maiden's sash. Today it makes me laugh—the country girl is not the equal of her cousin in the capital: for my age, I was as tall as I should be, if not so clever. I was a child, still unaware of what different creatures men and women are. Life was painless and carefree.

Then in the winter of my fifteenth year the cold currents carried rumors; before even I had understood the feelings in my heart, who could have recognized the truth? Soon Auntie caught wind of things: there was talk I was in love.

It is a world of mistakes we live in. Rumors break like waves from name-less rivers. The reason for these torrents, the cause of all my tears, was Katsuragi Ichirō, a teacher in my school.[3] He was from Tokyo, and as hand-some as could be. He lived a mere ten streets from me, to the north, in a cottage on the grounds of Hōshō Temple. Since my earliest schooldays he had been my teacher; I had always been his pet. Habits do not die easily. Some-times he would visit me, sometimes I would drop in at his lodgings. He always told me fascinating things, and I learned much from these talks with him. He treated me almost like a sister, and I, without brothers or sisters of my own, was of course delighted. At school I felt a certain pride, although, when I think of it now, our friendship must have seemed unusual to others. I would not have called it love between us.[4] But, after all, by this time I was wearing my hair in the young woman's fashion and had left behind the things of childhood. My teacher, Mr. Katsuragi, was now in his early thirties. The sages were indeed wise to separate boys and girls beyond the age of seven.[5] How friendly we were, how foolish!

Those who saw us began to censure us. Once the rumors started, they would not cease. "I could cry!" my aunt began to scold. "Even the purest gem becomes scratched! It will bring you a lifetime of unhappiness, you know. And all because you've forgotten how I raised you. To think the last daughter of the Usui family could turn out so slovenly. Don't you know what people are saying? 'If her parents were still living, she would never have come to this!' But it's your mother I feel sorry for. Looking up to me on her dying day and asking me to care for you—you could hardly hear her, her voice was so weak. Oh, it's more than I can bear . . . Whoever said that a parent suffers in the dark knew what he was talking about.[6] In spite of everything I've tried to do for you—we'll end up the laughingstock of the entire village. And then I don't know what I'll do, for your poor mother's sake, for the family name." At this point my aunt, who was usually a woman of few words, lowered her voice, as if remembering the neighbors: "I'm telling you, Tama, this friendship with Mr. Katsuragi has got to stop."

At first I didn't grasp what she was talking about.

Finally she became more explicit. "Listen to me, Tama. Mr. Katsuragi may very well be in love with you, and you with him. But you know that there are certain principles. In our family, no one has ever married someone from outside the village, let alone a man from Tokyo. No matter how fine a scholar Mr. Katsuragi may be, we know nothing of his background. It would be impossible to consider him as a son-in-law. I'm afraid it's hopeless, no mat-ter how much you may love him. Of course, if there's nothing to the rumors, all the more reason to avoid him. You mustn't have anything to do with him. You won't be needing lessons any more. It's only because you mean so much to me, you know, that I've treated him with any respect at all. I have no use for such a worthless stranger. All these years, I've brought you up so carefully. People have always said what a lovely girl you are. I've been so proud of you. Now he comes along to spoil everything. It can't be helped—what's done is done. You've got to restore your good name, and put my mind at rest. Remember, he's your enemy. If you have any respect for your family name, and for me, you'll forget that Katsuragi Ichirō exists. When you pass his gate, you must never drop in on him again."

Her repeated admonitions were too much for me to bear. I could not hold back the tears; hiding my face in my sleeves, I cried and cried. "How hateful of you! I don't care if the others gossip. If the whole town turns its back on me, that's one thing. I would have expected my own aunt to know I'm innocent. It's not as if I'd met Mr. Katsuragi yesterday. Our friendship is entirely proper. You ought to see that. How could you let yourself be swayed by silly talk? Go ahead and pass judgment on me. I've already shown my innocence."

What feelings lay lurking in my heart? I myself hardly knew. My emotions were like wild horses, and I could not rein them in.

A single bamboo blind, when drawn between two friends, becomes a painful barrier. In the ten streets that separated us, there were many watchful eyes to keep the two of us apart. The winds of late fall had arrived. How I envied the swirling maple leaves borne off in his direction! I watched to see how far they would travel, and the sight of the grove where he lived tempted me to follow. Memories of his house, there at the edge of the village, came back to me. The vespers tolled from Hōshō Temple. It was a mournful sound. My mind would wander toward him, but my aunt's words of warning weighed heavily. I could not bring myself to go to him. I waited, hoping he would come to me. But it seemed that the rumors had spread. No doubt they made him hesitate; I had no word from him. Every day we did not meet was like a thousand autumns.

Soon it was the New Year, a time of festivities and merriment. On the seventh day, my aunt went to visit relatives in the neighboring village. Since morning it had been cloudy, and gradually the sky grew darker. The wind eventually died down, but the cold was enough to sink into one's bones. I felt utterly alone. When I happened to look out, snow was falling. Auntie would be terribly cold. I felt sorry for her as I sat within the warmth of the *kotatsu*.[7] The snow was heavy now. It looked like tufts of cotton. Soon everything was hidden under it . . . the garden, the gate. I opened the window slightly. The fields and the rice paddies behind the house were all buried. The grove around the temple, that spot I watched every day, was the same color as the sky. I felt a stirring in my heart.

If there is a god of troubles, surely he had hold of me. What could I have been thinking of? Good and bad did not exist. Overcome with longing, I left the house where I had always lived.

It did not occur to me that I would never see my home again, those eaves that I had always known. I was too impatient as I rushed out into the garden.

"Miss, where are you going in the snow?" I was startled by our farmhand, Heisuke. He was a dull-witted man. "Aren't you going to take an umbrella?"

"I'm going to meet Auntie," I lied.

"In this weather? Don't you think she'll spend the night? If you want someone to meet her, though, let me go."

"No, no. I want to go and surprise her. She'll be delighted—in all this snow. You wait here and just pretend you never saw me leave."

"I think you're daft," Heisuke said with his usual guffaw. "You'd better take this, if your mind's made up." He handed me his umbrella. "Careful now you don't slip."

When there are bonds between two people, there is love, I thought, remembering the poem.[8] No matter how cold or uncaring Auntie may have seemed, no matter how strict she had been with me, everything she did was for my own good. Only later did I appreciate that her efforts were more than I deserved.

In spite of my love for Katsuragi, even in my dreams I had never imagined that he would become my husband, or that the two of us would run away. But together we wandered aimlessly. Like the black bamboo beneath the window, bent by the heavy snow, he and I were broken by the enormity of our offense. Abandoning my birthplace, discarding my beloved aunt—it was all the delirium of that snowy day.

Here in the splendor of the capital I miss my country friends, but at this late date it is futile to blame my husband for taking me away. "I am like the young grass in the shadow of the mountain trees," as the poets say. "The dew abounds, but companions I have none."[9] Even in the city, "life is as lonely as winter in a mountain village."[10]

When I question the past through my tears everything seems a mistake. Later, word finally reached me: so distraught was Auntie that in the autumn of that year she passed away.

My regrets come too late, and my illusions have all fled. I have tried to sustain a melody I never knew; the man I have been faithful to has disappointed me. Indeed, there is truth to Murasaki's poem: "The first snow falls on a world of rising sorrows."[11] Again this year it comes, oblivious to all the sadness it brings, so proud of itself for decorating, even for the moment, a broken, ruined fence. There was a time when I loved it, the first snow, but I was younger then.

The Sound of the Koto [1]
(Koto no Ne, 1893)

The sun and moon shed their light impartially on all who dwell under heaven. The flowers in spring bloom for everyone. Is it only in this treetop, then, that storms rage? For fourteen cruel years the child, an innocent, had seen his family dispersed like the leaves that scatter from the autumn tree. Battered by the wind and rain, he was the last leaf clinging to the branch. But in fact he had nothing to hold on to; he was adrift in a world of uncertainty.

His mother had abandoned him when he was four. She would have liked to save him, too, from suffering, but her parents insisted she forsake her husband and her home. The fortunes of her husband's family were in such decline that nothing could retrieve them. Her parents refused to see her spend her life in tears over a man who would never come to anything. They knew how hard it was for her to leave her child, but they urged her to make the break before there were other children. The argument sounded reasonable enough to their daughter's foolish ears. She herself was still a girl.

She had no regrets for her husband, but her own child she could not so easily discard. When she tried to leave him, in her pain she felt as if she might cough blood. In the end, her sense of duty drove her to obey parental admonitions. She was too fainthearted to resist. Knowing her husband's family was collapsing—like a pillar of ice slowly melting in the sun[2]—she left everything behind: home, husband, child.

Afterward her husband would come to her parents' house. Sometimes he came alone, sometimes he brought the child, sometimes he would leave the boy with her. "It doesn't matter what becomes of me," he pleaded. "The only thing I want is to see our son get ahead in life. Won't you try coming back?" He would not ask her to stay forever—just five years or so, until the child had reached the age of reason. He coaxed and begged. The heartache was almost too much for her; where was the mother who did not worry for her child? But the man was relying on the most unpromising of hopes if he expected her to apologize and return. He passed the days in futile expectation that perhaps she would come back the fifteenth, certainly the twentieth. If she didn't come today, then she would have to come tomorrow. Finally, when he went to implore her one last time, she was nowhere to be found. Had the woman gone off to be a nursemaid somewhere? Had she become another man's wife? The vows of a hundred years of faithfulness were empty words indeed.

Soon a half-year went by. The boy's father was not the man he had been. Many praised his wife as wise for having left him, while there were few, alas, to sympathize with those she had abandoned. Perhaps this was as it should be. Now drink was all that could dispel, if only for a moment, the clouds gathering in his heart. Every time he drank, his disposition grew darker, his will more violent. Small wonder, then, that there were few to side with him.

The year drew to a close. Father and son had no blanket of their own in which to wrap themselves, much less a roof to protect them from the rain. Still, the child had his father. He looked up to him, as to a great tree providing shade. The covers were thin in the lodging house where they spent their nights, but a father's love would keep him warm.

One year, before the boy was even ten, his father went off to a celebration at the house of a wealthy friend, where the kegs were opened and the wine flowed freely. This was the very stuff the gods themselves enjoyed. The man was ready to entrust himself to it, as if it were his guide to heaven. He drank to his heart's content and on his way home passed out beneath a pine, where he met his pitiful end.

Nowhere was there anyone to take the boy in, to care for him and see him to adulthood. And the boy himself had no hopes for his future. At first he ached with envy toward those who had their parents. He knew his mother was, no doubt, still living, but her whereabouts and her life were to him a mystery. In spite of everything, he still felt love for her. But then, with his father's death and the shock of knowing that he was now the last of his entire family, he grew to hate his mother for a deed as evil as the devil's own.

He used to cry when asked where his mother was, or whether it was true he had no father. But that was in the past. He understood now that there was no compassion in this world, no sincerity in men's hearts. Those who did show half-hearted pity for the boy only disgusted him; he suspected they were making fun. Let life be hard. What did it matter? His heart had become twisted. The gods and buddhas were his enemies. He had no one to appeal to. He was no longer an ordinary child.

His beady eyes seemed to pierce whatever he looked at through his mop of tangled hair, and, if there was anything handsome about his dirty face, no one would know it. Everyone mistrusted him. They were sure the urchin never missed a chance to do some harm. He was glared at even by the police. At festivals and holidays, wherever people gathered, he was always the object of suspicion. How he hated them, with their shouts and accusations, "Pickpocket!" "Thief!"

Eyes clouded with doubt whenever he was near. Would these rumors spread even to remote parts? There would be no undoing false reports. Now word had it the boy was a bandit. Before long they were calling him the Thief of the Meiji Era, or some name terrible enough to give everyone a scare, most of all himself. He wanted to flee. He couldn't bear the bitterness in his heart; he wished that he could die. He stared into the river and wondered if he should jump, but death does not come easily.

Alone and without hope, the boy found it increasingly difficult to sustain himself. He wandered here and there and sometimes managed to find work. At night, he stopped wherever he could. Life was like an unending nightmare. He drifted from day to day. The longer he lived, the taller he grew, but as his height increased his heart became more twisted.

Winds blew sadly beneath the Ogyō Pine. In Negishi late rice hung drying in the fields. The beggar-boy fixed his eyes upon the house of a woman named Morie Shizu: his manner had something strange about it, and the woman's maids were uneasy, whispering among themselves, although in fact there was little need to worry night and day over the locking of the gate. A month or so passed without incident. Branches of the persimmon tree hung low over the garden wall, but the boy had not so much as picked a single fruit. Here and there the mistress of the house heard talk about the ruffian. Her ears were sharp, and the stories were unsettling.

It was a night when the autumn rains poured down softly, and one knew all too well the sorrow of things. Alone by the lamplight, she played her koto. The songs had a cheerless ring, but the instrument was her one companion. She heard the bell toll through the woods in Ueno, and she put her music aside. The rain dripped from the eaves, the wind rustled the treetops. Several times she thought she heard some other sound.

From beneath the overhanging roof could be seen the tall pine, constant in its year-round coat of green. And to whom, one might ask, had this woman pledged *her* fidelity, living in this solitary nest? Music was her only master. She was nineteen; one wondered how many years she had already devoted to perfecting the gentle tones and shadings of her melodies. She was as thin and graceful as the willow branches ruffled by the wind, and, though she might appear too delicate, when she took up her box of plectrums and arranged herself to play, what did it matter, the tumult in this floating world of dust?[3] It was as if the Mountain Princess[4] herself guided the woman's hands over the strings, the way the pine breeze blows across the threadlike branches of the willow tree.[5] The look of serenity upon her face as she would play was almost dreamy. She was oblivious to the wind, the rain, the sound of the roaring thunder.

In the tenth month, at the first frost, the moon shone brightly on the fallen leaves. So did it illumine all it touched that one could well comprehend the old saw: the light of the moon is as frightening as the rouge on a crone's cheeks. Nothing under heaven escaped its beams—great homes and lofty mansions, humble huts and doghouses—all were enveloped in the moonglow: the frost upon the withered reeds; the pond here where a young woman lived out her days like a hidden stream, unknown to anyone; the lonely mountain hut, whose only visitor was the spring flowing in the trough; the fields, the scarecrows, the water in the ditch; the legendary spots of moonlit beauty—Suma, Akashi, Matsushima.[6] But the light of the moon did not deceive. The pure remained pure. The tainted did not lose its flaws. Selflessly, the moon beamed its light in all directions, a veritable eight-faceted jewel. Amid this radiance the sound of the koto rose into the night. Who knows how far it carried, with its comely, intriguing sounds, its clear and noble harmonies? It seemed the very music of the heavens.

On this night the sound of the woman's playing helped another to be reborn. Through fourteen springs and fourteen autumns, the boy had been buffeted by the rains. His heart had gradually toughened until it had become as hard as stone. No arrow could penetrate it. He seemed destined to follow the example of his father, to die among the fields or in the mountains, where his remains would be bleached by the elements. Some were convinced the boy's life would end in prison chains, while his bad name spread to every roadside.

But now, at once, the tenderness buried in his heart was freed by the midnight strains of the koto. For the first time in many years, he felt tears come to his eyes. Or were they jewelled drops of dew? He would not exchange them for anything.[7]

He, who had known neither love nor compassion, and who had no idea what the player of these refrains could even look like, felt a moment of happiness as the music drifted over the garden wall. He was embarrassed at his own emotions. He was overcome with a longing for his mother, the way he used to be, before he began to revile her as a demon. Now, all at once, he was loath to give up the world so lightly.

On this night of an ever-brighter moon, the scent of chrysanthemums along the hedge caressed his sleeve. How could a stormy wind blow now? The clouds in his heart had disappeared. Once more the woman began to play. The sound of the koto would be his friend for a hundred years, the seed for a hundred years of yearning. He had entered a world where a hundred different flowers were in bloom.

Encounters on a Dark Night
(Yamiyo, 1894)

People often wondered just how large the compound was, surrounded by its garden wall. How long had the front gate been boarded up? Storms had had their way with the place, and what remained was disquieting. There were none of the proverbial ferns running rank among the ruins, but on the rooftop weeds now choked the tiles.[1] Who was it who lived there mourning the past?

The time for silk brocades was clearly gone.[2] Now, one was fortunate just to cross Miyagi Plain, somehow to make it through the autumn fields of *hagi*, where the lonely call of the deer echoes for his mate.[3] Even a princeling can fall from favor, left to doubt if they were not a dream, those days when he rubbed elbows with the Court on mats spread out for a viewing of the summer moon. The November winds are cold, nothing lasts for long. From a silent pool, the Asuka River suddenly becomes a torrent.[4]

Malicious rumors lingered, and no one came to call. How moving—three lonely people, a mistress and her servants. They dwelt in the capital but they could well have been hiding in a mountain hut.

"That's where the swindler met his end," people said, pointing at the house. There was evidence, however, that if indeed the man had speculated, it might not have been from sheer greed. He left little wealth behind. The censure that lived on after him was because the good things to his credit he had done quietly. Few were witness to his kindness. Scandal, rather, would long remain attached to the house, the garden, the old pond. Best not say any more—it was horrid, people thought. And yet on rainy nights talk would often turn to the details of Matsukawa and his house. Everyone agreed: somehow or other it was an eerie place.

From the very beginning, there had been little sign of life in the big house. It had increasingly taken on the appearance of some deserted temple, a ruin where every sound rang ominously. Scant effort was expended to maintain the place. Rooms not in use were closed off, and the shutters were fastened tight for days on end. It was like the empty villa where Prince Genji's love, Yūgao, had died of fright.[5]

The mistress of the house, Oran, though no heroine from the old romances, was all the same a young woman to whom her servants were devoted. Unlike Yūgao, she was possessed by no demons, yet her existence was a strange and lonely one. An air of mystery shrouded her quiet life.

The nights were especially sad. In her dark rooms burnt a single candle. Only the shadow on the wall kept her company. Alone and disconsolate, she sat up through the nights, heard the bells toll daybreak. The woman's past and the question of her future would have troubled the toughest of men. The most awesome of gods would have spilt tears for her.

It was the fifth month by the lunar calendar, the twenty-eighth day. No moon graced the evening sky. Only a moment before it had been dusk, but already the night was black. The wind whistled fiercely through the big oak behind the house. It was like a woodland there, dense and overgrown. Almost without noticing it, she heard the sound of waves rising on the pond in back. Who could guess how deep its waters were? The noise seemed near enough to touch. She sat with her elbows on her desk of sandalwood, lost in thought, her eyes half-closed as if in sleep. Now and then her eyebrows would ripple in a frown, a look of infinite sorrow.

The heat of these past few days had been enough to melt gold. How bothersome her abundant hair became in summer weather! She had washed it that morning. It fell to her shoulders with a luster so rich that the black took on a shade of green. It brushed the edges of her cheeks, themselves so pure that snow would suffer in comparison. Connoisseurs of female beauty would surely have lamented her seclusion. There was a radiance about her reminiscent of the goddess Kannon,[6] but she looked more forlorn and still more beautiful.

Suddenly there came a sound of commotion from the front hall. The voice was unfamiliar. The young beauty rose from her languid state and listened carefully. Was it a fire? A quarrel between the old couple who served her? Highly unlikely, she said to herself. But she was suspicious and she straightened her collar, trying all the harder to hear whatever was transpiring. The sound of flurried footsteps reached her.

"Oran, are you reading? Excuse me for bothering you—but do you have some medicine I might borrow?" It was the old woman's voice, speaking from outside the door.

"What's happened? Is your husband sick? The medicine will depend on what's the matter. Calm down and tell me what's happened."

The woman stood in the doorway and spoke with deference. "Oh, no, ma'am, it's not Sasuke. Tonight, just now, like always, he finished making his rounds in the garden and went to check to see that the gates were closed. The side gate isn't shutting properly, and he's always hurting himself on it, so he thought he would fix it. He was opening and closing it, to see what he could do about it, when a rickshaw came along the main road and lit up the night. It had a lantern with an arrowhead crest, so right off he thought it must be

Namizaki coming to see you. He left the side gate open and waited for him, but it seems it wasn't Namizaki after all.

"Just as the rickshaw passed in front of the gate, a young man appeared in the road. Even Sasuke has no idea where he came from, but the wheels of the carriage hit him. Sasuke heard him cry and dashed out, forgetting all about his forehead. (It was sore, you see, from where he bumped it on the gate.) Awful though! The rickshaw flew right by and never even stopped!

"The man who was hit doesn't look too badly off, but he seems mighty weak for such a youngster. He doesn't even have the strength to wobble. The poor thing looks half-dead. Of course, Sasuke wouldn't think of leaving him there, lying in the road. 'I don't know if Oran will approve,' he said to me when he brought him in. 'It's hard to tell whether the boy's conscious. See what you can do for him.' That's what he told me. I'm not exaggerating. The poor thing!"

From days of hunger and fatigue, the boy's body was as tattered as a cotton rag. Now from the accident he had the wounds where the wheels had hit him, and his fright. It was as if his soul had left him. He barely breathed; for a while he floated in a trance. Balmy scents were in the air. He felt cool and refreshed. Gradually he began to return to his senses, as the veil curtaining his head slowly lifted. Opening his eyes, the boy looked around him. "He's coming to. I'll give him some medicine." He heard her speak and he wondered if he hadn't entered paradise. Beside his pillow was a goddess such as he had never seen.

"What a weakling!" Sasuke scolded. "All he has is a scratch on his little finger. Boys get that much when they slip chasing butterflies. It's nothing to faint over, for heaven's sake. Get hold of yourself, boy, and take your medicine."

"Don't be so harsh," Sasuke's wife rebuked him. "He's tired out all the same, no matter what it's from. He needs looking after."

"Don't worry about staying here," Oran said to soothe the boy. "Just relax and go to sleep. It doesn't matter how long you stay. If you want to let your family know, I'll send someone. This kind of accident could happen to anyone, but we don't want your family to worry. Just tell me if there's anything we can do. You're already recovering nicely, but do stay the night. I'll send word. Otherwise, your parents will go imagining terrible things have happened. We must let them know you're safe. Where do you live?"

He did not answer. It was painful for him to raise himself. His face was emaciated. His wide eyes looked leaden, and the bridge of his rather handsome nose was sunken. In contrast, his forehead was prominent and strong.

The hairline was thin, but his hair was long and covered his collar. He seemed about to speak. Instead, tears fell. His colorless lips quivered, and he was overcome.

Quietly Oran drew closer. "Here," she proffered him medicine.

"No. I'm all right." He waved it away. "I don't have a home to return to. I don't have any parents. It doesn't matter whether I'm killed in an accident like tonight's, or fall somewhere at the roadside . . . nobody's going to mourn for *me*. When people do show me any kindness, it only makes me more unhappy. You should've left me lying at the gate. As long as I go on living, I only see the sadness in the world. I'd as soon die and let the dogs feed on me. It was dark tonight, but I remember the man's face and the crest on his damned rickshaw, and I'll get even with him—even if I can't repay you for being so nice to me. Please let me go now." He started to rise but his step was uncertain, and he staggered as he moved.

"Watch out! Don't be a fool!" Sasuke, who had suffered with his own child, began to berate the boy. "Even if you don't have any parents, show some respect for their memory. They *did* give birth to you. You can't throw everything away so easily. It's because of children like you, who know nothing, that parents worry so." The old man made him sit and listen to the scolding as if he were his own son, and the boy hung his head.

"He looks faint, Sasuke," the old woman warned her husband. "That's why he says these funny things. We have to keep him here tonight and let him get a good rest."

The boy put himself in their care, and Oran returned to her apartments.

The morning glory by the fence blooms in splendor for a single day, and this is all it lives for. Why should he who knows the limits of his fate tremble over things that might have been?

The boy's family had enjoyed good fortune through his grandfather's generation. Around the region, the man had been revered as a great physician. When his palanquin approached, even the village children would come running across the rice fields to pay homage. Who, then, had led ill fortune down the road toward the boy?

His father died young and his mother was forced to hide in the shadows, for the two had never married. The world is not an easy place. The man's family had their means of preventing her from pressing any claims. The woman knew a protest would avail her nothing. Even if she swore by the gods[7] and by her lover's departed soul that the child she was carrying was his own, in his kinsmen's eyes she would be speaking from greed.

She blamed her suffering on her humble origins, but she wiped away her

tears and returned to her family's home. She was already seven months
pregnant. It was the second week after her lover's death.[8] Her choices were
limited indeed. She soon wearied of a world of growing enmity and she
longed to leave this life. The first birth, even in the best of times, is no easy
thing. When the child was born she bled profusely, and without ever seeing
her baby's face the poor woman died at twenty-one. The autumn rains had
taken her away.

From the child's first days, before he had his bearings in the world, he
grew up without a father or a mother. The only warmth he knew was when
he nestled in the arms of his grandfather, resting his head against the old
man's chest. The spring ice thawed and children came out into the fields to
play, but he was always excluded from their games. He hid behind trees; he
became more and more difficult.

His grandfather was the only one to take pity on the boy. "Poor child! The
world's against you!" he sympathized. "No wonder you are twisted—when
you grow up like a flower on the edge of the field, with nothing to protect
you. You're just unlucky; there's nothing you've done wrong. If people want to
look down on you for being an orphan, they're the ones with something
wrong. Maybe there *are* no gods in this world.[9] If everyone wants to be our
enemy, we'll have to be prepared to fight. After I'm dead, wherever you go
they'll be cruel. You can't trust anyone. When they're mean, answer them in
kind. They're going to be against you anyway, so don't bother playing up to
them. People are worthless. They'll only treat you like a worn-out pair of
sandals."

There were tears of anger in the man's eyes. His resentment toward the
world would never leave him. The more sympathy he showed his grandson
the worse people seemed to treat the child. From now on, the old man
vowed, anyone who tried to hurt the boy would have his grandfather to
contend with. He didn't care who it was—even the son of the village headman. He would see that justice was done.

And so the behavior of the two became increasingly unruly. The attitude of
the old man—approaching senility and without any farmland of his own to
till—was to get even, to show them all. In the end, he was despised by all the
farmers who did own land and whose existence was secure. It seemed certain
that the lives of the old man and the boy would be snuffed out soon, like
night candles put out by the wind.

Not long after the thirteenth anniversary of his daughter's death, the man
fell seriously ill. He knew that he was dying and that medicine could not help
him. The poor boy and the stubborn old man watched their fortunes ebb still
lower. They could see the moon peeking in through the holes in their
thatched roof.

Had others heard the way he faced the end, they would have been as tonished. The man was determined to go quietly to his death. "No gods will come to greet me with their songs," he joked with a smile on his face. "I wonder where I'm going—heaven or hell?" These were his last words.

Thenceforth the boy was completely alone in the world.

His name was Takagi Naojirō, and he had now reached the age of nineteen. It would be painful even to guess at all the suffering he had known. Of late he had decided to abandon the foothills of his childhood, where Mount Kano had always loomed above him, in the district of Amaha where he was born. Did he have to sacrifice a lifetime, he would ask himself, because he had no relatives? He remembered what he had heard of the traditions of his father's family. The sons had all studied medicine in Tokyo. With both his parents gone and no guardian to advise him on his future, he relied on his own judgment. Perhaps there were evil people in the capital, but surely he had talents he could put to use there. Let people think it rash of him—he was going off to Tokyo. The city would be pleased with him. He was sure that people there would find him capable.

Were he alive today, perhaps Meng Ch'ang-chün[10] would have given the boy a warm reception, but with others Naojirō did not fare well. His quirks were like kinks in a thread already braided. He wanted for any of the qualities that one might call appealing; he was a clumsy fellow into the bargain. Before learned men and the heads of temples where he called, eager to find work, he did not make a favorable impression.

Who could take him seriously? He was ready to sell himself in return for an easy life with food and lodgings. One house mistook him for demented and treated him most shamefully. Another, thinking him a beggar, invited him into the kitchen and offered him a meal. If that's what they think I am! he raged, and, with a breach of manners that was scandalous, he shrieked and overturned the tray of food they offered him and bolted from the house.

He had the courage of a wild boar, but wisdom he lacked. Anyone could see that he was something of a fool. There were naturally some who felt sorry for him. "Calm down, calm down," people would say. "Don't be afraid of an honest day's work. If we have anything for you to do, we'll be glad to help you."

He worked for a time gathering kindling for the furnace at the public bath, and for a while he delivered meals for the noodle shop. He worked as a cook. He was hired as a gardener. In one year, he had been taken in for a trial period by thirty different homes. It was bad enough when, after a mere three days or so, he left without so much as a good-by, but there were partings worse than this. The come-hither looks of a disheveled mistress would turn his stomach, and he would answer her overtures with a slap as he absconded. The woman, afraid to tell her husband, took the matter up with the police—one more enemy against him.

His latest job was at a flophouse in the dingy back streets. For the past few days he had been manning the front desk, until the owner said something he didn't like. His old temper flared again. Why the hell should he put up with this? He broke his writing brush in two and hurled the inkstone at his boss. He had no idea where to go; his defiance was going to cost him. Now how would he feed himself? He would bite his tongue and bleed to death before he begged for food. As he heard the bells toll at dusk, he felt worse off than the crows. When they left a place, they could build a new nest.

And so fate brought him to the Matsukawa house. Just in front of the tumble-down gate he was hit by the passing rickshaw. It bore an arrowhead crest, something Sasuke had likewise noticed.

Three days went by. The boy did nothing but sleep. He could remember little of what happened during this time, save the goddess whom he had seen on the first night, appearing at his pillow to attend him. It was all a blur, and yet he remembered something of her beauty and the lovely voice that had consoled him. When she held him in her gentle arms, it was like being born again in heaven. Would he wake to find that he had only dreamt of feeling like a butterfly among the flowers?[11]

"Take my hand when you are lonely," he heard her say. "Rest your head in my lap when the world is cruel to you. Together we can play among the mountains and the fields. The tears you hide from others you need not conceal from me—my sleeve will dry them all. I shall never hold you in contempt as others have, and, even if your character is flawed, I shall never despise you for your weaknesses. If there are secrets troubling you, offenses in the past that still torment you, tell me of them. It will cleanse your heart and make you feel better.

"I shall always be beside you. When you are angry, when you are disappointed. When you feel ashamed. When you have failed and know discouragement. When all you want to do is flee the world and hide among the mountains. When murderous or thieving instincts have the better of you. When you yearn for the distinction of high rank and high office. When your life seems bereft of beauty and you long to see the flowers and the moon. When you are waiting for a wind to cool you, or a cloud to bring some rain. When your boat is adrift upon the waves, or your little hut amid the mountains is oppressed by raging storms. When you are buried deep within a valley where the sun can never shine. Or when the summer sun pounds down upon the earth. I am your water; I shall quench your thirst. When sleet and snow are falling, let me be your fur robe on cold winter nights. We were never meant to be apart. Who cares what the world has to say? Forget distinctions of good and bad and beautiful and ugly. There is nothing you should hide from me. You must come to feel at home here. In my arms, in my lap."

The voice echoed in his head. Who was she? For these gentle words of hers he was ready to bow down before her.

It was then that he returned to consciousness. He felt consumed with the most intense heat. For a week he had slept, waking only to drift off to sleep again. Now he was in full control of his senses and could eat the gruel set before him. The couple were kind almost to a fault. The way they fussed over everything was enough to make him cry. They told him how wildly he had behaved while he was sick. The cut on Osoyo's forehead, they recounted, was from a cup Naojirō had thrown. But they bore him no resentment; they laughed as they told him these things. He was sorry for what he had done. He broke out into a sweat. Thoughts of regret came to him. His old shame returned again. What could he say? Timidly, he tried to ask if there had been another one besides the two of them looking after him while he was sick.

Sasuke laughed loudly. "If you want to ask a question, go ahead and ask. Nobody's going to hear you—just the mice in the ceiling and the lizards on the wall. There are only the two of us, and the young lady, rattling around the place. No dog, even. We go for a whole year without a visitor, never see a neighbor. In an empty house like this, you don't have to worry about asking questions. You won't be able to stand it here now that you're getting better. You've been dreaming all this time, but now you'll have trouble sleeping— when you lie awake and hear the wind in the pine. Poor fellow. I'll bet you're not used to such a lonely place."

"The young lady you talked about—was she the one looking after me while I was sick?"

"Yes, indeed."

Then he had not been dreaming.

Still, he wondered if the soft, soothing voice had actually been real. Was it not perhaps a dream that such a woman had caressed him?

Several days after he regained consciousness, Oran visited him, and the same questions returned to Naojirō. If Oran was the goddess of his dreams, then she had changed herself into an ordinary mortal. She was not without compassion, but there seemed to be a fence between them now. There was something punctilious in her manner. Could this be the woman who had held his hand? Who had petted his head in her lap?

"Dry your tears," she had said, and he could vaguely remember how their hands had touched: he was breathless and trembled with embarrassment— and fear. Everything about the woman in his dreams made him think of the mother he could not recall—her beauty and her elegance and the yearning he felt for her. The Oran now before him inspired the same sort of yearning. She was charming, if slightly intimidating. Was it possible she had ever said all those tender things?

Her hair was different now, though her face had the same beauty as the woman in his dreams, and her comforting voice had the same pleasant tones.

He doubted, however, that she and the goddess were one and the same. He was in a stranger's house, then, a stranger he could not altogether trust. Oran had been kind to him, but he sensed that it was time for him to go.

Naojirō had made up his mind to be off. He would go as quickly as the arrow leaves the bow. He went to say good-by to Sasuke and then to Oran.

"Wait a minute." Oran was shocked. "Take a look at yourself in the mirror. How far do you think you'll get when you're as pale as that? You can be stubborn if you want when you're well, but don't expect to have your way while you're still sick. Don't be so impatient. If you don't take things easy until you're better, you won't be able to do anything. I told you when you came here—you should feel at home with us. Don't think you have to go. I want to see you looking strong and healthy. In this last week or so we've already grown accustomed to having you around. You belong here, it seems. You know the saying, 'When sleeves touch, it means there is a bond between two strangers.'[12]

"You said yourself, Naojirō, you have no home to go to. So what am I to think? You're not going to have an easy time of it. As you can see for yourself, my own fate, like this crumbling house, is uncertain enough. When I compare my plight with yours, though, it scares me. You'll be tossed by the waves—it's a world of uncertainty. You'll grow weary of life. I suppose you won't listen to what a woman has to say. But I feel the same way you do. I, too, have suffered at the hands of others. I, too, have seen better days. If you don't want to discuss these things with me, talk to Sasuke. Or Osoyo. They have experience. They know what life is about. They are the ones to discuss it with. This is not a haunted house, you know," she said, smiling at him. "There aren't any goblins here to trick you. Don't be so afraid to stay."

"I hope you're not teasing just because you know how weak I am. You're right—I have nowhere to go. There won't be anyone to help me if I fall down along the road." He was mortified at his own frailty. The bravado was gone, and there was nothing he could say.

The old man and woman added their own urgings to those of Oran. He ought to stay at least until he had recovered. It was what they wanted, and it was what Oran wanted. He was their guest. Why did that embarrass him? He could be a great help to them with the work. And for a young man like him, surely that was better than a life of idleness.

Sasuke and Osoyo began to give him tasks to do, first easy ones that would not tax his weakened condition and gradually more strenuous chores as his health improved. He was treated as a member of the family. Caught up in the work, his spirits rose. The days passed, and, though he had never committed himself to staying, gradually he put down roots. Before he was aware of it, he had been there some time. He settled down, and the days went by.

He often worked in the gardens, which, as one might expect of such extensive grounds, were badly in need of repair. Trees and bushes had grown tangled. There were many broken branches. Weeds were everywhere. Ferns and wildflowers grew rank among the grasses. Gradually Naojirō worked his way round to the back garden, uprooting the weeds as he went. There a huge, gnarled pine dominated the scene. It would take several men just to reach around its trunk, he imagined. The lower branches grazed the surface of the old pond, which gave the tree the appearance of a great snake peering into water. It was impossible for him to tell how deep the pond might be.

Once there had been a summer house, but it was gone now. On the hill a few remains still stood. No autumn breezes blew. The setting sun shimmered in the dusk. The sight summoned strange feelings in the boy's heart. It was not a place to be alone. As far as the eye could see, the view was awesome. Even without such a distressing scene, Naojirō was inclined toward the melancholy. He was always lonely, and he felt ever more detached from the world.

Not only when the moon shines, but on dark nights, too, it is said that in summer it is the night that is most beautiful.[13] How lovely Oran's house was by moonlight. And how lovely, too, the vine of "evening faces" that grew beneath the eaves.[14]

Oran's rooms were at some distance from the others, down a corridor that turned several times before it reached her suite. It was the innermost part of the house. Here, if Oran, alone in thought, had anything to say, there was only the pine breeze to answer her. Naojirō and the old couple had rooms near the front hall. They lived beneath the same roof, and yet there was a barrier between Oran and the others. Once he had recovered, Naojirō had little chance to open his heart to her.

Sasuke and Osoyo revered the young woman as if she were a deity. They served her with complete devotion. For her, they were ready to throw their lives away as bits of dust. Loyalty is of course commendable, but what they felt toward Oran was more like awe. She was a single, splendid flower they wanted to protect from losing its petals or from being plucked and taken from the garden. They threw up a rope around her and stood watch. No one could approach her, and so Oran had no intimacies with anyone. In time,

Naojirō came to share the couple's attitude. He felt more like a servant to Oran, although in fact he was her guest. There were none of the usual opportunities to see her, for she did not indulge in the pastimes common to young women. She was not one to sit on the veranda in the evening with a book of stories and a fan to cool herself beneath the moon. Nor was she given to lolling away her summer afternoons burning incense, perfuming the breeze in the bamboo grove and exorcising the mosquitoes.

Naojirō knew nothing of her life and nothing of her family. He could as easily grasp a cloud as he could know the truth about Oran. Sasuke and Osoyo told him bits of things, but they did not amount to much: her father had been a rich man by the name of Matsukawa something. He had taken to speculating, where money is so easily lost. His wealth had evaporated like the clouds on a mountain peak when they try to come too close to the flowers on the ground. All that remained was his daughter Oran and a legacy of burdens. How sad it was. Even the house was not her own.

Dew was in the garden and gentle breezes blew. It was still the dim hours of the dawn. Oran awoke early; today was the anniversary of her father's death, and she wanted to pick flowers for his grave.

As she went into the garden with her scissors, Naojirō followed after her. "The baby's breath in back are pretty," he said. Perhaps this would be his chance to find out more about her. He spoke more freely than usual, and she was in good humor. Gathering a handful of lilies and baby's breath and a spray of other flowers, she seemed to enjoy strolling in her own garden, as if it were all new to her.

"Is today the memorial service for your father?" Naojirō asked her off-handedly. "How old were you when he died? You're like me, I guess," he smiled. "We've both been orphans since we were young."

"Let's go down the hill and rest a minute over there. I'm too tired to talk."

"Do you want to go back, then?"

"No, no. Just let's rest a while." They started down a mossy path. "It's slippery; let me hold on to you." All at once she was very close to him as they went down the hill.

When they came out at the bottom, they were standing at the edge of the pond. The ground was level there, and the bushes had been cut back. Oran cleared away some of the remaining debris. "Let's sit here."

Naojirō was delighted. She was treating him almost like a brother.

"Come over and sit down," she urged, making room for him in the clearing.

"That's all right. I'll sit over here," he said, squatting amid the withered grass.

"So you lost both parents early, too?" she asked him. "I don't even know what my mother looked like. My father raised me by himself. I miss him so much. It's bad enough ordinarily, but on days like this—I wish I could find some distraction, some way to forget. You probably have the same memories."

"Yes, I do." The boy's eyes glistened. "How many years ago did you lose your father? Your parents must have been young."

"No, they weren't so young. My father died eight years ago. It was a parting like something in a nightmare."

"From a sudden illness?" The boy kept pressing for details.

"Illness? No. My father drowned in this pond."

Naojirō turned white with surprise and looked away.

With her cool eyes, Oran seemed to be smiling. She had no idea how the nun felt when she took her grandson, the Emperor Antoku, with her to the bottom of the sea,[15] but she knew that her father had had enough of the sadness of living, and had sought a quiet place to sleep. Waves might disturb the surface, but, when one thought about it, the depths of the water were at peace. There, at the bottom of the pond, was a better refuge from the world than any mountain hut or cabin by the sea.

Silently Oran stared at the ripples on the pond, gathering momentum as a wind came up through the pines. It sounded in the tops of the trees and made the grasses stir, but Oran did not attempt to leave.

"Naojirō, why are you so quiet about yourself? Don't make me do all the talking. It's your turn to tell me something."

The boy felt words stick in his throat. He looked down into the grass.

"That won't do at all," Oran laughed at him. "Don't be like a girl."

It scared him that he should still feel such emotion. Was she laughing because he showed this on his face? He was a sissy next to her. It didn't upset her in the least to go on and on telling him about these things, while it sent a chill through him just to hear her story. He couldn't speak, and he tried to keep her from seeing his discomfort. Was he imagining it? Surely the color had gone out of his face.

"I suppose such talk is not for others' ears," she sighed. "Telling everything one knows may be the usual way, but I'm sorry I mentioned these things. I don't have to say it, I suppose; I guess you find it repellent to talk about your family, too. I won't say anything more." Her coloring had changed.

"No, it's natural that you want to talk about your father. Don't be upset."

She had spoken to him with the frankness of an old friend. "I'm a little embarrassed all the same; please forget what I've told you," she said as she stood up to leave. "Let's be going now."

"I'll carry the flowers for you."

"No. That's all right. Give me your hand instead."

They started back along the same path. Her white hand held Naojirō's shoulder. He looked slight of build, but she recognized that he was, after all a tall young man.

"How old are you, Naojirō? Nineteen, twenty? You're young enough to be my younger brother. How old do you think I am?"

"I don't know—one or two years older?"

"Hardly. I'm twenty-five. I'll be thirty soon, and then it's all downhill."

"Really? You look younger."

"Is that a compliment, or are you making fun of me?" Her face flushed as she walked along.

If a woman is gentle and submissive, one need ask for nothing more.[16] If she has some gifts and develops them, all the better. But there are those who, faced with adversity and standing at a fork in the road, are resolute and fan the flames of their problems until they spread in directions that were previously safe. Even if Buddha or Confucius were to take her hand and offer her advice, "Save your lectures," she would say, "I'm not interested." She would turn away and hide her tears. This, truly, is someone who is headstrong.

When a woman is blessed not only with a pretty face but also with a lovely bearing and a gentle education, once she has found a husband she cannot be faulted on any grounds. She seems flawless, complete.

But how fragile good fortune is! Oran had come so close to this perfection. Her father, all that she had left in life, had died. It would have been bad enough had he succumbed in due course to an illness, after nursing and medicine had done all they could and his allotted time was up. But such was not the case. The charges of speculation and shady business deals lingered long after they had prompted him to act. Oran herself did not accept the accusations, and when she tried to reckon with whatever offense had led her father to his suicide, she found it hard to believe that heaven made no distinction between right and wrong. The one who had committed a crime was not her father, but the unctuous gentleman with his fancy clothes and his neat little beard. Her father had been only his assistant. Her father was the one who had had to run ahead and clear the path. He was the one to be sacrificed, like the taster swallowing the poison, while his master survived to sleep on soft pillows and dream of flowers on a spring night. At the very least, he might have felt compassion for the daughter of the man he was indebted to. But now when he passed her gate, he was loath to stop for fear of rumors. Disgusting, indeed, is the human heart!

Oran was adrift on a wild stream.[17] In her young woman's heart, sadness and fear and bitterness mingled. But she was her father's child, she told herself, and she had to do something. If it seemed evil, so be it. Her character had never been a virtuous one, in any case. She must be sure to look calm, at peace on the surface, while she went about seeking revenge. She was ready to accept the consequences. Her father summoned her from the afterworld. Never mind if it was not the highest realm of paradise;[18] she could find a home in hell. Oran vowed to carry out her dreams. She was not acting on a whim. She would often force a smile when in fact she felt like crying, and she would look up toward the eaves to disguise her emotions. She felt the pain of sadness, but her actions belied it skillfully. There was a sorrow there that people did not see.

Love was something she did not believe in. One hides one's feelings for a man, but eventually they come out as clearly as the random patterns on a cloth. And then, there are the barriers that keep the two apart. One suffers waiting for a man who does not come. It is not a pleasant thing, love.[19]

Hooking up with Namizaki had proved as painful for Oran and her father as being caught is for a fish. Relations between the men were based solely on money. But she had been sincere in her feelings for Namizaki, though in the end he ignored her. She felt like a single piece of thread, unwound and discarded.[20]

Namizaki Tadayou. A handsome man he was, and a member of the Lower House of the Diet. He lived over in Banchō, and his name was often heard these days. He came from a prefecture not far away, but no rumors had circulated to mar his chances of election. His secrets had been kept between himself and Matsukawa. One did wonder, though, where half his present fortune came from.

When a man is active in the world he has many acquaintances, and rumor had it that her father had an excellent husband in mind for Oran. Then clouds appeared and evening fell on the hibiscus tree.[21] Namizaki had said he would marry her. After matters had proceeded that far, he went abroad. The months passed, and by the time he returned her father was dead. Today Namizaki was a man of influence. He had cleared away the clutter of his former life. But perhaps she ought to fish it out again—the promise he had made.

The halls of government and administration were things she knew nothing of. Yet Oran could well imagine that Namizaki's recent marriage into the aristocracy had helped him get ahead, along with his talent for rhetoric. Indeed, she herself had fallen prey to his palaver. Regrettably, until the autumn of her twenty-fifth year, she had been living in a dream. For whose sake had she remained chaste? Her fidelity was worth no more than the color of the evergreen when there is no one in winter to appreciate it.

She had contemplated her position, and she could not see doing any of the usual things. She was not about to abandon the world for the dark robes of a nun, off somewhere in the fields of Saga,[22] tamely viewing the autumn scenery while she nursed a grudge against her former love and read the sutras out of some half-baked belief in enlightenment.

If she were going to engage in anything so extreme, she wanted to show the world, to do something she would be remembered for. If she could not have the repute of a thousand years, she would settle for a moment's glory, even if it meant difficulties later. Oran herself was startled to acknowledge how much of the demon she had in her, but she was prepared to accept it as her true nature.

The notion that life can be lived without rancor or regret is an illusion only love leads us to believe. How frightening is the mind of a woman with a broken heart!

Winds rustled the reeds as summer yielded to fall. Nothing had changed at the Matsukawa house, except for Naojirō's decision: he was giving up his ambition to become a doctor.

Before, he had always been determined; he was ready, he believed, for the most arduous tasks in order to attain his goals.[23] With his mind made up, nothing was beyond his reach. He was a man, and when he said he would do something he did not go back on his word. Until now he had been despised by every good-for-nothing in every village where he had lived, and, lately, even by Sasuke and his wife. They took him for a fool and told him he could never be a doctor. But he would show them. If he didn't, he could hardly claim to be a man. Did they think he had no backbone?

Whenever he got onto the subject, the veins stood out on his temple and he pounded his fist.

"You don't know yourself," Sasuke told him scornfully. "Becoming a doctor and planting potatoes are two different things. Give up these plans of yours—they'll never come to anything."

Oran, who felt sorry for the boy, was a more sympathetic audience: "If you have your heart set on it, it's not impossible, I suppose. Remember, though, the competition is severe, Naojirō. Failure is quite common. There are so many people in the world, and, my goodness, more every year. Not to mention the tuition. Where will that come from? You say your mind's made up, but I wonder if resolution alone is enough. Your good qualities—your earnestness and your integrity—I'm afraid aren't worth much in today's world. Things don't always go smoothly. Success is not automatic. If you keep that in mind, and if you still go ahead and accomplish your goals, why, it would be wonderful, of course. But I can't help worrying about all the difficulties."

Ever since he left home, he had been running blindly, never looking back.

How could he recant his vow to be a doctor? But he had stumbled through life, he was menaced and rebuffed. And then he was hit by the rickshaw. From one misstep he had sustained an injury that might well deform him for life.

His benefactor, too, suffered in this same floating world, in the same autumn wind. The gate and walls around her house were crumbling. She lived hidden like a jewel buried in the dust. She looked perpetually sad. And so Naojirō began to have his doubts. Perhaps heaven did not, in fact, look out for the good.

No one in his family—not his father nor his mother nor himself—had ever even harmed the smallest insect. When he saw a starving puppy, he was always ready to share his food. He had not expected, then, that he would go through life creating enemies, hated by others, without a place to live. But he would not grovel to achieve his goals. Trailing around like a dog on the muddy heels of some patron did not appeal to him. It would be sleazy to rise in the world that way and then assume the air of the benevolent healer. He would give it up, this dream of his. He would not become a doctor after all. He'd sooner live like a monkey, with no skills to depend upon, than compromise his own integrity. Once he had given up his hopes, he would never mention them again.

But it meant that he had nowhere to go. The world was his enemy. Without a dream to sustain him, what was he to do? There was only Oran to turn to. And her fences were in ruin. The autumn grasses ran wild in her yard. Her garden resembled an open field. She was a wild flower[24] damaged by the storm, with a pitiful enough future herself.

He had always been a simpleton. Oran, however, was another story. She was a woman, and yet she had incredible will. No doubt there were not many people as cowardly as he, but Oran had enormous strength. Nevertheless, she was isolated from the rest of the world. She had no one to depend upon. A single pillar could not support an entire house.[25] Sasuke and Osoyo were completely dedicated to Oran, but, in Naojirō's eyes, they alone could not save her. In a strong wind this flower of theirs was defenseless; the petals would scatter.

The couple had been serving Oran's family through several generations. How many years, then, must they have known the young woman's kindness? By comparison, Naojirō's debt to Oran dated from only yesterday. But he was ready to lay down his life for her. If it sounded like big talk, he meant it. When he thought about all the uncertainties in life, he would gladly let Oran's wishes determine his fate. He had not yet pledged his loyalty to her,[26] but his intentions were apparent in his face.

People react strangely to things. The fonder Naojirō became of Oran, the cooler Sasuke and Osoyo grew. Their kindness to him when he was wounded—before they even knew him—had been totally sincere; there was no reason why it should have disappeared. But Oran came first. And Oran came second. In their eyes, anyone who interfered as Naojirō had done was a dolt who didn't know what's what. Even Sasuke himself, who had held Oran in his arms when she was just a baby, never forced his opinions on her. He kept half his thoughts to himself. Oran's wish was law. This was as it should be. But a boy without a home falls down, receives aid, and does not know gratitude. He starts acting like the young lady's brother! It was detestable. The only thing to do with someone like that was to look him in the eye and set him straight. Sasuke didn't hesitate to do so.

The upshot was frequent bickering. One would have thought Sasuke too old for such a thing; it troubled Oran, and for the life of her she could not decide who fared better in the arguments.

In autumn, the last glow of sun sinks into the dusk, and crows returning to their nest give out a plaintive cry.[27]

A messenger in dark livery arrived with a letter box from Namizaki. It was a rare occurrence.

Oran sat watching the sun's parting rays reflected on chrysanthemums along the bamboo fence. Suddenly Osoyo came running in. "Oran, you have a letter!"

"What a surprise! 'Then they are not the sleeves of my beloved,'" she said ironically, reminded of the poem, 'these white chrysanthemums before me.'"[28] She took the letter from Osoyo and went into her sitting room.

The letter was lengthy and infuriating: he began without so much as an apology for the long absence.

All kinds of things had kept him busy, he said. Yet he often thought of her. He was like a little boat just trying to navigate among the reeds that overran his life these days. But tonight, at last, he was free, and by himself at the pied-à-terre he kept in Somei. She would know why he was there. No one would trouble them. He had things he wanted to tell her. There were too many eyes watching at her place, too many noses sniffing around. He had sent his rickshaw for her.

The man hadn't lost his way with words, Oran mused as she showed the letter to Osoyo. Nor had he lost his talent with the brush. In the old days, a letter like this in his pale and elegant hand would have sent Oran into paroxysms of delight. Tonight she had her guard up.

"Well, you can be carefree about it, miss. But I can tell by reading this, that's not how he feels. It's obvious how eager he is to see you again, after all this time. Hurry up—I'll help you get ready. His man is waiting."

"Do you mean you think I should go? Oh, you are naive," Oran smiled.

There was a time when she had been bewitched by his letters. If he hoped that it would happen again, however, he was living in the past. The Oran of today had put away her girlishness. She was wise to the old tricks. Shyness was not what kept her from visiting him tonight. Oh yes, she knew it was common practice for a man to stop seeing a woman suddenly, contemptible as it might be. She was resigned to that. But she would not reconcile herself to his arrogance. He was too smug about his rise in the world. He was trifling with her. She had to live with her father's bad name, but she had no need of a jester's reputation.

He said they had to be discreet, but that was only his excuse. Why couldn't they have met on dark nights? When a man loves a woman, he will travel a thousand miles barefooted to be with her. She didn't have to read the newspapers to know how many nights a month he spent at the house in Somei—a stone's throw away from here. If anything, he went out of his way to avoid her. When he had to pass her gate, his rickshaw went faster. She pitied him, if the prospect of meeting a young woman could cause him so much anxiety. It would seem she had restricted his little universe.

But she saw through him now. The invitation was a ploy to relieve his conscience, to undo the fetters hampering his movement, to expand his world again. He wanted to deceive her and hear her say once more how she loved him. He would tell her not to worry. If he couldn't take her for his lawful wife in this world, they would be together in the next. He wanted her to live quietly in the shadows. Then he would be at ease again. Oh, she knew him well. Indeed, he must be worrying a great deal. How could she have caused him all this apprehension? They were not two people from the same back alley who had tired of each other and had nowhere to retreat. They had positions in society, after all, and they ought to refrain from acting disgracefully. For her part, she would keep her bitterness to herself. In her heart of hearts, she smiled with indifference to the man.

In reply to the letter, Oran complained of a cold and a lamentable appearance. She begged pardon, but in her present dishevelment she could not bring herself to call on someone so important. On the surface, then, it was a gracious letter, and she sent it off with his messenger.

The rickshaw Namizaki had dispatched for her pulled away from the front gate. On the messenger's coat was the same arrowhead crest that Naojirō had seen on the rickshaw lantern the night he was run down. Could it be the same carriage? The man's arrival had piqued Naojirō's curiosity, since Oran so seldom had a visitor. He kept his eyes on the messenger as the fellow waited for Oran's reply. And then, suddenly, the man turned to leave. On the back of his jacket was the same mark: the arrowhead crest.

"Who was that?" Naojirō asked Sasuke.

"You're full of questions, aren't you? Just a messenger—they do come now and then, you know."

The chilly answer left Naojirō without a rejoinder. Sasuke might at least have told him where the man was from, there was no harm in that. He was not trying to start a fight. Naojirō began to leave the room when Sasuke said more:

"What good would it do you to know? It's Oran's letter, so you'd have to ask her what it's all about. I guess I can tell you who the man was, though. He works for Namizaki, the Diet member you read about in the papers."

"Is he a relative of hers? I've never seen him visit. Or maybe he used to come before I was here?"

"Nosy, aren't you? What are you asking all the questions for?" Sasuke was laughing at him.

"Nothing. I was just curious. The messenger had the same crest on his jacket that I saw on the lantern of the rickshaw the night I was hit."

"So what do you want to do? Cut off his little finger? Like to get even, eh? I'll bet you were a snake in the last life. I have to hand it to you, though. You don't forget. You're dependable. The man who forgets the wrongs people do him is the same kind to forget a debt of gratitude. Yes, I have to admire you for that." Sasuke was often irritated with Naojirō and said things that he later regretted. But now he had spoken from the heart.

Naojirō was for once speechless.

The day's developments weighing on his mind, the boy went to visit Oran's rooms that night. Sasuke listened from outside, and he heard things he had never expected. With his head nestled in her lap, tearfully Naojirō confessed his feelings to Oran. The two of them consoled each other, while, behind the door, Sasuke could just make out the young man's shadow.

A poem with feeling and taste can still want for a true expression of the heart. Where does it go, youthful sincerity? We seem to take it for the mark of a fool.

The night had worn on. Oran was sitting by her lamp when Naojirō surprised her. She could tell he had been crying, as he bowed down before her with a great show of respect. It was no casual visit he was paying.

"What's all this about?" she asked impatiently. "Don't be so formal. What's troubling you?"

Her words only elicited fresh tears from the boy. He took a deep breath. "I'm going to be leaving you."

Oran was completely startled. "Why? Did you have a fight with Sasuke? I know he's stubborn and his complaints get on your nerves, Naojirō, but he means well. You shouldn't let it bother you so much. He's always upset about something."

"No, it's not that. He didn't say anything. And the fights—I'm used to

them. I just don't have anything to look forward to in life. I'm tired of living."
He bowed low again and wept.

"What are you saying?" Oran sat up straight. "That you want to die?"

"You don't think I'd joke about it, do you? I keep thinking about what you told me in the garden that day. About your father drowning in the pond. You said it was the only quiet place, away from the world. Well, I'm someone who's never had any peace of mind, any quiet. Ever since I was born I've been unhappy and unlucky. I'm tired of it. What's the point? I can't hope to repay you. You've been so kind to me, Oran, for months now. I owe you everything, the way you've taken care of me. It's been wonderful for me. It's the first time I've really been a part of the world—and the last. I feel as if I've seen enlightenment, all of a sudden, and I can't take this world any longer. You're the only one I'll miss. You've done so much for me. I couldn't leave without thanking you. There are so many things I wish I could say . . . I can't put them into words. I hope you have a long and happy life, Oran; I hope you get everything you want. Me, I was born a fool. I guess I was never meant to spend life with someone as fine as you are. I'll look out for you, though, when I go to the next world."

His words were choked with tears. "You see, I couldn't live without your affection, Oran. I feel more dependent on you all the time. If I could be content just to see you and hear your voice—but I can't any more. I have feelings I don't even understand myself. It's as if there were a fire in my heart. I sometimes wonder where these embarrassing thoughts of mine come from. Now I think I understand. Tonight, when I found out whose messenger that was, I knew I wanted to die.[29] It's uppity of me to say it, but I was jealous. I felt hatred as I watched him. And, to make it worse, he had the arrowhead crest on his jacket—the one I wish I'd never seen. I was almost crazy that night it happened, but I do remember, just for a second, seeing the man with the little beard riding in the rickshaw that hit me. Now I know his name. Namizaki. I hear he's a member of the Diet. He must be important. But that's not how I think of him. He's a good-for-nothing, as far as I'm concerned. My mind keeps coming back to what he did that night. Nothing would make me forget. I hate him, and yet he's the man you're in love with! I guess that makes us enemies. I don't know what to do. It frightens me. I want to kill myself. But I don't want to cause *you* any grief.

"If by some chance I'm wrong—I mean, if there's no connection between the man who hit me and the man who sent the letter tonight—it doesn't really make any difference. It only shows how depraved I am. My suspicions come from bad thoughts. I could do terrible things, Oran. Even if I hide how I feel, in my heart I follow you everywhere. The shame of it! I'll go to hell,[30] and that soft voice of yours will be there with the flames to torture me. I'm alone . . . When I think of all the changes that have come over me, I feel like a different person. I don't know myself what awful things I might do. I'm going to die without repaying any of your kindness. At least I won't be causing you any more trouble. You probably loathe me. After I'm gone, do you think you could find it in your heart to pray for me?"

His voice quavered and tears welled in his eyes as he knelt before her.

Who was it who said love is a transitory thing? Who said there is no fidelity?

Oran was abashed to look back on the life she had led until yesterday. Had Naojirō really been so in love with her? She'd felt sympathy toward him, yes, but she had never expected he would want to give up his life for her. Only now did she begin to appreciate him. No one had ever expressed his love with such sincerity. No one had ever offered to sacrifice his life. In the past, what had captivated her childish heart had always been the externals: a handsome face, a clever mind, things as temporary as a spring breeze. And so she had fallen in love with Namizaki. She did not like the thought of being inconstant, but certainly she was not the one who had been unfaithful. Namizaki had dropped her like a fan he didn't need when fall came, a remnant of summer forgotten in the autumn wind.[31]

"I'll tell you something, Naojirō. I know it's stupid for a woman to hold a grudge against a man who abandons her. But life has made sport of me. I feel as if some wicked god has taken over my heart. I can't hold my head up in front of you. I'm on the road to evil. You must detest me. Don't you find it frightening? If you don't, and if you're not afraid of devils, then consider me your wife. From tonight on, you will be my husband.

"Oh—and yet you're right to give up the world, Naojirō. Some day I'll do the same. There have been times when I've known happiness. What are they, though, compared to all the sadness? This world! I tell you, it's a gathering of the damned.

"Naojirō, listen—if you're truly fond of me, perhaps there is something you could do.[32] What I'm going to ask may sound unkind, or cold-hearted. Between casual acquaintances, such things could never be said, but you and I are different. I understand now completely how you feel. You must imagine how painful it is for me to make this terrible request.

"The man who wrote me tonight—I was once in love with him. Not any more, though: he's my enemy. He's the one responsible for this shackled life I live. I'll be bound to him until these ties are cut. I don't know—maybe this too is part of being in love. All I know is that I hate him now. The resentment I have against him is with me day and night. I'd like to kill him with these two hands of mine. But I can't. Put yourself in my position. Unfortunately, I have to take care of things for my father. God knows, it's not from any desire on my part. There are the instructions in his will to be carried out, you see. But you—if you're going to take your life anyway—you could do it in my place. Why don't you wait for a chance on a dark night and do the killing for me? It doesn't matter how you do it. Ah! When did I turn into such a witch? If only I could die, I would!" She was a woman who never cried, but now there were dewlike tears on her sleeve.

"The arrowhead crest you hate so much—I'm sure it belonged to Namizaki. He would have been on his way that night to the house he keeps in Somei. And he wouldn't want anyone to know about the accident. Especially since it happened in front of where *I* live. That's why he fled like lightning.[33] Yes, I'm sure it was Namizaki. In a way, it was my fault, since he was trying to avoid me. When you think of it, I'm the one to blame for all this. I haven't really rescued you; I've led you down the road to death. Now everything depends on your pledge. Give your life for me, Naojirō! At least kill Namizaki. With luck," she whispered, "you can escape. But be sure to wait till dark before you come back. We don't want anyone to see you. Once you're in here again you're safe. There's no one here. No one ever visits, not even stray dogs. A woman living alone like me—the police will never suspect. So you must try to escape."

Naojirō had listened speechlessly. "I understand. You don't need to say any more. I never expected to hear this from you. I didn't intend to live out the night. It never occurred to me that in dying I could answer your prayers. I'll show you I can do it! I've never completed anything before. I've been the model of a coward. But this time I will! My heart's set on it! I'm ready to give up my life. So long as *you* at least think I'm brave, then I'll be happy. Even if he gets me instead, or the police take me and hang me, I'll have no regrets. The only thing I regret is your telling me to escape. You shouldn't have said that, Oran. I'll never succeed with one eye on my getaway. It's cowardly. I'm not a clever man. I don't know any tricks. If my heart is undecided, when the time comes, your advice will only make me hesitate and keep me from concentrating on what I've got to do. I'll be too concerned about making my escape. Talk like that will spoil the purity of the whole mission. Let him kill me—that will be the end of it. If I do kill him, and live to be captured, I won't mention your name, ever. Don't worry. It'll be my crime alone. There's only one chance in ten thousand that the gods will protect me and bring me back to you. We won't see each other again. If I'm caught, I couldn't stand to let the blame fall on you. So don't expect to see me again. We can't associate. Pretend I'm already dead. Listen for rumors if you want to find out what happens. This is the end. I'm ready to die like a man."

He was resolute. There were no tears, but as he left his shadow fell somberly against the sliding door.

It was not a night Oran would soon forget.

That night Naojirō left the Matsukawa house under cover of darkness.

The next morning Sasuke and Osoyo seemed startled to find him gone. There had been arguments and complaints, but Osoyo had never imagined he might up and leave them. Each morning she would pray to the different gods for Naojirō's safety. The months passed, and winter came.

One day there was an incident in front of Namizaki's house in Banchō. The distinguished parliamentarian was returning in a drunken, sleepy state from an important political rally. It was a meeting he had organized. He had been among the speakers, and the applause was still ringing in his ears. As his rickshaw drew up to the front gate, a man leapt out of nowhere and grabbed the hood of the carriage. It overturned, and the man seized hold of Namizaki, pinning him against the ground. He flashed a dagger and made as if to slit his victim's throat. But perhaps the blade was dull. It grazed Namizaki's cheek, leaving only a superficial cut. "That'll do you for now!" the man yelled savagely and was gone. Namizaki had no idea where he fled, who he was.

There were headlines in the morning paper. A suspect was apprehended, a roughneck member of a rival faction, but eventually he was released for lack of evidence. The assailant was never found.

In a month all talk of the incident died down. Namizaki's wounds healed even faster, within two weeks. Regrettably, his reputation did not suffer. He flaunted his scar as if it were a battle wound.

Once again, Naojirō had failed in a world where others were more cunning. Once again, he was forced to hide in the shadows. How did he fare? His life was no doubt further circumscribed. Perhaps he found a river where he could drown himself. Perhaps he hid away somewhere in the mountains. Or perhaps this final failure forced him to become a new man.

But even stranger was the fate of the Matsukawa house. Within three months, the pavement round the front gate had been handsomely repaired. Each day gardeners and carpenters were busy there. It seemed that someone new was living in the house. And where were Sasuke, Osoyo, and Oran? It's a wide world, after all. These days the trains run everywhere.

On the Last Day of the Year
(Ōtsugomori, 1894)

Omine found that a servant's life was never easy. At the well, it took a long time to haul the bucket up. In the kitchen, on the north side, the winter wind whistled through the room. Yet, the way her mistress looked at things, a minute's warming by the fire was an hour's-worth of idleness.

How well Omine recalled the advice of the woman at the employment agency. There were six children in the family. Usually the only two at home were the eldest and the youngest. The mistress was strong-willed. Once she got used to the woman's glare, however, she would not find her so intimidating. And the woman was easily flattered. With that in mind, the girl would never want for a proper uniform, at any rate. They were the wealthiest family in the neighborhood, and also the tightest. Fortunately, the man of the house was less severe than his wife, and Omine was told she could hope for a little pocket money from the husband.

"If you don't like it there," the employment agent counseled, "just send me a note. You don't have to go into details. I'll see what I can do to help you find another house. I can tell you this, though—the secret of a servant's success lies in saying only what her mistress wants to hear. Even if the lady rants and raves, keep your feelings to yourself. Otherwise she'll have no use for you. So long as you work hard, there's no reason why you shouldn't suit her."

Three days after the end of Omine's trial period, the mistress was standing beside her bed, banging on the ash pot and yelling, "Wake up! Wake up!" (Who needed an alarm clock?) The woman's seven-year-old daughter had her dancing lesson in the afternoon, and there was the bath to be prepared, and this and that. "Come along! Come along!" Her bed felt so warm in the icy daybreak, but Omine arose without a murmur. With her sleeves pushed up and ready for work before her sash was even tied, she went off to the well for the bath water. The moon was still out. The cold wind stung her cheeks and drove away her drowsiness.

The wooden tub was not enormous. Still, filling it took Omine thirteen trips to the well and back. As she struggled along with a bucketful in each hand, her sandal strap came loose. She was unsure of her footing; the heavy load made things worse. She lost her step and slipped on the ice. Before she

205

could let out a scream, she fell and bumped her leg against the well. The buckets went flying, and one of them rolled into the well. Her skin, so white it put the snow to shame, was black-and-blue.

At the breakfast table her mistress glared at her as if the loss of a bucket had forever diminished the family treasures. The veins along the woman's temple were a frightening sight. All day she said nothing, but the next day whenever Omine lifted a chopstick the mistress would berate her. "Nothing in this house came free, you know. If you don't start taking better care of things, you'll pay dearly." Soon it was her standard refrain, repeated for the benefit of every visitor. Young Omine was humiliated. She became meticulous in every task she undertook.

There were many families that employed a serving girl; none, however, had the turnover the Yamamuras did. Two girls a month was nothing: some lasted three or four days, some fled after a night. Ask the woman how many maids they had hired since the Creation, and she'd wear her sleeves away trying to count them on her fingers.[1] In this light, Omine appeared long-suffering, for she took the abuse heaped upon her as heaven's punishment. Even in a city the size of Tokyo, it seemed there was no one willing to serve the Yamamuras any more. Omine, then, was to be lauded for her determination. Nothing wrong with the way the girl looked, either—men were quick to add.

In the fall her only uncle had taken sick. He was forced to close his vegetable shop on the main street and move to cheaper lodgings in the alley. Unfortunately, Omine could not return to look after him. Her salary had been paid in advance, and she might as well have been in bondage. It wasn't of her own volition that she kept away. If she went on an errand, her mistress all but clocked her. So many minutes, so many steps. How, then, could she sneak a visit home? Bad news traveled fast. The woman would know about it before Omine could return. It wouldn't do to risk being fired; her perseverance would be for naught, only adding to her uncle's worries. And she did not want to burden his poor household any longer, not even for a day. Letters, then, would have to suffice. Though she lived with the Yamamuras, her heart was with her uncle.

What a busy time December is: new clothes to be made for the holidays, new plays opening with a cast of all one's favorites. The daughters of the Yamamura house couldn't stand the thought of missing any of it. After much commotion, they persuaded their father to let them have their way. A theater party was arranged for the fifteenth, and, most unusual, notice of the coming event went round to every member of the house. In ordinary times, how delighted Omine would have been at the prospect of a trip to the theater. But now she felt a little guilty. She had not seen her uncle since he had taken sick, and he was, after all, like a father to her. If it put her mistress out, it was still worth venturing a request to spend the day with her family instead.

True enough, the woman conceded, Omine had gone without a holiday for quite a while. All right, tomorrow she could go, but she would have to promise to return promptly. Omine was much obliged. Soon, she found herself riding in a rickshaw bound for Koishikawa, and wondering what on earth was taking so long.

That the section of town where her uncle lived should be called "First Song" was indeed amusing. It was the poor part of the city. Here pleasures were as scarce as the warbler's first song of the new year.[2] They came to Tamachi and Chrysanthemum Hill, where her uncle used to sell his radishes and eggplant. Honest Yasubei, everybody called him. He was a landmark around here, with his bald head shining like a copper kettle, big enough to house all the gods of integrity.[3] Somehow Yasubei always seemed to lack the capital for laying in a proper stock. People would tease him for never offering any of the delicacies, or the first pick of the season—the baby cucumbers in their "little-boat" wrappers, the early mushrooms tied into a bunch with straw. Instead one could count on vegetables that were cheap and distinguished only for their bulk. Let them joke; he was always grateful for their patronage. It wasn't easy, but he managed to feed a wife and child. His boy Sannosuke had turned eight that year. Yasubei was seeing to it that his son received the compulsory education. Tuition was only five *rin*[4] a month, and even that seemed hard to come by.

But at the end of September, Yasubei had awakened one morning with a cold. On his way back from the central market in Kanda, his fever increased and he began to feel the first pains of palsy. It had gone on for three months now, and needless to say it had kept his business closed. Every day there was less to eat. Finally he had to sell the pole he used to carry vegetables. They had left the shop on the main street and moved to a place in the alley where the rent was only fifty *sen*.[5] Here, at least, there was no need to worry what the neighbors thought. And if he ever got better, perhaps they could afford to move back. It had not been easy coming here—a sick man like him carrying their belongings, such as they were. (Everything they owned could almost fit into one hand.) Now they lived hidden in a dark corner of the poorest part of town.

Omine left the rickshaw and began to look for signs of her family. Perhaps Sannosuke would be over there, at the candy store, where the group of children were playing. Kites and paper sailing ships swung from the eaves of the shop. She didn't see him, though, and gazed absent-mindedly at passersby. On the other side of the street was the scrawny figure of a child carrying a bottle of medicine. He was taller than Sannosuke and he looked too thin to be her cousin. And yet he did resemble him. She ran toward him for a closer look.

"Omine!"

"Sannosuke—it *is* you! How lucky!"

They set off together for her uncle's house, past the saké shop and the potato stand, farther into murky alleyways, over planks covering ditches in the road.

Sannosuke ran ahead. "Father! Mother! Omine's back!"

"Omine!" Yasubei sat up in bed.

Her aunt dropped the sewing she took in for extra money. "What a surprise!" she clasped the girl's hand for joy.

Omine looked around her. There was one room of six mats and one closet.[6] It was not a house that required much furniture. She did not even see the long brazier they had always had; instead there was a cheap-looking square one. What furnishings there were seemed to have come with the house. The place lacked so much as a chest to keep the rice in, her aunt told her, although, in fact, these days there was no rice anyway.[7] What a pass things had come to! Omine could not help remembering that on this same day others were enjoying the theater. Her eyes glistened.

"Uncle Yasubei, you must get your rest." She pulled the blanket up around him. It was as thin as a salted cracker. "How you've suffered! And Auntie, you've lost weight. You mustn't worry so much. Uncle Yasubei is getting better, isn't he? I had to come and see for myself. I've waited a long time for this day off. What? No, I don't care what the Yamamuras think. The important thing is for him to get well as soon as possible. Then you can move back to the main street. I know I should have brought you something, Uncle Yasubei, but it was such a long way, and I was impatient to get here. The driver was the slowest thing I've ever seen. And I didn't know where to find a pastry shop.[8] It's not much, but here's some extra money I earned from a relative of the Yamamuras. She lives in Kōjimachi. The old woman had stomach pains, and I stayed up all night massaging her. She gave me this and told me to buy an apron. The Yamamuras are pretty stingy, but luckily others have been good to me. So I'm glad for you to have it. Besides, the work isn't that hard. This purse and my neckpiece—they were gifts. I thought you might like the collar, Auntie. It's not too loud. And if you altered it a little, you could use the purse as a lunch bag for Sannosuke. You are going to school, aren't you, Sannosuke? Why don't you show me one of your compositions?" There was no dearth of things Omine had to say.

Her father had died when she was seven, while he was working on the construction of a storehouse. With his trowel in hand, he had climbed the scaffolding to give the building its second coat of plaster. When he turned around to talk to one of the men below, just then—it must have been a black-star day in the almanac, perhaps the anniversary of Buddha's death— he lost his footing in spite of years of experience, and he fell and fell toward the ground. The pavement had been torn up for the construction, and he hit his head against a pile of jagged stones. Nothing could be done. He had just been approaching that climacteric forty-second year.[9] No wonder people dreaded it.

Her mother, Yasubei's sister, had come to live with him after her husband's death. Two years later, however, the woman caught a cold going round and died very suddenly. After that, Yasubei and his wife were like parents to Omine. Until today, in her eighteenth year, the debt of gratitude Omine felt was beyond putting into words. Sannosuke called her "sister" and she loved him like a brother.

"Come here, Sannosuke." She gave her little cousin a smile and a love-pat. "It must be pretty lonely. I'll bet it's hard for you with your father sick. Would you like me to buy you something for New Year's? I don't want you bothering your mother for things."

"Bother? Omine—he's been a real help to us," her uncle said. "He's only eight, you know, but he's a strong boy. Ever since I've been sick, I haven't been able to earn a thing, and our expenses have been climbing. You can guess how difficult things are for us. But Sannosuke's been working with the fish dealer over on the main street. Why, he goes with Yarō to buy shellfish and keeps right up with him on the rounds. When Yarō sells fish for eight sen, Sannosuke can sell it for ten. The gods know what a wonderful son he is! It's Sannosuke that's paying for my medicine. You ought to praise him, Omine." Her uncle put his head beneath the covers to stifle the emotion in his voice.

"And he's good in school, too," her aunt was quick to add. "We never have to coax him. After breakfast, he's off to school in the morning like an arrow, and he comes straight home at three. He never stops to play. I'm not boasting, either—you should hear his teachers praise him! Just imagine how we feel, then," she said with tears in her eyes. "It's because we're poor that he has to trudge around in straw sandals, with a basketful of shellfish. And in this kind of weather!"

Omine hugged her cousin. "There aren't many boys like you, Sannosuke. Even if you are big for your age, you're still only eight. Doesn't that pole for carrying the fish hurt your shoulders? And I'll bet you get plenty of blisters, wearing straw sandals all the time. Just be patient a little longer. I'll come home to take care of Uncle Yasubei. I'll help you. I wasn't aware how bad things are. How could I have felt sorry for myself working at the Yamamuras'? What's a cold trip to the well compared to what you have to do! I don't know why I should have it so easy while you're out selling fish. Just at the age when you ought to be concentrating on your school work. Uncle Yasubei," Omine began to cry, "I want to quit my position."

Sannosuke, too, felt like crying. He looked down at the floor. The seam of his jacket was torn along the shoulder. It was a sad sight, this blunt reminder of the load he carried every day.

Her uncle would hear nothing of Omine's plans to quit. "I know you mean well, and it makes me happy. But what kind of money could you earn back here? You're a woman. Besides, we have the advance from the Yamamuras. No, it won't do. It's your first position, and it's very important. What if people thought you couldn't take it? No. You've got to do your best. I won't be sick forever. Once I get a little better, I'll be able to go back to work myself. The year's almost over. Spring will be here in no time, and our luck will change.[10] We'll all just have to be patient." He had managed to bring his emotions under control. "For such a special visitor I wish we had more to offer. We do have the muffins and the taro that you like.[11] Have all you want." To extend even this little hospitality seemed to raise her uncle's spirits.

But soon he was glum again: "Omine, I never wanted to cause you any hardship. New Year's is coming, and all our troubles seem to be pressing in on us at once. It isn't only illness that's causing this pain in my chest. It's worry. You know, when I was laid up in September, I had to borrow money to keep going. From a loan shark in Tamachi—he gave me ten yen on a three-month loan. I paid him one-and-a-half yen advance interest and now I've got to repay the other eight-and-a-half by the end of the month. I don't know what I'm going to do. Your aunt and I have been beating our heads together. Oh, sure, she takes in sewing. But for all the blood the needle draws from her fingers, it doesn't amount to ten sen a day. I can hardly ask Sannosuke to do more.

"The man you're working for, though, Omine, he's a rich man. He must own a hundred houses in Shirokane that he rents. The family lives in luxury off those investments of his. I saw his place once, when I had business over there. I got as far as the front gate, and I could see the new storehouse they were putting up. Why, you couldn't build something like that for a thousand yen. He's a rich man! What I'd give for a fraction of his wealth! But listen, you've been working there for a year now. If a nice serving-girl like you—I'll bet he's fond of you—were to ask a little favor of him, how could he turn you down? If you went up to him with a sad face and told him your uncle had to extend the payments on a loan—if he would pay the one-and-a-half yen interest on the extension, I'd have another three months to pay back the principal. I may sound greedy, but that's not it at all. What good are we as parents if we can't even buy little Sannosuke some New Year's rice cakes?[12] It's not easy for me to ask you this, Omine, but we need the money by the thirty-first."

Omine reflected for a moment and then agreed. "All right. If I can't get a loan, I'll ask for an advance on my salary. Even at the Yamamuras' house they know what money problems are. It isn't a great sum, anyway. If that little bit will help you tide things over, I don't see how they can say no. But it won't do to have them mad at me for getting home late. I'd better go. The next time I get a chance to see you, it will probably be spring, when the days are longer. I hope we'll all be laughing, for a change. Leave everything to me. I'll send the money somehow. Or why don't you have Sannosuke come for it? Yes, if he could do that . . . If it weren't the holidays, I'd come myself, but I'm not going to have a minute to spare. I don't like to ask Sannosuke to come so far, but if he could . . . I'll have the money ready by noon on the thirty-first."

With promises made, Omine started back for the Yamamuras'.

Ishinosuke was the eldest son and original heir to the Yamamura house. His mother was dead, however, and his father's other children were by the second wife. To make matters worse, the man lost little love on Ishinosuke. For the past ten years, there had been talk of having him adopted into another family and naming a younger sister heir. The whole affair was a bit unseemly, and made one recognize anew how odd was the government's decision to outlaw disinheritance.[13]

The young man amused himself exactly as he pleased. He brought grief to his stepmother and ignored his father. Ever since fifteen, he had been up to no good. Although he lacked an actor's fair complexion, with his rugged good looks and his clever eyes, he was a handsome fellow. Little wonder there were rumors about the Yamamura boy and the daughters of the neighborhood. His wildest exploits, however, he saved for the quarters of the night. He was addicted to the houses in Shinagawa; fights would erupt on his midnight rounds in Shiba. "Buy us a drink, buy us a drink!" his sidekicks would demand, and when he treated he would empty his purse. The man's excesses defined the art of dissipation.

"Naming Ishinosuke heir is like setting fire to the oil in the storehouse," his stepmother would complain to her husband. "The whole estate will go up in smoke. What will the rest of us do? Have a little pity on your other children. And yet, I know—who would want to adopt him?"

By way of solution to this dilemma of theirs, Yamamura and his wife decided to put aside a certain amount of money and to set the boy up as a separate branch of the family. Ishinosuke paid no heed; he was not about to fall into the trap of being severed from the family wealth. In the end, he laid down his conditions: a settlement of ten thousand yen plus a monthly allowance, no interference in his visits to the pleasure quarters, and the promise that he would succeed to the house on his father's death, with all the deference that was due him. (In the future, when he decreed it was time to put up pine boughs in honor of the kitchen god, they had better well go up!) If all these requirements were satisfied, yes, of course he would agree to live away from home for now. He didn't much feel like working for the family anyway.

Everything he said was a provocation. "You can certainly afford to meet my terms. You own more houses than ever, and I know you make double what you did last year. Everybody says how rich you are—that's how I know these things. It's nonsense: who do you think's going to end up with your money? Fires start at home, you know, from oil in the nearest lamp. You might as well admit you've got an explosion on your hands—me! Sooner or later, I'll have all your money anyway. Then what a New Year's bash I'll throw for everyone!" He had already planned the feast he would spread for his ne'er-do-well friends in Shiba.

"Ishinosuke's home!" His sisters dreaded their elder brother, and treated him as gingerly as they would dress a boil. His word was law.

He collapsed beneath the kotatsu and demanded water for his hangover. When it came to being rude, Ishinosuke had no peer.

He would have to come! Mrs. Yamamura grumbled to herself. At times the duties of a mother were more than she had bargained for, but she concealed her poison tongue behind an imitation of maternal thoughtfulness. "Now, don't catch a cold, Ishinosuke. Here's a blanket and a pillow for you. I'll visit with you later. The fish for the holidays still has to be prepared. If I leave it for the maids, they won't do it properly. You should see the perfectly good pieces they throw away!" She made a point of stressing economy as she passed by the profligate's pillow.

It was almost noon already, and Omine was beginning to worry about her promise to her uncle. Time was running out. She could ill afford to wait for the mood of her mistress to improve. In her first free minute she took her kerchief off and went to Mrs. Yamamura.

"I know it's inconsiderate of me to bother you at such a busy time . . ." As she spoke, she rubbed her hands nervously. "But I wonder if you remember the request I made the other day? You know—the money? That I promised my uncle I'd try to find by noon today? If I could ask you for it—you don't know what it would mean to him. And to me. I'd never forget your kindness . . ."

The first time she had mentioned it to her mistress, the woman had hesitated with a vague "I suppose . . ." She hadn't said no, at any rate, and that was what Omine was counting on. For the time being, Omine had thought it best to leave things as they were. The woman's moods were changeable, and badgering her would have the opposite effect from what Omine wanted. Until today she had held her tongue, but now the deadline was approaching. This was the last day of the year; it would soon be noon. Had her mistress forgotten? Why hadn't she said anything? Omine had begun to feel edgy. It was hard for her to repeat her request, but—there—somehow she had done it.

The woman acted as if the matter were a surprise to her. "Well, yes. You did mention that, didn't you? About your uncle's being sick, and the money. But at a time like this![14] I certainly couldn't have promised you an advance.

You must have misunderstood me. No, I don't recall saying any such thing."
It was one of her usual tricks.[15] Mrs. Yamamura was the most cold-hearted
person she had ever met.

Omine could scarcely have timed things more awkwardly. The mistress
was anxious to see her daughters dressed in their holiday finery—the wonderful robes in patterns of cherry blossoms and falling leaves, the matching
collars, the new skirts. How she wanted to show them off! An impossibility
with Ishinosuke around. One look at them, and he would know his mother
was not practicing the frugality she preached. Why didn't he leave? Hurry up
and go! she wanted to say. It was all she could do to control her famous
temper. A learned monk might perhaps have perceived that she was enveloped in flames; her eyes were smoldering. The girl's financial problems
were the last thing she wanted to hear about.

As a tonic, Omine reflected, money could be lethal.

In fact, the woman did remember having led Omine to believe that a loan
would be forthcoming. But what was that to worry over? "You misunderstood," she cut the girl off, blithely blowing smoke rings in the air. Omine
did not exist.

As if it were a great sum! Omine told herself. Two yen! And, besides, she
had already agreed to it. Had the woman gone daft in a mere ten days?
Suddenly, Omine remembered the writing chest. The Yamamuras always
kept money in it. An untouched packet would have ten or twenty yen; all she
needed was two. And her uncle would be overjoyed. Her aunt would smile.
Sannosuke would have his New Year's treats. The thought of it made her
recognize anew the importance of money. She was filled with loathing for
her mistress; she felt mortified and speechless at the woman's cruelty. For
once Omine was not her docile self. She was convinced of the justness of her
cause. She stood ready to act as she saw fit, even if her heart was heavy. The
cannon boomed, it was twelve o'clock noon. The sound reverberated in her
heart.

"Mother, please come at once." It was a message from the mistress's
daughter. She had gone into labor that very morning, and the birth of her
first child was imminent. The girl's husband was too excited to be of any use.
Worse, there was no one older and experienced to supervise the delivery.
According to the messenger, the pandemonium was beyond describing.
"Please hurry," the girl entreated. In the first birth every minute counts. The
rickshaw was waiting to take her to her daughter's house in Saiōji. It was the
day before the New Year—no time to dawdle. Yet she was leaving money in
the house, and her good-for-nothing stepson was still there sleeping. It gave
her pause. She could not be in two places, and her concern for her daughter
won out. She boarded the rickshaw and sped off, furious at her husband. He
was so relaxed about everything. Today of all days he was off fishing! A
thoroughly undependable man.

Sannosuke passed the mistress as she left. After asking several times along the way, he had at last found the house. Now he could understand what it must be like for Omine, how shabby she must feel in such surroundings. Timidly he peeked in through the kitchen door.

"Who's there?" Omine had been crying by the hearth, and she tried to hide her tears. Sannosuke! She was too upset to greet him. What was she to do?

"Omine, they won't scold me if I come in, will they? Did you get the money? Father told me to be sure to thank the Yamamuras." His beaming face knew nothing of the circumstances.

"Wait here a minute. I've something to do before I give it to you." Omine checked the rest of the house. The daughters were all in the garden playing shuttlecock; the errand boy had not returned as yet; the sewing girl was upstairs, and she was hard of hearing; Ishinosuke was asleep under the kotatsu in the sitting room. If the gods and the buddhas were watching, she prayed they might forgive her. She did not want to do it, but she had no choice. If anyone deserved to be punished, it was only she. Even if they used the money, her aunt and uncle were innocent. She hoped they, at least, would be spared. It was irreverent of her, she knew, but she begged the gods to let her take the money.

She had seen the writing chest before. She opened the drawer and from a packet of bills withdrew two of them. Hardly believing what she had done, Omine handed the money to Sannosuke and sent him on his way. She was foolish enough to assume that her deed had gone unnoticed.

It was almost evening when the master returned from fishing, with a catch and a grin like Ebisu himself.[16]

In a jolly mood at the safe delivery of her first grandchild, the mistress came home soon after. She was even cordial to the driver. "Once tonight is taken care of, I'll come again.[17] Tell her someone will be there in the morning. I'll send one of her sisters. Thanks again." She gave him a tip as she sent him off. "Well, we've got a lot to do! Someone lend me a hand. Who's free? Omine, did you boil the greens? And the herring roe, is it ready? Is the master back yet? What about Ishinosuke?" She lowered her voice. "Has he left? He's still here!" Her forehead wrinkled in displeasure.

That evening Ishinosuke seemed well behaved. "I suppose I ought to stay home and celebrate the New Year with you. But you know how lax I am. I would only be in the way when people come to call, all starched up in their best clothes. To tell the truth, I'm tired of what they have to say. And I don't imagine most of our kinfolk want to see much of me. Besides, I have plans already—with some friends from the back streets. I ought to be going now. We'll have more time to visit after the holidays."

It was only the hope of a reward that had held him there this long. He had slept the day away, waiting for his father's return. With the happy event in the family, gifts were certain to be distributed. Just as people said, a parent was never free of the burden of his child,[18] and how true when the boy was wayward! The bonds between father and son could not be cut, and this made Ishinosuke confident. No matter how depraved the young man became, the world would not allow his father to ignore him. To protect the Yamamura name, the old man would have to open up his treasured storehouse to his son.

Ishinosuke was banking on this. He had signed his name as guarantor for a friend, and the loan fell due tonight. If his friend could not recoup his money at the playing table—well, when the winds blew in the wrong direction, the cards, like the cherries, would be scattered everywhere.[19] In other words, he needed money.

Just what his mother had suspected! Ever since he showed his face! "How much?" She did not mince words.

She had little patience, either, with her husband and his easy attitude toward everything. But her hands were tied. She knew Ishinosuke could out-argue her. She could not handle him as easily as she had disposed of Omine and her problem. She was just waiting to see how her husband would react, and she glared in his direction.

Quietly he went over to the safe and withdrew a sheaf of fifty yen. "I'm not doing this for you. I'm doing it for the sake of your sisters. They are still your sisters, you know. And I, for one, have pity on them. I've got to think about your older sister's husband, too. Our family has always been completely honest and upstanding. Through all these generations, there's never been a breath of scandal. And there's no reason for one now. But you—you're like the devil. The one bad apple. For a little money, there's no telling what you'd do. I could see you going for another man's purse. And the grief that would bring! It wouldn't end with this generation, I can tell you that. I prize the Yamamura name more than I do money. So take it. And don't cause your family any more shame. I suppose all these words are lost on someone like you. If you were an ordinary son, you wouldn't go tarnishing your family's name so cavalierly. You'd start helping your father with his New Year's greetings. But you—all *you* do is bring me tears. I'm almost sixty years old, Ishinosuke. It's a sin, what you're doing to your family. I don't know why you don't understand. When you were little, you read enough books. You ought to know what's what. Well, the hell with you! Get out of here, and don't bring us any more disgrace."

He walked away from his son, into one of the back rooms. Ishinosuke stuffed the money into his pocket.

"Good-by, Mother! Happy New Year!" He took his leave with a show of great respect. "Omine, would you get my shoes?" And from the front hall he added, "Don't worry—I'll be back. I'm just going out for a while." Ishinosuke could wave good-by and make it a show of insolence.

Where was he off to now? Tonight there would be trouble sleeping, his father mused. He could easily have done without this prodigal son of his. And he could have done without a wife who would raise her stepson to turn out so feckless.

They did not spread salt to purify the room,[20] but they immediately swept the place clean after Ishinosuke had left. The mistress was delighted to have him gone. Hard as it was to part with money, it was harder still to suffer Ishinosuke. Getting rid of him was worth almost anything. "How could anyone be so arrogant?" she railed. "I'd like to see the woman who gave birth to him!" She was filing her sharp tongue, as usual.

No doubt Omine heard something of what was going on. But she was mesmerized with fear at the thought of her own crime. She could hardly believe what she had done. Would it be discovered? They would notice, even if only one note were missing from ten thousand. The minute the money was counted, the theft would be detected, and the missing amount would correspond to the money Omine had requested. If they questioned her, what would she say? What could she do? To lie would be another grave offense. To confess would bring ignominy upon her uncle. Even if she were prepared to admit her guilt, her uncle, an upright man, would be falsely accused. There would be no means of exonerating him. That was the way when one was poor. People were sure to accuse him, too. How wretched she felt! What could she do? She must not let her actions scar her uncle. Maybe suicide was the answer . . . She followed her mistress about her work, but her mind kept returning to the writing chest.

Accounts were settled on this evening of the last day of the year. Money on hand was sealed and stamped with the family insignia.

In the midst of all the bustle, the mistress suddenly remembered something: the money in the writing chest. Tarō, the roofer, had returned the money he had borrowed. Twenty yen, there ought to be.

"Omine! Bring the writing chest in here." The words rang out from the back room.

This was it, Omine told herself. She might as well confess, no matter how little sympathy her mistress showed. There was no other way. Honesty had always been what protected her. She wouldn't try to run away or to hide what she had done. She would own up to it and let them know it was not from greed that she had stolen. The important thing was for them to understand it was not her uncle's fault. If they didn't listen to her, she would bite her tongue and bleed to death. If she gave her life, perhaps then they would believe her.

She managed to get her courage up and walked toward the back room, a sheep going to the slaughter.

She had taken two yen from the drawer, so there ought to be eighteen yen left. But what had happened? The entire packet was gone. When her mistress turned the drawer upside down and shook it, there was nothing. Instead, how strange, a scrap of paper fell out. It was a note, a receipt. When had this been written?

"I have borrowed the money in the drawer. Ishinosuke."

Everyone looked at each other in amazement. That good-for-nothing!

So Omine had escaped interrogation.

Did Ishinosuke take the money without noticing what Omine had done? Or perhaps he did know. Perhaps he decided to let his own theft cover hers. In any case, he had saved her, and Omine knew she would always adore him.

Who can tell what happened afterward?

Troubled Waters
(Nigorie, 1895)

"Hey! Shin! Kimura! Come here! When you say you're coming over, why don't you come, then? I know you—you're off to Futaba's or somewhere for a drink without even stopping in. I'll come after you whether I'm invited or not—I'm warning you. Stop by on your way back from the bath—if that's really where you're going. You're such liars, both of you, I never know what to believe."

The two men, it would seem, were regulars. The woman's harangue as they went by did not appear to disturb them in the least. "Later, later," they assured her in passing.

She gave a click of the tongue as they went off. "They won't come later. They've no intention of coming," she grumbled to herself on her way back inside. "Once they get married, that's the end of it."

"Otaka, I don't blame you. But don't be upset," one of the other girls consoled her. "He hasn't forgotten you. It'll be just like before, after he's been married a while. Don't worry. Patience, and a little magic, and he'll be back again."[1]

"I'm not like Oriki, you know. I don't have any special talents, and I can't afford to let anyone slip away. For someone as unlucky as I am, magic isn't going to work. I suppose I'll have to stand out in front again tonight, trying to snare a customer. What kind of life is this?" In a fit of anger, she sat down in the front of the shop and kicked at the earthen floor with her sandals. She was a woman of perhaps twenty-seven, perhaps thirty. She had plucked her eyebrows and painted a dark line in their place and had outlined her widow's peak in black. A thick layer of powder covered her face. Her lips were rouged a shade of crimson so deep they lost their charm and suggested more a man-eating dog than a courtesan.

But the woman Otaka had referred to as Oriki was a true beauty, slender and of average height. Her hair, just washed, was done up in a great chignon knotted with a twist of new straw. Her white complexion seemed in need of no make-up. Even on her neck, the use of powder was not obvious. Her kimono was loosely tied, as if to show off the fairness of her breasts. Rather indecorously, she sat with one knee hoisted up and puffed away on her long pipe. She was fortunate there was no one to scold her.

One didn't have to ask her line of work. She had the uniform of all the girls in the district. Her summer kimono bore a bold pattern. Her sash of black satin was lined with less impressive satinette, and stitched with scarlet thread that showed all too clearly where she had tied the sash above her waist.

Otaka looked at her as if remembering something. "Oriki—" She scratched the base of her hairdo with a copper bodkin. "Did you mail the letter?"

"Mm," she answered absent-mindedly. "But he still isn't going to come. I was just being polite," Oriki laughed.

"Who are you kidding? You took all that paper to write him. And two stamps on the envelope! Don't tell me you were just being civil. You've known him ever since Akasaka, haven't you? So what if you've had your misunderstandings? You can't afford to break with him. It's up to you. Why don't you make more of an effort and try to keep him? You can't treat people that way and expect to do all right."

"Thanks for the advice, but he's not my type. You'd better get used to it—there's nothing between us." She talked as if the topic were of no concern to her.

"You astonish me," Otaka laughed. "You're as selfish as a grand lady. Ah, but me—there's no hope for me," she sighed, reaching for her fan to cool her feet. "I used to be a flower of a girl . . ."

From the window she could see men passing in front of the shops. Calls of solicitation vied with each other in the night.

The house was a two-story building twelve-feet wide in front. A festival lantern hung beneath the eaves, and a little pile of salt, for good luck, invoked prosperity. Bottles of one of the better brands of saké lined the shelf above the bar, but whether there was anything in them was another question. Now and then came busy sounds of someone starting a fire in the clay stove in the kitchen. At best, one might expect a chowder or a stew, served up by the lady who owned the place, although according to the sign in front the house aspired to the status of a full-fledged restaurant. What on earth would they do if someone actually came and ordered something? They could hardly claim to have just run out of their entire stock. Nor would it do to fall back on the excuse that they were only in the business of entertaining men. A good thing people seemed to know better! No one was boorish enough to order any side dishes.

Oriki was the number-one attraction of the house. She was also the youngest, and already the most adept at drawing customers. There were those among the other girls who found fault: she could be a little friendlier, some of the gentlemen were nervous, she was too willful. And that look on her face! Too self-satisfied! After all, she wasn't really *that* pretty.

Nevertheless, when you got to know her, Oriki was surprisingly kind. Even women found themselves attracted to her. A person cannot, in the end, hide his heart, and the bloom in Oriki's face bespoke her character. Not a man visited the new quarter who didn't know of Oriki at the Kikunoi House. One hardly knew whether it was Oriki of the Kikunoi or the Kikunoi of Oriki, such was the success of this recent and rare find. Thanks to her, the fledgling quarter had blossomed with bright lights, and envious neighbors thought the owners of the Kikunoi would do well to offer special thanks before their family altar.

It had quieted down now. There were no passersby, Otaka noticed, and she was free to speak her mind. "Oriki, I suppose I shouldn't meddle in your affairs. But I can't help putting myself in your place. And I can't help thinking of Genshichi. I know he's had some hard times, and he's not that great a customer any more. But when the two of you were so taken with each other . . . it's no good trying to forget him. He may be a lot older than you, and he may have a wife and child, I know, but are these reasons to give him up forever? What's to stop you from seeing him? Invite him back again. It's different in my case. If some two-timing fellow turns fickle on me, that's it—I'm helpless. All they have to do is look at my face, and men run the other way. I'm used to it by now. I just start searching all over again. But that's hardly your problem. Genshichi can divorce his wife any time he takes it into his head. You're so highfalutin—I suppose he's not good enough to be your husband. I still don't think it would hurt to ask him over. Write him a note. The delivery boy from the Mikawaya will be coming, and you can send it with him. You're not a schoolgirl, you know. Don't be coy. Your problem is you give up too easily. At least write a letter to him, poor Genshichi."

Oriki was busy cleaning out her pipe. She looked down intently into the bowl and did not respond to Otaka. When she had it cleaned, she drew on it once, gave it a tap, and filled it with tobacco. Lighting it, she handed the pipe to Otaka. "Careful how you talk. These aren't private quarters. People will hear us. I don't want anyone to get the wrong idea. What if they start saying I have a workman for a lover? The whole thing's a figment of your imagination. It's in the past. I've put him out of my mind. I barely remember the man's name. You're not to bring the matter up."

She walked toward the window as she spoke. A group of students were passing in front of the shop, and she called out to them. "Say! Mr. Ishikawa! Mr. Muraoka! Have you forgotten where Oriki lives?"

"Hah! Of course not! How could we ignore that voice?" No sooner had they spoken than the young gallants were inside the house.

At once there was a flurry of footsteps along the corridor as the maids came bringing saké and inquiring what was to be served. Soon there were the lively strains of the samisen, and dancing and revelry.

One rainy day a man in his thirties appeared in front of the Kikunoi. He was smartly dressed, complete with bowler hat. He looked like a man with time on his hands. Oriki soon spotted him and knew that a better guest would hardly come her way, especially in the rain. She rushed out to him and clung to his sleeve. "I won't let you go!" Her beauty entitled her to act as petulantly as she pleased.

The man who followed her into the house was considerably more impressive than the usual client. She led him to a small room on the second floor. There the two of them talked quietly, in no need, it seemed, of any musical diversion. He asked her age, what her name was, where she came from. Was she the daughter of a samurai?

'I can't tell you."

"So you're a commoner?"

"Perhaps . . ."

"A noblewoman?" he chuckled.

"How did you guess?" She filled his cup of saké to the brim. "Please allow a princess to attend you."

"What bad manners you have for a princess. Pouring saké without even lifting the cup from the tray! What is that, the Ogasawara school of etiquette?"[3]

"No, no, no, of course not. It's the Oriki school. That's what we follow here. There's an even more esoteric school where we pour saké on the floor and let the mats soak it up. We serve it to guests in the lid of a big bowl. And if we don't like someone, we don't serve him at all."

She was not the least bit shy with him, and he seemed to enjoy it. "Tell me about yourself," he asked. "I'm sure you've quite a story. You don't look as if you've had an ordinary upbringing. Am I right?"

"See for yourself. I don't have horns growing out of my forehead," she laughed. "I'm not that hardened."

"Come on, now, don't evade the question. If you won't talk about your past, let's hear about the future."

"That's a tall order. If I told you, you'd be shocked. My ambitions are as grand as those of Ōtomo Kuronushi,"[4] she smiled.

"Why don't you stop teasing and be serious for a moment? I suppose joking is the way in your world, but even so there are times for a little sincerity. Did you lose your husband? Or maybe you're doing this for your parents?"

As the man's questioning grew more earnest, Oriki began to feel depressed. "I am a human being, you know. There are things that weigh on my mind, too. My parents died when I was young. I'm alone. Oh, there have been men who didn't let my profession stop them from asking me to marry them, but I've never had a husband. I come from such a worthless family, I'll probably spend the rest of my life like this." She was not flirting or trying to win his sympathy, but speaking from the heart.

"Just because you come from poor circumstances doesn't mean you can't get married, a beauty like you. In a single bound, you could marry into a

great family. Or would you prefer to wed some hot-blooded young workman?"

"You're getting warm. But, unfortunately, the men I like are never interested in me, and the ones who are I don't seem to care for. I suppose you
don't think much of a woman who lives from day to day like this."

"You shouldn't talk that way. You must have plenty of attractive suitors.
Didn't one of the girls just say there was someone out in front sending his
regards? I'm sure there are lots of things going on in your life. Aren't there?"

"You're another one with too many questions! Yes, as a matter of fact, I
have more patrons that I can count. The exchange of all those love letters is so
much waste paper, as far as I'm concerned. If you want me to write you a
pledge of love, I'll write you one, too. Whatever you like. I do it all the
time—even promises of marriage. There's no risk. Before I have a chance to
break a vow, the man is always quick to show how lightly he takes the whole
business. He's more afraid of his master, or his parents. When he stops
coming to see me, why should I run after him? I let things die of their own
accord. Oh, yes, I have any number of admirers—and not one I can depend
upon."

Indeed, she looked forlorn and alone in the world, the man thought to
himself.

"Let's stop talking like this," she said. "We ought to be having a good time.
I can't stand to be gloomy. Let's have a little fun!" She clapped her hands to
summon the other girls in the house, and they soon came running.

"Oriki, you've been so quiet in here," said a woman in her thirties, amply
made up for the evening.

"Hey," the man asked her, "tell me the name of Oriki's boyfriend."

"I haven't heard it myself yet."

"Don't lie, or you won't be able to pay your respects to Enma on the Day of
Souls."[5]

"But we've just met! How can I go telling you secrets? You should be nice to
me—I was about to come and say hello when Oriki called."

"Why's that?"

"I wanted to learn the name of our distinguished guest."

"Don't be so obsequious," he chided. "Oriki won't like it."

This bantering had put Otaka in high spirits. "Shall I guess your occupation?"

"Sure." He offered her his palm.

"No, I don't need that. I can tell by your face." She looked at him intently.

"Stop. I don't think I can bear your taking inventory. You may not know it,
but, in fact, I'm a government official."

"What a lie! Since when do government officials take holidays in the middle of the week? Oriki, what do you think he is?"

"Well, I'll tell you this much," he scoffed, "I'm not a ghost." He took his wallet out from the folds of his kimono. "There'll be a prize for the one who guesses."

Oriki laughed at the two of them. "Otaka, don't be rude to our guest. He's an aristocrat. He has to make these visits on the sly. Why should he have an occupation? He doesn't need to work." She picked up his wallet from the cushion. "Why don't you leave me in charge of this? I'll see that everyone gets the proper tip." She did not wait for his reply before taking the money out.

He leaned back against the pillar with indifference. "Do what you want with it." Here was a generous man.

Otaka looked startled by Oriki's audacity. "You'd better stop before you go too far!"

"He said it's all right. Here, this is for you. And this is for you," she said, turning to another of her friends. "Take this down to the desk and pay the bill. You can keep the change and divide it among you. He said so," she assured, showering them with money. "Now you'd better thank him." This was one of Oriki's favorite tricks,[6] they all knew, and they did not demur.

"Is it really all right?" one of the girls asked perfunctorily. "Thank you very much!" In no time, she had gathered up the money and was gone.

The man watched her leave. "She looks old for nineteen."

"You say such nasty things," Oriki said, opening the window. She sat down against the railing and rubbed her forehead to relieve the headache that was coming on.

"What about you?" he asked. "Don't you want any money?"

"No, there's something else I want. If I could just keep this." She took his calling.card from underneath her sash, as if it were already hers.

"When did you take that? You'll have to give me your picture in exchange."

"Come next Saturday, and we can have our picture taken."

He was ready to leave now, and she did not try to detain him.

"Please forgive my bad manners today," she said as she helped him with his jacket. "I'll be waiting for you."

"You don't have to say that. Spare me the empty words. Well, then—" he smiled and started down the stairs.

Oriki followed after him, carrying his hat. "If you want to know whether they were empty words or not, you'll have to come another ninety-nine nights.[7] I don't say things just to be polite. I'm not cast in the mold you think I am!"

When they heard him leaving, the other women of the house came running with good-bys. The owner of the Kikunoi left her place behind the counter, and everyone thanked him in unison. "Please do come again!"

The rickshaw was waiting, someone said. He went out, and they all followed behind him. A chorus of "come again's" rang out cheerfully.

The effulgence, he was well aware, was the afterglow from his tips.

Once he had gone, the girls poured out an endless stream of thanks to Oriki, their own private goddess of wealth.

His name was Yūki Tomonosuke.[8] He described himself as something of a playboy, but now and then his serious side came out. Without work or wife and family to encumber him, he was just at the age for enjoying life.

Ever since his first visit, he had been coming to the Kikunoi two or three times a week, and, imperceptibly, Oriki found herself growing fond of him. If three days passed without a visit, she would dispatch a letter.

The situation caused a certain amount of jealousy and teasing among her friends. "How happy you must be, Oriki, with such a handsome and generous man! He's the kind to be successful. He'll probably ask you to marry him. You should be more careful, though—stop stretching your legs out and gulping saké out of teacups. He'll think you're coarse."

"What will Genshichi say?" another asked. "It'll drive him mad."

"You know," Oriki answered, "this road is going to ruin Yūki's carriage. I'd like to get it fixed. The way the gutter boards rattle, I'm ashamed to have him park in front. I do hope you'll all try to watch your manners with him, so that you can wait on him without embarrassing me."

"How terrible you are, Oriki. If you don't learn a little humility, no one will ever take you for a wife! When Yūki comes, I've a mind to tell him what you're really like."

Just then he appeared, and they launched into a diatribe against Oriki. "She's the most selfish thing you've ever seen! You ought to give her a talking-to."

"She keeps on drinking her liquor out of teacups—it's not good for her."

The expression on his face turned grave. "Oriki, you mustn't drink so much."

"You should know better than to scold me," she pouted. "Can't you tell? The only way I keep going in this business is with the help of drink. If I didn't have that to fall back on, the Kikunoi would become as quiet as a temple. Imagine what it's like for me!"

"Of course . . ."

One night of a full moon, Oriki and Yūki sat together in their usual room on the second floor, listening to a party of workers down below. The men were drumming away on empty bowls and dancing and carrying on with most of the girls in the house. Yūki stretched out on the floor in complete content. He would say things to Oriki, but she seemed not to listen, as if she were annoyed by the conversation.

"What are you thinking about?" he finally asked. "What's the matter? Do you have a headache?"

"No, it's not a headache. It's an attack of what I always get."

"What's that? A temper tantrum?"

"No!"

"Your nerves?"

"No."

"Well, what is it?"

"I can't tell you."

"You can tell me. Come on, what's wrong with you?"

"Nothing's *wrong* with me. Sometimes I just get to thinking—"

"What an impossible woman you are! You have too many secrets. Tell me about your father."

"No, I can't."

"All right, your mother."

"No."

"Come on, tell me about yourself."

"I can't."

"Well, make something up, then. Most women would be glad for the chance to talk about their troubles. It's not as if we'd only met. What harm is there in telling me? Look, I know there's something on your mind. A blind man could figure that much out. Come on. I already know something's the matter—so tell me. What's this attack of yours that you say you always get? Explain that, at least."

"Will you please stop interrogating me? If I told you, you'd see it's nothing to get excited about."

Just then one of the girls came in carrying a trayful of glasses and whispered to Oriki, asking her to come downstairs.

"No—I don't want to. Tell him I have a guest tonight and I've had too much to drink. I wouldn't be good company."

"That won't do!" she frowned.

"Yes it will. He'll understand." Oriki toyed with the plectrum of her samisen as the girl shook her head and left the room.

"Don't decline on my account," Yūki chuckled. "Why don't you go down for a while? Really, go ahead. You can't send your boyfriend away without even seeing him—it's too mean. Run down there and see him. Or do you want to call him up here? I'll go over in the corner and leave you two alone."

"Don't make fun, Yūki. I might as well tell you, I guess. For a long time the man downstairs, Genshichi, was a patron of mine. He used to have a great reputation around here. He was a bedding dealer, but now he's a pauper living like a snail in a shack behind the vegetable stalls. Once his influence was wider than the mattresses he sold, but now . . . He has a wife and child. He's really too old to be coming to see a woman like me. I guess there's still a bond between us, after all. He still finds some excuse or other to call every now and then. I'm not going to start having him thrown out, of course, but what's the use of seeing him . . . when it would only cause problems? It's better to send him away, before we do each other any harm. Even if he hates me for it. Oh, I'm resigned to that. In the end, he'll think I'm some sort of witch. It's better that way." She laid the plectrum down on the floor beside her and stretched to look out the window.

"Do you see your beloved?"

"I guess he's already left." Her voice was devoid of any emotion.

"Your chronic 'attacks' are because of him, then, aren't they?"

He had penetrated her defenses. "Well, yes, you could say that. I'm afraid no doctor or mineral waters are going to cure what ails me." She smiled wanly.

"I'd like to see this idol of yours. Who does he look like? If you had to pick an actor, say?"

"You'd be disappointed. He's big and swarthy—like the Fire God."[9]

"I take it that it was his personality, then—"

"He's the kind of man who empties his purse at a house like this. A good-natured man. That's about all you can say for him. He's not the least bit entertaining or amusing."

"What made you lose your head over *him*? That's what I want to know," he said, sitting upright.

"I'm the type of person who's always falling in love, I suppose. Lately, there's not a night I don't dream about you. Sometimes I dream you're married; sometimes I dream you stop coming. Sometimes I have even worse dreams, and my pillow ends up soaked with tears. A girl like Otaka starts snoring the minute she crawls into bed. How I envy her! No matter how tired I am, as soon as I pull the covers up, my eyes open wide and I start to think about everything. You, at least, understand there are things weighing on my mind, though I doubt you could guess what they are. It's no good brooding. I try to be cheerful in front of others. And then what happens? People think I'm carefree and thoughtless! There are men who come here who think I've never had a worry in my head. It's my fate, I guess. I wonder if anybody suffers more than I do."

He had never heard her talk so bitterly. Without knowing more, he was at a loss as to how to console her. "If it's reached the point where you're dreaming of me, why haven't you asked me to marry you? It's old-fashioned, but you know what they say: 'No one meets purely by chance.'[10] If you hate the life you're leading, you should have told me so. I assumed, with your tempera-ment, that this was what you wanted—that you found it comfortable to drift through life this way. Are there other reasons? Tell me, if you don't mind talking about it."

"I'd been thinking of telling you. But I can't tonight."

"Why not?"

"Don't ask me. I'm stubborn, that's why. I'm not going to tell you until I'm ready to." Suddenly, she stood and walked out onto the balcony.

The moon shone cool in the cloudless night. In the street below echoed the footfall of passersby, their shadows wavering here and there along the road.

"Yūki."

"What?" He came over and stood next to her.

"Sit down," she said, taking his hand. "See the child buying peaches at the fruit stand? The cute little one, about four? He's the son of the man who was here tonight. I must be hateful to him. He calls me a demon when he sees me. Do I look that evil?"

Oriki gazed up at the sky and took a deep breath. In her sigh, one could hear all her suffering.

On the outskirts of the new quarter, where a narrow alley ran between the greengrocer's and the hairdresser's shops, the eaves hung so close together that the passageway all but had its own roof, and the space between the crowded tenements on each side of the lane was so tight that on a rainy day one could scarcely open an umbrella. Missing sewer covers left gaping holes in the middle of the road. It was not an easy path to navigate. At the end of the road stood a rubbish pile and a small, ramshackle house. The rain shutters no longer closed properly, and the place looked quite unsafe. It did, however, have both a front and a back door, unlike the other houses in the alley. Removed as it was, fortunately, from the center of town, it boasted a porch some three-feet wide, which overlooked an empty lot in back. There, weeds grew with abandon and begonias and China asters and bean vines entwined themselves around a makeshift bamboo fence. It was here that Oriki's Genshichi lived.

His wife, Ohatsu, was twenty-eight or -nine. Poverty had left her worn and gaunt, and looking a good seven years older than her age. The dye on her teeth was beginning to chip off,[11] and her unshaven eyebrows gave the woman a tired, hapless look. Her cotton kimono, faded from too many launderings, she wore reversed, tied tightly with a narrow sash, and patched about the knees in such a way that the stitches barely showed. To bring in extra money, she was busy making wicker sandal pads. It was seasonal work, just before the Day of Souls, when the heat was at its worst. She would sweat over her labors, the pieces of rattan she needed suspended from the ceiling to save her time. The woman was so diligent and so delighted with her little pile of handiwork that it was, somehow, a sad spectacle.

By now the sun had gone down. Why wasn't Takichi home, she wondered.

And where was Genshichi? The woman gathered up her work and lit her pipe. Her troubled eyes blinked several times. She dug out some embers from the clay pot and put them in the brazier. Perhaps it would drive the mosquitoes away, she hoped, carrying it out onto the three-foot-wide veranda. She picked up needles that had fallen from the cedar tree and placed them in the fire and blew on it to get it going. Gradually smoke rose. The mosquitoes, driven off by the scent, swarmed under the eaves with a loud buzz.

Just then Takichi came running home, his sandals clattering on the drain boards in the alleyway. "Mommy, I'm home! I brought Daddy with me."

"You're awfully late, aren't you? I was beginning to wonder if you'd gone up to a temple in the hills, I was so worried. Hurry up now and come in."

Takichi entered first, followed by Genshichi. Her husband looked tired.

"Oh, you're home, too. It must have been sweltering at work today. I thought you'd be home early. The bath water's ready. If you're all sweaty, why don't you take one now? You, too, Takichi."

"Sure," the little boy said, untying his sash.

"Just wait while I check the water." She placed a tub near the kitchen sink and filled it with hot water, stirred it, and put out washcloths for them. "All right, it's ready. Give Takichi a bath with you. You look dead-tired. I hope you're not sick from the heat. Soak for a while and you'll feel better. Then you can have a nice dinner. Hurry up, Takichi's waiting."

"Oh, that's right," Genshichi said, as if coming to his senses. As he untied his waistband and walked over to the tub, he felt memories of his old self suddenly come back to him. He had never dreamed the day would come when he would have to bathe in the kitchen of a nine-by-twelve house, let alone that he would wind up as an assistant to a crew of construction workers, pulling a cart around all day. Surely his parents had not brought him into the world for this.

He forgot all about the bath as he stood there absorbed in his thoughts.

"Daddy, would you wash my back?"

"You'll get eaten by mosquitoes if you stand there like that," his wife warned him. "Hurry up, and get dressed when you're done."

"Mmmn. All right."

He finished washing Takichi and quickly bathed himself. When he stepped out of the tub, his wife handed him a kimono, threadbare but freshly starched.

He put it on and sat by the veranda, where he could feel the breeze.

Ohatsu carried in an old tray. The lacquer had begun to peel at the edges and it wobbled when she set it down. "Here. I've made you one of your favorites." Cubes of chilled bean curd floated in a small bowl. There were fresh-smelling green leaves sprinkled over it.

Takichi had grabbed the rice bucket while they weren't looking and was parading around the room chanting "Yotchoi! Yotchoi!"

"Come here, you." He patted his little son on the head and took up his chopsticks to eat. He wasn't sure exactly what was wrong, but the food had no taste to him and his throat felt swollen. "I can't eat any more," he told his wife, putting the bowl down.

"What do you mean, you can't eat any more? Men who do heavy work like you gulp down three servings without batting an eye. Aren't you feeling well? Are you tired, or what?"

"No. I don't think there's anything wrong with me. I just don't have any appetite."

"Ah—your usual regrets, I suppose." His wife had a plaintive look in her eyes. "You don't have to tell me—the dishes at the Kikunoi were tastier. But what good is it thinking about them now, in your present circumstances? If you earned a little money again, they'd fawn over you the way they used to. All you have to do is walk by those places and you can tell: it's their business to put on powder and pretty clothes and seduce every man who wanders by. If you'd only see, it's because you're poor now that she ignores you. This grudge you have against her—I mean, it's a dead giveaway, Genshichi, how much she's still on your mind. You know what happened to the boy who worked at the saké shop in the back street. He was so taken with Okaku, at Futaba's, that he spent all the money he'd collected from the bills. And when he tried to make it up gambling—novice that he was—he was driven into a corner. Things got worse and worse, and he ended up breaking into some-one's storehouse! He's in jail now, I believe, living on prison rations. His old girl friend, Okaku, couldn't care less. And you can be sure no one upbraids her for living free and easy! Oh no—she's thriving beautifully, thank you. Think about it. Women in that profession have all the advantages. If a man is stupid enough to let himself be fooled, it's his own fault. You're not going to get anywhere brooding. You've got to change your attitude. Make up your mind and put your energy into business. Save up some money to get going. When you're weak, Takichi and I are helpless. We'll end up begging at the roadside. Be a man, Genshichi, and get over it! All you need to do is make some money, and you can have any woman you want. Komurasaki, Agemaki[12]—not to mention Oriki. You can build her a house in the country. Wouldn't that be nice? So stop pining away. Eat up! You're making even little Takichi downhearted."

The child had put his dinner aside and was looking back and forth at his parents. He was too young to understand what was going on, but he was troubled all the same.

"I don't know why I can't forget her, that witch,[13] when I've a wonderful boy like this." Genshichi's heart was wrenched, and he blamed himself for not being able to get over Oriki. "What an idiot I am! Don't even mention her name again—I only remember all the mistakes I've made. Pretty soon, I won't be able to hold my head up. When I've sunk so low on her account, I don't know how I can have any feeling left for the woman. I'm too tired to have any appetite tonight. Don't worry, though. Let Takichi eat everything."

Her husband lay back on the floor and fanned himself furiously. He felt on fire with emotion. It was not the smoke from the mosquito smudge that was choking him.

White demons, someone had dubbed them. And, in fact, there was an air of the nether reaches to it all.[14] Even those who appeared guileless were ready to drive a man into a pool of blood, or chase a debt-laden customer up the side of a mountain of needles.[15] If they enticed men with their soft voices, they could also sound as shrill as a pheasant being swallowed by a snake.

Still, these girls had once spent the same ten months in the womb as everybody else.[16] When they were small, they too clung to their mothers' breasts and were fondled and coaxed to babble their first words. When they were offered their choice of money or candy, like any other child they held out a hand for the sweets.

In the trade, one did not look for honest women. One girl in a hundred shed tears of true love for a man.

"Take Tatsu, the dyer," a woman says, to prove her loyalty. "Again yesterday he was carrying on with that chatterbox Oroku at Kawada's. A disgusting sight! He pulls her out into the street and she slaps him and he hits her back—right in front of everybody. How old do you think he is, anyway? He turned thirty, year before last! I tell him to save his money, so we can get married. And he says 'Yes, yes.' He doesn't mean it, though. He's not the least bit concerned about the future. His father's getting on in years. His mother's eyes are bad. He ought to hurry up and settle down. It would put their minds at rest. Why, I'm ready to wash his jacket and mend his breeches. But the way he plays around all the time, I wonder if he'll ever take charge of things. Just thinking about it . . . I've had it with this work. I don't care about bringing in customers any more. It all depresses me." Oh, she complains about her lover's cruelty, all right, but ordinarily she's the one who does the deceiving. Now her head aches, she's at wits' end.

"Ah," another one sighs, "today's the sixteenth, the Day of Souls. All the children are off to the shrine to pay their respects to Enma.[17] They look so happy, with their pretty clothes and money jingling in their pockets. (You can tell they all have able parents.) I suppose my own little boy, Yotarō, is spending the day somewhere with his father. But it won't matter what festive things they do; he'll always envy the others. A drunkard for a father . . . no home of his own . . . a mother who has to doll herself up with powder and rouge in order to make a living . . . Even if he knew where I was, he wouldn't come to see me. I remember when I ran into him last year at Mukōjima when the cherries were in bloom. I was dressed up just so and wore my hair in a nice chignon. I was out for the day with friends. I saw him at a teahouse by the river bank and called his name. He seemed surprised to see me looking so young. 'Is it you, Mother?' he asked. I could tell he was startled. How surprised he would be to see me today, with my hair done up in a bouffant bun and spangled with the latest flowered bodkins! If he heard me joking with one of my customers, how sad he would be! When I saw him last year, he told me he had been apprenticed to a candlemaker in Komagata. He said he'd stick to it no matter how hard it got. And when he grows up, he said he'll see that his father and mother live in comfort. 'Try to support yourself till then,' he told me, 'and don't remarry.' Unfortunately, a woman isn't going to feed herself making matchboxes. And I'm not strong enough to be a scullery maid. I'm no better off doing this for a living, but at least it's easier. I certainly didn't choose the profession lightly. I suppose my boy despises me for it, though. This fancy hairdo of mine—I don't usually think anything of it—but today I'm embarrassed to be wearing it." With tears in her eyes, she sits before her evening mirror, repeating her woes to herself.

Oriki of the Kikunoi was another girl unlikely to be mistaken for a demon. There were reasons why she had fallen into the stream, where she now spent her days telling lies and bantering with men who came to call. Love, compassion—in her world, these were things as flimsy as a sheet of mulberry paper, about as steady as the flickering of a firefly. Here, people were not apt to be moved by another's tears.[18] A man could kill himself over a woman, and the lady would mutter, "What a pity," and look the other way. There were times, of course, when a woman felt truly sad or frightened. Afraid to let emotions show, she would fling herself down in a room upstairs and sob quietly to herself. So it was with Oriki. She kept her problems to herself. Others considered her strong and independent. They did not perceive that she was as vulnerable as a spider's web. Touch it, and it disintegrates.

It was night on the sixteenth of July, and every house in the quarter was full of customers, singing songs, making rhymes. In the first-floor room at the Kikunoi, five or six shop clerks had gathered. They sang the Kiinokuni song completely off key, and someone with no voice for it had the temerity to attempt an all too affected rendering of "The hill is shrouded in the mist."[19]

"Oriki, it's your turn to sing for us."

After some coaxing, she began one of their favorite songs. "I shall not say his name, but there is someone here tonight . . ."

They responded to her usual way of flattering them with enthusiastic bursts of applause.

"My love is like a bridge of logs across the Hosotani River," she went on. "I'm afraid to cross to the other side; I'm afraid to stay where I am." But suddenly, as if the song had reminded her of something, she fell silent. "Excuse me. I'm sorry." She put her samisen aside and left the room.

"Where are you going?" they all began to shout. "You can't run out on us!"

"Teru, Otaka, cover for me, will you? I'll be right back." She hurried through the hallway and slipped into her shoes. Without looking back, she ran out into the street and down the alley on the other side.

Oriki ran from the house as fast as she could. If only it were possible, she would keep on going, to China, to India. How she hated her life! She never wanted to hear another human voice, or any sound at all. She needed a quiet place, where her mind could relax, where there were no worries. How long would she be stuck in this hopeless situation, where everything was absurd and worthless and cruel? Was this what life was supposed to be? She hated it! She hated it! She felt almost delirious and leaned against a tree at the side of the road. "I'm afraid to cross to the other side; I'm afraid to stay where I am." It was her song and her voice, but where was it coming from?

"I have no choice," she whispered. "I will have to cross the bridge by myself. My father fell treading it. They say my grandfather stumbled, too. I was born with the curse of many generations, and there are things I have to undergo before I die. No one's going to feel sorry for me, that much I know. If I complain about how sad I am, 'What's wrong?' people say, 'Don't you like your work?' Oh, it doesn't matter any more what happens—I haven't the slightest idea what will become of me. I might as well go on as Oriki of the Kikunoi. Sometimes I wonder if I've lost all sense of kindness and decency. No. I mustn't think such things. It won't do me any good. With my station in life and my calling and my fate, I'm not an ordinary person any more. It's a mistake to think I am. It only adds to my suffering. It's all so hopeless and discouraging. What am I doing standing here? Why did I come here? Stupid! Crazy! I don't even know myself," she sighed. "I'd better get back."

Oriki left the darkness of the alley and walked along a street lined with shops. They were all doing a lively business. If only some of the gaiety would rub off, she mused. As she trudged along, the faces of passersby seemed tiny to her. Even those of people who walked directly in front of her seemed somehow very distant. She felt as if she were hovering ten feet above the ground. She could hear the din of voices, but it sounded more like the echo of someone falling to the bottom of a well. She was lost in her own thoughts and paid no heed to the voices about her. Nothing distracted her. She passed a crowd gathered round a husband and wife who were arguing, but this, too, failed to interest her. It was as if she were walking in a great, open field laid bare by winter. There was nothing to capture her attention. She felt unsure of her step, as if she might faint. She wondered if she was losing her mind. No sooner did she stop than someone tapped her on the shoulder. "Oriki, where are you going?"

She had told Yūki Tomonosuke she would be waiting for him on the sixteenth, but the appointment had completely slipped her mind. Only now when Oriki saw him did she remember.

"Oh!"

He laughed at the look of astonishment on her face. It was not like her to be flustered.

"I had something on my mind. I didn't expect to see you so suddenly! But I'm glad you came."

"After promising you'd be waiting for me, here you are out galavanting—"

"Say what you like. I'm not going to explain until we get out of here." She took his hand.

"Careful of the crowd. It's pretty rowdy tonight."

"It's all right. This way," she said, leading him through the holiday throngs.

At the Kikunoi, the guests in the front room were still roistering; things had become even more raucous after her departure. Now they saw her come in.

"Oriki—you're back!"

"Is that any way to treat your guests, running out on us? Come in here, now that you're back! We're not going to forgive you till we see your face again."

She ignored their swaggering voices and led Yūki to the room on the second floor. "Tell them I can't drink with them tonight," she asked one of the girls. "I have a headache. I'll pass out if I even smell any more liquor. Perhaps after I've rested a while I'll feel better. Right now, they'll just have to excuse me."

"Can you do that?" Yūki asked. "They won't be angry? What happens if they start insisting? Won't that cause trouble?"

"Those pasty melons![20] What can they do? Let them get angry!" She ordered some saké from one of the serving girls and waited impatiently for it to come. "Yūki, I'm not myself tonight. Something's been bothering me. I hope you'll understand. I need a few drinks. You mustn't stop me. If I get drunk, you'll look after me, won't you?"

"I've never seen you drunk. If it makes you happy, it's fine with me. But what if it gives you another headache? Why are you in such a bad mood? Can't you tell me?"

"Mmmn. I'm going to tell you, after I have a few drinks. You mustn't be shocked, though." She smiled and filled a large teacup with saké, which she drained two or three times.

Ordinarily, she didn't pay much attention to his appearance, but tonight, for some reason, she thought Yūki looked a little different. He was a very tall, broad-shouldered man. When he spoke, it was quietly and with assurance. His sharp eyes seemed to look right through her. Altogether, he was most impressive, and the discovery delighted her. His dark hair was closely cropped in a cleancut line at the nape of the neck. She was fascinated by his looks, as if she had met him for the first time.

"What are you daydreaming about?"

"I was looking at your face."

"You are an odd one!" he scowled.

"And you're intimidating," she laughed.

"All right, enough of the jokes. You don't look like your old self tonight, Oriki. Are you going to get mad at me again if I ask you what's wrong? Something's happened, hasn't it?"

"No, nothing's happened. Nothing unusual—even if I did have a bit of trouble with someone. I haven't given it a thought. Why should I? It's my own fault. I'm flighty, I guess. I get this way from time to time, and no one's to blame. Look, you're a gentleman, I'm of low birth. Your view of things and mine may be very different. I don't know whether you will sympathize with me or not, I just don't know, but I don't care, even if you laugh at me. I don't mind at all. Tonight I'm going to tell you everything. Ah . . . but where to begin? I'm so upset, I can barely talk." Again she took a swig of saké.

"First of all, there's no point in beating around the bush. I'm nothing but a slut. You know that. I'm not some innocent young maiden. To put it politely, if a woman like me *weren't* tainted by these surroundings—like a lotus flower flourishing in the middle of a swamp—do you really think I would have any callers? Do you think this place would be in business? You're different from most of the men who come here. Imagine what the others are like. Sometimes I wonder how it would be to live a normal life, and then I start to feel bitter and ashamed. I think to myself maybe I too could get married and settle down in a little house somewhere. But it will never happen.

"As long as I'm here, I can't be rude to the men who come to see me. I have to think of something nice to say to all of them—how cute this one is, how sweet that one is, how I've never seen anyone so handsome. Some even take me seriously. Do you know, some of them ask a good-for-nothing like me to marry them? I wonder, would I be happy if I accepted one of their proposals? Would that be the answer to my prayers? You, I've liked from the very start. When I don't see you for a day, I miss you. But if you asked me to be your wife, I don't know . . . I doubt it would work, and, yet, when we're not together . . . In a word, I guess you could say I'm fickle. And what do you think made me this way? Three generations of failure, that's what. My father's life was miserable, too." Tears were in her eyes as she spoke.

"Tell me about him."

"He was a craftsman. His father was a learned man. My grandfather even read Chinese. But he was mad. In other words—like me. He wrote worthless scraps of things; they were banned, and he starved to death, I've been told.[21] He knew what he wanted to do with his life from the age of sixteen. He was a poor boy who threw himself into his studies with all his heart. He never had any success, though. He lived on into his sixties, and in the end people laughed at him. Today no one would know his name. When I was little, I used to hear all the sad stories about him from my father—who had problems of his own. When my father was three, he fell from the porch, and it left him crippled. As a result, you see, he never enjoyed being around other people. He became a silversmith, so that he could work at home. But he was a proud and unfriendly man, my father, and he never had many customers.

"I remember one winter when I was seven. It was freezing cold, and the only things the three of us had to wear were our old summer kimonos. My father didn't seem to notice the cold so much. He had his work to absorb him; he would spend hours leaning against the post designing something. One night my mother was standing over the tiny hearth, cooking dinner in one of the broken pots we had. She asked me to go buy some rice, and I ran off with my usual enthusiasm, carrying the bean-paste strainer and the few coins she gave me. On the way home, my hands and feet felt numb from the cold. I was about five or six houses away when I slipped on an icy sewer cover and fell, and all the rice spilled and went down an opening into the gutter. It was filthy down there where the water flowed. I kept looking into the hole, but how could I retrieve the rice? I was only seven. I knew, though, what the circumstances were at home. I knew how my father would feel. How could I go home with an empty strainer and no rice? I stood in the middle of the road and cried. No one stopped to ask me what was wrong. Naturally, no one offered to help me buy more rice. If there had been a river or a pond in the neighborhood, I would have thrown myself into it. I can't begin to tell you how I felt. (I think that's when my mind began to go haywire.) My mother must have worried when I didn't get back, so she came looking for me. We went home together, but no one said anything. No one scolded me. The house was as still as a forest. Once in a while I could hear them sigh, and I could hardly bear it, it made me so sad. I didn't breathe, I think, until my father finally spoke. 'Well, we'll fast tonight.'"

Oriki stopped without finishing, unable to hold her tears back. She buried her face in her crimson handkerchief. She bit on the end of it to control herself. The room fell silent. Nearly half an hour seemed to pass. The only sound was the buzzing of mosquitoes drawn by the smell of saké.

After a while, she looked up at him. Her face was still streaked with tears, but she smiled wistfully. "So you see, my people were poor; craziness has a long history in my family. It comes out now and then. But how bothersome for you to have to listen to all this! I won't say any more. I hope I haven't annoyed you. Let's call some others in and liven things up a bit."

"No, don't worry about it. Tell me what happened to your father. Did he die young?"

"Yes. My mother died of consumption after a long illness, and he followed her not a week later. If he had lived, he would be just fifty. I know I shouldn't praise my own parents, but he was a great craftsman. A master, really. Oh, what difference does it make how good he was? When you're born into a family like his, what chance do you have? It's the same with me, of course." Oriki's mind seemed to wander.

"You want to be successful, don't you?"

"Hm?" The question startled her. "Oh, I suppose I have my dreams. Though I know the best *I* can hope for: to marry a poor man and buy rice every day by the strainer-full. I don't expect to see myself riding in a palanquin."

"You don't have to be modest with me. I've understood you from the first night. You're not the least bit convincing when you try to hide your ambition. What's wrong with it, anyway? If it's success you want, admit it and go after it."

"Spare me the pep talk. It's ridiculous to think that someone like me—" She was too crestfallen to continue.

The night had grown late. At some point the revelers downstairs had departed. Soon the maid would be locking up. Yūki Tomonosuke was surprised at the hour, and Oriki suggested that he spend the night. His shoes had already been put away. How did he think he would get out? Slipping barefoot through a crack in the door, like some midnight apparition? Swayed by her argument, he pulled the shutters closed with a clap that rang out for a moment in the dark. No longer could they see the flickering of street lamps through the window. Outside, beneath the eaves, the only sound was a pair of footsteps. It would be the night watchman making his rounds.

What good did it do to dwell on the past? He had made up his mind to forget her. But memories have a way of coming back. He remembered times like the Day of Souls last summer. They had visited the shrine at Kuramae together, wearing the same cotton kimonos. Now, when the festival came round again, he did not have the energy to bestir himself.

"You mustn't be this way," Genshichi's wife chided him.

"Don't lecture me. Just be quiet." He rolled over on his side, irritated at the woman.

"If I kept quiet, we wouldn't make it through another day. If there's really something the matter with you, you might try taking some medicine. Not that I think a doctor's going to cure what's wrong with you. If you'd just change your outlook, you'd be perfectly all right. Come to your senses, for heaven's sake, and apply yourself."

He was inured to her admonitions. "Why don't you go get me some saké? A drink might lift my spirits."

"Listen, if we could afford to buy saké, I wouldn't ask you to go to work against your will. Here I am, doing piecework morning, noon, and night for a grand total of fifteen sen! We're not going to get enough to eat on that. How can you be so asinine—telling me to go buy you saké? The festival is here, and I can't even make little Takichi a dumpling or put out any offerings in honor of the dead. It was all I could do to light a votive candle. And whose fault do you think that is? Yours, for being such a fool over a woman like Oriki. I suppose I shouldn't say it, but you're being an undutiful son to your dead parents and an irresponsible father to your child. Think about Takichi's future and pull yourself together, Genshichi. Drinking isn't the solution. You've got to change your whole way of thinking. If you don't, I don't know how we're going to get by."

Genshichi did not answer. He lay absolutely still, gazing at the ceiling. Every so often he would breathe a deep sigh of regret.

"You still can't forget Oriki, can you?" she felt like asking him. "Even after all you've suffered on her account!"

She had lived with Genshichi for ten years and had given him a son, and yet he had caused her so much sorrow that she could barely stand it. His own child was dressed in rags. They lived in a one-room shack no better than a doghouse. People had come to treat her husband as an outcast, an idiot. At the spring and autumn equinox, everyone else exchanged rice cakes and dumplings, but no one came to call on them. You could say the neighbors were being kind, knowing that Genshichi's family could not afford to reciprocate, but they were the one house on the block that everyone ignored. He was a man and was out all day. He didn't know what it was like for her—ostracized by her own neighbors. The humiliation she felt! Day after day she could see the chill in their eyes whenever she said hello to one of them. He never considered such things. All he ever thought about was that girl friend of his, though how he could love anyone as heartless as Oriki was beyond her. Even when he dozed off for a nap, he would babble Oriki's name. It was disgusting. Had he completely forgotten that he had a wife and a child? Was he going to give his whole life to her? What a cruel person she was married to! How she wanted to tell him all this! Tears of bitterness and frustration welled in her eyes.

The silence between the two of them cooped up in the tiny house was oppressive, and the oncoming twilight only deepened the feeling of gloom in the already shrouded back street.

Ohatsu lit one of the lamps and set out a smudge to drive off the mosquitoes. Discouraged, she stood by the doorway, watching the alley. Takichi was just coming home. He skipped along the road, a large package in his hands. She could not make out what it was.

"Mother! Look what I've got!" he smiled as he came running.

Why, it was a sponge cake from the new pastry shop, the Hinodeya. "Where did you ever get such a nice cake? I hope you thanked them."

"I did. The demon-lady at the Kikunoi gave it to me."

His mother's face went white. "What nerve she has! Hasn't she done enough already? How much more does she want to torment us? Now she's using you as a go-between to your father. What did she say to you?"

"I was playing over on the main street. There were big crowds of people going by, when she came along with a man and told me she'd buy me some sweets if I came with her. I said no, but she hugged me and picked me up and carried me to the cake shop. Can't I eat it?" Uncertain what his mother wanted him to do, he watched her and waited.

"You're too young to understand. Don't you know the woman is a demon? Look what she's done to your father. She's turned him into a wastrel. It's because of her that you don't have any clothes to wear, that we don't have our own house any more. Everything is her doing. She's devoured us, and still she isn't satisfied. How can you take anything from her? How could you want to eat it? It makes me sick—that filthy, slimy piece of food. I don't want it in my house. Throw it away. Will you throw it away! What are you waiting for? Is it so precious? Stupid!"

She grabbed the package from him and flung it into the vacant lot. The bag ripped and the cake fell out, rolling through a hole in the rough bamboo fence and landing, from the sound of it, in the gutter on the other side.

Genshichi sat bolt upright. "Ohatsu!"

"What?" she said over her shoulder, glaring at him out of the corner of her eye.

"I've had enough of your lip! What are you raising such a ruckus about, just because somebody gives the boy a piece of cake? She's no stranger, why shouldn't he accept it? Don't take your anger out on Takichi. Where did you learn to insult a father through his son? And don't slander Oriki. If she's a demon, you're the Queen of Hell. Everyone knows a courtesan will deceive a man, but no one ever talks about what a wife does. You should be ashamed of yourself for being so spiteful. I may only be a workman, but I'm still the head of this household, and I won't have anyone here I can't get along with. I don't care where you go, but I want you out of here! You're a tiresome woman."

"You're being unfair. Don't jump to conclusions. Why would I insult you? I lost patience with Takichi for being so innocent. It's just that my anger at Oriki has been building up. But that's no reason to throw me out. It's too mean! I only said those things because I was thinking of our family. If I'd wanted to leave," she sobbed, "I wouldn't have waited all this time, through thick and thin."

"If you're so tired of the way we live, go wherever you want. Nobody's keeping you. I won't have to lead a beggar's life once you're gone. Then maybe Takichi will grow up properly. I've had it with your carping all the time—I can't seem to do anything right in your eyes—and your jealousy of Oriki. If you want to stay here, I'll leave. It's all the same to me. I could take Takichi away from here and never miss the place. Then you can squawk your head off all you want. So which is it? Are you going, or am I?"

Ohatsu had never seen her husband like this, so hot with anger. "Do you really want a divorce?"

"How perceptive of you."

Ohatsu was beside herself. She could barely speak as she swallowed her tears. "It was wrong of me. Forgive me. I shouldn't have thrown the cake away, after Oriki was kind enough to give it to us. It was wrong. You're right—for the things I've said about Oriki, I'm the one who's a demon. I'll never say anything bad about her again, ever. I'll never mention her after this, I swear. I'll never gossip about her. Please reconsider. You know I have no parents or brothers and sisters, only my uncle, the caretaker, who stood in at our wedding. If we're divorced, I'll have nowhere to go. Please forgive me. Even if you do hate me, at least consider Takichi. Please. I'm sorry, Genshichi." She bowed down on the floor and wept.

"No, it won't work." He looked toward the wall, with no intention of listening to any further argument.

He had never been so cruel. Was this what happens to a man when a woman bewitches him? Not only was he prepared to cause her anguish, for all she knew he might let their adored son starve to death. No amount of begging or apologizing was going to save the marriage, but she might at least still save the child.

"Takichi, Takichi," she called. "Who do you like? Your father or your mother?"

"I don't like Daddy. He never buys me anything."

"So you'd rather be with me? Wherever I go?"

"Yes. I'll go too," he said innocently.

"Did you hear that? He wants to go with me. He's your only son. You want him to stay, don't you? Well, I can't let you have him. I'm taking him with me, no matter where we go. Do you understand? He's going with me."

"Do what you want! I don't need the child or anything else. If you want to take him, take him wherever you like. You can have the house and furniture, too. I don't care what you do."

"What are you talking about? What furniture? The house isn't even ours. Just what is it that I'm supposed to do what I want with? You'll be all alone from now on, Genshichi. You can indulge all your vices. But don't come asking me to return Takichi, because I never will."

She rummaged in the closet for her things and found a scarf to wrap them in. "I'm only taking Takichi's coat and sash and his pajamas. I know you haven't said these things out of drunkenness, so I don't expect there'll be any sobering up or changing your mind; but you ought to think carefully about what you're doing. You know what they say. With both parents by his side, a poor child has all the advantages of a rich boy. Won't you feel sorry for Takichi, with only a mother? It's a depraved man who doesn't appreciate his own son. This is the last you'll ever see of either of us."

She took up her bundle and went out.

"Good riddance!"

Lanterns were still up, dangling stale and melancholy, long after the Festival of Souls had ended. Through the gate to the new quarter, two coffins were being carried out, one borne by palanquin and the other thrown like baggage over the shoulders of two men. The bier had been taken quietly from the lodgings of the Kikunoi.

"What a pity the girl fell in love with such a man," onlookers whispered along the main street.

"No. People say it was a love suicide. There's a witness who saw them talking at the temple on the hill that evening just before."

"She must have felt she had to do it. He was the one she really loved."

"That whore feel a sense of duty? Love suicide? Ha! I'll bet he was someone she met on her way home from the bath. She probably couldn't shake him, and went on walking a little too long."

"Mm. She was slashed across the back, down from the shoulder. There were bruises on her cheek and cuts on her neck. She had wounds all over! Obviously she tried to flee, and that's when he killed her."

"He, on the other hand, did a splendid job of it! Hara-kiri and the whole business. Who would have thought he had it in him? Ever since the days he lost his bedding shop, at least. But he died like a man. Went out in a blaze of glory."

"What a loss to the Kikunoi."

"Yes. Think of the men she attracted! To let all those clients slip through your fingers!"

And so the neighbors talked, half-joking, half-sad. There were all sorts of rumors, but nothing that was known with any certainty. There were even those who said they sometimes saw a light flickering in the temple on the hill. It would rise and leave a trail in its wake, and some said it was a soul, denied the repose of the dead.

The Thirteenth Night
(Jūsan'ya, 1895)

Ordinarily, Oseki rode in a handsome black rickshaw, and, when her parents heard the sound of it approaching their gate, they would run out to greet her. Tonight, however, she had hired a rickshaw on the street corner. She paid the driver, sent him away, and stood dejectedly at the door to her parents' house.

Inside, she could hear her father talking in the same loud voice as always. "You could say I'm one of the lucky ones. We have good children. Never a speck of trouble when they were growing up. People are always praising them. And we've never wanted for a thing, have we? Don't think I'm not thankful."

He would be talking to her mother, then. It gave Oseki pause. How was she going to broach the question of divorce when they were so happy, so unaware of things? What a sermon there would be! She was a mother herself, and it wasn't easy, God knows, leaving little Tarō behind. It was a bit late now to be bringing her parents such startling news. The last thing she wanted was to destroy their happiness, as if it were so many bubbles on a stream. For a moment, she felt the urge to go back without saying anything. She could go on just as before—mother to Tarō, wife to Isamu—and her parents could go on boasting of a son-in-law with an imperial appointment. So long as she was careful, nothing would have to change. The little gifts of food they liked, the spending money now and then, all the filial courtesies would continue. But if she had her way and went through with the divorce, it would be the end of everything. Tarō would be miserable with a stepmother. In a single instant, her parents would lose the only reason they had to hold their heads high. There was no telling what people would think of her. And her brother's future—any basis for his success in life—would be swept away by her selfishness and her caprice. Perhaps she *should* go back home to her husband. No! She couldn't. He was inhuman, and she trembled at the thought of him and reeled against the lattice at the gate.

Inside they heard the noise. "Who's there?" her father called out. "Some urchin at the wrong house, I suppose."

But the sound outside turned to laughter. "Papa, it's me." It was a lovely voice.

"Who is it?" Her father pushed back the sliding door. "Oseki! What are you doing here? And without a rickshaw, or your maid? Hurry up—come in.

241

What a surprise! No, we certainly weren't expecting you. Don't bother about the door, I'll get it. Let's go into the other room. We can see the moon from there. Here, use a cushion. No, no, use a cushion, the mats are dirty. I told the landlord, but he says we have to wait till the matting people can get around to making new ones. Don't be so polite with us—you'll get dirty if you don't take a cushion. Well, well, it's awfully late for you to be visiting. Is everyone all right?"

Her father treated her with the usual courtesy, and it made Oseki feel uncomfortable. She disliked it when they deferred to her as the wife of someone important.

"Yes, everyone's fine, in spite of the weather." There, she had managed to bring her emotions under control. "I'm sorry for not coming sooner. How are you?"

"I've been fine. Not so much as a sneeze. Your mother has one of her fainting spells now and then, but it's nothing to speak of. If she lies down for a few hours, it goes away." From his hearty laugh, she could tell he was in good health.

"I don't see Inosuke. Has he gone out somewhere? Still studying hard?"

"He's just left for night school. He's had a promotion, Oseki, thanks to you," her mother said ebulliently as she served the tea. "His supervisor is quite fond of him. Everything seems to be going well. It's thanks to our having Harada Isamu for a son-in-law, of course. Not a day goes by we don't acknowledge it. Ino isn't very good with words, and I know that when he sees Isamu, he probably doesn't express his gratitude as fully as he might. You know about these things, Oseki. I hope you'll let Isamu know how grateful we are to him, and always do your best to make him happy. See to it that he keeps on taking an interest in Ino. How is Tarō in this weather? This change in the seasons! I could do without it. Is he still up to his old tricks? You should have brought him with you tonight. Grandpa and I would have liked to see him."

"I thought I would, but he goes to bed so early. He was already asleep when I left. He really is full of the dickens, and he never listens to reason. When I go out, he wants to go too. He follows me around the house and keeps a good eye on me. He's a handful, all right! I don't know what makes him that way."

She felt overcome with remorse at the thought of the little son she had abandoned. In her resolve to find a new life, she had left him sleeping in his bed. He would probably be awake by now, and calling for her, giving the maids no end of trouble. No treats[1] would placate him tonight. His nurse-maid and the housekeeper would end up threatening to wash their hands of him and feed him to the devil if he didn't behave himself. "The poor thing!" she wanted to cry out. But seeing her parents in such a happy mood, she held her tongue. Instead, she took several puffs on her pipe, coughing into her sleeve to hide her tears.

"By the old calendar, it's the thirteenth night.[2] You may think I'm old-fashioned," her mother said, "but I made some dumplings to offer to the moon, like the old moon-viewing parties. I know you like them. I thought I'd have Inosuke bring you some. But you know how self-conscious he is, he didn't want to have any part of it. So I didn't send you any on the fifteenth, and then I didn't think I ought to start in now.[3] Still, I did want you to have some—it's like a dream, that you've come tonight. It's as if you read my mind! You must have all kinds of good things to eat at home, Oseki, but it's not often you can have your mother's cooking, is it? Let's see you eat some beans and chestnuts—you used to like them so when you were little. Tonight you can forget you're a married woman. Be your old self, don't worry about your manners.

"You know, your father and I are always talking about your success. What an extraordinary match you've made, how wonderful it is, the circles you move in, how impressive you are. But I'm sure it's not easy being the wife of someone as important as Isamu. Why, it's hard just to have people under you—maids to manage, guests to entertain. Not to mention the problem of coming from a poor family like ours. I'll bet you have to be on your toes all the time to make a good impression. Your father and I are well aware of all this. That's why we don't want to make a nuisance of ourselves, much as we would like to see more of you and little Tarō. Sometimes, you know, we pass in front of your gate, in our cotton clothes and carrying our old umbrellas, and we look up at the bamboo blinds on the second floor and wonder to ourselves what you're doing. Then we walk on by. If only your own family were a little better off, you wouldn't have to be so ashamed of us. With all your other problems, if your father and mother were from a higher station, it would be one less thing for you to worry about . . . But what good does it do to talk like this? I can't even send over any dumplings for moon-viewing without being ashamed of the box. I know how you must feel."

Delighted as she was with her daughter's visit, all too quickly the woman had recalled anew how seldom these occasions were, how little freedom she had to see her own daughter.

"I really am an undutiful child," Oseki said, as if to allay her mother's regrets about their humble station. "I may look grand dressed up in soft silks and riding in a private rickshaw, but I can't even help my own parents. I've only helped myself. I'd be much happier doing piecework and living at home with you."

"Don't be a fool!" her father said. "You should never talk that way. What married woman supports her parents? When you were here, you were our daughter. But you're married now, you're the wife of Harada Isamu. Your only responsibility is to Isamu—to make him happy and to manage his household. It's a big job, to be sure, but it was your fate to marry a man who's somebody, Oseki. You have to take the bad with the good. Women are always complaining. Your mother is the same way. What a nuisance it is. She's been irritable all day, just because she couldn't give you any of her dumplings. She's made such a fuss over those dumplings, you'd better eat them up and put her mind at ease . . . Good, aren't they?"

When her father made a joke of things, how could Oseki introduce what she had come to talk about? Dutifully, she began to eat the chestnuts and soybeans her mother had prepared.

In the seven years she had been married, Oseki had never called on them at night. For her to come alone and without a gift was completely unprecedented. Somehow, too, she did not seem quite as well dressed as usual. In their joy at seeing her, at first her parents failed to detect any difference. But she had brought not one word of greeting from their son-in-law, her smile seemed forced. It appeared that something was troubling her.

Her father glanced at the clock on the desk. "Say, it's almost ten. Is it all right for you to stay the night? If you're going back, you'd better be off pretty soon." As he watched Oseki, he tried to fathom what was on his daughter's mind.

There was no more time for pleasantries, and she looked him in the eye. "Papa, actually, I've come to ask you something. Please hear me out." Stiffly, she bowed before him. A tear trickled down her cheek. She was about to reveal now the layers of sorrow she had been keeping to herself.

Disconcerted, her father leaned forward. "What is it?"

"I came here tonight vowing never to return to Isamu. He knows nothing about it. When I put Tarō to bed, I knew I would never see him again. He won't let anyone else take care of him, but I tricked him. I waited for him to fall asleep, and then, as he dreamt, I crept away like an evil spirit. Papa! Mama! Please put yourself in my place! Until today, I've never mentioned our relations to anyone. I've had second thoughts a hundred times, a thousand times, but now my mind's made up, for once and for all. I can't go on another day like this. I must leave Isamu. Please help me. I'll take on any kind of work. I'll do anything to help Inosuke. I just want to live life alone." She burst into sobs and bit her sleeve to try to hold them back. It seemed as if the black bamboo pattern on her robe would turn purple from her tears.

"What happened?" her mother and father asked, drawing closer to Oseki.

"I haven't said anything until now, but if you could see us together for half a day, you'd understand. The only time Isamu talks to me is when he has something for me to do. And even then, he's always hostile. In the morning when he wakes up and I ask him how he slept, he turns the other way and makes a point of showing his indifference. 'The garden is doing well,' he'll say, or something like that. This alone would suffice to make me angry, but he is my husband, so I hold my temper. I've never argued with him. He starts in at me at the breakfast table, and it never stops. In front of the maids even he complains how I can't do anything right, how ill-bred I am. If that were all, I could endure it, but he never lets up. He slights me for my lack of learning. You should hear him dismiss me as 'a woman without any education.' Nobody ever said I went to school with the nobility. I admit I can't hold my own in a discussion of flower arranging or the tea ceremony or poetry or art with the wives of his friends. But if it embarrasses him so much, why doesn't he let me take some proper lessons? He doesn't have to announce publicly how lowborn I am, so that my own maids stare at me!

"You know, for the first six months or so after we were married, he was always at my side, doing everything he could for me. But as soon as Tarō was born—it's frightening how much a man can change! After that, I felt as if I'd been thrown into a dark valley, and I haven't seen the sunlight since. At first I thought he must be teasing. But then I began to understand: he had tired of me, and that was that. He bullies and bullies me in the hope that eventually I'll run away or ask for a divorce.

"Even if he were making a fool of himself over some geisha or keeping a mistress, I would control my jealousy . . . I hear rumors from the maids, but that's the way men are. When a man works as hard as Isamu, you have to expect he'll want to play sometimes. When he goes out, I lay out his clothes carefully, to please him. But no matter how hard I try, nothing I do satisfies him. The reason he doesn't spend more time at home, he says, is because I do everything so badly. I can't even seem to hold my chopsticks to suit him. If he would just tell me what it is he doesn't like, it wouldn't be so bad, but all he ever says is how boring I am, how worthless. He sneers and says he can never have a conversation with me because I don't understand anything, and that, as far as he's concerned, I'm just a wet nurse for Tarō! He's a monster, not a husband. He doesn't come right out and tell me to go away. I'm such a coward, and so attached to Tarō, that I listen to his complaints and never speak up. Then he calls me a slug and says how can he care for anyone with so little spirit or self-respect? On the other hand, if I do stand up for myself in the slightest, then he *will* tell me to go. Mama, it means nothing to me to leave him. He's a great man in name only, and I won't have a moment's regret at being divorced.

"But when I think of Tarō, who can't possibly understand any of this, left with only one parent, that's when my resolve weakens, and I go on apologizing for myself and trying to humor Isamu, and trembling at the least little thing. That's how I've lived until today—quietly enduring everything. How unlucky I've been!" In pouring out her sorrows to them, Oseki had already said much more than she had intended.

Her parents looked at each other in amazement. "We never dreamt things were like this between you."

For a while no one spoke.

Like any mother, she was partial to her children, and, the more she had listened to Oseki, the more distressed her mother felt. "I don't know what your father thinks but, in the first place, we didn't ask Isamu to marry you. What gall he has, complaining about your schooling, or your family's position! Perhaps he's already forgotten how things were, but *I* haven't. You were seventeen and it was New Year's when he first saw you. It was the seventh day of January, in the morning. I remember it very clearly. The pine boughs were still up on the gate. We lived in the old house then, in Sarugakuchō. You were playing badminton out in front with the little girl next door. She hit the shuttlecock into Isamu's carriage as it was passing by, and you went running after him to fetch it. Oh, he was taken with you the minute he saw you. Those go-betweens of his began arriving fast and furious. He had his heart set on you. I don't know how many times we refused. Why, we told him over and over again that our social standing was no match for his, that you were still a child, that you hadn't had the proper training yet—that, given our circumstances, we could hardly arrange for a big wedding. But he wouldn't hear of it. No, no. He had no parents, he said, so there wouldn't be any in-laws making demands to worry about. It was his choice alone, and, as far as he was concerned, no need to fret about social status or anything of the kind. As for training in the polite accomplishments, he said you could take lessons after you were married. He was so persuasive in his arguments. What care he said he'd lavish on you! We never asked him for it, but he even provided funds for your trousseau. You really were the girl of his dreams.

"The reason we don't visit you more often," her mother went on, "is certainly not because we're intimidated by Isamu's standing. You're not his mistress, after all. You're his lawful wife. He begged us for your hand. We have nothing to be embarrassed about on that account. Still, he is so successful. We live a simpler life. We're not about to start hanging onto the coattails of our son-in-law. I couldn't stand to have people think of us that way. It's not out of false pride that we want to be correct in our relations with Isamu. That's why we haven't called on you as often as we would have liked.

"How stupid of us! When he treats you like some foundling! How arrogant he is! He has no right to grumble that you're not cultivated. Oseki, if you don't protest when he criticizes you, it will only get worse. It will become a habit, this abuse of his. First of all, he shouldn't say such things in front of the maids. When a wife's authority is questioned, before you know it, none of the servants will even listen to her. And in front of Tarō! What will happen if he starts to lose respect for you? I think you should speak your mind. If Isamu won't listen, walk out. Tell him you have a family of your own to turn to. I think you've made a terrible mistake in keeping quiet until now. You're too well-mannered. He's taken advantage of that. It makes me sick, just hearing about this. There's no reason to take any more from him. I don't care what our 'status' is—you *do* have a father and mother, and a brother, even if he is still young. Why should you have to suffer like this? Isn't that so, Papa? I'd like to see Isamu once and tell him a thing or two!" In her wrath the woman had lost all perspective.

For some time, Oseki's father had been listening with arms folded and eyes closed. "Now, Mother, don't say anything rash. Hearing all this for the first time, I've been trying to think what we should do. I know Oseki wouldn't say these things without a good reason. It's plain how you've suffered. Does Isamu know you're here tonight? Was there a new flare-up?" He spoke to his daughter in measured tones. "Has he mentioned a divorce yet?"

"Isamu hasn't been home since the day before yesterday," Oseki said. "But that doesn't mean anything. Sometimes he stays away for five or six days. Before he left, he got angry with me for the way I'd laid out his clothes. I apologized profusely, but he wouldn't listen. He ripped the kimono off and flung it on the floor and changed into a suit, one he took out himself. He yelled at me as he went out. 'There couldn't be another man as unhappy as I am,' he said, 'with a woman like you for a wife!' Why is he like this to me? Three hundred and sixty-five days a year, he says almost nothing. Then, on the rare occasions when he does speak, it's to heap abuse upon me. In the face of all this, do you think I want to go on being the wife of Harada Isamu? How can I go on being Tarō's mother? How can I go on wiping the tears away year after year in secret? I don't understand why I should have to suffer so. I've finally made up my mind to forget him, and my child, too.

"You know, when I think back to the days before I was married, I have no unpleasant memories. But the way I feel now, miserable enough to abandon innocent little Tarō as he lies sleeping, I know I can't go on living with Isamu. 'A child grows up even without his parents,' they say. He might be better off without such an unfortunate mother. A stepmother or a mistress—someone who gets along with Isamu—might do Tarō more good than I can. His father might grow to like the boy. In the long run, it's for his own benefit. After tonight, I'll never set foot in Isamu's house again." She spoke bravely, but her voice quavered. It was not so easy to cast off the affection she had for her child.

"Well, no one can say you're being unreasonable," her father sighed. "I'm sure it's been hard on you. It sounds like a dreadful marriage." For a long time he studied Oseki's appearance. Almost without a father's recognizing it, his daughter had become the perfect matron: the proper hairdo fastened with a gold circlet, the black crepe jacket, it was all very tasteful. How could he watch her throw these things away? How could he let her change into a work coat, with her sleeves tied up and her hair pulled back, the better to take in washing or to tackle the scrubbing? And there was Tarō to think of. A moment's anger could dismantle a hundred years of good fortune, and she would then be the butt of ridicule. Once she went back to being the daughter of Saitō Kazue, all the laughter and tears in the world could never reinstate her as the mother of Harada Tarō. She might well have no fondness for her husband, but forgetting her child would not be so easy. After they were separated, she would find herself yearning for him more and more. She would come to long for those days when she endured the ordeal for the sake of being with Tarō. It was Oseki's misfortune to have been born so beautiful, and to have married above herself.

When he thought about her hardships, the man's pity for his daughter doubled. "Oseki, you may think I'm heartless, that I don't understand your situation. But I'm not saying any of this to scold you: when people come from different backgrounds, it's only natural their ways of thinking aren't always going to be the same. I'm sure you're doing your best to please Isamu. But that doesn't mean everything is fine and dandy—not in his eyes, anyway. Isamu is a smart man. He knows what's what. I don't think he means to be unreasonable with you. It's often the case, though: men who are hard-working and admired by the world can sometimes be very selfish. Away from home they hide their swollen heads. With their families they let their hair down; they take out all the discontent they bring home from the office. It must be terribly hard on you to be the target of all Isamu's grievances.

"On the other hand, your responsibilities as the wife of a man like Isamu are of another kind altogether. You're not married to someone in the ward office, you know—some fellow who lights the fire underneath the kettle for you and goes off to work every day with lunch box tied to his waist. You can't compare Isamu's place in society with an ordinary office worker's. Even if he is fussy and a little difficult sometimes, it's still a wife's duty to humor her husband. You can never tell, but I'd be surprised if there are many wives who enjoy completely happy relations with their husbands. If you think you're the only one in a bind like this, Oseki, it'll only embitter you. Fact is, it's a burden many people have to bear. What with the difference in your backgrounds, it's natural you'd meet with more suffering than a wife whose husband comes from the same class.

"Your mother talks big, but remember: the fine salary your brother is making is all thanks to Isamu. They say the light a parent sheds on his child is sevenfold.[4] In that case, the benefits we've received from Isamu must be tenfold! His way of helping out is to do things behind the scenes, but we're indebted to him nonetheless. It's trying for you, Oseki, I know. Think what your marriage means to us, though, and to Inosuke, and to Tarō. If you've been able to put up with things this long, surely you can continue. And how do you know a divorce is the answer? Isamu would have custody of Tarō, and you'd be my daughter again. Once the bonds are cut, there's no going back—even for a glimpse of little Tarō. If you're going to cry over spilt milk, you might as well do your crying as the wife of Harada. All right? Wouldn't that be better, Oseki? Get hold of yourself and go home tonight as if nothing had happened. Go on beingjust as careful as you have been. Even if you don't tell us anything more after this, we'll know now, we'll all understand how you feel. We'll share your tears with you." As he urged his daughter to bow to the inevitable, he too wiped a tear from his eyes.

Sobbing, Oseki gave in to his advice. "It was selfish of me to think of a divorce. You're right. If I couldn't see Tarō, there'd be no point in living. I might flee my present sorrows, but what kind of future would I have? If I could think of myself as already dead, that would solve everything . . . Then Tarō would have both his parents with him. It was a foolish idea I had, and I've troubled you with the whole unpleasant business. From tonight I will consider myself dead—a spirit who watches over Tarō. That way I can bear Isamu's cruelty for a hundred years to come. You've convinced me, Papa. Don't worry. I won't mention any of this again." No sooner had she wiped her eyes than fresh tears came.

"Poor child!" her mother sobbed.

At that moment even the bright moon looked disconsolate. Even the wild grasses in the vase, picked by her brother Inosuke from the thicket along the back bank, swayed as if to offer their sympathy.

Her parents' house was at the foot of Shinzaka in Ueno, on the road toward Surugadai. It was a shady, secluded spot. But tonight the moon shone brilliantly, and on the main street it was as light as midday. Her parents were not patrons of any of the rickshaw stations; from their window they hailed a rickshawman as he went by.

"Well, then, if you agree, Oseki, I think you'd better be off. Going out without permission while your husband's away, you'll have a lot of explaining to do. It's getting late. It won't take long by rickshaw, though. We'll come soon and talk about things. But tonight you'd best get back." Her father led her by the hand as if to drag her out. The pity he felt for Oseki did not preclude his desire to see the matter settled quietly.

Oseki was resigned to her fate. "That's the end of it, this talk. I'm going home. I'm still Harada's wife. Isamu mustn't know about tonight. Inosuke still has the backing of an important man. Don't worry. As long as you are all happy, I won't have any regrets. I won't do anything rash, so please, you mustn't worry. From now on, I'll consider myself Isamu's property. I'll do whatever he says. Well, I'd better go. Say hello to Inosuke when he comes home. Take care of yourselves. The next time, I'll come with happy news." It was apparent in the way she rose to leave that Oseki had no choice in all of this.

Taking her purse, with what little money she had, Oseki's mother went out to the rickshaw driver. "How much is it to Surugadai?"

"No, Mother. I'll pay. Thank you anyway." Her voice was subdued as she touched her sleeve to her face to brush a tear. Quietly, she passed through the front door and stepped into the rickshaw.

Inside the house, her father coughed to clear his voice, and, from the sound
of it, he too was crying.

The faint cry of crickets sounded mournful in the moonglow and the autumn
wind. No sooner had they reached Ueno than Oseki was given a start.

"I'm sorry," the man said, abruptly putting down the poles of the
rickshaw. "I can't take you any farther. I won't charge you anything."

Oseki was astonished. "What? What am I supposed to do? I'm in a hurry.
I'll pay you extra, please try. I'm not going to find another rickshaw in a
lonely place like this, now, am I? Come on, do stop grumbling and take me
home." She trembled slightly as she implored him.

"I'm not asking you to pay double. I'm asking you to let me stop. Please get
out. I can't take you any farther. I'm too tired."

"Are you sick? What's the matter?" She began to raise her voice. "You can't
just drop me here and say you're tired."

"Forgive me. I'm too tired, really." He held the lantern in his hand and
stepped aside from the poles of the rickshaw.

"What a selfish man you are! All right, I won't ask you to take me all the
way, just to where I can find another rickshaw. I'll pay you—at least go as far
as Hirokōji." She spoke in a soft voice to cajole him.

"Well, you are a young lady. I suppose it wouldn't be very nice of me to
leave you here, in this forsaken spot. It was wrong of me. All right, let's go. I'll
take you there. I must have scared you."

When he picked up the lantern to be off, he did not seem so rough, and
Oseki breathed a sigh of relief. Feeling safe in his charge, she looked into the
man's face. He was twenty-five or -six, of dark complexion and a wiry build.
He was not very tall. Wait—that face now turned away from her in the
moonlight! She knew it! His name was on the tip of her tongue, but she
hesitated to utter it.

"Is it you?" she asked before she knew what she was saying.

"Hm?" Surprised, he turned around to look at her.

"Goodness! It *is* you. Surely you haven't forgotten me, have you?" She
slipped down from the rickshaw, never taking her eyes from him.

"Saitō Oseki? I'm ashamed for you to see me like this. How could I have
known it was you—without eyes in the back of my head? I should have
recognized you from your voice. I guess I've gotten pretty stupid," he said,
avoiding her look.

Oseki studied him from head to toe. "No, no. If we had met walking in the
street, I wouldn't have recognized you. Until just now I thought you were a
stranger, only a rickshawman. Why should you have recognized me? Forgive

me. How long have you been doing this? You're not overworking yourself, are you? You look frail. I heard somewhere that your aunt closed the shop in Ogawamachi and moved to the countryside. I'm not the person I used to be, either. Things get in the way of what we want," she sighed. "I haven't been able to visit you or even write you a letter. Where are you living now? How is your wife? Do you have children? Now and then I go to see the shops[5] in Ogawamachi. The old store looks the same as always. It's the same tobacco shop, only it's called the Notoya now. Whenever I go by, I look at it and think to myself, 'That's where Kōsaka Roku lived when we were children.' Remember how we used to sneak a smoke on the way to school? What little know-it-alls we were! I've always wondered where you'd gone, what you were doing now. Anyone as gentle as you would be having a hard time of it. I worried about you. When I go home to see my parents, I ask if anyone's heard what became of you. It's been five years since I moved away from Sarugakuchō, and all that time I've never heard a thing.[6] How I've missed you!" She seemed to have forgotten that she was a married woman as she deluged him with her questions.

"I'm ashamed how low I've fallen," he said as he took his towel and wiped the sweat from his forehead. "I don't even have a place I can call home any more. I sleep upstairs in a cheap inn in Asakusa run by a man named Murata. Some days I spend the whole day there, doing nothing. Some days, like tonight, I work until late pulling the rickshaw. Then when I get tired of it, I loaf again: my life's just going up in smoke. I heard that you were still as beautiful as ever, Oseki, and that you were someone's wife now. I always hoped that, by some slim chance, I'd see you again and we'd be able to talk once more. My life isn't worth anything, I didn't think it mattered what happened to me—but if I hadn't gone on living, I couldn't have met you tonight. Gosh, I'm glad you recognized me! Thank you, Oseki." He looked down at the ground.

There were tears in her eyes as Oseki tried to console him. "You're not the only one to suffer in this sad world . . . Tell me something about your wife."

"You probably knew her. She was the daughter of the Sugitas, kitty-corner from us. The one people were always complimenting for her fair skin and her pretty figure. Well, I was leading a bad life—out carousing, never coming home—which one of my pig-headed relatives mistook for proof that I ought to get married. Mother put her glasses on and began looking for candidates and soon settled on the Sugita girl. She kept pestering me, so I finally gave in. We were married just about the time I heard that you were expecting. And then, a year later, people were congratulating us. But you don't think a few baby's toys were enough to make me change my ways, do you? People think that with a pretty wife a man will stop playing around, and with a child he'll become more serious. But it wouldn't have mattered what beauty of a wife I had. Ono no Komachi, Lady Hsi Shih, Princess Sotoori herself dancing before my eyes—my bad habits wouldn't have changed.[7] Why should a little thing that reeks of its mother's milk inspire some sort of religious awakening in a man? I fooled around to my heart's content and drank myself silly. I neglected my family, I had no use for work. It got to the point where I didn't have a chopstick to my name. That was three years ago. My mother went to live with my sister, who had gone to the provinces to marry. My wife took the baby and returned to her folks. We haven't had a thing to do with each other since. The baby was a girl, anyway, so I never missed her much. I heard she died late last year of typhoid. Girls are precocious, though—I bet she didn't die without remembering her papa. If she'd lived, she would have been five this year. I don't know why I'm telling you all this—it's not really very interesting."

A smile played across his somber face. "If I'd known it was you, Oseki, I wouldn't have been so gruff tonight. Come on, get in and I'll take you home. I must have given you a good scare. You know, I'm not much of a rickshaw-man, even. I don't get any thrill out of clutching these poles, I'll tell you that. What does a fellow like me have to look forward to? Making a living like a horse, like some ox! You think I'm happy when I get a few coins? You think a little wine's going to drive my sorrows away? I'm really fed up with it. Who cares if I have a passenger? When I'm tired, that's it! I don't go any farther. Pretty selfish and disgusting, aren't I? Well, come on, get in."

"What! Do you think I could ride now that I know who you are? It was different when I didn't know it was you. But I will ask you to walk with me as far as Hirokōji. *Please.* I'm afraid to stay here alone. We can talk along the way." Oseki held up the bottom of her kimono as she walked. The clatter of her lacquered sandals rang despondently against the cobblestones.

Of all her friends, he was the one she had never quite forgotten: Kōsaka's boy at the tobacco stall in Ogawamachi, where everything was always ship-shape. Now his skin was dark and he looked pretty shabby, but in the old days he had cut a different figure, in his fine matched cottons and his snappy apron. What a charmer he was then! So friendly and grown-up. He was just a boy, but the store did better under him than it had when his father was alive. Everyone thought so highly of him, he was so intelligent. He had certainly changed . . . After her engagement was announced, as she remembered it, he had become another person, wild and dissipated. The decline was so extraordinary, it seemed as if some evil spirit had taken hold of him. That's what people said. And tonight he looked it. It was pitiful . . . She would never have dreamt that Kōsaka Roku would end up living in a cheap rooming house.

He had been in love with her once, and, from the time she was twelve until she was seventeen, they saw each other every day. She used to imagine what it would be like to sit behind the counter of the tobacco shop, reading the paper and waiting on customers. But then a stranger came along and asked her to marry him. Her parents pressed her, how could she defy them? She had always hoped to marry Roku, though he had never made any overtures, it was true. In the end, her parents persuaded her, and she told herself that her dreams of helping Roku run the shop were only that—the dreams of a schoolgirl, puppy love. She put him out of her mind and resigned herself to marrying Harada. It had not been easy; until the last moment, there were tears in Oseki's eyes for Kōsaka Roku. He must have yearned for her, too. Perhaps she was even the cause of his ruin. How repellent he must find it to see her tonight, looking smug and matronly. She was not as happy and contented as she might look, she wanted to tell him. She turned to him, wondering what he was thinking, but his face was blank, and he did not appear to be rejoicing in this rare encounter.

They came out into Hirokōji. Here Oseki would be able to find a rickshaw. She took some money from her purse and gently wrapped it in chrysanthemum paper. "Forgive me, Roku, for being rude," she said, offering it to him. "Please buy yourself some paper handkerchiefs or something. I haven't seen you in so long—there are so many things I'd like to say. It's hard to put them into words . . . Take good care of yourself, Roku, so your mother doesn't worry. I'll pray for you. I want to see the old Roku I used to know, with that fine shop again. Good-by."

He took the paper from her. "I shouldn't accept this. But since it's from you, I will. As a keepsake. I hate to say good-by to you, Oseki. It's been like a dream, seeing you again. Well, I'll be going too, then. It's lonely on the road late at night, isn't it?"

He started off with the empty rickshaw behind him, and when he had gone a little way he turned back to look at her. He was heading east; she would be going south. The branches of the willow trees trailed beside her in the moonlight as she walked, dispirited, along the main road. One living on the second floor of Murata's boardinghouse; the other, the wife of the great Harada: each knew his share of sadness in life.

Child's Play
(Takekurabe, 1895–96)

It's a long way round to the front of the quarter,[1] where the trailing branches of the willow tree bid farewell to the nighttime revellers and the bawdyhouse lights flicker in the moat, dark as the dye that blackens the smiles of the Yoshiwara beauties.[2] From the third-floor rooms of the lofty houses the all but palpable music and laughter spill down into the side street.[3] Who knows how these great establishments prosper? The rickshaws pull up night and day.

They call this part of town beyond the quarter "in front of Daion Temple." The name may sound a little saintly, but those who live in the area will tell you it's a lively place. Turn the corner at Mishima Shrine and you don't find any mansions, just tenements of ten or twenty houses, where eaves have long begun to sag and shutters only close halfway. It is not a spot for trade to flourish.

Outside the tumble-down houses everyone works madly: cutting up paper into queer little pieces, slopping them with paint, spearing them on funny-looking spits. Whole families, the whole neighborhood is wrapped up in the production of these strange, bright paper skewers. They dry the painted scraps in the morning and assemble them at night. And what are these things that have everyone so preoccupied? "You don't know?" a merchant will reply in astonishment. "*Kumade* charms![4] On Otori day, you ought to see the big-wishers buy them up!"[5]

Year in, year out, the minute the New Year pine bough comes down from the front gate, every self-respecting businessman takes up the same sideline, and by summer hands and feet are splattered with paint. They count on the earnings to buy new clothes for the holidays. If the gods grant prosperity to mere purchasers of these charms, the men who make them figure they stand to reap a windfall. Funny thing, no one hears of any rich men dwelling in these parts.

Most of the people here, in fact, have some connection with the quarter. The menfolk do odd jobs at the less dignified houses. You can hear them in the evenings jiggling their shoe-check tags before they leave for work, and you'll see them putting on their jackets when most men take them off. Wives rub good-luck flints behind them to protect their men from harm. Could this be the final parting? It's a dangerous business. Innocent bystanders get killed when there's a brawl in one of the houses.[6] And look out if you ever foil the double suicide of a courtesan and her lover! Yet off the husbands go to risk their lives each night like schoolboys to a picnic.

Daughters, too, are involved in the quarter: here, a serving girl in one of the great establishments; there, an escort plying back and forth between the teahouse and the brothel. They bustle along with their shop's lantern, an advertisement for all to see. But what will become of these girls once they have graduated from their present course of training? To them, the work is something grand and gala, as if they were performing on a fine wooden stage. Then one day before they know it they have reached the age of thirty, trim and tidy in their cotton coats with matching dresses and their sensible dark blue stockings. They carry their little packages under their arms, and we know what *these* are without asking. Stomp, stomp, they go with the heels of their sandals—they're in an awful hurry—and the flimsy drawbridges flop down across the ditch. "We'll leave it here at the back," they say, setting down their bundles, "it's too far round to the front." So they are needle-women now, apparently.

Customs here are indeed a little different. You won't find many women who tie their sashes neatly behind their waists. It's one thing to see a woman of a certain age who favors gaudy patterns, or a sash cut immoderately wide. It's quite another to see these barefaced girls of fifteen or sixteen, all decked out in flashy clothes and blowing on bladder cherries, which everybody knows are used as contraceptives. But that's what kind of neighborhood it is. A trollop who yesterday went by the name of some heroine in *The Tale of Genji* at one of the third-rate houses along the ditch today runs off with a thug. They open a lean-to bar, though neither of them knows the first thing about running a business. They soon go broke. The beauty begins to miss her former calling. Her assets are gone with the chopped-up chicken bones left from last night's hors d'oeuvres. Unlike the chicken, however, our charmer can still return to her old nest.[7] People around here, for some reason, find this kind of woman more alluring than your ordinary one.

In such a world, how are the children to escape being influenced? Take the autumn festival.[8] Mother Meng[9] would be scandalized at the speed with which they learn to mimic all the famous clowns; why, there's not a one of them who can't do Rohachi and Eiki.[10] They hear their performances praised, and that night the smart alecks repeat their rounds. It starts at the age of seven or eight, this audacity, and by the time they're fifteen! Towels from the evening bath dangle from their shoulders, and the latest song, in a nasal twang of disrespect, dribbles from the corner of their lips. At school, any moment, a proper music class is apt to lapse into the rhythms of the quarter. Athletic meets ring with the songs of geisha—who needs the school cheer? One sympathizes with their teachers, who toil at the Ikueisha, not far from here. It may be a crowded little schoolhouse—a private school, actually[11]—but the students number close to a thousand, and the teachers who are popular there soon become known. In these parts, the very word *school* is synonymous with the Ikueisha.

Listen to them walking home from school: "Your father sure keeps an eye on the teahouse by the bridge!" they shout at the fireman's boy. It's the wisdom of the street. Children know about the quarter. They scramble over garden walls, imitating firemen. "Hey! You broke the spikes on the fence to keep the thieves away!" A two-bit shyster's son begins his prosecution: "Your old man's a 'horse,' isn't he? Isn't he?" The blood rushes to the defendant's face. The poor boy—he'd sooner die than admit his father collected bills for a brothel. And then there are the favorite sons of the big shots of the quarter, who grow up in lodgings at some remove, free to feign a noble birth. They sport the latest prep-school cap, they have a look of leisure, and they wear their European clothes with style and panache. All the same, it's amusing to watch the others curry favor. "Young master, young master," they call them, when "spoiled brat" would do.

Among the many students at the Ikueisha was Nobuyuki of Ryūge Temple.[12] In time, his thick, black hair would be shorn, and he would don the dark robes of a priest. It may well have been his own choice, and then again perhaps he had resigned himself to fate. His father was a cleric, and already like his father Nobu was a scholar. By nature he was a quiet boy. His classmates considered him a wet blanket and they liked to tease him. "Here—this is your line of work," they would laugh, stringing up a dead cat. "How about offering the last rites?" All that was in the past, however; no one made fun of him now, not even by mistake. He was fifteen[13] and of average height, his dark hair was closely cropped in schoolboy fashion, and yet something about him was different from the others. Although he had the ordinary-sounding name of Fujimoto Nobuyuki, already in his manner were suggestions of the cloth.

The Festival of Senzoku Shrine was set for the twentieth of August, and not a block would there be without a float of its own jostling for glory. Over the ditch and up the side of the embankment they charge: all the young men, pushing, pulling, bent on taking the quarter. The heart beats faster at the mere thought of it. And keep an eye, mind you, on the young ones—once they get wind of what the older boys are up to. Matching kimonos for the whole gang are only the beginning. The saucy things they dream up will give you goose bumps.

The back-street gang, as they preferred to call themselves, had Chōkichi for their leader. He was the fire chief's son—sixteen and full of it. He hadn't walked without his chest puffed out since the day he started policing the fall festival with his father: baton swinging, belt low around the hips, sneering whenever he answered. The firemen's wives all griped among themselves, "If he weren't the chief's boy, he'd never get away with it."

Selfish Chōkichi saw to it that he always got his way. He stretched his side-street influence wider than it really went, until in Shōta, the leader of the main-street gang, Chōkichi knew that he had met his match. Though Shōta was three years younger, he was the son of Tanaka, the pawnbroker; his family had money, he was a likable boy. Chōkichi went to the Ikueisha; Shōta, to a fancy public school.[14] The school songs they sang may have been the same, but Shōta always made a face, as if Chōkichi and his friends at the Ikueisha were poor relations.

With his band of admirers—even some grown-ups numbered among them—for the last two years Shōta's plans for the festival had flowered more luxuriantly than the efforts of Chōkichi's gang. There had been no contest, and, if he lost again this year, all his threats—"Who do you think you're dealing with? Chōkichi from the back streets, that's who!"—would no longer garner even enough members for a swimming team at the Benten Ditch. If it were a matter of strength, he knew he would prevail, but everyone was taken in by Shōta's quiet ways and his good grades. It was mortifying—some of his own gang had gone over on the sly to Shōta's side. Tarokichi and Sangorō, for instance.

Now the festival was only two days away. It looked more and more as if Chōkichi would lose again. He was desperate. If he could just see that Shōta got a little egg on his face, it wouldn't matter if he himself lost an eye or a limb. He wouldn't have to suffer defeat any more if he could recruit the likes of Ushi, the son of the rickshawman, and Ben, whose family made hair ribbons, and Yasuke, the toymaker's boy. Ah, and better still: if he could get Nobu on his side—there was a fellow who'd have a good idea or two.

Near dusk on the evening of the eighteenth, hoping for a chance to persuade Nobu, Chōkichi made his cocky way through the bamboo thicket of the temple. Swatting the mosquitoes that swarmed about his face, he stole up to Nobu's room.

"Nobu? You there? I know people say I'm a roughneck, and maybe I am. But it's no wonder, with the way they goad me. Listen, Nobu, I've had enough of them—ever since last year when that jerk from Shōta's gang picked a fight with my little brother and they all came running and jumped on him and threw him around. I mean, what do you think of something like that? Beating up a little kid and breaking his festival lantern! And then that Donkey from the dumpling shop, who's so big and awkward he thinks he can go around acting like a grown-up! He comes and starts insulting me to my brother behind my back. You know what he said? 'Think Chōkichi's so smart, huh?

And your father's fire chief? Well, your big brother isn't head of anything. He's the tail end—a pig's tail end!' That's what he said! All this time I'm off in the parade, pulling our float. When I heard about it later, though, I was ready to get even! But my father found out, and *I'm* the one who got in trouble. And you remember the year before that, don't you? I went over to the paper shop, where a bunch of kids from the main street were putting on their slapstick.[15] You know what snide things they said to me? 'Doesn't the back street have its own games?' And all the while they're treating Shōta like king. I don't forget these things, Nobu . . . I don't care how much money he has. Who is he, anyway, but the son of a loan shark? I'd be doing the world a favor to get rid of such a creep. This year, no matter how tough I have to be, I'll see to it that Shōta eats his words. That's why, Nobu—come on—for a friend, you've got to help. I know you don't like this kind of rough stuff. But it's to get our honor back! Don't you want to help me smash that snooty Shōta with his stuck-up school songs? You know when they call me a stupid private-schooler, it goes for you too. So come on. Do me this one favor and help us out. Carry one of the lanterns around at the festival. Listen, I'm eating my heart out, this has been bothering me so much. If we lose this time, it'll be the end of me." Chōkichi's broad shoulders trembled with anger.

"But I'm not very strong."

"I don't care whether you're strong or not."

"I don't think I could carry one of the lanterns."

"You don't have to!"

"You'll lose even with me—you don't care?"

"If we lose, we lose. Look, you don't have to do anything. Just so you're on our side. All we have to do is show you off. It'll attract others. Build up our morale. I know I'm not very smart, but you are. So if they start using big words and making fun of us, you can answer right back in Chinese. I feel better already. You're worth the whole lot of them! Thanks, Nobu." It wasn't often you heard Chōkichi speak so softly.

The one the son of a workman, with his boy's belt and his smart straw sandals; the other like a priest in his somber jacket and his purple band— they were the opposite sides of a coin. More often than not, the two boys disagreed. Yet it was true that Nobu's own parents had a soft spot for Chōkichi. Why, the venerable Head Priest and his wife had heard Chōkichi's first cries as a babe outside the temple gate. And, after all, they did both go to the same school. If people made fun of the Ikueisha to Chōkichi, it reflected on Nobu too. It was a shame that Chōkichi wasn't better liked, but he never had been what you'd call appealing—unlike Shōta, who attracted everyone, even the older boys, for his allies. Nobu wasn't showing any prejudice. If Chōkichi lost, the blame would rest squarely on Shōta. When Chōkichi came to him like this, out of a sense of decency Nobu could hardly refuse.

"All right. I'm on your side. But you'd better keep the fighting down . . . If

hey start things, we won't have any choice. And if that happens, I'll wrap
hōta around my little finger." Nobu's reticence had already been forgotten.
Ie opened his desk drawer and showed Chōkichi the prized Kokaji dagger his
ather had brought him from Kyōto.
    "Say! That'll really cut!" Chōkichi admired.
    Look out—careful how you wave that thing.

Jndone, her hair would reach her feet. She wore it swept up and pulled into a
eavy-looking roll in the "red bear" style[16]—a frightening name for a maiden's
airdo, but the latest fashion even among girls of good family. Her skin was
air and her nose was nicely shaped. Her mouth, a little large perhaps, was
irm and not at all unattractive. If you took her features one by one, it is true,
hey were not the classic components of ideal beauty. And yet she was a
vinsome girl, exuberant, soft-spoken. Her eyes radiated warmth whenever
he looked at you.
    "I'd like to see her three years from now!" young men leaving the quarter
vould remark when they noticed her returning from the morning bath, her
>wel in hand and her neck a lovely white above her orange kimono of boldly
atterned butterflies and birds, her stylish sash wrapped high at the waist[17]
nd her lacquered slippers more thickly soled than what one usually saw,
ven around here.
    Her name was Midori and she was from the Daikokuya. She was born in
ishū,[18] though, and her words had the slightest southern lilt. It was charm-
ig. There were few who did not enjoy her generous, open nature.
    For a child, Midori had a handsome pocketbook, thanks to her sister's
uccess in the quarter. The great lady's satellites[19] knew how to purchase
ood will: "Here Midori, go buy yourself a doll," the manager would say. "It
n't much, honey," one of the attendant girls would offer, "but it'll buy you a
all, anyway." No one took these gifts very seriously, and the income Midori
ccepted as her due. It was nothing for her to turn round and treat twenty
lassmates to matching rubber balls. She had been known to delight her
·iend the woman at the paper store by buying up every last shopworn trifle.
he extravagance day after day was certainly beyond the child's age or sta-
on. What would become of her? Her parents looked the other way, never a
·ord of caution.
    And wasn't it odd, how the owner of her sister's house would spoil her so?
ie was hardly his adopted child, or even a relation. Yet ever since he had
>me to their home in the provinces to appraise her older sister, Midori and
er parents had found themselves here at the Daikokuya. They had packed up
ieir belongings, along with her sister, to seek their fortunes in the city.

What lay behind it all would be difficult to say, but today her parents were housekeepers for the gentleman. On the side, her mother took in sewing from the women of the district; her father kept the books at a third-rate house. They saw to it that Midori went to school and that she learned her sewing and her music. The rest of the time she was on her own: lolling around her sister's rooms for half the day, playing in the streets the other half. Her head was full of the sounds of samisen and drum, of the twilight reds and purples of the quarter.[20] New to the city, Midori had bristled when the other girls made fun of her, calling her a country girl for wearing a lavender collar with her lined kimono. She had cried for three days then. Not now, though. It was Midori who would tease when someone seemed uncouth—"What kind of dress is that!"—and no one had quite the nimble wit to return her rebukes.

The festival was to be held on the twentieth, and this year they would have to outdo themselves. Midori's help was needed. "All right. Everyone plan something. We'll take a vote. I'll pay for everything," she responded with her usual generosity. "Don't worry about the cost."

The children were quicker than adults to seize an opportunity. The beneficent ruler seldom comes a second time.

"Let's do a show. We can borrow a shop where everyone can watch us."

"No—that's stupid! Let's build a little shrine to carry around. A good one like they have at Kabata's. Even if it's heavy, it won't matter, once we get it going to a nice beat."

"Yatchoi! Yatchoi!" danced a youth already in the mood, his towel twisted into a festive headband.

"What about us?" "You think Midori's going to have any fun just watching while you're all roughhousing?" "Come on, Midori, have them do something else." The girls, it seemed, would prefer to forgo the celebrations for an afternoon of vaudeville.

Shōta's handsome eyes lit up. "Why don't we do a magic lantern show? I have a few pictures at my house. Midori, you can buy the rest. We can use the paper shop. I'll run the lantern, and Sangorō from the back street can be the narrator. What do you say, Midori? Wouldn't that be good?"

"I like it! If Sangorō does the talking, no one will be able to keep from laughing. Too bad we can't put a picture of him in the show."

Everything was decided. Shōta dashed around to get things ready.

By the next day, word of their plans had reached the back street.

The drums, the samisen! Even in a place never wanting for music, the festival is the liveliest time of year. What could rival it but Otori day? Just watch the shrines try to surpass one another in their celebrations.

The back-street and the main-street gangs each had their own matching outfits, Mōka cotton emblazoned with their street names. "But they're not as nice as last year's," some grumbled.[21] Sleeves were tied up with flaxen cords stained yellow from a jasmine dye. The wider the bright ribbons, everyone agreed, the better. Children under fifteen or so weren't satisfied until they had accumulated all the trinkets they could carry—Daruma dolls, owls, dogs of papier-mâché. Some had eight or nine, even eleven, dangling from their yellow armbands. It was a sight to see them, bells of all sizes jingling from their backs as they ran along gamely in their stockinged feet.

Shōta stood apart from the crowd. Today he looked unusually dapper. His red-striped jacket and his dark-blue vest contrasted handsomely with his boyish complexion. He wore a pale blue sash wrapped tightly round the waist. A second look revealed it to be the most expensive crepe. The emblems on his collar were exceptional enough to draw attention by themselves. In his headband he had tucked a paper flower. Though his well-heeled feet beat time to the rhythm of the drums, Shōta did not join the ranks of any of the street musicians.

Festival eve had passed without incident. Now at dusk on this once-in-a-year holiday, twelve of the main-street gang were gathered at the paper shop. Only Midori, a long time with her evening toilette, had yet to appear. Shōta was getting impatient.

"What's taking her so long?" He paced in and out the front door. "Sangorō, go and get her. You've never been to the Daikokuya, though, have you? Call her from the garden, and she'll hear you. Hurry up."

"All right. I'll leave my lantern here. Shōta, keep an eye on it; someone might take the candle."

"Don't be such a cheapskate! Stop dawdling."

"I'm off."[22] The boy didn't seem to mind being scolded by his juniors.

"There goes the god of lightning,"[23] someone said, and the girls all burst out laughing at the way he ran. He was short and beefy, and, with no neck to speak of, his bulging head suggested one of those wooden mallets. Protruding forehead, pug nose, big front teeth—no wonder he was called Bucktooth-Sangorō. He was decidedly dark-skinned, but what one noticed even more was the expression on his face, dimpled and affable and ready for the clown's role. His eyebrows were so oddly placed as to suggest the final outcome of a game of pin-the-tail-on-the-donkey. He was an amusing child, without a mean streak in him.

To those who did not know how poor he was, Sangorō shrugged off his everyday cotton clothes. "Couldn't get a matching kimono made in time."

He was the eldest of six children. Their father contrived to feed them all by clinging to the handles of a rickshaw. True, he worked the prosperous street in front of the quarter, lined with the teahouses. But somehow the wheels of his cart never turned a real profit. Fast as they spun, they only kept the family going hand-to-mouth.[24]

"Now that you're thirteen, I'm counting on you to help out, boy," Sangorō's

father had told him the year before last. He went to work at the printing shop
over in Namiki but, in his lackadaisical way, in ten days he had tired of the
job. Seldom did he last more than a month anywhere. From November to
January he worked part-time making shuttlecocks for the New Year's games.
In summer he helped the iceman near the hospital. Thanks to the comical
way he had of soliciting customers, the two of them did a brisk business. A
born hawker, the iceman said.

Ever since he had pulled a float last year at the Yoshiwara carnival, his
disapproving friends had dubbed him "Mannenchō." He was as bad, they
said, as the jesters from that lowliest of slums.[25] But everyone knew Sangorō
was a buffoon. No one disliked him; this was his one advantage.

The pawnshop Shōta's people ran was a lifeline for Sangorō and his family,
whose gratitude toward the Tanakas was no small thing. True, the daily
interest rates they were obliged to pay bordered on the exorbitant; yet without the loans they could scarcely have kept going. How, then, could they
begrudge the moneylender his due?

"Sangorō," Shōta and the main-street gang were forever urging him,
"come over to our street and play." And how could he refuse Shōta, to whose
family they were all indebted? On the other hand, he was born and raised in
the back streets, he lived on land belonging to Ryūge Temple, Chōkichi's
father owned their house. It wouldn't do to turn his back openly on Chōkichi.
When in the end he quietly went over to the main street, the accusing looks
were hard for him to bear.

Shōta sat down in the paper shop, tired of waiting for Midori, and began to
sing the opening lines of "Secret Love."

"Listen to that!" laughed the shopkeeper's wife. "Singing love songs
already—we'll have to keep an eye on this one."

Shōta's ears turned red. "Let's go!" he called to the others in a loud voice he
hoped would cover his embarrassment. But as he ran out of the shop, he
bumped into his grandmother.

"Shōta—why haven't you come home for dinner? I've been calling and
calling, but you're so busy playing you don't even listen. You can all play
again after dinner. Thanks," she added in a curt word of parting to the
shopkeeper's wife.

Shōta had no choice but to follow her home.

Whenever he left, how lonely it seemed. Only one less person than before,
and yet even the grown-ups missed Shōta. It was not that he was boisterous
or always cracking jokes, like Sangorō. Such friendliness, though—you don't
usually find it in a rich boy.

"But did you see the nasty way his grandmother has?" housewives gossiped
on the street corner. "She's sixty-four if she's a day. And her hair done up like
a young floozy! At least she doesn't wear all that powder any more."

"You ought to hear her purr and coax to get her loans back. Nothing stops her. You watch—the borrower could die, and she'd be at the funeral to collect. She's the kind who'll try to take her money with her when she goes."

"We can't even hold our heads up to her—that's the power of money."

"Don't you wish you had a little of it?"

"They say she even lends to the big houses in the quarter."

What they wouldn't give to know how much the old crone had.

"How sad it is for one who waits alone by the midnight hearth." The love songs do have a way of putting things.[26]

The breeze felt cool on that summer evening. In the bath Midori had washed the heat of the day away, and now she stood before her full-length mirror getting ready. Her mother took charge of repairing the girl's hairdo. A beauty, even if she did say so, the woman thought, inspecting her daughter from every angle. "You still don't have enough powder on your neck." They had chosen for the occasion a silk kimono in a cool, pale blue. Her straw-colored sash was flecked with gold threads and custom-made to fit her tiny waist. It would be some time, though, before they could begin deciding on the proper sandals.

"Isn't she ready yet?" Sangorō was losing his patience. He had circled the garden wall seven times. How much longer could he go on yawning? The mosquitoes around here were a local specialty; no sooner had he brushed them away than they would buzz back again. A bite on the neck, a bite on the forehead. Just as he had had about all he could take, Midori finally appeared.

"Let's go," she said.

He pulled her sleeve without answering her and began to run.

Midori was soon out of breath. She could feel her heart pounding. "Well, if you're in such a hurry about it, go on ahead."

Sangorō arrived at the paper shop just before her. Shōta, it appeared, had gone home for dinner.

"This isn't going to be any fun. We can't start the lantern show without Shōta," Midori complained, turning to the shopkeeper's wife. "Any checkers? Cut-outs? We'll need *something* to keep us busy till he comes."

"Here we are." The girls immediately began to cut out the paper dolls the shop lady handed them.

The boys, with Sangorō in the lead, replayed entertainments from the Yoshiwara carnival. Their harmony was odd, but they knew the melodies:

> "Come see the thriving quarter—
> The lights, the lanterns under every eave,
> The gaiety of all five streets!"[27]

In fact, they remembered perfectly the songs and dances of a year, two years before. They didn't miss a beat; they had every gesture down. A crowd gathered at the gate outside to watch the ten of them, carried away by their own side show.

"Is Sangorō there?" called a voice from among the onlookers. "Come here a minute, quick." It was Bunji, the hairdresser's boy.

"Just a second," yelled Sangorō without a care.

No sooner did he run through the doorway than someone punched him in the face. "You double-crosser! This'll teach you! Who do you think I am? Chōkichi! I'll make you sorry you ever made fun of us!"

Sangorō was dumbfounded. He tried to escape, but they grabbed him by the collar.

"Kill him! Shōta too! Don't let the chicken get away. And Donkey from the dumpling shop—don't think you're going to get off so easy!"

The uproar swelled like the rising tide. Paper lanterns came crashing down from the eaves.

"Mind the lamp. You mustn't fight in front of the shop." The woman's yell was loud enough, but who was listening?

There were fourteen or fifteen of them in the attack, streamers round the heads, their oversize lanterns swinging. Blows were struck in all directions, things trampled underfoot. The outrage of it! But Shōta—the one they were after—was nowhere to be found.

"Hide him, will you? Where is he? If you don't tell us, you'll answer for it." They closed in around Sangorō, hitting and kicking, until Midori couldn't stand to watch. She pushed her way to the front, past the restraining hand of the shopkeeper's wife.

"What are you taking it out on him for? If you want to fight with Shōta, fight with Shōta. He didn't run away and he's not hiding. He's not here, that's all. This is our place. Why do you have to go sticking your noses in? You're such a creep, Chōkichi. Why don't you leave Sangorō alone? There—you've knocked him down. Now stop it! If you want to hit someone, hit me. Don't try to hold me back," she turned to the shopkeeper's wife, shouting abuse at Chōkichi all the while she tried to free herself.

"Yeah? You're nothing but a whore, just like your sister," Chōkichi shot back. He stepped around from behind the others and grabbed his muddy sandal. "This is all you're worth." He threw it at Midori.

With a splatter, it struck her square on the forehead. She turned white, but the shopkeeper's wife held her back. "Don't. You'll get hurt."

"Serves you right," Chōkichi gloated. "By the way, guess who's joined our side. Nobu from Ryūge Temple! So try and get even any time you want." He left Sangorō lying in the shop's front door. "You fools! *Weak*lings! Cowards! We'll be waiting for you. Be careful when you walk through the back streets after dark."

Just then he heard the sound of a policeman's boots. Someone had squealed on them. "Come on!" As fast as they could, Ushimatsu, Bunji, and the ten or so others all scattered in different directions, crouching in hiding places among the alleyways until the coast was clear.

"Damn you, Chōkichi! You bastard. Damn you! Damn you, Bunji! Damn you, Ushimatsu! Why don't you just kill me? Come on. Just try and kill me. I'm Sangorō—and maybe it's not so easy! Even if you did kill me, even if I turned into a ghost, I'd haunt you for the rest of your lives. Remember that, Chōkichi!" Sangorō began to sob. Hot tears rolled down his cheeks. He looked as if he must be aching. His sleeves were torn. His back and hips were covered with dirt.

The force of his anger, beyond his power to control, kept the others back. But the shopkeeper's wife rushed over to him. "It's all right," she soothed him with a pat and helped him to his feet. She brushed the gravel from his clothes. "Don't be upset. There were just too many of them, the rest of us weren't much help, not even a grown-up could do anything. It wasn't a fair match—don't be ashamed. It's lucky you weren't hurt, but you won't be safe going home alone. I'll feel much better if the policeman takes you; it's a good thing he's come. Officer, let me tell you what happened."

As she finished her account, the policeman reached for the boy's hand in his professional way. "I'll take you home."

"No. I'm all right. I can go by myself." He seemed to cringe with shame.

"There's nothing to be afraid of. I'll just take you as far as your house. Don't worry." He smiled at Sangorō and patted him on the head.

But Sangorō shrank back farther. "If my father hears about the fight, I'll get in terrible trouble. Chōkichi's father owns our house."

"How about if I take you as far as the front gate? I won't say anything to get you into trouble." He managed to coax the downcast Sangorō and led him off toward home.

The others felt relieved. But as they watched the two depart, at the corner leading to the back streets, for some reason Sangorō shook loose and broke into a run.

It was as rare as snow falling from a summer sky, but today Midori couldn't brook the thought of school. She wouldn't eat her breakfast. Should they order something special? It couldn't be a cold, she had no fever. Too much excitement yesterday, probably. "Why don't you stay home?" her mother suggested. "I'll go to the shrine for you."

Midori wouldn't hear of it. It was *her* vow to Tarō-sama for her sister's success.[28] "I'll just go and come right back. Give me some money for the offering."

Off she went to the shrine among the paddy fields. She rang the bell, shaped like the great mouth of a crocodile, and clasped her hands in suppli-cation. And what were they for, these prayers of hers? She walked through the fields with her head downcast, to and from the shrine.

Shōta saw her from a distance and called out as he ran toward her. He tugged at her sleeve, "Midori, I'm sorry about last night."

"That's all right. It wasn't your fault."

"But they were after me. If Grandmother hadn't come, I wouldn't have left. And then they wouldn't have beaten up Sangorō the way they did. I went to see him this morning. He was crying and furious. I got angry just listening to him talk about it. Chōkichi threw his sandal at you, didn't he? Damn him, anyway! There are limits to what even he can get away with. But I hope you're not mad at me, Midori. I didn't run away from him. I gulped my food down as fast as I could and was just on my way back when Grandmother said I had to watch the house while she went for her bath. That's when all the commotion must have started. Honest, I didn't know anything about it." He apologized as if the crime were his, not Chōkichi's. "Does it hurt?" Shōta examined Midori's forehead.

"Well, it's nothing that will leave a scar," Midori laughed. "But listen, Shōta, you mustn't tell anyone. If Mother ever found out, I'd get a real scolding. My parents never lay a hand on me. If they hear a dolt like Chōkichi smeared mud on my face with his filthy sandal—." She looked away.

"Please forgive me. It's all my fault. Please. Come on, cheer up. I won't be able to stand it if you're mad at me." Before they knew it, they had reached the back gate of Shōta's house. "Do you want to come in? No one's home. Grandmother's gone to collect the interest. It's lonely by myself. Come on, I'll show you those prints I told you about the other day. There are all kinds of them." Shōta wouldn't let go of her sleeve until Midori had agreed.

Inside the dilapidated gate was a small garden. Dwarf trees were lined up in their pots and from the eaves hung a tiny trellis of fern with a windbell, Shōta's memento from the holiday market.[29] But who would have picked it for the wealthiest house in the neighborhood? Here alone by themselves lived an old woman and a boy. No one had ever broken in: there were cold, metal locks everywhere, and the neighboring tenements kept an eye on the place.

Shōta went in first and found a spot where the breeze blew. "Over here," he called to Midori, handing her a fan. For a thirteen-year-old, he was rather too sophisticated. He took out one color print after another. They had been in his family for generations, and he smiled when Midori admired them. "Shall I show you a battledore? It was my mother's. She got it when she worked for a rich man. Isn't it funny? It's so big. And look how different people's faces were in those days. I wish she were still alive . . . My mother died when I was three, and my father went back to his own family's place in the country. So I've been here with Grandmother ever since. You're lucky, Midori."

"Look out. You'll get the pictures wet. Boys aren't supposed to cry."

"I guess I'm a sissy. Sometimes I get to thinking about things . . . It's all right now, but in the winter, when the moon is out and I have to make the rounds in Tamachi collecting the interest, sometimes when I walk along the ditch, I sit down on the bank and cry. Not from the cold. I don't know why . . . I just think about things. I've been doing the collecting ever since year before last. Grandmother's getting old. It's not safe for her at night. And her eyes aren't so good any more. She can't see what she's doing when she has to put her seal on the receipts. We've had a lot of different men working for us. But Grandmother says they all take us for fools—when it's only an old lady and a boy they have to answer to. She's just waiting for the day when I'm a little older and we can open the pawnshop again. We'll put the family sign out in front, even if things aren't as good as they used to be. Oh, I know people say Grandmother's stingy. But she's only careful about things for my sake. It really bothers me, to hear them talk that way. I guess the people I collect from over in Tōrishinmachi are pretty bad off, all right. I suppose it's no wonder they say things about her. When I think about it, though, sometimes I just can't help it if I cry. I guess I am a weakling. This morning when I went to see Sangorō, he was sore all over, but he still went right on working so his father wouldn't find out about last night. I didn't know what to say. A boy looks pretty silly when he cries, doesn't he? That's why the back street makes fun of Sangorō." He seemed ashamed at his own unmanliness.

Occasionally their eyes would meet.

"You looked so handsome yesterday, Shōta. It made me wish I were a boy. You were the best dressed of them all."

"*I* looked good! *You* were beautiful! Everybody said you were prettier than any of the girls in the quarter, even your sister Ōmaki. Boy, I'd be proud if you were my sister! I'd hold my head up with a girl like you alongside me. But I don't have any brothers or sisters. Hey, Midori, what do you say we have our picture taken? I'll wear what I did yesterday and you can put on one of your best striped kimonos, and we'll have Katō in Suidōjiri take our picture! Won't Nobu be jealous! He'll turn white, he'll be so envious—a milquetoast like him wouldn't know how to turn red. Or maybe he'll just laugh at us. Who cares? If Katō takes a big one, he might use our picture in the window! What's the matter? Don't you like the idea? You don't look very excited." The boy's impatience was disarming.

"What if I look funny? You might not like me any more." Her laugh had a beautiful ring, her spirits had obviously improved.

The cool of the morning had given way to the summer sun. It was time for Midori to be going: "Shōta, why don't you come over this evening? We can float candles on the pond and chase the fish. It'll be easy now that the bridge is fixed."

Shōta beamed as he saw her out. What a beauty Midori was.

Nobu of Ryūge Temple and Midori of the Daikokuya both went to school at
the Ikueisha. It had all started at the end of last April, at the spring athletic
meet in Mizunoya-no-hara. The cherries had fallen and the wisteria was
already in bloom in the shade of the new green leaves. They played their
games of tug-of-war and catch and jump rope with such ardor that no one
seemed to notice the sun going down. But what had come over Nobu? He had
lost his usual composure. He stumbled over the root of a pine by the pond
and landed hands-first in the red mud.

Midori, who happened to be going by, took one look at his dirty jacket and
proffered her crimson handkerchief. "Here, you can wipe it off with this."

There were those, however, who were jealous of this attention from
Midori. "For a priest's son, he sure knows how to flirt. Look at him smile
when he thanks her! What's he going to do—take her for his wife? If she goes
to live at the temple, then she really will be Miss Daikoku: from Midori of the
Daikokuya to Daikoku, goddess of the kitchen! That ought to suit a priest."[30]

Nobu couldn't stomach all the talk. He had never been one to enjoy idle
gossip and had always shunned tales about others. How, then, could he
tolerate it when he found himself the target of the rumors? He began to dread
hearing Midori's name. He was snappish whenever anyone mentioned field
day. "You're not going to bring that up again, are you?" It never failed to put
him in a bad mood. Yet what reason was there, really, for this loss of temper?
He knew he would do better feigning indifference. A stoic face, wait it out, he
told himself. He could silence his tormentors with a word or two, but the
embarrassment was still there. A cold sweat followed every confrontation.

At first, Midori failed to notice any change. On her way home from school
one day she called out with her usual friendliness. Nobu trailed behind
amid a cluster of people. The blossoms at the roadside had caught her eye,
and she waited for him to catch up. "See the pretty flowers, Nobu? I can't
reach them. You're tall enough—won't you pick me some?"

She had singled him out from his younger companions. There was no
escaping. He cringed at what he knew the others would be saying. Reaching
for the nearest branch, without even choosing, he picked the first flower he
saw, a token effort. He flung it at her and was gone.

"Well, if that's how he's going to be! Unsociable thing!"

After several of these incidents, it dawned on Midori: Nobu was being
mean to her deliberately. He was never rude to any of the others, only
her. When she approached, he fled. If she spoke to him, he became angry. He
was sullen and self-conscious. Midori had no idea how to please him, and in
the end she gave up trying. Let him be perverse; he was no friend of hers. See
if she'd speak to him after he'd cut her to the quick. "Hello's" in the street

were a thing of the past. It would take important business indeed before she would deign to talk to him. A great river now stretched between them that all boats were forbidden to cross. Each of them walked alone on separate banks of the stream.

From the day after the festival, Midori came to school no more. She could wash the mud from her face, but the shame could not be scrubbed away so easily.

They sat together side by side at school—Chōkichi's gang and the main-street gang—and one might have expected that they could get along. But there had always been a sharp division.

It was the act of a coward to attack a weak, defenseless girl. Everyone knew Chōkichi was as violent and as stupid as they come. But if he hadn't had Nobu backing him, he could never have behaved so brazenly. And that Nobu! In front of others he pretended to be gentle and wise, but a look behind the scenes would reveal that *he* was the one pulling all the strings. Midori didn't care if he was ahead of her in school, or how good his grades were. So what if he was the young master of Ryūge Temple! She, after all, was Midori of the Daikokuya, and not beholden to him in the slightest. She had never borrowed a single sheet of paper. So who were they to call her a tramp, or those other names Chōkichi had used? She wasn't about to be impressed just because Ryūge Temple had a prominent parishioner or two.

What about the patrons her sister Ōmaki had? The banker Kawa, a steady customer for three years now; Yone, from the stock exchange; and that short one, the member of parliament—why, he'd been all set to buy her sister's contract and marry her, till Ōmaki decided she could do without him. And he was somebody! Just ask the lady who ran Ōmaki's house. Go ahead and ask, if you thought she was making it up. Where would the Daikokuya be without her sister? Why do you think even the owner of the house was never curt with Midori and her parents? Just take that porcelain statue of Daikoku, the one he kept in the alcove. Once when she was playing shuttlecock, she knocked over a vase accidentally and smashed the master's favorite statue to smithereens. He was sitting right in the next room drinking. And all he said was, "Midori, you're turning into a little tomboy." Not one word of reproach. Had it been anyone else, you can be sure, he wouldn't have stopped there. The maids were green with envy. No question about it, the child's privileges derived from her sister's position. Midori knew it, too. Her parents were mere caretakers for the master's house, but her sister was Ōmaki of the Daikokuya. She didn't have to take insults from the likes of Chōkichi. And too bad for him if the little priest wanted to be mean to her. Midori had had enough of school. She was born stubborn and she was not about to suffer anyone's contempt. That day she broke her pencils and threw away her ink; she would spend her time playing with her real friends. She wasn't going to need her abacus or her books.

In evening they rush into the quarter, at dawn they leave less cheerfully. It's a lonely ride home, with only dreams of the night before to keep a man company. Getaways are under cover. A hat pulled low, a towel around the face. More than one of these gentlemen would rather that you didn't look. To watch will only make you feel uneasy. That smirk of theirs—not half-pleased with themselves as the sting of their lady's farewell slap sinks in. After all, she wouldn't want him to forget her. Careful when you get to Sakamoto. The vegetable carts come barreling back from the early morning market. Watch out when you hit Crazy Street. Until Mishima Shrine, you won't be safe from those who wander home all gaga and enraptured from the night before. Their faces never look so resolute the morning after. It's rude to say it, but don't they all suggest love's fools? The fishwives seldom hesitate to sum them up. Look, there goes a man with money. But that one over there, he couldn't have a penny to his name.

One need hardly cite the Chinese "Song of Everlasting Sorrow"[31] and the heights to which Yang's daughter rose to see that there are times when daughters are more valuable than sons. Many a princess comes into the world among the shanties of the back street. Today she calls herself "Snow" in one of those swank geisha houses over in Tsukiji, a celebrated beauty whose accomplishments in dance have entertained a nobleman or two. But yesterday she was a mere delinquent and she earned her spending money making playing cards, you know. "What kind of tree does rice grow on?" she asks, as if she'd grown up in the lap of luxury. Around here, of course, she is not the celebrity she used to be. Once they leave, they're soon forgotten. Already she has been eclipsed by the dye-maker's second daughter, Kokichi, a home-grown flower of a girl, whose name you'll hear throughout the park. The lanterns are up these days at The New Ivy, in Senzoku, where that one works.

Night and day, it's the daughters that you hear of. A boy is about as useful as a mutt sniffing round the rubbish. Every shopkeeper's son is a wastrel. At seventeen, the age of insolence, the young men band together. Before they go completely gallant—you don't see any flutes tucked into sashes yet—they join up with a leader whose alias is invariably a solemn, grandiose affair. They deck themselves out with matching scarves and matching paper lanterns. It won't be long now before they learn to gamble and to window-shop the quarter. Bantering with the courtesans will begin to come more easily. Even with the serious ones, the family business is only something for the day. Back from the evening bath they come in kimonos of a rakish cut, sandals dragging. "Hey, did you see the new one? At What's-Its-Name? She looks like the girl at the sewing shop, over in Kanasugi. But, with that funny little nose of hers, she's even uglier." It's the only thing remotely on their minds. They bum tobacco, a piece of tissue at every house. The pats and pinches they exchange with each beauty along the way: *these* are the things that bring a lifetime of renown. Even the sons of perfectly upstanding families decide to style themselves as local toughs. They are forever picking fights around the Gate.

Ah, the power of women. One need hardly say more. In the quarter, prosperity makes no distinctions between the autumn and the spring. Escort lanterns are not in vogue these days, and still the men are carried away. All it takes is the echo of a pair of sandals. Here she comes! The little girl from the teahouse who will take them to their ladies. Clip-clop, clip-clop. The sound mingles with the music of the theater. They hear it and they stream into the quarter. If you ask them what they're after, it's a flowing robe, a scarlet collar, a baroque coiffure, a pair of sparkling eyes and lips with painted smiles. The beauties may in fact have little of the beautiful about them. The minute they are courtesans, they climb the pedestal. Those of you from other parts may find it all a little hard to understand.

Needless to say, Midori, who spent her days and nights immersed in such a world, soon took on the color of the quarter. In her eyes, men were not such fearsome things. And her sister's calling was nothing to disparage. When Ōmaki was on the verge of leaving for the city, how Midori had cried. Not in her wildest dreams had she hoped to accompany her sister. And now here they were. Who wouldn't envy a sister like Ōmaki? What with her recent success, it was nothing for her to repay all the debts she had ever owed her parents. Midori had no notion of what price Ōmaki might have paid to reign supreme in her profession. To her it was all a game. She knew about the charms and tricks the girls would use. Simpering to summon men they longed for, like mice grabbing cheese. Tapping on the lattice when they made a wish. She knew the secret signals they would use to give their guests a parting pat. She had mastered the special language of the quarter, and she didn't feel the least embarrassed when she used it.

It was all a little sad. She was fourteen. When she caressed her dolls, she could have been a prince's child. But for her, all lessons in manners and morals and the wifely arts were topics to be left at school. What never ceased to capture her attention were the rumors of her sister's suitors—who was in and who was out of favor—the costumes of the serving girls, the bedding gifts that men would lavish on Ōmaki,[32] the teahouse tips for the introduction of a patron. What was bright and colorful was good, and what was not was bad. The child was still too young to exercise discretion. She was always taken with the flower just before her eyes. A headstrong girl by nature, Midori indulged herself by fluttering about in a world that she had fashioned from the clouds.

Crazy Street, Sleepy Street. The half-witted, groggy gentlemen all pass this way as they head home. At the gate to this village of late risers, the sweepers and the sprinklers have already cleaned the streets. But look down main street. They have roosted for the night among the slums of Mannenchō or Yamabushichō, or perhaps Shintanimachi, and now here they come: what for want of any other word one might as well call "entertainers." The singing candy man. The two-bit player. The puppeteers. The jugglers and the acrobats. The dancers with their parasols. The clowns who do the lion dance. Their dress is as varied as their arts, a gauze of silk, a sash of satin. The clowns prefer the cotton prints from Satsuma, with black bands round the waist. Men, pretty women, troupes of five, seven, even ten, and a lonely old man, all skin and bones, who totters as he clutches his battered samisen. And, look, there's a little girl of five or so they've got to do the Kinokuni dance.[33] Over there, with the red ribbons on her sleeves. But none of them stop here. They know where the business is, and they hurry to the quarter. The guest who has lingered at the teahouse, the beauty in a melancholy mood—these are the ones it pays to entertain. The profits are too good to give it up, or to waste time with benefit performances along the way. Not even the most tattered and suspicious-looking beggar would bother to loiter around here.

A lady minstrel passed before the paper shop. Her hat all but concealed her striking face, yet she sang and played with the bearing of a star. "It's a shame we never get to hear the end of her song," the shopkeeper's wife complained. Midori, bright from her morning bath, was lounging on the shop's front step, watching the parade pass by. She pushed her hair up with her boxwood comb. "Wait here. I'll bring her back!"

The child never mentioned slipping something in the lady's sleeve to coax her to perform but, sure enough, back in tow she came to sing the requested song of thwarted love. "Thank you very much for your patronage," she concluded in her honeyed tone, and even as it echoed they knew that they were not about to hear its likes again.

"To think—a mere child could have arranged it!" bystanders marveled, more impressed with Midori than with the minstrel.

"Wouldn't it be fun to have them all perform?" Midori whispered to Shōta. "The samisen and the flute and the drums! The singers and the dancers! Everything we never get more than just a glimpse of!"

Even for Midori, the proposal was ambitious. "Don't overdo it, girl," Shōta muttered.

"Thus have I heard it spoken," the reverend priest intoned the sutra. As the holy words were carried from the temple by the soft breeze through the pines, they should have blown away all dust within the heart.

But smoke rose from fish broiling in the kitchen. In the cemetery diapers had been seen drying over tombstones. Nothing wrong here in the eyes of the Order, perhaps; those who fancied their clerics above worldly desires, though, found the doings at Ryūge Temple rather too earthly for their tastes.[34]

Here the fortunes of the head priest were as handsome as his stomach. Both had rounded out nicely through the years. The man's glow of well-being beggared description: not the sunny pink of the cherries, not the deep pink of the peach; from the top of his freshly shaven pate to the bottom of his neck, he shone like burnished copper. When he whooped with laughter—bushy, salt-and-pepper eyebrows floating heavenward—the noise of the old man's excess could have toppled Buddha from the altar.

The priest's young wife (she was only in her forties) was not an unattractive woman. Her skin was fair, and she wore her thinning hair in a small, modest bun. She was always cordial when people came to pray. Even the florist's wife outside the temple gate held her tongue where the reverend's wife was concerned—the fruit, you may be sure, of the temple lady's kindliness: a hand-me-down here, a leftover there. At one time, she herself had been among the parishioners. But her husband died young, and, having nowhere to turn, she came to do the sewing at the temple. In exchange for meals, she took over the washing and the cooking. Before long she was out in the graveyard, sweeping away with the best of the groundsmen. The priest was quick to offer his compassion, and quicker still to calculate the advantages. The woman knew full well that the difference in their ages, some twenty years, might make the arrangement appear a bit unseemly. But she had nowhere else to go, and she came to consider the temple a good place to live out her days and to meet her end. She learned not to lose too much sleep over prying neighbors.

Some in the congregation found the situation shocking. Soon enough, however, they began to acknowledge that in her heart the woman was a good person, and they ceased to censure her. While she was carrying their first child, Ohana, the priest finally made an honest woman of her. A retired oil dealer over in Sakamoto, one of the parishioners who went in for such things, acted as the go-between—if you want to call it that.

Nobu was their second child. Someday he would do his father proud, but at the moment he was a taciturn, moody boy who preferred to pass the day alone in his room. Ohana, on the other hand, was quite the opposite, a lovely girl with fine skin and a soft, plump little chin. To call her a beauty would be going too far, perhaps, but since adolescence she had had her share of admirers. It seemed a shame to waste such a girl, for she might have been a geisha. Who knows? There may be worlds where even Buddha enjoys the music of the samisen. In this world, at any rate, there was the matter of what others said, and talk they would if the daughter of a temple became an

entertainer with her skirt hitched up. What the priest did instead was to
establish Ohana in a little tea shop in Tamachi. He put her behind the
counter, where she could vend her charm. Young men with no idea in their
heads how tea was weighed and measured began to gather at the shop.
Seldom was Ohana's empty before midnight.

But his holiness was the busy one. Loans to collect, the shop to oversee,
funerals to arrange, not to mention all the sermons every month. When he
wasn't flipping through accounts, he was going through the sutras. If things
didn't let up, he'd wear himself out, he would sigh as he dragged his flowered
cushion onto the veranda, where he fanned himself, half-naked, and enjoyed
his nightly hooch. He was a fish-eater, and Nobu was the one he sent over to
the main street for the broiled eels that he liked. "The big oily ones, if you
please." It galled Nobu. His eyes never left his feet as he trudged over to the
Musashiya. If he heard voices at the paper shop across the street, he would
keep on going. Then, when the coast was clear, he'd dart into the eel shop.
The shame he felt! He would never eat the smelly things.

The reverend was nothing if not practical. There were some who might
call him greedy, but that never bothered him a whit. He was neither a timid
soul nor an idler: give him a spare moment and he'd set about fashioning
kumade charms. On Otori day he would have his wife out peddling them.
Whatever doubts she may have had about the venture, they were short-lived
once his holiness started to bemoan the killing everybody else made, rank
amateurs up and down the street. He soon persuaded his reluctant wife, set
up a booth not a stone's throw from the temple gate, and installed her there
to sell his charms and good-luck hairpins. She tied her hair back with a
headband, just like the vendors and all the young men. In the daytime, she
knew enough to stay out of sight and mingle with the crowd, leaving the
florist's wife to manage things. But when the sun went down—who would
have guessed it?—the woman had a field day. At dusk she took over for
herself, quite forgetting what a spectacle she made with her sudden itch for
profit. "Everything marked down! Prices slashed!" she barked after a customer who backed away. Buffeted and dizzy from the throngs, the victim
soon lost his powers of appraisal. They had fled along with memory: two
days earlier he had come to this very temple as a pilgrim. "Three for only
seventy-five sen." But her price left room to negotiate. "How about five for
seventy-three?" "Sold!"

There were, of course, all kinds of sharp practices. Even if no one from the
congregation heard, Nobu wondered, what would the neighbors think? And
his friends? He could just hear them. Ryūge Temple is selling hairpins now.
Nobu's mother is out huckstering like a lunatic. Really, didn't they think they
ought to stop?

The reverend priest would hear nothing of it. "Knock it off. You don't know
what you're talking about." The mere idea sent the man into paroxysms.

Prayers in the morning, accounts at night. His father's face beamed whenever his fingers touched the abacus. It was enough to turn the boy's stomach. Why on earth had the man become a priest?

There was nothing in his upbringing to make Nobu such a gloomy child. He had the same parents as Ohana. They were part of the same cozy, self-contained family. Yet he was the quiet one. Even when he did speak, his opinions were never taken seriously. His father's schemes, his mother's conduct, his sister's education—to Nobu everything they did was a travesty. He had resigned himself to knowing that they would never listen. How unfair it was. His friends found him contrary and perverse, but in fact he was a weakling. If anyone maligned him in the slightest, he would run for the shelter of his room. He was a coward utterly lacking in the courage to defend himself. At school they called him a brain; his family's station was not lowly. No one knew how weak he really was. More than one of his friends considered Nobu something of a cold fish.

The night of the festival Nobu was sent on an errand to his sister's tea shop in Tamachi, and he was late coming home. Not until the next morning did he learn of the fight at the paper shop. When Ushimatsu and Bunji and the others gave him the details, the full impact of Chōkichi's violent ways startled him anew. What was done was done—but in name he was included in the violence, and it rankled. Now people would be blaming him for the trouble.

It was three days before Chōkichi had the nerve to face Nobu. For once he must have felt a little sheepish about the damage he had done. He did not look forward to Nobu's scolding. "I know you're probably angry," he ventured, having waited for the storm to pass. "I couldn't help it, though. Everything got out of hand. I hadn't meant it to happen. You won't hold it against me, will you, Nobu? How were we to know that you'd be gone and Shōta would fly the coop? It's not as though I planned to beat up Sangorō and pick a fight with that tramp Midori. Things just happened. You don't run away once the lanterns start swinging! All we wanted was to show a little muscle, show 'em who's boss. It's my fault, I know. I should have listened to you. But come on Nobu, if you get mad now, how's it going to look? After I've gone around telling everybody you're on *our* side. You can't leave us in the lurch. Okay, so you don't approve of this one thing. You be the leader, and next time we won't botch things up." Gone was the usual swagger.

Nobu couldn't turn his back on Chōkichi. "All right," he sighed. "But listen—bully the weak ones, and we'll be the ones in disgrace. We're not going to gain anything fighting Sangorō and Midori. If Shōta and his flunkies want to stir up trouble, we can cross that bridge when we come to it. But let's not egg them on." Chōkichi had to promise: no more fights. For a rebuke, it was rather mild.

The innocent one was Sangorō. They had kicked and beaten him to their hearts' content, and he still ached two, three days afterward. He couldn't stand up, he couldn't sit down. Every evening when his father picked up the empty rickshaw and headed for the teahouses, someone would ask him what was wrong with the boy. "Say, your Sangorō looks a little peaked these days," the caterer remarked, almost accusingly. "Somebody give him a pounding?"

Groveling Tetsu they called his father, head always lowered before his betters. It didn't matter who—the landlord or someone with money or the owner of one of the houses in the quarter, where Tetsu pulled his cart—any of them could make the most impossible demands, and the rickshawman would acquiesce. "Indeed, of course, how right you are." Small wonder, then, what his reaction was to the incident with Chōkichi. "He's the landlord's son, isn't he? I don't care if you were right. I won't have you getting into scraps with him. Now go apologize. You ought to know better!" There was no avoiding it. His father made sure that he got down on his knees in front of Chōkichi.

Within a week Sangorō's wounds healed and his temper cooled. He was ready to forget what he'd been angry about. For the price of a carriage ride, he was baby-sitting again for Chōkichi's little brother, walking round with the child on his back and lulling it to sleep with nursery rhymes. Sangorō was sixteen, that age when boys get cocky, but the lumpish figure he cut failed to trouble him. He wandered over to the main street, unconcerned as always. "Hey, Sangorō. Have you forgotten you're a boy?" Midori and Shōta were great ones when it came to teasing. "Some sight you make, with that baby on your back!" It didn't matter, they were still his friends.

In spring the cherry trees blossom in profusion. In summer the lanterns twinkle in memory of the late Tamagiku.[35] In fall the festival streets overflow with rickshaws. Count them: seventy-five down the road within the space of ten minutes. Then the autumn holidays are over. Here and there a red dragonfly bobs above the rice fields. Before long, quail will be calling out along the moat. Mornings and evenings, the breeze blows cold. At the sundries shop, pocket warmers now take the place of mosquito incense. It's sad, somehow, that faint sound of the mortar grinding flour at Tamura's, over by the bridge. The clock at Kadoebi's has a melancholy ring. Fires glow through all four seasons from the direction of Nippori. It's in autumn that one begins to notice them. Smoke rises each time one more soul embarks on the journey to the other shore.

Deftly, a geisha plays on the samisen. The refrain reaches the path along the bank behind the teahouses. A passerby looks up and listens. Not much of a song, really, but moving all the same. "Together we shall spend our night of love."[36] Women who have done time in the quarter will tell you—it's the men who begin visiting in fall who prove to be the truly faithful ones.

Talk, talk: in this neighborhood, there is always grist for gossip. The details are tedious, but the stories make the rounds. A blind masseuse, she was only twenty, killed herself. With a handicap like hers, love was out of the question. Well she couldn't stand it any more. Drowned herself in Mizunoya Pond. Then there are the incidents too commonplace to rate a rumor. Missing persons: Kichigorō, the greengrocer, and Takichi, the carpenter. How come? "They picked them up for this," a fellow whispers, and pantomimes a gambler dealing out the cards.

A moment ago there were children there, down the street. "Ring-a-ring-a-rosy, pocket full of posies."[37] Suddenly it's quiet now, before you notice. Only the sound of rickshaws, loud as ever.

It was a lonely night. Just when it seemed the autumn rains would go on and on falling softly, with a roar a downpour came. At the paper shop they were not expecting anyone. The shopkeeper's wife had closed up for the evening. Inside, playing marbles,[38] were Shōta and Midori, as usual, and two or three of the younger ones. All at once, Midori heard something: "Is that a customer? I hear footsteps."

"I don't hear anything," Shōta said. He stopped counting out the marbles. "Maybe someone wants to play."

Who could it be? They heard him come as far as the gate, but after that, not a word, not a sound.

"Boo!" Shōta opened the door and stuck his head out. "Hey, who's there?" He could just make out the back of someone walking along beneath the eaves two or three houses up ahead. "Who is it? Do you want to come in?" He had slipped Midori's sandals on and was about to run after him, in spite of the rain. "Oh, it's him." Shōta cupped his hand above his head, mimicking a bald monk. "No use—we can call him all we want, he won't come."

"Nobu?" Midori asked. "That old priest! I'll bet he came to buy a writing brush and scurried off the minute he heard us. Nasty, stupid, toothless, old-maid Nobu! Just let him come in. I'll tell him what I think. Too bad he ran away. Let me have the sandals. I want a look." This time Midori poked her head out. The rain dripped down from the eaves onto her forehead. It gave her a chill. She pulled back, staring at the shadowy figure as he made his way around the puddles. He was four or five houses away by now, and he seemed to cower in the gaslight. His paper umbrella hugged his shoulders. She looked and looked.

Shōta tapped her on the shoulder. "Midori, what is it?"

"Nothing," she said absent-mindedly, returning to the game. "I hate that little altar boy! He can't even conduct his fights in public. He makes that pious, old-maid face of his and goes sneaking round corners. Isn't he awful? My mother says people who are straightforward are the good ones. She's right, don't you think, Shōta? It's a sure thing Nobu has an evil heart, the way he lurks around."

"But at least he knows what's what. Not like Chōkichi, there's a real moron. The boy's a total ignoramus," Shōta said knowingly.

"Cut it out. You and your big words." Midori laughed and pinched him on the cheek. "Such a serious face! Since when are you so grown up?"

Shōta was not amused. "For your information, it won't be long before I *am* grown up. I'll wear a topcoat with square-cut shoulders like the shopkeeper at Kabata's, and the gold watch Grandmother's put away for me. I'll wear a ring. I'll smoke cigarettes. And for shoes—you're not going to see me in any clogs. Oh, no. I'll wear leather sandals, the good kind, with triple-layered heels and fancy satin straps. Won't I look sharp!"

"You in triple heels and a square-cut overcoat?" Midori couldn't help snickering. "Mm, sure, if you want to look like a walking medicine bottle."

"Oh, quiet. You don't think I've stopped growing, do you? I won't be this short forever."

"Seeing is believing. You know, Shōta," Midori said, pointing a sarcastic finger at the rafters, "even the mice laugh when you keep making these promises." Everyone, the shopkeeper's wife included, shook with laughter.

His eyes spun; Shōta was completely serious. "Midori makes a joke of everything. But everyone grows up, you know. Why is what I say so funny? The day will come when I go walking with my pretty wife. I always like things to be pretty. If I had to marry someone like that pock-marked Ofuku at the cracker shop, or the girl at the firewood store with the bulging forehead—no thank you. I'd send her home. No pockmarks for me!"

"How good of you to come, then," the shop wife laughed. "Haven't you noticed my spots?"

"Oh, but you're old. I'm talking about brides. Once you're old, it doesn't matter."

"I shouldn't have said anything," the woman sighed. "Well, let's see now. There's Oroku at the flower shop. She has a pretty face. And Kii at the fruit stand. And who else? Who else, I wonder? Why, the prettiest one is sitting right next to you. Shōta, who will it be? Oroku with those eyes of hers? Kii and her lovely voice?[39] Tell us who."

"What are you talking about? Oroku, Kii—what's so good about them?" Shōta's face turned scarlet, and he backed away from the light, into a corner.

"Does that mean it's Midori, then?"

"How do I know?" He looked away, tapping out a song against the wall. "The water wheel goes round and round."[40]

Midori and the rest had begun another game of marbles. *Her* face was not flushed in the slightest.

There would have been no problem if he hadn't taken the short cut. But every time Nobu went off to Tamachi he took the path along the ditch. And every time he saw it: the lattice gate, the stone lantern, the thatched fence. The summer bamboo blinds were rolled up now along the veranda. He couldn't help remembering things. Behind the glass windows,[41] her mother would be there, like some latter-day widow of Azechi at her rosary; and she would be there too, straight from the ancient tales, a young Murasaki with her hair bobbed.[42] This was the house of the man who owned the Daikokuya.

Yesterday and today the autumn rains had continued. The winter slip Ohana had requested was ready, and Nobu's mother was anxious for her to have it. She didn't like to ask in such weather, but would he mind taking it to the shop in Tamachi on his way to school? The poor girl was waiting for the package. Diffident Nobu could never say no. He took the bundle under his arm, stepped into his clogs, and started out, clinging to his umbrella as the rain lapped at his feet.

He followed the ditch around the quarter, the same path he always took, but today luck was not with him. Just in front of the Daikokuya, the wind came up. He had to tug to keep his umbrella from flying off. He braced his legs against the wind, when the strap on one of his clogs tore clean away. Now what was he to do?

It was almost enough to make him swear. He had no choice but to try repairing the clog himself. He propped his umbrella against the gate and sought shelter underneath its eaves. Yet how was a fledgling cleric to accomplish this sort of handiwork? He was flustered, and no matter how hard he tried, he couldn't fix it. He grew more and more irritated. From his sleeve he took out the draft of his school composition and tore it up, twisting the strips of paper in hopes of somehow fashioning a new strap. But the confounded storm grew worse again, and his umbrella began to roll away in the wind. This was more than he could tolerate! He reached out to grab the umbrella—but it was just his luck—his sister's package fell from his lap into the mud. There, now he had mud on his sleeve, too.

A pathetic sight he made, without an umbrella and stranded barefoot in the downpour. From the window, Midori saw the sad figure beyond the gate. "Look, someone's broken his sandal. Mother, can I give him something to fix it with?" She found a piece of Yūzen crepe in the sewing drawer and hurried into her clogs. Grabbing an umbrella from the veranda, she dashed out across the stepping stones toward the front gate.

Then she saw who it was. The blood rushed to Midori's head. Her heart pounded as if she had encountered a dreaded fate. She turned to see, was anyone watching? Trembling, she inched her way toward the gate. At that instant Nobu, too, looked around. He was speechless, he felt cold sweat begin to bead. He wanted to kick off the other sandal and run away.

Had Midori been herself, she would have seized on Nobu's predicament to tell him what she thought. She would have sneered at his cowardice and heaped upon him every bit of abuse that he deserved. Didn't he think he owed her an apology? Bossing everyone around from backstage, ruining all the fun at the festival, just because he was angry at Shōta. And letting them beat up helpless Sangorō! He was the one who had incited Chōkichi to call her those names. And what was wrong with being a courtesan, anyway, even if she were one? She didn't owe him anything. With her parents and her sister and the man from the Daikokuya—what did she need to ask favors of a broken-down priest for? He had better stop calling her names. Something to say, was there? Then he could come out in the open, like a man. Any time, any time. She'd meet him. What did he have to say to that? She would have grabbed him by the sleeve and given him a piece of her mind, all right. Nobu would not have had a prayer.

But instead she cringed in the shadows of the gate. She didn't move, her heart throbbed. This was not the old Midori.

Whenever he came near the Daikokuya, timorous Nobu hurried past without so much as looking left or right. But today, the unlucky rain, the unlucky wind, and, to make matters worse, the broken sandal strap! There was nothing for it but to stop and make a new one. He was upset enough already, and then he heard the sound of steps on the flagstones—he felt as if ice water had been poured down his back. Even without looking, he knew who it would be. He shivered and his face changed color. He turned away and pretended to be hard at work. But he was panic-stricken. It didn't look as if the clog would ever be of use again.

From the garden, Midori peered at him. How clumsy he was; he could never do anything right. Who ever heard of trying to make a strap out of anything as flimsy as a piece of paper—or straw, is that what he was using? Old ladies, maybe. It would never hold. Oh, and didn't he know he was getting mud all over the bottom of his jacket? There went the umbrella. Why didn't he close it before he propped it up? How it irritated her to watch his fumbling. "Here's some cloth to fix it with." If only she could have said it. Instead, she stood rooted to the spot, hiding, staring. The girl was oblivious to the rain soaking through her sleeves.

Midori's mother, unaware of what was happening, called out. "Midori, the iron's ready. What are you doing out there? Don't you know better than to play in the rain? You'll catch another cold."

"All right, coming." If only Nobu wouldn't hear. Her heart raced, her head seemed to reel. The last thing she could do was open the gate, but she could not turn her back on him, either. What was she to do? There—she hurled the rag outside the lattice without saying anything. Nobu pretended not to notice. Oh! He was his same old nasty self! It crushed her, the tears welled up. Why did he have to be so mean? Why didn't he just tell her what it was? It made her sick. But her mother kept on calling. It was no use. She started for the house. After all, why should she be sentimental? She wasn't going to let him see Midori eat humble pie.

He heard her walk away; his eyes wandered after her. The scarlet scrap of Yūzen silk lay in the rain, its pattern of red maple leaves near enough to touch. Odd, how her one gesture moved him, and yet he could not bring himself to reach out and take the cloth. He stared at it vacantly, and as he looked at it he felt his heart break.

He bungled everything. Nobu sighed and took the cord from his jacket and wrapped it round the clog. It was unsightly and makeshift, but perhaps it would do, perhaps he could stumble along. But all the way to Ohana's? It was a little late to be wondering that, he thought as he stood up, his sister's package tight under his arm. He had only gone two or three steps when he looked back again at the tatter of silk, bright with autumn maples. It was hard for him to leave it there.

"Nobu, what's the matter? Break your strap? What a sight you are!"

Nobu turned around to see who owned the unexpected voice. It was obnoxious Chōkichi, decked out like a young gallant. He had on his best-dress kimono,[43] and he wore his orange sash profligately low on the hips. His new jacket had a fancy black collar, and the umbrella he carried was festooned with the trademark of one of the houses in the quarter. His high clogs were sporting lacquered rain covers—this was something new. What pride there was in the young man's swagger.

"The strap broke, and I was wondering what to do," Nobu answered helplessly. "I'm not very good at these things."

"No, you wouldn't be. It's all right, wear mine. The straps won't give out."

"But what will you do?"

"Don't worry. I'm used to it. I'll just go like this," he said, tucking up the bottom of his kimono. "Feels much better than wearing sandals, anyway." He kicked off his rain clogs.

"You're going to go barefoot? That won't be fair."

"I don't mind. I'm used to going barefoot. Someone like you has soft feet. You could never walk barefoot on the gravel. Come on, wear these," he urged, arranging his sandals obligingly. What a spectacle: Chōkichi was more detested than the plague god himself, and here he was with soft words on his tongue and bushy eyebrows moving solicitously. "I'll take your sandals and toss them in at the back door. Here, let's switch."

Chōkichi took the broken clogs, and they parted, Nobu bound for his sister's in Tamachi and Chōkichi for home before they met again at school.

The silk shred lay abandoned by the gate. Its red maple leaves shimmered in the rain.

This year there were three Otori fair days.[44] Rain had spoiled the second, but today, like the first, was perfect for a festival. Throngs packed Otori Shrine, young men surged into the quarter through the side gates. They say they've come to pay a visit to the shrine. They are pilgrims, but, ah, the roar of young laughter is loud enough to rend the pillars holding up the heavens, to tear away the very cord from which the earth hangs. Front and back of the main street of the quarter look as if they've been reversed. Today, the side drawbridges are down clear around the moat, and the crowds keep pouring in. "Coming through, coming through." What have we here? Some flat-bottomed boat trying to navigate these waves of people? Who will soon forget the excitement in the air? Peals of laughter, incessant chatter echo from the little shops along the ditch. Strains of the samisen rise from the first-class pleasure houses towering several stories in the sky.

Shōta took a holiday from collecting interest. He dropped in at Sangorō's potato stall, and then he visited his friend Donkey at the dumpling shop. "How are you doing? Making any money?" The sweets looked pretty uninviting.

"Shōta! You're just in time. I've run out of bean jam and don't know what to do. I've already put more on to cook, but they keep coming and I don't want to turn them away. What should I do?"

"Don't be stupid. Look what you've got on the sides of the pot. Add some water and some sugar, and you can feed another ten or twenty people. Everybody does it—you won't be the first. Besides, who's going to notice how it tastes in all this commotion? Start selling, start selling." Shōta was already at the sugar bowl.

Donkey's one-eyed mother was filled with admiration. "You've become a real merchant, Shōta. I'm almost afraid of you."

"This? I saw Clammy do the same thing in the alley. It's not my idea." The woman's praise did not go to his head. "Hey, do you know where Midori is?

I've been looking for her since this morning. Where'd she go off to? She hasn't been to the paper shop. I know that. I wonder if she's in the quarter."

"Oh, Midori, she went by a little while ago. I saw her take one of the side bridges into the quarter. Shōta, you should have seen her. She had her hair all done up like this." He made an oafish effort to suggest the splendor of Midori's new grown-up hairdo. "She's really something, that girl!" The boy wiped his nose as he extolled her.

"Yes, she's even prettier than her sister. I hope she won't end up like Ōmaki." Shōta looked down at the ground.

"What do you mean—that would be wonderful! Next year I'm going to open a shop, and after I save some money I'll buy her for a night!" He didn't understand things.

"Don't be such a smart aleck. Even if you tried, she wouldn't have anything to do with you."

"Why? Why should she refuse me?"

"She just would." Shōta flushed as he laughed. "I'm going to walk around for a while. I'll see you later." He went out the gate.

> "Growing up,
>   she plays among the butterflies
>   and flowers.
> But she turns sixteen,
>   and all she knows
>   is work and sorrow."[45]

He sang the popular refrain in a voice that was curiously quavering for him, and repeated it again to himself. His sandals drummed their usual ring against the paving stones, as all at once his little figure vanished into the crowd.

Inside the bustling quarter, Shōta found himself swept along into a corner of the compound. It was there he saw Midori. Why, it certainly was Midori of the Daikokuya; she was talking to an attendant from one of the houses, and, just as he had heard, her hair was done up in the glorious *shimada* style of a young woman.[46] And yet she looked shy today. Colored ribbons cascaded from her hair, tortoise-shell combs and flowered hairpins flickered in the sun. The whole effect was as bright and stately as a Kyōto doll. Shōta was tongue-tied. Any other time, he would have rushed over and taken her arm.

"Shōta!" Midori came running up. "If you have shopping to do, Otsuma, why don't you go on ahead? I'll go home with him." She nodded good-by to the lady.

"Oh, you don't want me around, now that you've found another friend, is that it?" Otsuma smiled as she headed down a narrow street of shops. "I'll be off to Kyōmachi, then."

"You look nice, Midori." Shōta tugged at her sleeve. "When did you get that new hairdo? This morning? Why didn't you come and show it to me?" He pretended to be angry.

Midori had difficulty speaking. "I had it done this morning at my sister's. I hate it." Her spirits drooped. She kept her head down; she couldn't bear it when a passerby would gawk.

When she felt so awkward and unhappy, flattery only sounded like an insult. People turned to admire her and she thought they were jeering.

"Shōta, I'm going home."

"Why don't you play? Did someone scold you? I bet you had a fight with your sister."

Midori felt her face color. Shōta was still a child, clearly. Where did one begin to explain?

They passed the dumpling shop, and Donkey called out theatrically, "You two sure are friendly." It made her feel like crying.

"Shōta, I don't want to walk with you." She hurried off ahead of him.

She had promised to go with him to the festival, and now here she was, headed in the opposite direction. "Aren't you going to come?" he yelled, running after her. "Why are you going home? You might at least explain!"

Midori walked on without answering, hoping to elude him. Shōta was stunned. He pulled at her sleeve. It was all so strange. Midori's face only turned a deeper red. "It's nothing, Shōta." But he knew that this was not the truth.

He followed her in through the gate at her house and onto the veranda. There was no need to hesitate; he had been coming here to play for years.

"Oh, Shōta," her mother greeted him. "Nice to see you. She's been in a bad mood all day. I don't know what to do with her. See if you can cheer her up."

Shōta became quite the grown-up. "Something the matter, is there?"

"No, no." Her mother gave an odd smile. "She'll get over it in no time. She's just spoiled. I suppose she's been grumpy with her friends, too? I tell you, sometimes I've had it with that girl." Her mother turned to look at her, but Midori had gone into the other room. Her sash and her outer kimono were discarded on the floor and Midori lay face-down underneath a quilt.

Shōta approached her gingerly. "Midori, what is it? Don't you feel well? Please tell me what's the matter." He held back as he spoke to her. What should he do? He folded and unfolded his hands in his lap. Midori said nothing. He could hear her sobbing into her sleeve. Her bangs, too short still for sweeping up into the great hairdo, were matted with tears. Something was terribly wrong, but, child that he was, Shōta had no idea what it could be, or how to console her. He was totally bewildered. "Please tell me what it is. You've never said anything to me, so how can you be angry with me?" He looked at her warily.

"Shōta, it isn't you." Midori wiped her eyes.

But when he asked her what it was, then, she couldn't answer. There were just sad things, vague things. Feelings . . . She couldn't put them into words. They made her cheeks burn. Nothing she could point to—and yet lately everything discouraged her. So many thoughts; none of them would ever have occurred to the Midori of yesterday. This awkwardness all of a sudden! How was she to explain it? If they would just leave her alone . . . she'd be happy to spend night and day in a dark room. No one to talk to her, no one to stare. Even if she felt unhappy, at least she would be spared the embarrassment. If only she could go on playing house forever—with her dolls for companions, then she'd be happy again. Oh! She hated, hated, hated this growing up! Why did things have to change? What she would give to go back a year, ten months, seven months, even.

They were the thoughts of someone already old.

She had forgotten that Shōta was there. But he kept on pestering her until she wanted to drive him away. "For God's sake, go home, Shōta. I feel like dying, with you here. All these questions give me a headache. They make me dizzy. I don't want anybody here! Just go *home!*"

She had never treated him so cruelly; Shōta could make no sense of it. He might as well have been groping through a cloud of smoke. "You sure are acting strange, Midori. I don't know why you talk this way. You must be crazy." The regrets were too much for him. He spoke calmly enough, but now his eyes smarted. This wouldn't help matters.

"Go home! Go home, will you! If you don't get out of here, you're not my friend at all. I hate you, Shōta."

"If that's the way you feel, I'm sorry to have bothered you." He darted off through the garden without so much as a farewell to Midori's mother, who had gone to check the water in the bath.

Shōta made a beeline for the paper shop, ducking, dodging his way through the crowds.

Sangorō was there, his holiday stall sold out and the take jingling in his pocket. Shōta burst in upon them just as Sangorō was playing the part of big brother. "Anything you want—it's yours!" The younger ones jumped up and down with glee. "Hey, Shōta! I was looking for you. I made a lot of money today. I'll treat you."

"You idiot. Since when do you treat me? Don't start talking big." These were rough words for Shōta. "That's not what I came here for." He looked dejected.

"What happened? A fight?" Sangorō shoved a half-eaten doughnut into his pocket. "Who was it? Nobu? Chōkichi? Where? The temple? Was it in the quarter? It won't be like the last time! This time, they won't take us by surprise. There's no way we can lose. I'm ready. Let me lead. We can't chicken out, Shōta."

The call to arms only infuriated him. "Take it easy," Shōta snapped. "There was no fight."

"But you came in here as if something terrible had happened. I thought it was a fight. And besides, if you don't do it tonight, we won't have another chance. Chōkichi's losing his right arm."

"Huh?"

"His accomplice, Nobu. Didn't you hear? I just found out. My father was talking with Nobu's mother. Any day now, he's going off to learn how to be a monk. Once he puts those robes on, they'll cover up his fighting arm. Those long, floppy robes—how can he roll up his sleeves in them? But you know what that means. Next year, you'll have the front and the back street to yourself."

"All right, quiet. For a few coins they'll go over to Chōkichi. I could have a hundred like you, and it wouldn't excite me in the least. They can go where they like for all I care. I'll fight my own battles. It was Nobu I wanted to beat. But if he's running off on me, it can't be helped. I thought he was going next year, after he graduated. What a coward—why is he going so soon?"

But it wasn't Nobu he was worried about. Tonight, there were none of the usual songs from Shōta. Midori was on his mind. The throngs of merrymakers passing in the street only left him feeling lonely. What was there to celebrate?

The lamps went on, and Shōta rolled over on his side. Some festival, everything had ended in a mess!

From that day on Midori was a different person. When she had to, she went to her sister's rooms in the quarter, but she never went to play in town. Her friends missed her and came to invite her to join them in the fun again. "Maybe later. You go on ahead." Empty promises, always. She was cool even to Shōta, once her closest friend. She was forever blushing now. It seemed unlikely that the paper shop would see the old dancing and the games a second time.

People were puzzled. Was the girl sick? "No, no. She'll be her old self again," her mother assured them. "She's just having a rest. One of her little vacations." The woman smiled. And yet there seemed to be more to it.

There was praise for Midori now from some quarters. So ladylike, so well-behaved. Yes, but what a shame, others mourned: she was such a delightful, saucy child.

The front street was quiet suddenly, as if a light had gone out. Seldom did Shōta sing his songs any more. At night you could see him with his lantern making the rounds for the interest payments. The shadow moving along the moat looked chilly, somehow. From time to time, Sangorō would join him, and his voice rang out, comical as ever.

Everyone talked about Nobu, but Midori had not heard any of the rumors. The former spitfire was still closeted away somewhere. With all these changes lately, she hardly knew herself. She was timid now, everything embarrassed her.

One frosty morning, a paper narcissus lay inside the gate. No one knew what it was doing there, but Midori took a fancy to it, for some reason, and she put it in a bud vase. It was perfect, she thought, and yet almost sad in its crisp, solitary shape. That same day—she wasn't sure exactly where—Midori heard of Nobu's plans. Tomorrow he was leaving for the seminary. The color of his robes would never be the same.

Separate Ways
(Wakare-Michi, 1896)

There was someone outside, tapping at her window.

"Okyō? Are you home?"

"Who is it? I'm already in bed," she lied. "Come back in the morning."

"I don't care if you are in bed. Open up! It's me—Kichizō, from the umbrella shop."

"What a bothersome boy you are. Why do you come so late at night? I suppose you want some rice cakes again," she chuckled. "Just a minute. I'm coming."

Okyō, a stylish woman in her early twenties, put her sewing down and hurried into the front hall. Her abundant hair was tied back simply—she was too busy to fuss with it—and over her kimono she wore a long apron and a jacket. She opened the lattice, then the storm door.

"Sorry," Kichizō said as he barged in.

Dwarf, they called him. He was a pugnacious little one. He was sixteen, and he worked as an apprentice at the umbrella shop, but to look at him one would think he was eleven or twelve. He had spindly shoulders and a small face. He was a bright-looking boy, but so short that people teased him and dubbed him "Dwarf."

"Pardon me." He went right for the brazier.

"You won't find enough fire in there to toast any of your rice cakes. Go get some charcoal from the cinder box in the kitchen. You can heat the cakes yourself. I've got to get this done tonight." She took up her sewing again. "The owner of the pawnshop on the corner ordered it to wear on New Year's."

"Hmm. What a waste, on that old baldie. Why don't I wear it first?"

"Don't be ridiculous. Don't you know what they say? 'He who wears another's clothes will never get anywhere in life.' You're a hopeless one, you are. You shouldn't say such things."

"I never did expect to be successful. I'll wear anybody's clothes—it's all the same to me. Remember what you promised once? When your luck changes, you said you'd make me a good kimono. Will you really?" He wasn't joking now.

"If only I could sew you a nice kimono, it would be a happy day. I'd gladly do it. But look at me. I don't have enough money to dress myself properly. I'm

288

sewing to support myself. These aren't gifts I'm making." She smiled at him. "It's a dream, that promise."

"That's all right. I'm not asking for it now. Wait until some good luck comes. At least say you will. Don't you want to make me happy? That would be a sight, though, wouldn't it?" The boy had a wistful smile on his face. "Me dressed up in a fancy kimono!"

"And if you succeed first, Kichizō, promise me you'll do the same. That's a pledge I'd like to see come true."

"Don't count on it. I'm not going to succeed."

"How do you know?"

"I know, that's all. Even if someone came along and insisted on helping me, I'd still rather stay where I am. Oiling umbrellas suits me fine. I was born to wear a plain kimono with workman's sleeves[1] and a short band around my waist. To me, all 'good luck' means is squeezing a little money from the change when I'm sent to buy persimmon juice.[2] If I hit the target someday, shooting arrows through a bamboo pole,[3] that's about all the good luck I can hope for. But someone like you, from a good family—why, fortune will come to greet you in a carriage. I don't mean a man's going to come and take you for his mistress, or something. Don't get the wrong idea." He toyed with the fire in the brazier and sighed over his fate.

"It won't be a fine carriage that comes for me. I'll be going to hell in a handcart."[4] Okyō leaned against her yardstick and turned to Kichizō. "I've had so many troubles on my mind, sometimes it feels as if my heart's on fire."

Kichizō went to fetch the charcoal from the kitchen, as he always did.

"Aren't you going to have any rice cakes?"

Okyō shook her head. "No thank you."

"Then I'll go ahead. That old tightwad at the umbrella shop is always complaining. He doesn't know how to treat people properly. I was sorry when the old woman died. *She* was never like that. These new people! I don't talk to any of them. Okyō, what do you think of Hanji at the shop? He's a mean one, isn't he? He's so stuck-up. He's the owner's son, but, you know, I still can't think of him as a future boss. Whenever I have the chance, I like to pick a fight and cut him down to size." Kichizō set the rice cakes on the wire net above the brazier. "Oh, it's hot!" he shouted, blowing on his fingers. "I wonder why it is—you seem almost like a sister to me, Okyō. Are you sure you never had a younger brother?"

"I was an only child. I never had any brothers or sisters."

"So there really is no connection between us. Boy, I'd sure be glad if someone like you would come and tell me she was my sister. I'd hug her so tight . . . After that, I wouldn't care if I died. What was I, born from a piece of wood? I've never run into anyone who was a relative of mine. You don't know how many times I've thought about it: if I'm never, ever going to meet anyone from my own family, I'd be better off dying right now. Wouldn't I? But it's odd. I still want to go on living. I have this funny dream. The few people who've been the least bit kind to me all of a sudden turn out to be my mother and father and my brother and sister. And then I think, I want to live a little longer. Maybe if I wait another year, someone will tell me the truth. So I go on oiling umbrellas, even if it doesn't interest me a bit. Do you suppose there's anyone in the world as strange as I am? I don't have a mother or a father, Okyō. How could a child be born without either parent? It makes me pretty odd." He tapped at the rice cakes and decided they were done.

"Don't you have some kind of proof of your identity? A charm with your name on it, for instance?[5] There must be something you have, some clue to your family's whereabouts."

"Nothing. My friends used to tease me. They said I was left underneath a bridge when I was born, so I'd be taken for a beggar's baby. It may be true. Who knows? I may be the child of a tramp. One of those men who pass by in rags every day could be a kinsman. That old crippled lady with one eye who comes begging every morning—for all I know, she could be my mother. I used to wear a lion's mask and do acrobatics in the street," he said dejectedly, "before I worked at the umbrella shop. Okyō, if I were a beggar's boy, you wouldn't have been so nice to me, would you? You wouldn't have given me a second look."

"You shouldn't joke like that, Kichizō. I don't know what kind of people your parents were, but it makes no difference to me. These silly things you're saying—you're not yourself tonight. If I were you, I wouldn't let it bother me. Even if I were the child of an outcast. I'd make something of myself, whether I had any parents or not, no matter who my brothers were. Why are you whining around so?"

"I don't know," he said, staring at the floor. "There's something wrong with me. I don't seem to have any get-up-and-go."

She was dead now, but in the last generation the old woman Omatsu, fat as a *sumō* wrestler, had made a tidy fortune at the umbrella shop. It was a winter's night six years before that she had picked up Kichizō, performing his tumbler's act along the road, as she was returning from a pilgrimage.

"It's all right," she had assured him. "If the master gives us any trouble, we'll worry about it when the time comes. I'll tell him what a poor boy you are, how your companions abandoned you when your feet were too sore to go on walking. Don't worry about it. No one will raise an eyebrow. There's always room for a child or two. Who's going to care if we spread out a few boards for you to sleep on in the kitchen, and give you a little bit to eat?

There's no risk in that. Why, even with a formal apprenticeship boys have been known to disappear. It doesn't prevent them from running off with things that don't belong to them. There are all kinds of people in this world. You know what they say: 'You don't know a horse till you ride it.' How can we tell whether we can use you in the shop if we don't give you a try? But listen, if you don't want to go back to that slum of yours, you're going to have to work hard. And learn how things are done. You'll have to make up your mind: this is where your home is. You're going to have to work, you know."

And work he did. Today, by himself, Kichizō could treat as many umbrellas as three adults, humming a tune as he went about his business. Seeing this, people would praise the dead lady's foresight: "Granny knew what she was doing."

The old woman, to whom he owed so much, had been dead two years now, and the present owners of the shop and their son Hanji were hard for Kichizō to take. But what was he to do? Even if he didn't like them, he had nowhere else to go. Had not his anger and resentment at them caused his very bones and muscles to contract? "Dwarf! Dwarf!" everybody taunted him. "Eating fish on the anniversary of your parents' death! It serves you right that you're so short. Round and round we go—look at him! The tiny monk who'll never grow!"[6]

In his work, he could take revenge on the sniveling bullies, and he was perfectly ready to answer them with a clenched fist. But his valor sometimes left him. He didn't even know the date of his parents' death, he had no way to observe the yearly abstinences. It made him miserable, and he would throw himself down underneath the umbrellas drying in the yard and push his face against the ground to stifle his tears.

The boy was a little fireball. He had a violence about him that frightened the entire neighborhood. The sleeves of his plain kimono would swing as he flailed his arms, and the smell of oil from the umbrellas followed him through every season. There was no one to calm his temper, and he suffered all the more. If anyone were to show Kichizō a moment's kindness, he knew that he would cling to him and find it hard ever to let go.

In the spring Okyō the seamstress had moved into the neighborhood. With her quick wit, she was soon friendly with everyone. Her landlord was the owner of the umbrella shop, and so she was especially cordial to the members of the shop. "Bring over your mending any time, boys. I don't care what condition it's in. There are so many people at your house, the mistress won't have time to tend to it. I'm always sewing anyway, one more stitch is nothing. Come and visit when you have time. I get lonely living by myself. I like people who speak their minds, and that rambunctious Kichizō—he's one of my favorites. Listen, the next time you lose your temper," she would tell him, "instead of hitting the little white dog at the rice shop, come over to my place. I'll give you my mallet, and you can take out your anger on the fulling block.

That way, people won't be so upset with you. And you'll be helping me—it'll do us both good."

In no time Kichizō began to make himself at home. It was "Okyō, this" and "Okyō, that" until he had given the other workmen at the shop something new to tease him about. "Why, he's the mirror image of the great Chōemon!" they would laugh.[7] "At the River Katsura, Ohan will have to carry *him*! Can't you see the little runt perched on top of her sash for the ride across the river? What a farce!"

Kichizō was not without retort. "If you're so manly, why don't you ever visit Okyō? Which one of you can tell me each day what sweets she's put in the cookie jar? Take the pawnbroker with the bald spot. He's head over heels in love with her, always ordering sewing from her and coming round on one pretext or another, sending her aprons and neckpieces and sashes—trying to win her over. But she's never given him the time of day. Let alone treat him the way she does me! Kichizō from the umbrella shop—*I'm* the one who can go there any hour of the night, and when she hears it's me, she'll open the door in her nightgown. 'You haven't come to see me all day. Did something happen? I've been worried about you.' That's how she greets me. Who else gets treated that way? 'Hulking men are like big trees: not always good supports.'[8] Size has nothing to do with it. Look at how the tiny peppercorn is prized."[9]

"Listen to him!" they would yell, pelting Kichizō across the back.

But all he did was smile nonchalantly. "Thank you very much." If only he had a little height, no one would dare to tease him. As it was, the disdain he showed them was dismissed as nothing more than the impertinence of a little fool. He was the butt of all their jokes and the gossip they exchanged over tobacco.

On the night of the thirtieth of December, Kichizō was returning home. He had been up the hill to call on a customer with apologies for the late filling of an order. On his way back now he kept his arms folded across his chest and walked briskly, kicking a stone with the tip of his sandal. It rolled to the left and then to the right, and finally Kichizō kicked it into a ditch, chuckling aloud to himself. There was no one around to hear him. The moon above shone brightly on the white winter roads, but the boy was oblivious to the cold. He felt invigorated. He thought he would stop by Okyō's on the way home. As he crossed over to the back street, he was suddenly startled: someone appeared from behind him and covered his eyes. Whoever it was, the person could not keep from laughing.

"Who is it? Come on, who is it?" When he touched the hands held over his eyes, he knew who it was. "Ah, Okyō! I can tell by your snaky fingers.[10] You shouldn't scare people."

Kichizō freed himself and Okyō laughed. "Oh, too bad! I've been discovered."

Over her usual jacket she was wearing a hood that came down almost to her eyes. She looked smart tonight, Kichizō thought as he surveyed her appearance. "Where've you been? I thought you told me you were too busy even to eat the next few days." The boy did not hide his suspicion. "Were you taking something to a customer?"

"I went to make some of my New Year's calls early," she said innocently.

"You're lying. No one receives greetings on the thirtieth. Where did you go? To your relatives?"

"As a matter of fact, I *am* going to a relative's—to live with a relative I hardly know. Tomorrow I'll be moving. It's so sudden, it probably surprises you. It *is* unexpected, even I feel a little startled. Anyway, you should be happy for me. It's not a bad thing that's happened."

"Really? You're not teasing, are you? You shouldn't scare me like this. If you went away, what would I do for fun? Don't ever joke about such things. You and your nonsense!" He shook his head at her.

"I'm not joking. It's just as you said once—good luck has come riding in a fancy carriage. So I can't very well stay on in a back tenement, can I? Now I'll be able to sew you that kimono, Kichizō."

"I don't want it. When you say 'Good luck has come,' you mean you're going off some place worthless. That's what Hanji said the other day. 'You know Okyō the seamstress?' he said. 'Her uncle—the one who gives rubdowns over by the vegetable market—he's helped her find a new position. She's going into service with some rich family. Or so they say. But it sounds fishy to me—she's too old to learn sewing from some housewife. Somebody's going to set her up. I'm sure of it. She'll be wearing tasseled coats the next time we see her, la-de-da, and her hair all done up in ringlets, like a kept woman. You wait. With a face like hers, you don't think she's about to spend her whole life sewing, do you?' That's what he said. I told him he was full of it, and we had a big fight. But you *are* going to do it, aren't you? You're going off to be someone's mistress!"

"It's not that I want to. I don't have much choice. I suppose I won't be able to see you any more, Kichizō, will I?"

With these few words, Kichizō withered. "I don't know, maybe it's a step up for you, but don't do it. It's not as if you can't make a living with your sewing. The only one you have to feed is yourself. When you're good at your work, why give it up for something so stupid? It's disgusting of you. Don't go through with it. It's not too late to change your mind." The boy was unyielding in his notion of integrity.

"Oh, dear," Okyō sighed. She stopped walking. "Kichizō, I'm sick of all this washing and sewing. Anything would be better. I'm tired of these drab clothes. I'd like to wear a crepe kimono, too, for a change—even if it is tainted."

They were bold words, and yet it didn't sound as if she herself fully comprehended them. "Anyway," she laughed, "come home with me. Hurry up now."

"What! I'm too disgusted. You go ahead," he said, but his long, sad shadow followed after her.

Soon they came to their street. Okyō stopped beneath the window where Kichizō always tapped for her. "Every night you come and knock at this window. After tomorrow night," she sighed, "I won't be able to hear your voice calling any more. How terrible the world is."

"It's not the world. It's you."

Okyō went in first and lit a lamp. "Kichizō, come get warm," she called when she had the fire in the brazier going.

He stood by the pillar. "No, thanks."

"Aren't you chilly? It won't do to catch a cold."

"I don't care." He looked down at the floor as he spoke. "Leave me alone."

"What's the matter with you? You're acting funny. Is it something I said? If it is, please tell me. When you stand around with a long face like that and won't talk to me, it makes me worry."

"You don't have to worry about anything. This is Kichizō from the umbrella shop you're talking to. I don't need any woman to take care of me." He rubbed his back against the pillar. "How pointless everything turns out. What a life! People are friendly, and then they disappear. It's always the ones I like. Granny at the umbrella shop, and Kinu, the one with short hair, at the dyer's shop. First Granny dies of palsy. Then Kinu goes and throws herself into the well behind the dyer's—she didn't want to marry. Now you're going off. I'm always disappointed in the end. Why should I be surprised, I suppose? What am I but a boy who oils umbrellas? So what if I do the work of a hundred men? I'm not going to win any prizes for it. Morning and night, the only title I ever hear is 'Dwarf' . . . 'Dwarf'! I wonder if I'll ever get any taller. 'All things come to him who waits,'[11] they say, but I wait and wait, and all I get is more unhappiness. Just the day before yesterday I had a fight with Hanji over you. Ha! I was so sure he was wrong. I told him you were the last person rotten enough to go off and do that kind of thing. Not five days have passed, and I have to eat crow. How could I have thought of you as a sister? You, with all your lies and tricks, and your selfishness. This is the last you'll ever see of me. Ever. Thanks for your kindness. Go on and do what you want. From now on, I won't have anything to do with anyone. It's not worth it. Good-by, Okyō."

He went to the front door and began to put his sandals on.

"Kichizō! You're wrong. I'm leaving here, but I'm not abandoning *you*. You're like my little brother. How can you turn on me?" From behind, she hugged him with all her might. "You're too impatient. You jump to conclusions."

"You mean you're not going to be someone's mistress?" Kichizō turned around.

"It's not the sort of thing anybody wants to do. But it's been decided. You can't change things."

He stared at her with tears in his eyes.

"Take your hands off me, Okyō."

Notes to Part One

Chapter One: The Family

1 Noriyoshi was the name he took two weeks after Ichiyō's birth. He had had at least seven other names, including Daikichi (the name he was given by his parents), but Noriyoshi is the name by which he is most commonly known.

2 This, again, is the most common of his several names. The same is true of Mashimo Sennosuke and Ueno Heizō below.

3 The "bannermen," or direct personal retainers of the *shōgun*, the military commander and head of the government in the Edo, or Tokugawa, period (1615–1868). Although the *hatamoto* held enfeoffments of under 10,000 *koku* (the minimum amount required for *daimyō*, or baronial, status), they were permitted the privilege of direct audience with the shōgun. (For *koku*, see note 7 below.)

4 In the case of Mashimo Sennosuke, they were: first, a clerkship in the office of the chief magistrate of Iwasa, in the Yashiro district (a position that again brought him into contact with the Higuchis, as his duties took him into the Nakahagiwara area), and then a similar clerkship in Kōfu. After this he returned to Edo and purchased samurai rank from a man named Mashimo who worked in the kitchens of Edo Castle.

5 Quoted in Wada Yoshie, *Higuchi Ichiyō* (Tokyo: Kōdansha, 1974), p. 72.

6 "Daikichi no Bannai," Daikichi being his name in youth and Bannai, a character in *Kanadehon Chūshingura* (A Copybook of Kana: The Treasury of Loyal Retainers, 1748) by Takeda Izumo, Miyoshi Shōraku, and Namiki Senryū. The popular puppet play, which depicts a bold vendetta by a band of loyal samurai avenging their fallen lord, was adapted for the *kabuki* stage and became the best-loved of all Japanese dramas.

7 Inaba Daizen was from a cadet branch of the Inaba clan, whose head was the *fudai daimyō* (a personal vassal of the shōgun) of Yamashiro Province and lord of Yodo Castle, and whose domain totaled 102,000 *koku*. Daizen's holdings were paltry by comparison. (One koku, the stipendiary unit in the Edo period, was the equivalent of approximately five bushels of rice and was considered the amount sufficient to feed one adult for one year.)

8 The *ryō* was the standard monetary unit for gold, the principal currency of Edo (the *monme* being the standard for silver, the principal currency of Kyōto and Ōsaka). One ryō was the equivalent of 17.86 grams, and at this time, in the late Edo period, would buy approximately one koku, or five bushels, of hulled rice.

Chapter Two: The Prodigy

1 *Hakkenden* (Biographies of Eight Dogs, 1814–41), Takizawa Bakin's sweeping account of samurai ideals in the fifteenth century, is the longest work of Japanese fiction. It is highly improbable that at age seven even a prodigy could read all 106 books in three days. The story does become more believable, however, if Ichiyō read the abridged *kana*—or Japanese-syllabary—version by Kanagaki Robun, *Kanayomi Hakkenden* (1866–68).

2 Wada Yoshie, *Higuchi Ichiyō* (1974), p. 14.

3 "Chiri no Naka," 10 August 1893, *Zenshū*, vol. 3-a, p. 315. One wonders if in describing her youth, the adult Higuchi Ichiyō was emulating, either consciously or unconsciously, the picture that Murasaki Shikibu drew in her eleventh-century diary of a precocious childhood, where we are presented with a Murasaki who learns faster than her backward older brother, delighting her father but prompting him to wish that *she* had been born the son.

4 Wada, *Higuchi Ichiyō* (1974), p. 18. I have not usually included the Japanese original in the text, but this poem seemed of sufficient curiosity to make an exception.

297

5 "Chiri no Naka," 10 August 1893, *Zenshū*, vol. 3-a, pp. 315–16.

6 The distinction by gender is that of the Japanese critics. The other two distinguished women poets who were always compared with Nakajima Utako were Saisho Atsuko and Tsuru Hisako.

7 The poem that won Natsuko first place was:

Uchinabiku	The willow tree
Yanagi o mireba	Sways in the night
Nodoka naru	Of a misty moon;
Oborozukiyo mo	Somewhere
Kaze wa arikeri.	Gentle breezes blow.

8 "Mi no Furugoromo," 19 February 1887, *Zenshū*, vol. 3-a, pp. 3–6.

9 The site near Kōbe where in 1184, during the Gempei War, the Taira forces were ambushed by the Minamoto.

10 "Mi no Furugoromo," 16 April 1887, *Zenshū*, vol. 3-a, pp. 6–7.

11 Ichiyō's description of the attitude of a character who shared her father's ambition, in "Hanagomori." The passage is quoted virtually in full in chapter 4, pp. 83–86.

12 Ibid.

13 In exchange value, the yen averaged U.S. $0.94 between 1874–81. In the summer of 1888, one koku of rice cost 4.91 yen.

14 Shioda Ryōhei, *Higuchi Ichiyō Kenkyū*, p. 178.

15 "Chiri no Naka," 10 August 1893, *Zenshū*, vol. 3-a, p. 315.

16 "Yamiyo," chap. 7, *Zenshū*, vol. 1, pp. 328–29.

Chapter Three: The Mentor

1 "Koto no Ne," chap. 1, *Zenshū*, vol. 1, p. 268.

2 "Fude-Susabi," undated entry, *Zenshū*, vol. 3-b, pp. 627–28.

3 By the Japanese count, one was a year older on the first of January; by Western reckoning she was still nineteen.

4 "Wakaba-Kage," undated preface (ca. 11 April 1891), *Zenshū*, vol. 3-a, p. 16.

5 Ibid., 15 April 1891, pp. 20–21.

6 His first impression is recounted in an article he wrote after her death, which forms the basis of the following description. See Nakarai Tōsui, "Ichiyō Joshi," *Chūō Kōron* (June 1907), p. 36.

7 Ibid., pp. 21–22.

8 "Chiri no Naka," 10 August 1893, *Zenshū*, vol. 3-a, p. 315.

9 Asai Ryōi, *Ukiyo Monogatari*, in Takagi Ichinosuke; Nishio Minoru; Hisamatsu Sen'ichi; Asō Isoji; and Tokieda Motoki, eds.; *Kana Zōshi Shū*, vol. 90 in Nihon Koten Bungaku Taikei series (Tokyo: Iwanami Shoten, 1965), p. 244.

10 "Wakaba-Kage," 22 April 1891, *Zenshū*, vol. 3-a, p. 23.

11 Ibid., 25 (actually 26) April 1891, pp. 23–25.

12 Ibid., 17 June 1891, p. 32.

13 Ibid., pp. 32–33.

14 Ueda Akinari (1734–1809) was a writer of the middle Edo period best known for his supernatural tales, of which the most famous are *Ugetsu Monogatari* (Tales of Moonlight and Rain, 1776) and *Harusame Monogatari* (Tales of Spring Rain, 1808). Takizawa (or Kyokutei) Bakin (1767–1848) was an extremely prolific writer of the late Edo period, whose output ranged over many genres but whose best-known work is the immense novel *Hakkenden* (Biographies of Eight Dogs, 1814–41), a work in 106 volumes, which Natsuko is reputed to have read for the first time at the age of seven. (See chapter 2, note 1.)

15 See *Makura no Sōshi* (The Pillow Book, ca. 1002), chapter 3, in the Nōinbon tradition:

On the third day of the third month, the sun shines bright and balmy, and the flowering peach begins to blossom. The willows are never more beautiful, each bud still asleep inside its cocoon. Only when the leaves spread does one tire of them. In fact, once they lose their blooms all trees begin to pall.

Matsuo Satoshi and Nagai Kazuko, eds.; *Makura no Sōshi*, vol. 11, in Nihon Koten Bungaku Zenshū series (Tokyo: Shōgakkan, 1974), p. 67.

16 "Waka-Kusa," 8 August 1891, *Zenshū*, vol. 3-a, pp. 44–46.

17 "Fude-Susabi," undated entry, *Zenshū*, vol. 3-b, pp. 628–29.

18 Ibid., pp. 620–21.

19 "Wakaba-Kage," 11 April 1891, *Zenshū*, vol. 3-a, pp. 17–18.

20 "Waka-Kusa," 21 July 1891, *Zenshū*, vol. 3-a, p. 41.

21 "Fude-Susabi," undated entry (ca. 7 September 1891), *Zenshū*, vol. 3-b, pp. 632–34.

22 Ibid., undated, pp. 619–20.

23 "Yomogifu Nikki, 1," 4 October 1891, *Zenshū*, vol. 3-a, pp. 60–61.

24 Ibid., 22 September 1891, p. 53.

25 "Yomogifu Nikki, 2," 24 November 1891, *Zenshū*, vol. 3-a, pp. 80–82.

26 Ibid.

27 See, for example, Wada Yoshie, *Ichiyō no Nikki*, pp. 97–101.

28 "Mori no Shita-Gusa, 1," undated entry (late 1891), *Zenshū*, vol. 3-b, pp. 722–23.

29 Or "Ichiyō joshi," "Miss Ichiyō."

30 Tōsui had chosen a suitably literary name for his journal. Musashino, or Musashi Plain, on the northwest outskirts of present-day Tokyo, is a site full of literary overtones. In classical Japanese poetry the name is inextricably linked with the imagery of love. The plain is invoked as a lovers' tryst, a place where the grasses yield a dye deep as the deepest love, and so forth. See note 17 to "Flowers at Dusk" and note 8 to "A Snowy Day," for example.

31 Two popular gesaku writers of the late Edo period. Tamenaga Shunsui (1790–1843) was the author of the novel *Shunshoku Umegoyomi* (A Plum Calendar for Spring Love, 1832), and Ryūtei Tanehiko (1783–1842), the author of *Nise Murasaki Inaka Genji* (A False Murasaki and a Rustic Genji, 1829–42).

32 Yamamoto Fumio, *Nihon Shinbunshi*, p. 116.

33 "Wakaba-Kage," 15 April 1891, *Zenshū*, vol. 3-a, p. 21.

34 *Kokkai Kaisetsu no Zengo* (1890), by one of the leading political novelists, Suehiro Tetchō (1849–96).

35 *Keikoku Bidan* (Praiseworthy Anecdotes of Statesmanship, 1883–84), by Yano Ryūkei: a historical novel written in *kanbun*, or Sino-Japanese, and based on a gleaning of translated descriptions of celebrated incidents in Greek history. The work was originally intended as pure history, but his lack of source material prompted the author to settle for historical fiction. The facts were changed to suit his own designs, which were, in essence, a conservative pitch for a sort of Greco-Confucian democracy. The ambidextrous Yano was a typical Meiji man: educator, journalist, bureaucrat, and editor-in-chief of the newspaper *Yūbin Hōchi* (The Post Dispatch); he was also responsible for introducing the Japanese to Unitarianism.

36 Of some 250 political novels published during the Meiji period, approximately 220 appeared in the decade 1880–90. See *Meiji Bunken Mokuroku* (Tokyo: Nippon Hyōronsha, 1931).

37 Nakamura Mitsuo, *Modern Japanese Fiction, 1868–1926* (Tokyo: Kokusai Bunka Shinkōkai, 1968), p. 55.

38 "Mekki." See *Kunikida Doppo, Tayama Katai Shū*, vol. 11, in Gendai Nihon Bungaku Taikei series (Tokyo: Chikuma Shobō, 1974), p. 435.

39 It is sometimes forgotten that *Shōsetsu Shinzui* was not entirely a repudiation of gesaku. By no means was the essay an advertisement for the wholesale adoption of the European novel. Shōyō maintained, rather, that a study of Western models would enrich the Japanese

literary tradition; novelists conversant with their Dickens and their Bulwer-Lytton would be in a position to reform native genres of fiction into a sort of "enlightened" gesaku.

40   Quoted in an unpublished paper by Andrew Laurence Markus, "Tsubouchi Shōyō's *Tōsei Shosei Katagi* and *Shōsetsu Shinzui*," 14 October 1978, p. 25.

41   See Marleigh Grayer Ryan, *Japan's First Modern Novel: Ukigumo of Futabatei Shimei* (New York: Columbia University Press, 1967).

42   "Mori no Shita-Gusa, 1," undated entry (late 1891), *Zenshū*, vol. 3-b, p. 722.

43   "Wakaba-Kage," 11 April 1891, *Zenshū*, vol. 3-a, pp. 18-20.

44   "Tamadasuki" (Jeweled Sleeve Band) was published on 17 April 1892 in the second issue of *Musashino*, and "Samidare" (Early Summer Rain) on 23 July 1892 in the third and final issue. Like "Flowers at Dusk" and the Heian classics, both stories are about sheltered maidens of good family who pine for men who are for one reason or another beyond their reach. The courtly atmosphere is thick with moonbeams and fireflies, handsome strangers glimpsed from garden walls, and love poems that the lovers themselves have trouble deciphering.

45   Tamenaga Shunsui's *Shunshoku Umegoyomi* (A Plum Calendar for Spring Love, 1832) was the most famous of the ninjōbon, and the model for many imitations. Its wanly handsome, feckless hero, Tanjirō, was the love-boy supreme. The adopted son of the owner of a Yoshiwara brothel, the Karakotoya, he is the object of fierce rivalry between the beautiful and determined Yonehachi, a geisha affiliated with the house, and the naive young Ochō, daughter of the owner.

The plot of *Umegoyomi*, with many a twist and turn, revolves around the overcoming of the endless, but not quite insurmountable, barriers to love. Both women give their all for poor Tanjirō, who has been implicated by the villainous head-clerk of the Karakotoya in the theft of a precious heirloom and has been forced into hiding when the story opens. Before the chronicle hurtles to its happy conclusion—with Tanjirō exonerated, Ochō chosen as his wife, and Yonehachi officially instated as his concubine—the reader is treated to a varied cast of flesh-brokers and extortionists, to alternating scenes of intense jealousy and noble self-sacrifice, to attempted rapes by bands of highwaymen and surrenderings of virginity in sleepy, moonlit gardens.

Shunsui makes repeated reference in *Umegoyomi* to the dependence of his amatory tales on the patronage of women readers (see the end of chapter 13, for example). In fact, the readership for the ninjōbon embraced, in equal numbers, proper young ladies of the upper class and downtown demimondaines. In spite of their different styles of living, both audiences were apparently thirsty for true love and a little excitement, and together the two groups made a very lucrative market for the publishers of the ninjōbon.

46   Ichiyō has sentences like: "Sashi mo shigekaru yaemugura ni sawaranu wa kuru toshi-tsuki zo kashi." ("All that made its way through the tangle of wild grass were the years and the months and the moonlight.") This echoes a description in the "Kiritsubo" chapter of *Genji*: "Tsuki-kage bakari zo yaemugura ni mo sawarazu sashi-iritaru." ("Only the moonlight made its way through the tangle of wild grass.") Further on, Ichiyō writes, "Dare ka wa yomogifu no oku made tazunen mono zo." ("Who is about to come calling when they have to struggle through a garden of overgrown weeds?") This, again, is too close to a passage in "Kiritsubo" to be coincidental. The sentence in *Genji* reads, "Kakaru mi-tsukai no, yomogifu no tsuyu wake-iri-tamau ni tsukete mo, ito, hazukashū namu." ("I am greatly ashamed that such an august messenger has had to struggle through the dew in this garden of overgrown weeds.")

Ichiyō also alludes to the poetry in the imperial anthologies. For example, when she describes the heroine's house, we are told that, although the moonlight is not yet shining in through holes in the roof, its state of disrepair is reminiscent of the dilapidated guardhouse at the abandoned barrier at Fuwa—a cliché in court poetry. Of the many possible candidates, the poem that Ichiyō's passage seems closest to is a selection in the *Shingosenshū*, the thirteenth of the anthologies, completed in 1303:

Akikaze ni	In the autumn wind,
Fuwa no sekiya no	The eaves of the guardhouse at Fuwa
Aremaku mo	Will be crumbling now,
Oshikaranu made	And the moon, cool and uncaring,
Tsuki zo morikuru.	Will be shining in.

The *locus classicus* is poem 1599 in the *Shinkokinshū*, the eighth of the imperial anthologies, completed in 1206:

Hito sumanu	No one lives there any more,
Fuwa no sekiya no	In the guardhouse
Itabisashi	At the barrier to Fuwa:
Are ni shi ato wa	The autumn wind echoes through the eaves,
Tada aki no kaze.	Left behind to founder.

47 Tanaka Jūtarō, cited in Hosaka Kōshi, "Ichiyō Bungaku to Koten," *Kokubungaku*, November 1957 (special issue, "Higuchi Ichiyō no Sōgō Tankyū"), p. 47.

48 "Nikki, 2" (untitled), 7 March 1892, *Zenshū*, vol. 3-a, p. 107.

49 Chaps. 1 and 2 in *Shunshoku Umegoyomi*, for example.

50 "Iro-otoko wa chikara mo kane mo nakarikeri" was the standard saying: "Neither strength nor money has the love-boy."

51 "Nikki Shinobu-Gusa," 7 June 1892, *Zenshū*, vol. 3-a, pp. 143–44.

52 Ibid., 14 June 1892, *Zenshū*, vol. 3-a, pp. 145–46.

53 When Ichiyō's diary was published in 1912, Tōsui's niece, Chiyo (the daughter of his brother and Tsuruta Tamiko), asked her uncle why he had never married Ichiyō. "She always hid in a corner," he replied, "and would never approach me. I had no idea she was in love with me until I read the diary. And besides, she wasn't all that beautiful" (quoted in a 1953 interview with Ishikawa Chiyo, in Shioda Ryōhei, *Higuchi Ichiyō Kenkyū*, p. 587). While this is precisely the sort of blasé disclaimer one might expect from the perpetual playboy, the number of such comments on Tōsui's part cannot help but suggest that, whatever the affection between them, the intensity of the affair was exaggerated by Ichiyō. See also Nakarai Tōsui, "Ichiyō Joshi," *Chūō Kōron*, June 1907, pp. 36–41.

54 Wada Yoshie, *Ichiyō no Nikki*, p. 106.

55 She was dressed up because of the mourning observances for Mrs. Nakajima's mother.

56 "Nikki Shinobu-Gusa," 15 June 1892, *Zenshū*, vol. 3-a, pp. 147–48.

57 She had been staying in Koishikawa helping Mrs. Nakajima since the death of her teacher's mother on 3 June.

58 "Nikki Shinobu-Gusa," 22 June 1892, *Zenshū*, vol. 3-a, pp. 148–51.

Chapter Four: The Yoshiwara

1 *Umoregi* is bogwood, or lignite, but the title suggests the idiom "Isshō o umoregi ni owaru," to lead an obscure life or end one's days in obscurity.

2 *Jogakusei*, 23 December 1892.

3 Nishio Yoshihito (*Zenshaku Ichiyō Nikki*, vol. 1, p. 126) estimates the 1890 yen to be the equivalent in purchasing power of ten thousand 1976 yen; at the mid-1979 exchange rate of two hundred and eighteen yen to the U.S. dollar, Ichiyō's royalties would have been the equivalent of approximately five hundred dollars, which was roughly one month's living expenses for the three women.

4 "Umoregi," chap. 1, *Zenshū*, vol. 1, p. 152.

5 "Taninaka no bijin," coined by Matsuzaka Toshio, cited in Seki Ryōichi, *Higuchi Ichiyō: Koshō to Shiron*, p. 218. In fact, this theme—the discovery of an intriguing, castoff maiden

living in secluded and derelict surroundings—was already becoming a cliché by the eleventh century. See chapter 2 of *Genji Monogatari*, for example, where Prince Genji and his friends discuss the allure of the neglected young beauty.

6   The metaphor describing the heroine of "Aketsukiyo."

7   The usual standard against which Ichiyō measured feminine beauty. Ono no Komachi was an accomplished poetess of the ninth century and a legendary femme fatale.

8   These are examples from "Wakarejimo" and "Yamiyo."

9   The image occurs in a description of the heroine in the story "Wakarejimo."

10 "Koto no Ne," *Zenshū*, vol. 1, pp. 268-73.

11 "Hanagomori," chap. 2, *Zenshū*, vol. 1, p. 277.

12 Ibid., chaps. 2 and 3, pp. 278-83.

13 "Nikki," undated preface (ca. 1 July 1893), *Zenshū*, vol. 3-a, p. 289.

14 Ibid., p. 290.

15 "Chiri no Naka," 15 July 1893, *Zenshū*, vol. 3-a, pp. 300-02.

16 "Takekurabe," chap. 1, *Zenshū*, vol. 1, p. 402.

17 "Chiri no Naka," 20 July 1893, *Zenshū*, vol. 3-a, pp. 303-04.

18 Ibid., 25 July 1893, *Zenshū*, vol. 3-a, pp. 306-07.

19 An allusion to Po Chü-i's "Ch'ang hen ko" (The Song of Everlasting Sorrow), in which the Chinese Emperor Hsüan Tsung (r. 712-56) yearns inconsolably for his deceased beloved:

> He would lengthen the lamp-wick to its end
>   and still could never sleep.
> Bell and drum would slowly toll the dragging
>   night hours
> And the River of Stars grow sharp in the sky,
>   just before dawn,
> And the porcelain mandarin-ducks on the roof
>   grow thick with morning frost
> And his covers of kingfisher-blue feel
>   lonelier and colder·
> With the distance between life and death
>   year after year;
> And yet no beloved spirit ever visited his dreams.

Cyril Birch, ed., *Anthology of Chinese Literature* (New York: Grove Press, 1965), vol. 1, p. 268.

20 "Chiri no Naka," 3 August 1893, *Zenshū*, vol. 3-a, pp. 310-12.

21 "Takekurabe," chap. 1, *Zenshū*, vol. 1, p. 402.

22 One *rin* equaled 1/1000 yen.

23 An allusion to the affair between her fellow student, Tanaka Minoko, who had opened her own poetry school, the Umenoya (Plum Arbor), and Koide Tsubara, a colleague of Mrs. Nakajima who went by the literary sobriquet Kuchinashi-zono (Jasmine Garden).

24 "Jinchū Nikki," 15 November 1893, *Zenshū*, vol. 3-a, pp. 339-41.

25 Ibid. The sentiments echo especially chapter 137 in *Tsurezuregusa* (Essays in Idleness, ca. 1330).

26 Yoshida Kenkō, *Tsurezuregusa*, chap. 71.

27 She was twenty-two by Western count. The birthdate she gives is according to the lunar calendar. By the Gregorian calendar the date was 2 May 1872.

28 The four elements constituting life are earth, water, fire, and wind. The five facets of human life are the *skandhas*, or "aggregates," of Buddhist philosophy: "Our physical form, feeling, ideation, dispositions, and consciousness are all transitory, and therefore suffering, and not permanent and good. That which is transitory, suffering, and liable to change is not the eternal soul. So it must be said of all physical forms whatever, past, present, or to be,

subjective or objective, far or near, high or low: this is not mine, this I am not, this is not my eternal 'soul' " (Mahāvagga I, p. 13f.).

29 "Small-sleeved garment": a short-sleeved robe, an undergarment adopted as outer wear in the Muromachi period (1334–1573), in elaborate patterns, usually of silk with cotton padding, and originally with rounded corners on the lower sleeve.

30 "Nikki Chiri no Naka," undated (23 February 1894), Zenshū, vol. 3-a, pp. 359–64.

31 "Takekurabe," chap. 1, Zenshū, vol. 1, p. 402.

32 After the Meiji Restoration in 1868, many Japanese viewed Korea as the natural outlet for their country's ambitions. They advocated intervention in the development of the Korean peninsula so that Japan's closest neighbor might share in the advances wrought by modernization but, more importantly, so that Japan could secure a new economic market and a sphere of influence to prevent both Chinese and Western hegemony in East Asia. Korea, on its part plagued by intriguing regents, sporadic revolts, and overly solicitous neighbors, was not always amenable to these plans. The Korean question remained a perennial subject of debate, particularly heated in these months prior to the outbreak of the Sino-Japanese War in the summer of 1894.

33 The Chishima had collided with a British battleship in November 1892. In a court ruling on 25 October 1893, the Japanese ship was held responsible for the accident.

34 "Jinchū Nikki," 2 December 1893, Zenshū, vol. 3-a, pp. 348–49.

35 The Genroku period (1688–1703) during the thirty-year rule of the fifth Tokugawa shōgun, Tsunayoshi (1646–1709) in the early Edo era, was an age of plebeian renaissance for Japanese art and literature. Not only did the great literary triumvirate of Saikaku, Bashō, and Chikamatsu create unparalleled works in fiction, poetry, and drama; in art as well, Moronobu and other major masters of early ukiyo-e produced some of Japan's finest woodblock prints. With advances in printing techniques and the rise of an affluent merchant class, the literary, theatrical, and graphic arts all dovetailed in the publication of a variety of handsome illustrated books, coveted in the Meiji period by connoisseurs like Awashima. It was Awashima's collection of Saikaku first editions that formed the basis for the first Saikaku zenshū, or complete works, the Teikoku Bunko edition of 1894.

36 None of them really had much in common with Saikaku. Kōyō perhaps came closer than Rohan to Saikaku's brand of realism, but he lacked the Edo writer's maturity. Kōyō must have realized this, for after 1895 he ceased to imitate Saikaku and began writing in a language that was more colloquial, less ornate. Kōyō nonetheless played an important role in the Saikaku revival, collating the texts for the first zenshū. Kōyō's main colleague in the revival, Kōda Rohan, would also eventually abandon his attempt to revive Genroku literature in the modern novel, though not before both the style and form of Saikaku's writing had had a beneficial effect on Rohan's prose. Mori Ōgai was to write only one work in the Saikaku manner, a short story called "Somechigae" (Different Dyes, 1897).

37 It was not, however, his first piece of extended prose. Two years earlier, in 1680, he had written Naniwa no Kao wa Ise no Oshiroi (A Debut in Ōsaka with Make-up from Ise), which belonged to the genre of hyōbanki, or critiques of actors and courtesans, one of the popular forms of kana zōshi. Only volumes 2 and 3 are extant, but it seems clear that the work was an experiment in prose for Saikaku, and it is considered the first hyōbanki to attain the level of creative literature.

38 The non-samurai class of merchants and artisans.

39 Saikaku's absence from the diary is not necessarily significant; these were frantic times for Ichiyō, and many things went unrecorded. In a letter dated 18 October 1894, Hirata Tokuboku, one of the Bungakkai writers, affirms that he will soon bring Ichiyō the "Kaku zenshū," the complete Saikaku, as he has promised. His Ichiyō no Omoide and Kuniko's Higuchi Ichiyō Ryakuden are among the memoirs that mention Ichiyō's enthusiasm for Saikaku. Kuniko says, for example, that her sister was particularly fond of Nippon Eitaigura, one of the later collections of chōnin stories.

40   The Ueno collection contains the first editions of seventeen works by Saikaku, including: *Kōshoku Ichidai Otoko, Shoen Ōkagami, Kōshoku Gonin Onna, Kōshoku Ichidai Onna, Nanshoku Ōkagami, Budō Denraiki, Buke Giri Monogatari, Yorozu no Fumihōgu, Nippon Eitaigura, Seken Munesan'yō, Hitome Tamaboko.*

41   Altogether, Saikaku produced three yakazu haikai series, always within twenty-four hours: 1,600 verses in 1677; 4,000 verses in 1680; 23,500 verses in 1684. He had previously composed solo sequences of linked verse, *Ōsaka Dokugin Shū* (Verses from a Solitary Poet in Ōsaka, written in 1673, published in 1675), and the sequence inspired by his wife's death, *Haikai Dokugin Ichinichi Senku* (One Day, One Man, a Thousand Verses, 1675). But these were not billed as yakazu haikai, which is to say they were not formal marathons with witnesses and scribes and the implicit challenge that makes it fair to call them "poetry competitions" in spite of the fact that only one poet took part. Saikaku is credited with inventing these "arrow-counting" haikai spectaculars. The name "yakazu" apparently comes from archery contests, dating from 1608, which were held at the Sanjūsangendō in Kyōto. The champion bowman was one Hoshino Kanzaemon of Owari, who in 1662 reputedly hit the target at the other end of the long corridor of the Sanjūsangendō 8,000 times in 10,542 attempts. The object, then, was quantity, whether the medium was arrows or poetry.

42   The extraordinary performance, which is mentioned almost ad nauseam in anything ever written about Saikaku, took place at Sumiyoshi Shrine in 1684. Although the poems produced at this last yakazu were never published (their sheer number might well have discouraged any patrons from underwriting publication), scholars evince little doubt that Saikaku did in fact accomplish this feat. It has been computed that with amanuenses to record the verses, Saikaku would have had approximately four seconds per verse, or one minute per fifteen links. At such speed, versification amounts to mindless monologue.

43   The rules, like the genre, came from haikai's more respectable sister, *renga* in the *ushin* (elegant, or serious) tradition. There were prescribed themes (*fushimono*), for example, and *sarikirai*—restrictions on what words and themes could be repeated, and where within a sequence. Haikai, or comic renga, were considerably freer, especially in the Danrin tradition. But nonetheless rules remained to keep haikai gatherings from degenerating into evenings of tipsy repartee. It was essential, for example, that the *hokku*, or opening verse, contain a *kireji* (a "cutting word" like *ya* to divide the verse into two complementing parts). In addition, the hokku had to fix the setting: the place, the season, the time of day. The second verse had to end in a *te* form, the third in a noun, and so forth. Certain words, especially in the ushin tradition, were considered so powerful or unsettling that they were not to be used more than once in a sequence of a thousand lines—words like *devil, dragon,* and *woman*. "Dutch" Saikaku, of course, didn't set much store by some of this.

44   As Saikaku devised the yakazu, however, seven of the *omote hakku* (front eight verses) for each set of one hundred links were furnished in advance by another poet. This had the advantage of providing even the virtuoso with a ready set of various images with which to begin each series.

45   See, for example, Richard Douglas Lane, "Saikaku," p. 114.

46   The first yakazu session was published as *Ōkukazu* (A Myriad of Yakazu Verses, 1677) and the second as *Saikaku Ōyakazu* (Saikaku's Great Yakazu, 1681).

47   See note 44 above.

48   Lane, "Saikaku," p. 115.

49   See G. W. Sargent's introduction to his translation of *Nippon Eitaigura.*

50   See, for example, Robert Leutner's comments on translation in "Saikaku's Parting Gift," p. 368.

51   Book 4:2. The work is composed of five books, each consisting of four chapters, or stories. In the *Teihon Saikaku Zenshū*, each story is approximately five pages in length.

52 Ben Befu, "Seken Munezan'yō" (Ph.D. diss., Stanford University, 1966), p. 16.

53 Sargent, introduction to *Nippon Eitaigura*, p. xxxvii.

54 Shinkei (1406–75), for example. Conventionally, there were three different types of linking in a haikai sequence: *monozuke*, word play, the only linking device recognized by Matsunaga Teitoku; *kokorozuke*, in theory, the capturing of the essence of the preceding verse and the responding to that inner meaning, usually by indirect allusion, the chief linking practice of the Danrin school; and *nioizuke*, emphasized by Bashō and his school, a kind of linking where the poet sought communion with the soul of his fellow poet, and with nature, marking a reversion from the facetiousness of Teitoku's style and a return to the seriousness of *waka*, or classical Japanese poetry.

55 Book 1:4.

56 *Kanoko* (dapple-pattern) dyeing is a form of tie-dyeing. To translate it by the other conventional Western equivalent, "random dyeing," is somewhat misleading, since the tied patches of the fabric were not chosen entirely at random. "Graded tints" in the translation refers to the effect achieved from a second-stage rinsing process. Immediately after the initial dyeing, the portions drawn together with thread to resist the dye are untied and the fabric is "washed" in water, so that the color runs into the undyed areas, producing a subtle gradation in the overall coloring of the cloth. See George E. Linton, *The Modern Textile Dictionary* (New York: Duell, Sloan and Pearce, 1963).

57 Book 2:3.

58 One *kanme* was 3.75 kilograms and equaled a thousand *monme*, the monetary unit for silver.

59 A pun on "yome o yobu" (call, or take, a wife). Instead of this, Saikaku says "kane o yobu" (summon the money).

60 The settlement of a dispute over the inheritance of a wealthy Kyōto merchant's estate. The only provisions the man had made were to leave each of his three sons a gourd. When Itakura Katsushige (1545–1624), the shōgun's deputy in Kyōto, learned of the dispute, he examined the three gourds. The third son was declared the heir, on the ground that his gourd alone would stand up on end, thus indicating the young man's promise, to Itakura's mind. He thereby inherited four-fifths of the estate, while his two older brothers shared the remaining fifth.

61 Presumably the equivalent of a massage.

62 There is a discrepancy between the name Saikaku gives here and that in the first subtitle, but it is obviously the same clerk who is referred to.

63 A many-pronged hook suspended above the hearth at New Year's for holding the holiday fish and fowl.

64 Gallants who had been detained from keeping their appointments in the Shimabara quarter would wait for the gates to reopen at dawn. This was referred to as *asagomi*, "morning visits."

65 In the original, "Sanjū kanme ga hana ni sakite, hanayome-sama to motehayashi."

66 "'Well, well,' you think, 'isn't this appealing!' . . . 'Well, well,' you sigh, 'wasn't that a fleecing!'"

67 This is one of the tenets of Lane's dissertation.

68 See *Munesan'yō*, Book 3:4, and *Eitaigura*, Book 4:5, Book 6:3.

69 *Munesan'yō*, Book 4:4.

70 Ibid., Book 5:4.

71 Ibid., Book 4:2.

72 *Kōshoku Gonin Onna*, Book 2:2.

73 Ibid., Book 4:2.

74 *Eitaigura*, Book 4:4.

75 *Munesan'yō*, Book 4:1.

76 Ibid., Book 1:4.
77 *Eitaigura*, Book 6:4.
78 *Kōshoku Gonin Onna*, Book 2:5.
79 Ibid., Book 3:4.
80 Quoted in Lane, "Saikaku" p. 64.
81 *Saikaku Shokoku Banashi*, Book 4:2, quoted in Lane, p. 159.
82 *Munesan'yō*, Book 3:3.
83 Ibid., Book 3:2.
84 Ibid., Book 3:3.
85 *Nanshoku Ōkagami*, Book 7:1, quoted in Lane, p. 243. See also *Munesan'yō*, Book 4:3.
86 *Kōshoku Gonin Onna*, Book 1:1.
87 *Eitaigura*, Book 4:3.
88 *Munesan'yō*, Book 3:2.
89 *Eitaigura*, Book 4:2.
90 *Kōshoku Gonin Onna*, Book 4:3.
91 He did idealize samurai in his earlier fiction. See, for example, the first half of *Nanshoku Ōkagami* (1687).
92 Quoted by Maxime du Camp, *Souvenirs littéraires* (Paris: Librairie Hachette, 1882), vol. 1, p. 230.

Chapter Five: The Bundan

1   *Shimazaki Tōson Zenshū* (Tokyo: Shinchōsha, 1948–52), vol. 4, p. 90.
2   Helen Craig McCullough, trans., *Tales of Ise: Lyrical Episodes from Tenth-Century Japan* (Stanford: Stanford University Press, 1968), pp. 87–88. The same episode also forms the basis of the nō play *Izutsu* (The Well Curb) by Zeami Motokiyo (1363–1443).
3   "Takekurabe," chap. 10, *Zenshū*, vol. 1, pp. 430–31.
4   Saitō Ryokuu, quoted in "Mizu no Ue Nikki," 15 July 1896, *Zenshū*, vol. 3-a, p. 517.
5   "Takekurabe," chap. 9, *Zenshū*, vol. 1, pp. 425–28.
6   Ibid., chap. 16, p. 445.
7   Ibid., chap. 13, pp. 438–39.
8   Edward Seidensticker, *Kafū the Scribbler* (Stanford: Stanford University Press, 1965), p. 44.
9   "Noki Moru Tsuki" (April 1895) and "Utsusemi" (August 1895), for example.
10 "Nigorie," chap. 1, *Zenshū*, vol. 2, p. 4.
11 Ibid., chap. 2, p. 8.
12 Ibid., chap. 6, p. 25.
13 Ibid., chap. 5, pp. 21–22.
14 "Jūsan'ya," chap. 1, *Zenshū*, vol. 2, p. 100.
15 Ibid., pp. 106–07.
16 "Wakare-Michi" was not Ichiyō's final story, but it is what I take to be her last completed work. In early February 1896 she published the first chapter of "Uramurasaki" in the journal *Shinbundan* (The New Literary World), but she left the work unfinished. In May, "Ware Kara" appeared in *Bungei Kurabu* (The Literature Club). This was a relatively long work for Ichiyō, thirty-six pages, and is generally considered the complete story as she intended it. The piece is riddled with inconsistencies, however, and concludes so abruptly that it cannot be accepted as a finished work. Ichiyō was already gravely ill by this time and, plainly, she abandoned the effort, ending the story but not really completing it.
17 "Wakare-Michi," chap. 3, *Zenshū*, vol. 2, pp. 140–42.
18 "Makoto no shijin." Mori Ōgai, Kōda Rohan, Saitō Ryokuu, "Sannin Jōgo," *Mezamashigusa* (April 1896), p. 48. *Mezamashigusa* (1896–1902) was the reincarnation of Mori Ōgai's first magazine, *Shigarami Zōshi* (1889–94), which was founded on his return from Ger-

many and disbanded with the outbreak of the Sino-Japanese War. Like its predecessor, *Mezamashigusa* became one of the most influential literary journals in the Meiji period. (*Subaru*, in turn, was the successor to *Mezamashigusa*, founded by Ōgai in 1909 and discontinued in 1913.)

19 Ibid.

20 This is an allusion to the scene in chapter 9 of *Genji Monogatari*, where Aoi and Lady Rokujō in their respective carriages compete for a spot to view Prince Genji as he passes in the procession celebrating the investiture of the Kamo priestess.

21 *Tsubo-ori sugata* were robes that billowed in such a way as to suggest the shape of a pot or bowl, and were worn by court ladies of lesser rank when they ventured outside the palace on foot.

22 "Mizu no Ue," 1 June 1895, *Zenshū*, vol. 3-a, pp. 438–40.

23 "Mizu no Ue Nikki," 7 May 1895, *Zenshū*, vol. 3-a, p. 417.

24 Ibid., 10 May 1895, *Zenshū*, vol. 3-a, p. 419.

25 "Mizu no Ue Nikki," 2 May 1896, *Zenshū*, vol. 3-a, pp. 481–82.

26 Koharu is the heroine, a courtesan who commits double suicide with her true love Kamiya Jihei, a paper merchant, in the popular puppet play by Chikamatsu, *Shinjū Ten no Amijima*, first performed on 3 January 1721.

27 Onoe Kikugorō V (1844–1904) belonged to one of the most illustrious families of kabuki actors.

28 Note that Mori Tokujirō is so carried away by the dramatic possibilities of the joint novel that he describes it as if it were a production for the stage and eventually declares, below, that they should abandon the novel altogether and present their collaboration on the boards.

29 All were famous kabuki actors.

30 Yokotani Shūmin was active in the mid-Edo period and died in 1733.

31 "Mizu no Ue Nikki," 20 July 1896, *Zenshū*, vol. 3-a, pp. 522–27.

32 He had died in November 1894.

33 Tōsui had often joked about the rain that inevitably accompanied their visits.

34 "Mizu no Ue," 3 June 1895, *Zenshū*, vol. 3-a, pp. 441–43.

35 "Mizu no Ue Nikki," 20 June 1896, *Zenshū*, vol. 3-a, pp. 507–08.

36 "Zakki" (Miscellaneous Writings), no. 8, *Zenshū*, vol. 3-b, pp. 678–79.

37 In both Europe and Japan, death rates for tuberculosis shot up to their highest levels just after the shift from an agrarian to an industrial economy. Statistically, then, Ichiyō's death fell at the beginning of the new wave. (Between 1900–20, the annual death rate from tuberculosis in Japan, per 100,000 population, leapt from 150 to 300.) Cf. Rene and Jean Dubos, *The White Plague: Tuberculosis, Man and Society* (Boston: Little, Brown and Co., 1952), pp. 232–33.

38 Shioda Ryōhei, *Higuchi Ichiyō Kenkyū*, p. 701.

39 Wada Yoshie, *Ichiyō no Nikki*, p. 316.

Notes to Part Two

Flowers at Dusk

1 Ichiyō's opening sentence is riddled with *engo*, or word associations.

Hedate wa nakagaki no kenninji ni yuzurite, kumikawasu *niwai* no *mizu* no majiwari no *soko, kiyoku fukaku*, nokiha ni saku *ume* hitoki ni ryōke no *haru* o misete, *kaori* mo wakachiau *Naka*mura, Sonoda to yobu yado ari.

The associations fall into two groups—water imagery: *niwai* (garden well), *mizu* (water), *soko* (depths), *kiyoku* (purely), *fukaku* (deeply); and spring imagery: *haru* (spring), *ume* (plum), *kaori* (fragrance). Both groups of imagery suggest purity, freshness, and, in the case of the water imagery, depth or steadfastness, the hallmark of the friendly relations between the neighbors. But more important, the associations set the tone for this short story of young and innocent love, implying the pure, budlike nature of the heroine, Chiyo, and the boy next door of whom she is enamored. The final clause of the sentence turns on a *kakekotoba*, or pivot word, "Nakamura," which can be parsed to read "kaori wakachiau *naka*" (a relationship in which both shared the fragrance [of the plum blossoms]) and "*Naka*mura, Sonoda . . ." (the two family names). Here, in her first published story, Ichiyō is faithful to her poetic heritage of a thousand years.

2 In the translations, ages are given by the Japanese count, which is at least one year older than it would be in the Western. A baby is one year old at birth, but, to further complicate the reckoning, until the modern period a newborn child was considered two years old at the coming of the New Year. The Japanese system of calculating has been retained, as there are instances where the Western age-equivalents would fail to convey the appropriate connotations.

3 An allusion to poem 750 by Fujiwara Michinaga in the *Shokushūishū*:

Ashitazu no	If you could live as long
Yowai shi araba	As the cranes
Kimi ga yo no	Who dwell among the reeds,
Chitose no kazu wa	Your reign, too,
Kazoetoritemu.	Might be reckoned at a thousand years.

4 Commentators have suggested an autobiographical element when they note that this difference of six years in Chiyo's and Ryōnosuke's ages corresponds to the age difference between Ichiyō and Shibuya Saburō, to whom she was briefly engaged. But this must be overinterpreting, since traditionally a difference of six years between man and woman was considered the ideal.

5 Ki no Tsurayuki, *Kokinshū* 2:

Sode hijite	Today the first breeze of spring
Musubishi mizu no	Will surely melt away
Kōreru o	The ice that has formed upon our sleeves.
Haru tatsu kyō no	In warmer days
Kaze ya toku ran.	We drew water from the stream.

In other words, hearts thaw with the coming of spring.

6 The original here is another example of Ichiyō's classical style, employing *engo* (word association) and poetic suggestion:

Kuretake no yo no uki to iu koto, futari ga naka ni wa hazue ni oku tsuyu hodo mo shirazu. . . .

308

The passage begins with the *makurakotoba*, or "pillow-word," *kuretake* (black bamboo). This was a conventional epithet suggesting darkness and used in poetry before such words as *yo* (knot, joint, melody, air), *yo* (world), *yo* (night), *munashi* (empty, fruitless). There is also an association at work between *take* and the latter *hazue* (the tips of leaves), so that the whole image is set within a somber bamboo grove. When rendered literally into English, such a sentence seems overwrought:

> The melancholy in [this] world of darkness, dark as the black bamboo [and caused by the indifference and cruelty that arise between lovers], was something the two of them had never experienced in their relations. They knew nothing more of such a thing than of the dew that forms on the tips of leaves [on the dark bamboo tree].

7 Marishiten, a Buddhist deity whose name derives from the Sanskrit *Marici*, also referred to in Japanese as Kagerō (shimmering heat). Originally, in Indian belief, she was an attendant goddess to the sun. In Japan during the Kamakura and Muromachi periods, she came to be worshipped as the patron goddess of samurai, protecting them in battle. In art she is often depicted as an impressive figure with three faces and three or four pairs of arms.

8 One of the heroines in Saikaku's *Kōshoku Gonin Onna* (Five Women Who Loved Love, 1686). Oshichi, a vegetable dealer's sixteen-year-old daughter, is utterly carried away by her first love. When a fire forces Oshichi and her family to flee their home and seek refuge in a temple, Oshichi loses her heart to one of the young attendants. She is distraught when her family's new house is completed and she must leave the temple. In her passion, Oshichi decides to destroy the house so that she can be reunited with her lover. But the conflagration that she starts also destroys much of Edo, and for her crime Oshichi is put to death at the stake. The story is the tale of shy and artless young love, and of the dark, incomprehensible force of desire, themes which "Flowers at Dusk" may be said to share. "Koigusa Karageshi Yaoya Monogatari" (The Greengrocer's Daughter with a Bundle of Love) was based on an actual event, the execution of a young woman under similar circumstances four years prior to the publication of *Gonin Onna*. Oshichi's tragedy became a popular theme for Edo writers, who also immortalized her love in *jōruri*, or puppet-play, and kabuki versions.

9 The commentators suggest that the "bear" was a come-on. The wild animal, supposedly captured in Tamba Province, was in fact a man with his face painted black crawling around on all fours. He was led on a stick by his partner, who did the hawking.

10 The koto is a musical instrument consisting of an oblong box with thirteen silk strings stretched over it and played by plucking with fingers or plectrum. Asagao is the heroine of *Asagao Nikki* (1832), a jōruri and kabuki piece about a young woman named Miyuki who is in love with one man but engaged to another. In her dilemma she decides to flee them both. She weeps herself blind and is forced to eke out a living as a minstrel under the name of Asagao. One day she meets her lover again and miraculously regains her sight.

11 An allusion to a song from the play discussed in note 10. The blind Asagao sings this song at an inn along the Tōkaidō to a man who turns out to be her former love. The song includes a play on her performing name, "Asagao," or morning-glory:

Tsuyu no hinu ma no asagao o,	Before the dew forsakes the morning-glory,
Terasu hikage no tsurenaki ni,	In the harshness of the shining sun,
Aware hitomurasame no,	How moving! A sudden shower!
Harahara to fure kashi.	Fall softly, rain, fall softly.

12 Ichiyō's use of language recalls her Edo forebears. In the original, the allusion to the preceding song ends in "aware, aware," followed by "awa no mizuame" (millet syrup)—a conscious repetition of sound, functioning almost like a *kakekotoba*, or pivot-word, to create a vibrant rhythm that suggests the lively, overlapping shouts of minstrels and street hawkers on an early spring holiday.

13 The confusion that accompanied love's awakening was a familiar theme in court poetry and prose. These opening lines may be an allusion to Taira Tadamori, *Kin'yōshū* 607:

Omoiki ya	Yearning for you so,
Kumoi no tsuki o	My eyes gaze upon your distant dwelling,
Yoso ni mite	As far away as the moon among the clouds—
Kokoro no yami ni	No wonder, then, I wander in a trance,
Madou beshi to wa.	My heart in darkness.

Further, it seems that Ichiyō was incorporating one of her own poems. Here is the sentence in the original: "Kinō wa, izukata ni yadoritsuru kokoro tote ka, hakanaku ugokisomete wa, nakanaka ni e mo tomarazu, ayashi ya mayou, nubatama no yami, iro naki koe sae mi ni shimite, omoiizuru ni mi mo furuwarenu." Here is Ichiyō's earlier poem:

Fumimayou	If you ask me, is it love
Koi no kokoro o	That has me wandering bewildered?
Hito towaba	I can only say
Tada ubatama no	I travel
Yamiji nari keri.	On a path that has no light.

With such passages, the story cannot but suffer in translation. The original Japanese is much less specific. What must be rendered in English as "his voice" is "iro naki koe." Ichiyō, and her heroine, are more reticent in admitting whose voice, whose presence, causes such consternation, and therefore the poetic sense of "nubatama no yami"—the world of darkness in which Chiyo suddenly finds herself—is that much more complete, and chilling, in the original.

14   Ki no Tsurayuki, *Kokinshū* 572:

Kimi kōru	If I had not shed tears
Namida shinakuba	Of love for you,
Kara-koromo	My heart,
Mune no atari wa	Beneath my China-robes,
Iro moenamashi.	Might still have been on fire.

In other words, somehow the tears have cooled my emotions.

15   Ono no Komachi, *Kokinshū* 552:

Omoitsutsu	I must have seen you
Nureba ya hito no	As I slept,
Mietsu ran	Lost in thoughts of love for you—
Yume to shiriseba	Had I known it was a dream
Samezaramashi o.	I would never have awakened.

16   Anonymous, *Kokin Rokujō, Zoku Kokka Taikan* 33576:

Koi koi te	Dawn comes,
Mare ni au yo no	The cock crows—
Akatsuki wa	How hateful!
Tori no ne tsuraki	Our nights of love
Mono ni zarikeru.	Are all too few.

17   Anonymous, *Kokin Rokujō, Zoku Kokka Taikan* 33710:

Haru wa mazu	Spring comes first
Azuma-ji yori zo	Along the eastern road:
Wakakusa no	The new grass
Koto no ha tsuge yo	Proclaims the season
Musashino no hara.	In the fields of Musashi Plain.

That is to say, the new grass announces spring, the season of love, and the words of the young proclaim the stirrings in their hearts. "Wakakusa" (new grass) is a metaphor for the young.

18   Minamoto Tōru, *Kokinshū* 724:

Michinoku no	I am not one to long
Shinobu mojizuri	For anyone but you,
Tare yue ni	My heart in turmoil
Midaren to omou	Like the tangled patterns
Ware naranaku ni.	On the cloth from Michinoku.

Shinobu, in Michinoku Province (present-day Fukushima Prefecture) was noted for its dyes, made from *shinobu-gusa* (hare's foot fern, *Davallia mariessi*). A length of cloth was stretched over a rock and rubbed with grasses or flowers to stain it. *Mojizuri* (lady's tresses, *Spiranthes sinensis*) the commentators believe here refers to the twisted pattern that this rubbing produced. By Heian times the method was considered rural and primitive; more sophisticated techniques were used in the capital.

The first two lines of the poem form a *joshi*, or preface, to "midaren" (be in turmoil), with their pun on "shinobu," which also means "endure," "contain one's emotions." The same pun is at work in Ichiyō's sentence. Ryōnosuke endures the turmoil in his heart; Chiyo's robe is dyed from shinobu-gusa. In fact, this play on "shinobu" was a convention in *waka*, or classical Japanese poetry. When the word "shinobu" appears in waka, "midaru" is seldom far behind.

19 Fujiwara Nagaie, *Shinkokinshū* 815:

Tama no o no	He, too, blessed with life
Nagaki tameshi ni	As long as the jeweled thread,
Hiku hito mo	Will one day vanish:
Kiyureba tsuyu ni	No more than gem-like drops of dew,
Kotonaranu kana.	A fine promise of eternity!

20 The tolling of the bell at dusk is a familiar image in Japanese literature, indeed the image par excellence of the sad and final end to things. One thinks of *Heike Monogatari* (The Tale of the Heike, mid-thirteenth century), for example, which opens and closes with the sound of the temple bell. The very first lines read:

> The bell at Gion Temple tolls the evanescence of all things. The faded flowers of the teak tree beside the deathbed of the Buddha bear witness to his teaching that those who flourish will one day also decay. The proud soon fall; their glory has no more substance than a dream on a spring night.

Ichiyō has incorporated these sentiments in her final sentence, with its imagery of bell and faded flowers. Her closing also resonates with the same mood of sadness, or *aware*, found in the final chapter of the *Heike*. (The ex-Emperor Go-Shirakawa has just paid a visit to Kenreimon-in, the sole surviving member of the decimated Taira clan, who has fallen in the world from Empress to cloistered nun at the Jakkō-in, a tiny temple on the outskirts of Kyōto.) Here is the opening of the last chapter:

> As the evening sun went down behind the mountain, the bell of Jakkō Temple began to toll day's end. The ex-Emperor, holding back his tears, departed with reluctance. Kenreimon-in wept bitterly as thoughts of the past came rushing back to her.

Ichiyō's closing sentence is probably also an allusion to Nōin, *Shinkokinshū* 116:

Yamazato no	I come upon
Haru no yūgure	A mountain village
Kite mireba	At eventide in spring—
Iriai no kane ni	The blossoms fall to earth,
Hana zo chirikeru.	A bell tolls in the temple.

Ichiyō composed her own poem on this theme in the spring of 1892, the same year she wrote "Flowers at Dusk."

Kaze no naki	No wind blows
Nokiba no sakura	Beneath the eaves
Horohoro to	Where the blossoms flutter to the ground
Chiru ka to mireba	Yet they scatter
Kuresome ni keri.	And take on the color of the night.

A Snowy Day

1 Ki no Tsurayuki, *Kokinshū* 323:

Yuki fureba	It snows,
Fuyugomoriseru	And flowers
Kusa mo ki mo	Unknown to spring
Haru ni shirarenu	Blossom on the trees and grass,
Hana zo sakikeru.	Still sleeping through the winter.

2 Fujiwara Tadafusa, *Kokinshū* 837:

Sakidatanu	The sadness I feel,
Kui no yachi tabi	With eight thousand regrets,
Kanashiki wa	Not to have gone before you!
Nagaruru mizu no	The water flows on
Kaerikonu nari.	And will never return.

3 Mibu no Tadamine, *Kokinshū* 628:

Michinoku ni	A river flows through Michinoku,
Ari to iu naru	From which it takes its name—
Natorigawa	How hateful,
Naki na torite wa	That I should be branded for a rumor
Kurushikarikeri.	As transient as the current.

Ichiyō alludes to the poem ("'Naki na tori' gawa") to establish an *engo*, or word association, with her "nami kake koromo" (robes dampened by the waves) and "nurenishi sode no aite" (the one who brought me tears or, literally, the companion of my moistened sleeves).

4 Fujiwara Yoshizane, *Shokukokinshū* 789:

Yuku mizu ni	Love lingers
Todomaru iro zo	Where the water flows—
Nakarikeru	The blossoms
Kokoro no hana wa	In my loveless heart
Chiritsumoredomo.	Fall and accumulate.

Ichiyō's "yuku mizu no iro naku to mo" is an allusion to this poem, difficult to retain in translation, where "yuku mizu no iro" becomes simply "love."

5 The *Li Chi* (The Book of Rites, or *Raiki* in Japanese), one of the five Confucian classics, compiled during the Han dynasty, prohibited the mingling of the sexes beyond the age of seven.

6 Fujiwara Kanesuke, *Gosenshū* 1103:

Hito no oya no	Nothing of the dark
Kokoro wa yami ni	Is there within a parent's heart—
Aranedomo	Yet worry over a child
Ko o omou michi ni	Will plunge him into confusion
Madoinuru kana.	With a blackness of its own.

7 The Japanese equivalent of the hearth. A table-and-quilt contrivance placed over charcoals (or today, an electric heater) around which family members gather in the winter months.

8 Anonymous, *Kokinshū* 867:

Murasaki no	Fond I am
Hitomoto yue ni	Of a single blade of *murasaki*,
Musashino no	And so I feel affection,
Kusa wa minagara	And sympathy,
Aware to zo miru.	For all the grasslands of Musashi Plain.

The poem is fairly intractable. *Murasaki* was prized as a source of purple dye, and the color purple was always associated in poetry with *en*, the bond between two human beings. Hence the implication of the poem is, "Because I love you, my love and sympathy extend to all who share a bond with you."

9 Lady Ise, *Shinchokusenshū* 715:

Miyamagi no	I am like the young grass
Kage no ogusa wa	In the shadow
Ware nare ya	Of the mountain trees—
Tsuyu shigekeredo	The dew abounds,
Shiru hito mo naki.	But companions I have none.

10 Minamoto Muneyuki, *Kokinshū* 315:

Yamazato wa	Winter in the mountain village
Fuyu zo sabishisa	Is especially lonely,
Masarikeru	When I think how
Hitome mo kusa mo	The grasses have withered
Karenu to omoeba.	And my love has gone away.

"Karenu" is a pun on "karu" (grow apart, be estranged) and "karu" (wither, die).

11 Murasaki Shikibu, *Shinkokinshū* 661:

Fureba kaku	The first snow falls,
Usa nomi masaru	Oblivious to this world
Yo o shirade	Of rising sorrows,
Aretaru niwa ni	And hides for now
Tsumoru hatsu yuki.	The withered ruins of the garden.

The Sound of the Koto

1 A thirteen-stringed instrument sometimes translated as "zither." See note 10 to "Flowers at Dusk."

2 "Shimobashira ima tafurenu beki." A variation on the proverb found in Saikaku: "hinata ni kōri" (ice [melting] in the sun), in *Seken Munesan'yō* 5:2, and "hinata ni kōri bimbō," in *Nippon Eitaigura* 4:3. The latter phrase, which Ichiyō probably had in mind, suggests the poverty that comes from overeconomizing, when a willingness to take risks might have paid off handsomely—i.e., letting one's assets melt away, rather than using them as the base upon which to build a fortune.

3 Apparently an allusion to "Midare" (Disorder), a song for the koto. Ichiyō writes, "Chiri no ukiyo no midare mo nani zo": "What of the disorder in this floating world of dust? [It vanishes when Morie Shizu takes up her instrument to play.]"

4 "Yamahime" (Mountain Princess), also the title of a nō piece.

5 An allusion to the nō play *Matsukaze* (Pine Wind) and to a song for the koto of the same name.

6 Three sites celebrated in literature for their beauty in the moonlight. Suma and Akashi are important settings in *Genji Monogatari*. In *Oku no Hosomichi* (The Narrow Road of Oku, 1690–94), Bashō praises the renowned Matsushima as indeed "the most beautiful spot in all Japan."

7 The original reads, "Tama naraba, Chōshi ga shiro no ikutsu ni mo kaegatashi" (If jewels they were, Chōshi would find it hard to trade them, no matter how many castles [in the offer]). The thought is based on a Chinese tale in which King Chao (Chōshi), of the Warring States period, is asked by the head of a more powerful domain to exchange a precious stone for some of his neighbor's territory.

Encounters on a Dark Night

1 An allusion to *Makura no Sōshi* (ca. 1002), chapter 83:

How desolate the Western city is! [The ladies-in-waiting recounted Fujiwara Tadanobu's words:] "Had I someone to view it with me, the [lonely] setting would have moved me all the more. The fences were all broken down, and overrun with moss." "And were there ferns among the tiles?" Lady Saishō asked.

The passage from Sei Shōnagon is itself an allusion to a poem by Po Chü-i (772–846) about the desolation of the old palace on Mount Li, to the west of Ch'ang-an, the capital of China during the T'ang dynasty. The relevant portion of the poem has been translated by Ivan Morris as follows (*The Pillow Book*, vol. 2 [New York: Columbia University Press, 1967], p. 70):

How many months, how many years, have passed
Since the Imperial banners last appeared!
The walls lie silent under moss
And the tiles are choked with fern.
His Majesty has been five years on the Throne.
Why has he not once paid a visit here?
It is not far from the city's western gate. . . .

Sei Shōnagon was equating the western part of the capital—which had fallen into early decline as Heian-kyō developed toward the east—with the abandoned palace west of Ch'ang-an. Ichiyō makes a similar comparison in her allusion by evoking these famous scenes of desolation from the classics. Furthermore, Tadanobu's visit to Shōnagon in this chapter of *Makura no Sōshi* comes only after he has been forced to spend part of the night in the western section of the city, in order to avoid an unlucky direction and the danger of remaining in, or moving in, the path of a malevolent divinity. Perhaps it is not too much, then, to read into Ichiyō's allusion a hint of the danger lurking in this dismal, unlucky house.

2 The Japanese proverb has it that the successful man returns to his hometown decked out in rich brocades: "Nishiki o kite kokyō e kaeru."

3 Kakuen, *Senzaishū* 315:

Miyagino no	Walking through
Kohagi ga hara o	The fields of *hagi*
Yuku hodo wa	On Miyagi Plain,
Shika no ne o sae	I try to clear a path away;
Wakete kiku kana.	Somewhere a deer cries.

The cry of the deer was associated with autumn (and particularly with the autumn rains, or *shigure*). It was a mournful sound, which the poets took to be the male calling for the female. Since the *Man'yōshū*, autumn in poetry has been a time of parting, and the image of the deer crying in the autumn rain is one of utter loneliness. The *hagi* (*Lespedeza japonica*) mentioned in the poem is sometimes translated as "bush clover."

4 Anonymous, *Kokinshū* 933:

Yo no naka wa	What is constant
Nani ka tsune naru	In this world of change?
Asukagawa	Yesterday

Kinō no fuchi zo   The Asuka River was a quiet pool,
Kyō wa se ni naru.   Today it is a torrent.

The Asukagawa, a tributary of the Yamato River (located near Nara), was immortalized as a symbol of flux in this and poem 341 of the *Kokinshū*.

5   "Zoku ni kudakishi Kawara-no-in mo kaku ya to bakari." "Kawara-no-in" alludes to "sono watari chikaki nanigashi no in" (the villa of someone nearby), in chapter 4 of *Genji Monogatari*, which the commentators of *Genji* identify as the Kawara-no-in, the former residence of the Minister of the Left, Minamoto Tōru (822–895), located in the sixth ward of Heian-kyō. Nettled by the noise of Yūgao's uncouth peasant neighbors, Genji takes her away to the more secluded, sedate Kawara-no-in. The new tryst is described in much the way Ichiyō depicts the Matsukawa house:

Waiting for the caretaker to be summoned, Genji looked up at the rotting gate and the ferns that trailed thickly down over it. The groves beyond were still dark, and the mist and the dews were heavy. [Murasaki Shikibu, *The Tale of Genji*, trans. Edward G. Seidensticker (New York: Alfred A. Knopf, 1976), p. 68]

They go inside and spend the night, though Yūgao is very frightened. The sun is high when Genji awakes, but the place is hardly less desolate.

He opened the shutters. All through the badly neglected grounds not a person was to be seen. The groves were rank and overgrown. The flowers and grasses in the foreground were a drab monotone, an autumn moor. The pond was choked with weeds, and all in all it was a forbidding place. [p. 69]

The second night, as Yūgao sleeps in this house that she finds "unbelievably strange," the jealous spirit of one of Genji's other loves, Rokujō, comes to kill her.

6   Although a male deity in India (Avalokiteshvara), in Japan, Kannon came to be worshipped as the goddess of mercy. She was one of the primary thirteen deities of Esoteric Buddhism in the Heian period (along with Fudō, Shaka, Monju, Fugen, Jizō, Miroku, Yakushi, Seishi, Amida, Ashiku, Dainichi, and Kokūzō). By late Heian, Kannon held a special place in the hearts of the Japanese. Statues of the goddess were enshrined at thirty-three sites of scenic beauty, making her one of the most widely honored deities and a favorite of pilgrims, from the imperial family on down. Kannon became the symbol of the female, as Fudō became the symbol of the male. Although she was not directly associated with beauty or love, as, say, Aphrodite was, she did come to stand for feminine perfection. In art she was often represented as having numerous heads and arms, the better to dispense mercy, but apparently this multidexterity was overlooked when writers invoked her name as a paragon of female beauty.

7   Literally, Hachiman, who was originally a Shintō deity but became accepted as a Buddha. By the Kamakura period he was regarded as a manifestation of Amida. Hachiman was often identified as the god of war, and the Minamoto shōguns enshrined him in Kamakura, the capital of their military government. The "divine winds" that frustrated the Mongol invasions of 1274 and 1281 were thought to be the work of Hachiman and the sun goddess, Amaterasu. Forever after, Hachiman became the god to call on in a pinch, as the woman does here.

8   One of the death days observed in Buddhism. These fell on the seventh, fourteenth, and forty-ninth days after the death. In addition, of course, the anniversary of a person's death is commemorated.

9   Literally, "it must be a world where no gods or buddhas dwell in our heads" (Yoshi, *warera ga kōbe ni yadoritamau kami* mo naki hotoke mo naki yo naru beshi), where the italicized words are a play on the saying "The gods dwell in the heads of the honest" (Shōjiki no kōbe ni kami yadoru), here used decoratively to modify the real meaning of the sentence, "kami mo naki hotoke mo naki yo" (It's a world without gods [who might have had compassion for us]).

10   Meng Ch'ang-chün was a Chinese nobleman of the Warring States period known for the warm reception he gave his guests, who at his banquets were said to number in the thousands.

11   A metaphor from Chuang Tzu, or Chuang Chou (ca. 369–286 B.C.). Ichiyō alludes to a famous passage from his collected writings, the *Chuang Tzu:*

Once Chuang Chou dreamt he was a butterfly, a butterfly flitting and fluttering around, happy with himself and doing as he pleased. He didn't know he was Chuang Chou. Suddenly he woke up and there he was, solid and unmistakable Chuang Chou. But he didn't know if he was Chuang Chou who had dreamt he was a butterfly, or a butterfly dreaming he was Chuang Chou. Between Chuang Chou and a butterfly there must be *some* distinction! This is called the Transformation of Things. [Burton Watson, *The Complete Works of Chuang Tzu* (New York: Columbia University Press, 1968), p. 49]

12   A proverb: "Sode no furiawase dani mo, tashō no en." (Even when only sleeves touch, [it is from] the bond of some previous existence.)

13   An allusion to the opening of *Makura no Sōshi.* Here is Ivan Morris's translation (vol. 1, p. 1):

In spring it is the dawn that is most beautiful. As the light creeps over the hills, their outlines are dyed a faint red and wisps of purplish cloud trail over them.

In summer the nights. Not only when the moon shines, but on dark nights too, as the fireflies flit to and fro, and even when it rains, how beautiful it is!

In autumn the evenings, when the glittering sun sinks close to the edge of the hills and the crows fly back to their nests in threes and fours and twos. . . .

In winter the early mornings. It is beautiful indeed when snow has fallen during the night, but splendid too when the ground is white with frost. . . .

14   An allusion to the "Yūgao" chapter in *Genji Monogatari.* Ichiyō's sentence reads, "Gojō watari no noki no tsuma naraba, yūgao no nao ya hanabanashikaru beki." "Evening faces" is Seidensticker's translation for "yūgao," the moonflower (*Lagenaria siceraria*), a night-blooming plant of the morning-glory family. It is from the moonflowers entwined beneath the eaves of her humble house that the heroine of the chapter takes her name. Genji has gone to visit his former nurse, now living as a nun in Gojō, the Fifth Ward. The house next door catches his eye. It is a modest abode, but the beautiful flowers on the vine and the outlines of the pretty foreheads through the shutters attract his attention. He is at once taken with both sorts of "evening faces."

The fate of Yūgao—who dies as a result of Genji's infatuation, from the jealousy it inspires on the part of her rival—is implicit in Ichiyō's allusion, suggesting Oran's own affinity for misfortune. Both women are as hapless as Yūgao's namesake. As in the earlier allusion to the Kawara-no-in (see note 5 above), this reference illustrates how Ichiyō depended on the connotations of classical allusion to heighten the mood she wanted to create (here, the desolation clinging to Oran's quarters), and to impart dignity, or poetic worthiness, to her characters (here, to underscore the mystery and elegance Oran shared with the best literary heroines of the past). In so doing, Ichiyō is continuing a venerable tradition in Japanese poetry, that of *honkadori,* or "allusive variation," which Brower and Miner define as "an echoing of an older poem or poems, not just to borrow material or phrasing, but to raise the atmosphere—something of the situation, the tone, and the meaning—of the original" (Robert H. Brower and Earl Miner, *Japanese Court Poetry* [Stanford: Stanford University Press, 1961], p. 14). In honkadori, as is often the case with Ichiyō, the allusion was not necessarily a direct quotation, or even an echoing of the same words, but a hinting at a situation or conception from a well-known earlier work. These references, when they approach true allusive *variation,* are not mere borrowings or embellishments, but fundamentally enhance the tone of the new work.

15   A reference to the drowning of Taira Kiyomori's widow and her grandson, the infant

Emperor Antoku, when the Taira clan was decimated by Minamoto Yoshitsune at the naval battle of Dannoura (1185).

16 Sentiments that hark back at least to *Genji Monogatari*, where the Shining Prince declares his preference for the passive type: "The clear, forceful ones I can do without. I am weak and indecisive by nature myself, and a woman who is quiet and withdrawn and follows the wishes of a man even to the point of letting herself be used has much the greater appeal. A man can shape and mold her as he wishes, and becomes fonder of her all the while" (Seidensticker translation, p. 80).

17 "Fukyō no mizu no ko no habune, kakaru nagare ni noritaru Oran...." (Oran, adrift on this [wild] stream, in a boat of leaves on the waters of Wu Gorge....) Ichiyō alludes to "T'ai Hsing Lu" (The T'ai Hsing Road), a poem by Po Chü-i which treats the inconstancy of the lord-vassal bond through the metaphor of unstable conjugal relations.

18 "Kuhonrendai no jōbon" (the highest of the nine realms, or lotus calyces, of the Pure Land).

19 These sentences contain several poetic conceits. The original reads: "Nasu majiki wa koi to ya, iro aru naka ni shinobu mojizuri, iza Michinoku ni ari to iu seki no, hitome ni todae o waburu wa yasashikaru beshi." "Shinobu" is a pun on "endure" (the pangs of love) and "conceal" (one's feelings). "Shinobu mojizuri" is a dyeing process (see note 18 to "Flowers at Dusk"). Michinoku is famous both for its barrier gate and for its grasses (which were used in the dyeing).

20 A pun on the fishing metaphor of the earlier sentences, which reads in part, "kakeraretsu tsurinawa no kurushiki wa" (the pain of being caught by a fishing line). Here, in the next sentence, the line has been unraveled, as has Oran's relationship with Namizaki: "Yoriawaneba kore mo kata-ito no omoi ya su ran." The pun is on "yoriawaneba," "yoru" meaning both "meet" and "twist" or "entwine."

21 I.e. "Then everything began to turn sour." The hibiscus (*fusō*, or *bussō-ge*) was considered by the Chinese to be a sacred tree, from which the sun emerged.

22 In the northwest corner of Kyōto.

23 Literally, "He would do anything [to achieve his goal], even if it pulverized his bones, like the relics of the Buddha" (Dō de mo yarimasuru, hone ga shari ni naru te mo yarimasuru).

24 Literally, an *ominaeshi*, a perennial plant with yellow flowers, of the *Valerianaceae* family.

25 "Taika no ichiboku nan to shite sasaen," based on the saying "Taika no taoren to suru wa ichiboku no sasouru tokoro arazu," which can be translated freely as, "A single man is powerless to save a great house from collapse."

26 This is couched in the language of the samurai. "Kono hitokoto o kinchō ni shite.... iwanedomo...." *Kinchō* was an oath on the sword, given when two men crossed blades. This gesture and the resulting sound constituted the oath.

27 An allusion to the first chapter of *Makura no Sōshi* (see note 13 above).

28 Ki no Tomonori, *Kokinshū* 274:

Hana mitsutsu	I gaze at the chrysanthemums,
Hito matsu toki wa	And wait for you to come,
Shirotae no	Are they your white sleeves
Sode ka to nomi zo	I see approaching?
Ayamatarekeru.	No—I am mistaken: only flowers.

29 Literally, "I am ready to be crucified or torn limb from limb" (Kono mi o yatsu-zaki ni shite, ki no sora ni mo kaketaki).

30 The original says "gakidō no kurushimi" (the pain and suffering along the path of hungry demons). The *gaki*'s realm was one of the six roads (*michi*) of hell in the Buddhist cosmology. As retribution for sins of gluttony and excess, the dead consigned to this realm became gaki (starving demons): gaunt creatures with grotesquely swollen stomachs and throats as narrow as needles in order to prevent them from swallowing food, which, in any case, would immediately burst into flames the moment it entered their mouths. Thus, the gaki suffered perpetual thirst and starvation.

31 A conceit from Chinese poetry. (In Ichiyō's original, "Mamoranu wa misao narade, Hannyo ga neya no ōgi no iro ni ware akikaze no tatareshi mi nari.") The fan discarded in the autumn breeze refers to a poem written in the *yüeh-fu* (folk-ballad) style and attributed to Lady Pan, whose personal name is not known but whose court title was *Chieh-yü*, or Lady-in-waiting. Lady Pan was a favorite concubine of Emperor Ch'eng (r. 32–7 B.C.) of the Han dynasty. (She was also the great-aunt of the historian Pan Ku.) Her poem, "A Song of Regret," is the first known example in the *shih*, or lyric, mode to take up the theme of the neglected palace lady, and it had a great influence on later literature. "A Song of Regret," it is said, was composed when the Emperor abandoned Lady Pan for a younger, more beautiful woman, sending his ex-favorite to live instead with the Empress Dowager. In the poem, which follows, the "paired-joy fan" is a symbol of auspicious union—the two, round silk faces of the fan having been sewn together—and a symbol of intimacy, for the fan would have been kept in the folds of her lover's robes. From this time on, "autumn fan" became synonymous with "deserted woman."

> To begin I cut fine silk of Ch'i,
> white and pure as frost or snow,
> shape it to make a paired-joy fan,
> round, round as the luminous moon,
> to go in and out of my lord's breast;
> when lifted, to stir him a gentle breeze.
> But always I dread the coming of autumn,
> cold winds that scatter the burning heat,
> when it will be laid away in the hamper,
> love and favor cut off midway.

[Burton Watson, *Chinese Lyricism* (New York: Columbia University Press, 1971), p. 94]

32 Literally, "Aren't you going to offer up your life here [i.e., for me]?" (Sono inochi o ima konoba nite tamawaru majiki ya).

33 Literally, "off to cover a thousand-and-one *ri*" (senri-hito tobi ni). One *ri* equals 2.44 miles.

On the Last Day of the Year

1 In the original, "Kaibyaku irai o tazunetaraba, oru yubi ni ano kami-sama ga sodeguchi omowaruru." The hyperbole of sentences like this some commentators ascribe to the influence of Saikaku.

2 Ichiyō employs a *kakekotoba:* "Yo o uguisu no bimbō machi zo kashi." "Yo o uguisu" can be parsed to mean "yo o u[shi]" (the world is hard, or sad, or, as I have translated it, a world where pleasures are few) and "yo o [naku] uguisu" (the warbler sings of this world), which forms an *engo* for the name of the district, Hatsunechō (Village of the First Sound, i.e. the first song of spring). The *uguisu* was associated in poetry with the early spring, as were plum blossoms, while the *hototogisu* was the bird associated with the coming of summer, whose flower was the *tachibana*, orange blossoms. Ichiyō, therefore, has her seasonal elements correctly in place. The time of the story is the New Year, which, by the lunar calendar, was also early spring.

3 A variation on the proverb "Shōjiki no kōbe ni kami yadoru" (The gods dwell in the heads of the honest). See also note 9 to "Encounters on a Dark Night."

4 One *rin* = 1/1000 yen. The boy went to what was called a *gorin gakkō:* a "five-*rin* school," or elementary school for the children of the poor, where the monthly tuition was only five rin.

5 One *sen* = 1/100 yen.

6 Each mat is approximately 3' × 6', or roughly 18 square feet. A six-mat room would be approximately 108 square feet.

7 "Komebitsu" has a double meaning: a rice chest and what in English would be called a breadwinner.

8 "Ameya," a shop selling *ame*, sweets made of rice jelly or wheat gluten.

9 "Yon-jū-ni no mae-yaku": *mae-yaku* (before the calamity) refers to the year preceding one's climacteric, which for men was thought to be the forty-second year and for women the thirty-third year. But the years immediately before and after were also jinxed, so that one had three years of potential bad luck: the *mae-yaku*, the *hon-yaku*, and the *ato-yaku*. In addition, there were other years of danger, though of lesser risk. For men these fell at the ages of twenty-five and sixty, and for women at the age of nineteen. This belief in "evil years" (*yaku-doshi*) dates from the Heian period.

10 "Spring is written with the characters for "new year" (*shinnen*) but glossed in *kana* as "spring" (*haru*). In the lunar calendar, spring and the New Year were one and the same.

11 *Imagawa-yaki* (hot muffins with bean jam) and *satoimo* (taro).

12 *Zōni*, a New Year's dish of rice cakes boiled in soup.

13 Disinheritance was prohibited by the Meiji government. In the Edo period, however, a family was allowed to disown a son who had disgraced it. In the case of a criminal act, the rest of the family would in fact be implicated if they did not disown the offending son (or daughter). A notice of intent to disinherit was circulated among relatives and among the *gonin-gumi* (one's neighborhood five-family group, whose members were supposed to keep an eye on one another) and then submitted to the *nanushi* (village headman), who presented the petition to the *machibugyō* (magistrate). Once the magistrate's authorization was granted, all ties with the family were severed, and the child became homeless.

14 The last day of the year was, financially, the most difficult time of year. In addition to the expenses for the coming holidays, all bills fell due. In this season even a prosperous family like the Yamamuras might experience some liquidity problems, although Ichiyō does not suggest that the family is really pressed for cash. The theme of the hardships men faced at New Year's, supposedly a time of joy, is a familiar one in Saikaku, especially in *Seken Munesan'yō* (1692), a collection of twenty stories that all take place at year-end. (The work is subtitled "Ōtsugomori wa ichinichi senkin"—The last day of the year is worth a thousand gold pieces.)

15 Literally, "number eighteen [in her repertoire]" (*jū-hachi ban*). The expression is based on the designation by the kabuki actor Ichikawa Danjūrō VII (1791–1859) of what in his opinion were the eighteen kabuki classics: *Kanjinchō, Shibaraku, Sukeroku, Gedatsu, Yanone, Kagekiyo, Narukami, Kamahige, Kenuki, Fudō, Fuwa, Kanu, Nanatsumen, Zōhiki, Oshimodoshi, Uwanari, Uirōuri,* and *Jayanagi*. Most of the "Eighteen Plays" selected by Danjūrō in 1840 are no longer performed, but at the time they were considered the choice vehicles for the Ichikawa family of kabuki actors. Hence, Ichiyō uses the term to mean one's specialty, one's tricks. See Gunji Masakatsu, *Kabuki Jū-Hachi Ban Shū*, vol. 98 in Nihon Koten Bungaku Taikei series (Tokyo: Iwanami Shoten, 1965).

16 "Danna tsuri yori Ebisu-gao shite kaerarureba . . ." Ebisu was one of the seven gods of good fortune (*shichi fukujin*). He is usually depicted carrying a fishing pole and a *tai* (sea bream), and Ichiyō plays on this convention. The *shichi fukujin* were a kind of grab-bag of good-luck deities. Ebisu (the god of work) and Daikoku (the god of prosperity) derived from Shintō. Benten (the god of love) and Bishamon (the god of happiness) were of Hindu origin. Jurōjin and Fukurokujū (gods of longevity) were of Chinese origin. Hotei was considered another incarnation of the Bodhisattva Maitreya.

17 The woman refers to the last-minute preparations for the holidays and the financial settlements that had to be completed by this night. See note 14 above.

18 Literally, "Ko wa sankai no kubikase" (A child is a pillory in all three worlds, i.e. the past, present, and future).

19 A pun on the popular card game *hanafuda* (flower cards): "hanami no mushiro ni kyōfū

ichijin" (a strong wind blows through the camp [and scatters blossoms] on the mats one brought to view the flowers from).

20 A Shintō ritual. Salt was spread in the entryway or placed in small piles at each side of the front gate to purify a dwelling.

Troubled Waters

1 In the demimonde, when a woman pined for a certain man, she would whisper his name and tap on the lattice, and supposedly, if she were patient enough, he would come. The practice is mentioned in chapter 8 of "Child's Play": "[Although Midori was just entering adolescence,] she knew about the charms and tricks the girls would use: simpering to summon men they longed for, like mice grabbing cheese, tapping on the lattice when they made a wish."

2 Ichiyō's annotators note that this is not the Akasaka in Minatoku, known today for its hotels, expensive restaurants, and geisha houses, but a less impressive section of the downtown.

3 The Emily Post of the Tokugawa period. The Ogasawara-ryū was the code of etiquette and ceremonial for the feudal military class. It was established by Nagahide (d. 1425), a member of the powerful Ogasawara clan, together with Ise Mitsutada and Imagawa Ujiyori.

4 In the tokiwazu ballad—a popular samisen narrative genre—entitled "Tsumoru Koi Yuki no Seki no To," the border guard at Ōsakayama, Ōtomo Kuronushi (one of the Six Poetic Geniuses of the early Heian period), aspires to seize the entire province for his own.

5 In traditional Buddhist belief, Enma was the ruler of hell and the judge of the dead. Sinners were brought before the formidable Enma, from whom nothing of one's past could be concealed. Every sin was reflected in a man's eyes, supposedly, and Enma would thereby decide which of the eight different regions of hell the person belonged in. Liars, it was said, were punished by having their tongues removed, and hence the guest's joke that, for lying, the woman will not be able to pay Enma his due on the Day of Souls (Obon, 16 July), when prayers were offered on behalf of deceased relatives and friends.

6 "Jū-hachi ban." See note 15 to "On the Last Day of the Year."

7 An allusion to the story of the love affair between Ono no Komachi and Fukakusa no Shōshō, a popular subject in Japanese theater. (See Kan'ami's Kayoi Komachi, Chikamatsu's Hyakuya Komachi, Takeda Izumo's Shichi Komachi.) Ono no Komachi demands of her admirer that he court her for one hundred nights to prove his love. Fukakusa no Shōshō vows to do so, but on the last night he is detained (or, in a variant legend, dies) and his pledge comes to naught. In the nō play Kayoi Komachi, for example, he appears as a spirit tortured over his failure to consummate the affair with the beautiful Komachi.

8 Wada Yoshie suggests that he is modeled after Nakarai Tōsui.

9 "Fudō-sama no myōdai," one of the five myōdai, or manifestations of the Buddha (along with Go Sansei, Dai Itoku, Gundari Yasha, and Kongō Yasha). The myōdai (or myō-ō), who protected the faithful by quelling passion and frightening off evil spirits, originated in late Indian Tantric Buddhism and were introduced into Japan by the Shingon sect. There were twenty-some gods in all, but these five (the go-myōdai) were the central deities. Fudō, the God of Fire, was considered the most important of the five and is usually depicted surrounded by flames, with a ferocious face of livid blue half hidden in his long hair, and wielding a sword to battle avarice, anger, and folly. Those who oppose the Buddha have Fudō to reckon with.

10 "Sode furiau mo sa" alludes to the proverb "Sode furiau mo tashō no en" (Even the touching of two people's sleeves is preordained).

11 Haguro was the black dye women used to darken their teeth in an effort to make themselves more beautiful.

12   Komurasaki and Agemaki were both renowned courtesans of the Edo period, who took their names, as many did, from heroines in *Genji Monogatari*. Agemaki flourished in the Yoshiwara ca. 1624, and Komurasaki, ca. 1655.

13   Literally "tanuki" (raccoon). In Japanese folklore, this was the form that cunning and evil would often assume.

14   "Mugen jigoku," in Buddhist belief the lowest of the eight hells.

15   These were among the tortures in *mugen jigoku*.

16   "Saritomo tainai tō tsuki no onaji koto shite." By the Japanese count, a fetus is ten months in the womb.

17   See note 5 above.

18   More literally, "People endured another's tears for one hundred years [without ever being moved by them]" (Hito no namida wa hyaku nen mo gaman shite).

19   "Kiinokuni" was a popular song. "The hill is shrouded in the mist" is a line from a *kiyomoto* ballad (a lyrical narrative played to the accompaniment of the samisen), entitled "Hokushū Sennen no Kotobuki" (Best wishes from the northern provinces for a thousand years of prosperity).

20   "Shiro-uri" was a derisive term for shop clerks, among others—those who were pale from their long hours of work and thus had complexions like muskmelons.

21   If the story is assumed to take place around the time it was written (1895), the ban would have been part of the Tempō Reforms of 1841–43. Instigated by Mizuno Tadakuni (1794–1851), Shōgun Ieyoshi's chief adviser, the reforms were modeled after two earlier attempts in the Edo period, the Kyōhō Reforms of 1716–36 and the Kansei Reforms of 1787–93. The purpose of the reforms was to shore up the coffers of the shogunate and its military dependents while curbing the power of the townsmen. The measures were thus a combination of sumptuary edicts, moral injunctions extolling austerity and the martial spirit, and sweeping economic reforms. The literary repercussions were not insignificant. Several prominent gesaku writers were reprimanded or jailed. Tamenaga Shunsui (1790–1843) was put in manacles in 1842 and upon his release forsook the ninjōbon for a heavily didactic fiction. In the same year Ryūtei Tanehiko (1783–1842) was castigated for writing *Nise Murasaki Inaka Genji* (A False Murasaki and a Rustic Genji, 1829–42) as conduct unbecoming a member of the samurai class. He died soon after in disgrace, perhaps a suicide. The theater was also threatened. For a time, the government considered abolishing kabuki altogether, and the most celebrated actors of the day—Nakamura Tomijūrō in Ōsaka and Danjūrō VII (then known as Ebizō) in Edo—were both sent into exile.

The Thirteenth Night

1   Literally, "rice crackers" (*osen[bei]*) and "millet-and-rice cakes" (*okoshi*).

2   By the old lunar calendar, it was the thirteenth night of the ninth month. On this night, along with the night of the fifteenth of the eighth month, moon-viewing parties were held, and delicacies, including special dumplings, were offered to friends and to the moon.

3   It was considered bad form to offer the dumplings on only one of the two moon-viewing dates.

4   "Nana hikari dokoro ka tō hikari mo shite" in the original, which alludes to the saying, "Oya no hikari wa nana hikari": The light (i.e. favors and influence) of one's parents is sevenfold.

5   *Kankōba*, the Meiji forerunner of the department store.

6   There would seem to be a discrepancy here. If one assumes that Oseki left Sarugakuchō when she married, then the number of years should be seven, not five.

7   All three women were legendary beauties. Komachi was the great poetess of the early Heian period, who was ranked by Ki no Tsurayuki as one of the Six Poetic Geniuses. Hsi Shih (Sei Shi in Japanese) was the beloved of a Chinese warlord in the Chou dynasty, who offered her to a

rival who defeated him in battle. The rival thereupon became so enamoured of Hsi Shih that he neglected his state and let it fall to ruin. Sotoori-hime was a consort to Emperor Ingyō (376–453).

Child's Play

1   The quarter is the famed Yoshiwara. The story takes place in Tokyo around 1895, but the licensed pleasure district known as the Yoshiwara dated from the early seventeenth century, when the military government decided to relocate all the houses of prostitution in Edo, as the city was then called, within one compound. (Similar licensed quarters existed in the other major cities: Shimabara in Kyōto, Shinmachi in Ōsaka, Maruyama in Nagasaki.)

The authorities had intended to keep prostitution both isolated from the city proper and as simple and unostentatious as possible. The original petition advocating the creation of a segregated pleasure zone asserted that the government would gain greater control over the establishments of the demimonde and hence over the morality and finances of its denizens. Visitors were to be prohibited from staying in the quarter for more than twenty-four hours. Government surveillance would prevent further kidnapping and sale of young women into the profession. Checks on the coming and going of visitors would serve to keep tabs on the disenfranchised samurai, whose growing numbers and potential for mischief, if not rebellion, gave no end of worry to the new military government.

Originally, in 1617, the compound was situated to the east of the city on reclaimed marsh land that endowed the quarter with its name: Yoshiwara, or Reed Plain. Before long, both the orthography and the location of the Yoshiwara had changed. The homonymic character for "good luck" replaced "reed," so that the quarter was afterward known as the Plain of Good Fortune. Forty years after the founding of the Yoshiwara, officials decided that the land was needed for the expansion of the city and ordered the houses to remove to a new location still farther from the heart of Edo, in present-day Asakusa. In September 1657 the new quarter, the Shin-Yoshiwara, opened for business on the site where it was to flourish for the next three hundred years.

Soon the pleasure quarter became the exuberant center of social life and art. In a society where only the samurai had clout, both ordinary townsmen and affluent merchants had few approved outlets for their vitality and growing wealth; likewise, a low-ranking samurai had little recourse against the disappointments of a stymied career or a life of tedium in the newly pacified world of the Tokugawa shogunate, which had more need of civil servants than warriors. Add to these frustrations the fact that romantic love was deemed an aberration in marriage (where a wife's duty was to bear children and manage the household), and one begins to appreciate what the quarter meant. Here a man could express himself and find the affection and prestige denied him in the real world. All manner of townsmen and samurai congregated in the Yoshiwara, where they spent their earnings lavishly. Originally intended as an area over which the government could exercise strict control, in practice the Yoshiwara became a special enclave, where Confucian and martial strictures were temporarily forgotten. The patrons of the quarter were among the world's most impressive conspicuous consumers. Money squandered on dress or a favorite courtesan brought a man renown as a connoisseur, and the sumptuary edicts promulgated from time to time did little to dampen this freewheeling spirit of the Yoshiwara.

As a result, what was at first a cluster of bordellos blossomed into a luxurious entertainment district. The successful courtesan became the female counterpart of the kabuki actor. She reigned rather like the celebrated equivalent of the latter-day movie star; she was immortalized in woodblock prints by artists like Utamaro and Kiyonaga. She also acquired the trappings of culture: song and dance, calligraphy and tea entered her repertoire. As Donald Shively has explained, "The cultural accomplishments of the higher class of prostitute far exceeded those of the townsman's wife. Their rich dress and elaborate coiffures led the trend in fashion, and the influence of their styles reached even to the ladies of the shōgun's palace. A few of the girls of the highest rank attained a position of considerable independence. They would not bestow their favors lightly, but demanded a long and expensive courtship." (See Donald H. Shively, *The Love Suicide at Amijima* [Cambridge: Harvard University Press, 1953], p. 20 for the elaborate hierarchy of ranks within this earthly paradise.) Midori's older sister in "Child's Play" is such a woman. The heyday of the Yoshiwara was long past by the time of this story, but much of the rich tradition of the demimonde still endured.

Even in the golden age, however, for every courtesan of the first water many a more affordable girl sat in a cage at the front of the shop. Poor relations indentured young women into the profession, and one suspects that the tawdry side of the Yoshiwara increased as the quarter entered the modern day. (It was moribund long before postwar reforms outlawed prostitution.) But this demimonde had produced a culture and an etiquette all its own. And looming as it did on the hill just beyond the neighborhood that Ichiyō chooses for the setting of this story, the pleasure quarter became a symbol of escape, success, and even happiness to those who led more workaday, prosaic lives.

2 The opening sentences of "Child's Play" are replete with puns, as, indeed, is much of the story. The first clause reads "*Mawareba Ōmon no mikaeri yanagi ito nagakeredo.*" In this and subsequent quotations the italicized words are *engo* (related words) or *kakekotoba* (pivot words). "Mikaeri" has both the meaning of "looking back [when one leaves the main gate of the Yoshiwara]" and at the same time is part of the proper noun "mikaeri yanagi," the name of the willow tree that stood outside the front gate. "Ito" also has a double meaning. It is the adverb "very," modifying "nagakeredo" (long, but . . .) and the noun "thread," used in poetic diction to mean the slender branches of the willow tree. The "nagai" in "nagakeredo," then, means (1) it is quite a long way round to the front gate, and (2) the branches of the willow tree are very long. In English, it has been necessary to break what was one clause in the original into two in order to convey the multiple meanings. Such is frequently the case with Ichiyō.

Regarding the last two clauses of the opening sentence (". . . and the bawdyhouse lights flicker in the moat, dark as the dye that blackens the smiles of the Yoshiwara beauties"), the original reads, "*Ohaguro dobu* ni tomoshibi utsuru. . . ." "Ohaguro dobu" is a proper noun and a pun evoking the faces of the women in the Yoshiwara. Literally it means "the Tooth-Dye Ditch," which was named after the dye (ohaguro) the courtesans used to stain their teeth jet black. The ditch was originally a wide moat surrounding the quarter to prevent the escape of any courtesans, many of whom were more or less sold into the profession. Custom has it that the waters of the ditch had been sullied by the ladies' habit of tossing their dyes over the wall into the water. By Meiji times, the handsome moat had shriveled up into a putrid little trench some three feet wide.

Lest it seem that this first sentence has been unnecessarily expanded in translation, it should be pointed out that in Ichiyō's original, one clause flows into another (the entire first chapter has only one period at the very end), and, if certain puns are more compact in the Japanese, the stately, fluid cadence of the original is nonetheless not so very different from that attempted here.

3 In contrast to the sorry sight beyond the confines of the quarter, the three-story buildings within suggest, for their day (ca. 1895), great opulence. Aside from hotels and government buildings in the Western manner located in central Tokyo, structures of more than two stories would still have been rare. And certainly the humble dwellings outside the quarter, as described below, would never have risen to the lofty height of three floors. The brothels, with their electric lights and gaiety and their sheer height, were imposing edifices to the townsmen who lived on the other side of the ditch.

4 The charms were shaped like *kumade* (bear's paws), or bamboo rakes, usually with five

prongs. On this rake various trinkets were arrayed in a wreath. In the center was a child's smiling face of good fortune and around the edges were a *tai* (sea bream), the symbol of prosperity, pine boughs, also a sign of well-being, and a number of slogans invoking success and good luck. It was thought that the larger the charm, the more efficacious. Petty merchants and members of the demimonde were particularly superstitious, so there was a brisk trade in these charms on the fringes of the pleasure quarter.

5 There were two or three Otori days each November, when fairs were held at the various Otori shrines in Shinjuku, Shinagawa, Yoshiwara, and so on. The largest of the shrines was the one just outside the Yoshiwara, in Ryūsenji, the setting of this story. On fair days the side gates to the pleasure quarter were thrown open and women and children were allowed in to see the sights. "Otori" was written with the character for "bird," the tenth sign of the zodiac, under which the Otori days always fell. Through a pun on the character for "take," a homonym, Otori day became the day for "taking" good luck; hence the sale of kumade charms.

6 An example of Ichiyō's allusive and elliptical style. The original reads, "Jūnin-giri no soba zue." This is a reference to the kabuki play *Kagotsurube Sato no Eizame* (The Pleasure Zone, a Sharp Sword, and the Morning After, 1889) wherein a man spurned by a prostitute he loves cuts down not only the woman but other members of her establishment as well. The play was by Kawatake Shinshichi III (1842-1901).

7 To convey the puns involved here has required some expansion of Ichiyō's compact clause: "Shindai *tataki*-bone ni nareba futatabi *furusu* e no kamisama sugata."

8 "Aki wa kugatsu, Niwaka no koro no ōji o mitamae." *Niwaka* was the Yoshiwara's September festival. The word originally meant "impromptu," and the celebration, consisting at first of simple pantomimes, dates from the Edo period. The name is an abbreviation of *niwaka kyōgen*, an entertainment said to have originated in the years 1716-36 at the summer festival of Sumiyoshi Shrine in Ōsaka, where amateurs took turns performing improvised comic skits (later performed by professional comedians, ca. 1789-1801). These niwaka kyōgen inspired carnivals in the Shimabara and Gion pleasure quarters of Kyōto, which, in turn, inspired the Yoshiwara festival. There were actually two Niwaka festivals in the Yoshiwara, each lasting several days: one at the beginning of September and one at the end. Both geisha and *hōkan* (male jesters) would dance through the streets of the quarter, making the rounds of the teahouses and the brothels whose patronage they had enjoyed during the year. For several days, the Yoshiwara took on even more color than usual. Lanterns shaped like morning-glories were hung before the houses. At seven o'clock each night, festival floats (*yatai*) would begin to parade down the main street, the Nakanochō, each float fitted with a stage upon which the geisha and hōkan performed their comedies and "lion dances" (*shishimai*). These floats were approximately eighteen square feet in area and were decorated with backdrops painted on paper and silk and illuminated by a cluster of lanterns. Needless to say, geisha went to considerable expense to outdo each other in their dress; their costumes for the carnival were perhaps the gaudiest of the year. The Niwaka festival was at its most rococo from the end of the Edo period through the early Meiji. In 1897, the year after "Child's Play" was published, the festival suddenly fell into decline.

9 The mother of Mencius (Meng-tzu or Meng K'e), the Chinese philosopher (ca. 372-289 B.C.). Tradition has it that Mencius's mother was what today's Japanese would call a *kyōiku mama*, or "education mom":

> The mother of Meng K'e of Tsou was known as Mother Meng. Her house was near a graveyard, and the boy Mencius played at grave-digging and was most energetic at building and interring. "This is no place for my child," said Mother Meng, so she moved to live next to the market. Mencius played he was a hawker hawking his goods. Once more Mother Meng said, "This is no place for my child." Once again she moved to live near a school. Mencius played at sacrificial and ceremonial rituals. "This is truly a place

for my son," said Mother Meng and she settled there. When Mencius became a man, he studied the six arts and became known as a great Confucianist. In the opinion of the gentleman, Mother Meng knew the method of gradual transformation. [From the *Lieh Nü Chuan*, cited in D. C. Lau, trans., *Mencius* (Harmondsworth, England: Penguin Books, 1970), pp. 215–16]

10 Rohachi and Eiki were well-known mimics of the time. These jesters, or hōkan, as they were called, were comic male counterparts to the geisha.

11 In the Meiji period, when the government devoted a good deal of attention to developing a modern public secondary school system, it was the public school that was usually superior to the private. The latter suggested the old-fashioned temple schools. The implication is that the Ikueisha is an overcrowded, second-rate school for a down-at-the-heels neighborhood, a point that will have significance later in the story.

12 Names are sometimes a problem in "Child's Play." Here Nobuyuki is introduced to us as Shinnyo (the *on* reading of the characters used to write his name), although afterward he is usually referred to as Nobuyuki or, less formally, Nobu. For the sake of clarity, the more common name is anticipated here. With other names, too, I have imposed a consistency that is not always in the original.

13 Note that in citing his age, Ichiyō already suggests the contrast between Nobu and the others—the precocious fifteen-year-olds mentioned earlier, who affect the swagger and the latest songs of the visitors to the quarter. Nobu, on the contrary, is a true naif.

14 On the distinction between public and private schools see note 11 above.

15 "Chaban," from *chaban kyōgen*, were improvised pantomimes or comic skits. The term is also one of depreciation, to mean "a farce," "a waste of time."

16 The "red bear" (*shaguma*) was a popular hair style that had originated in the demimonde and spread in the 1890s to young women of the upper classes. It was a somewhat flamboyant hairdo, with a grand chignon and flowered hairpins, but it became quite the thing for fashionable schoolgirls.

17 Actually, a multicolored *obi* (sash), for everyday wear (among girls of the shitamachi, or the downtown), sewn half of black satin, half of another fabric, here probably cotton. It was considered very much in vogue at this time. The placement of the obi has significance. Decorous young ladies wore their sashes high up on the waist. As a married woman grew older, her obi moved down the waist. Geisha and courtesans wore their obi low and often tied in front; in contrast, the proper matron, as alluded to in chapter 1, would be expected to wear her sash fastened neatly behind her waist.

18 Present-day Wakayama Prefecture.

19 *Yarite* and *shinzō*. The yarite was the overseer of the brothel, the madam, as it were. The shinzō were assistants to the yarite and attendants to the courtesans, who were usually known in this period as *ane-jorō*, *oiran*, or *yūjo*. The full life cycle of a woman in the Yoshiwara would be: *kamuro* (handmaiden, ages five, six, or seven to thirteen), shinzō (apprentice, thirteen to late teens), oiran (courtesan, usually in her twenties), yarite (madam, in her middle age).

20 A typical example of Ichiyō's punning language: "Mi kiku wa sami ni taiko ni *ake*murasaki no nari katachi" (What she saw and heard were the sound of samisen and drum and the patterns [of robes] in dusk-red and purple). *Ake* is a pivot word, meaning both "at dusk" and "red."

21 This clause and the next are joined by a pun, or kakekotoba, on the word for "jasmine": *kuchinashi*. The "kuchi" of *kuchinashi* is also the word for mouth, which is modified by "kozo yori wa yokaranu kata to tsubuyaku mo arishi." Thus, "[There were] also mouths that muttered, '[This year's outfits] are not as nice as last year's.' "

22 Actually, he makes a pun on the name of a character in the kabuki play *Kagotsurube Sato no Eizame* (see note 6 above). He says, "Otto kita Sano Jirozaemon, ima no ma," or "I'll be

back before you know it (otto kita sa), like Sanno Jirozaemon," who flees over rooftops after cutting down the woman who has jilted him.

23 Idaten, the swift-footed heavenly warrior, who in legend pursued Ragetsu when he tried to make off with the Buddha's ashes. The disciples were too shocked to stop Ragetsu, but Idaten bounded after the demon and managed to retrieve the precious relics. The incident forms the theme of the nō play *Shari* (The Relics of the Buddha), attributed to Zeami Motokiyo (1363–1443). In art, Idaten is usually depicted in the uniform of a Chinese general, his hands resting on an impressive weapon. From the seventh century on, Idaten became a popular deity in Japan (as in China), albeit a subsidiary one. He was thought to guard the Buddhist law and to watch over the discipline and conduct of the monasteries.

24 "Naishō no kuruma wa shōbai mono no hoka nareba sen-naku." The sentence contains a play on "kuruma," alluding to "hi no kuruma" and the saying "Naishō wa hi no kuruma desu" (One finds oneself in straitened circumstances). Explicitly, the sentence says, "As the rickshaw he pulled to earn his living was different from those of professionals, there was no help for it." But implicitly, by suggesting the pun on "hi no kuruma," the sentence also implies, "And therefore the earnings from the rickshaw only kept the family going hand-to-mouth." The translation I have given is a good example of how an English rendering inevitably becomes wordier than Ichiyō's compact and elliptical original.

25 Mannenchō was a slum to the southwest of the Yoshiwara and Ryūsenji area. The floats in the Yoshiwara festival were usually pulled by men from this section, which was home for many of the jesters and street performers who worked the quarter. Troupes of entertainers from Mannenchō appear in chapter 8.

26 Ichiyō alludes to a popular song. She gives us a snippet ("Matsu mi ni tsuraki yowa no okigotatsu"), which Wada Yoshie identifies as part of the following song:

> Waga mono to omoeba karoki kasa no yuki
> Koi no omoni o kata ni kake
> Imogari yukeba fuyu no yoru no
> Kawa kaze samuku chidori naku
> Matsu mi ni tsuraki okigotatsu
> Hon ni yaruse ga nai wai na.

> The snow falls upon my frail umbrella,
> The burden of love weighs heavy on my shoulders;
> On a winter's night, I make my way to where my
>   lover dwells.
> The plover cries in the cold of the wind and
>   the river.
> And she who waits alone for me beside the hearth—
> How sad and helpless she must feel!

27 Ichiyō heard this song while she was living in Ryūsenji and recorded it in her diary entry for 14 November 1893. The full song as we have it is as follows (note the italicized words and the similarity to Ichiyō's opening lines in chapter 1):

> Hokkaku *zensei* miwataseba
> Noki wa *chōchin denkitō*
> Itsu mo nigiwau go-chō machi
> Mukashi ni kawaranu betsu sekai
> Haru wa sakura o uenarabe
> Aki wa tōrō ni hatsu-niwaka
> *Mainichi maiban kyaku no yama*
> Nichiyō hatabi wa nao no koto

Samisen taiko no taema-naku
Shan-shan-shan no te o soroi
Kore mo benkyō suru ga tame
Benkyō suru no mo sato no tame
Zensei ja ja, yukai ja ja
Banzai, banzai, ban-banzai.

Come see the thriving northern quarter—
The lights, the lanterns under every eave,
The gaiety of all five streets!
A world apart, unchanged from ages past:
In spring, the branches of the cherries are lined up in a row,
In autumn, the first of the festivals is lit with paper lanterns;
Day and night, a mountain of visitors,
Sundays and holidays, the usual throngs.
Incessant is the sound of samisen and drum,
Shan, shan, shan—
It makes a man step lively,
And the quarter reaps rewards.
To joy and to good fortune,
Cheer after cheer after cheer!

28   Tarō-sama was the god enshrined at Tarō Inari Jinja, in Shitaya. The shrine was especially popular during the Edo period.

29   *Uma no hi*, fair days associated with the Inari shrines. Merchants would set up stalls along the main thoroughfares, offering toys, snacks, and the flowers and produce of the season. Goldfish and other pets were also sold, to the delight of children.

30   "Daikoku" was a euphemism for the wife, or mistress, of a Buddhist priest, who until the Meiji period was expected, by law if not by custom, to be celibate. The sobriquet derived sarcastically from Daikoku, one of the seven gods of good fortune (*shichi fukujin*) and the patron saint of family hearth and pocketbook. (For the shichi fukujin, see note 16 to "On the Last Day of the Year.") Nobu's tormentors are also playing on the name of the brothel where Midori's sister is employed, the Daikokuya, itself no doubt named for the god of prosperity, who was a favorite deity among merchants of the downtown. In art, Daikoku was usually depicted holding the hammer of wealth and a bag of riches, and straddling two hefty sacks of rice.

31   By Po Chü-i (772–846), the T'ang poet. The poem, "Ch'ang Hen Ko" (or "Chōgonka" in Japanese), concerns the immoderate love of the Chinese Emperor Hsüan Tsung (r. 712–756) for his beautiful young consort, Yang Kuei-fei, and the grief into which he is plunged by her death. (The poem exerted considerable influence on the opening chapter of *Genji Monogatari*.) A portion of "Ch'ang Hen Ko" follows, from Cyril Birch, ed., *Anthology of Chinese Literature* (New York: Grove Press, 1965), vol. 1, p. 266.

China's Emperor, craving beauty that might
    shake an empire,
Was on the throne, for many years, searching,
    never finding,
Till a little child of the Yang clan,
    hardly even grown,
Bred in an inner chamber, with no one knowing her,
But with graces granted by heaven
    and not to be concealed,
At last one day was chosen for the imperial household.

If she but turned her head and smiled,
     there were cast a hundred spells,
And the powder and paint of the Six Palaces
     faded into nothing.
....

The cloud of her hair, petal of her cheek,
     gold ripples of her crown when she moved,
Were sheltered on spring evenings by warm
     hibiscus-curtains;
But nights of spring were short
     and the sun rose too soon,
And the Emperor, from that time forth,
     forsook his early hearings
And lavished all his time on her with feasts and
     revelry,
His mistress of the spring, his despot of the night.
....

Her sisters and brothers were all given titles;
And because she so illumined and glorified her clan,
She brought to every father, every mother
     through the empire,
Happiness when a girl was born rather than a boy.

32 *Tsumi-yagu*, the presentation and display of bedding gifts, was a major event in the pleasure quarter. A courtesan's regular patrons were expected to finance new sets of nightgowns and bedding for each of the five holidays (the *go-sekku*): *matsu no uchi* (New Year's week), *momo no sekku* (3 March), *obon* (13–15 July), *higan* (23 September, 21 March), and *tori no ichi* (the Otori days in November, see note 5 above). These gifts were an expensive proposition, and the display of new bedding became, naturally, a demonstration of a courtesan's status within the demimonde. Her completed set was exhibited with great show on a special stand just inside the door to the house, in plain view of every passerby. Those beauties with the most ardent and affluent suitors would brandish the most elaborate tsumi-yagu. In the earlier days of the quarter, the piles of quilts and bedclothes were of fine brocades, but by the time of "Child's Play," damasks and crepes were more common. The practice was generally limited to the best houses, the *ō-mise* and some of the *chū-mise*, although occasionally a woman of a smaller house would attempt to demonstrate her standing with a handsome collection of coverlets. It was apparently not uncommon for a woman between patrons to borrow, if necessary, in order to keep up the pretense of her popularity. It even reached the point where second-hand tsumi-yagu could be rented at exorbitant rates, and perhaps the loud colors of the fabrics detracted from the wear around the edges. Ōmaki, we can be sure, never had to make do with any hand-me-downs.

33 This was a well-known popular song that went: "Out in the deep blue sea the white sails pass: / The tangerine boats from Kinokuni" (Oki no kurai no ni shiraho ga mieru / Are wa Kinokuni mikan-bune). Kinokuni, also written "Kiinokuni," was one of the former provinces, today Wakayama Prefecture.

34 Until 1872, with the exception of those who were members of the sect known as Jōdo Shinshū, Buddhist monks were forbidden to marry or to eat fish (or meat, for that matter). By the time of this story, however, these taboos had been abolished for some twenty years. Therefore the priest of Ryūge Temple was committing no offense against the letter of the law, but the religious practices and attitudes of centuries were slow to die.

35 Tamagiku was a celebrated courtesan whose death in 1726 was mourned each year with a festival of lanterns. The observation, from mid-July to mid-August, became an important attraction in the Yoshiwara. In her diary entry for 3 August 1893, Ichiyō mentions going to

see the lanterns. For similarities between this passage in the story and her entry in the journal, see pp. 93–95.

36 A line from a song dating from the mid-1850s, "Kaori ni Mayou" (Bewildered by the Scent [of Love]). It belonged to the Edo genre of popular music known as *utazawa:* lyric ballads sung to the accompaniment of the samisen. The song went as follows:

> Kaori ni mayou
> Ume ga nokiba ni nioi tori
> Hana ni ōse o matsu toshi no
> Akete ureshiki kesōbumi
> Hiraku hatsune no hazukashiku
> Mada tokekaneru usugōri
> Yuki ni omoi no fuka-gusa no
> Momo yo mo kayou koi no yami
> Kimi ga nasake no karine no toko no
> Makura katashiku yomosugara.

> Bewildered by the scent of plum beneath the eave,
> A thrush begins his tentative announcement of
>   the spring.
> Shyness and joy mingle in his song:
> A lover opening a billet-doux.
> Has it come?
> The time we have waited for to meet among
>   the flowers?
> Thin ice still covers the ground,
> The grasses are deep in snow—
> Deep as my thoughts of love,
> As one hundred nights I journey through darkness,
> To be by your side:
> Where you have spread your sleeve to make
>   a pillow for me,
> Together we shall spend our night of love.

37 "Hiraita hiraita, nan no hana hiraita," from the rhyme that children sang while holding hands in a circle. They would dance back and forth, expanding and shrinking the size of the circle, like a flower, now blooming, now wilting. The song went:

> Hiraita,
> Hiraita.
> Nan no hana hiraita?
> Renge no hana hiraita.
> Hiraita to omottara,
> Itsu no ma ni ka,
> (Yattoko-sa to)
> Tsubonda.

> They blossom
> And bloom—
> But what flowers are they?
> The buds of the lotus!
> We only admire them,
> And then they are gone—
> They fade
> And they wilt.

38   Actually, a game played with snail shells (kishiyago), perhaps more like tiddlywinks.

39   Literally, "Or the *kiyomoto* [songs] of Kii-san?" (Kii-san no kiyomoto ka). Kiyomoto was a narrative samisen genre originating in the Edo period. Aficionados like Nagai Kafū (1879–1959) admired kiyomoto ballads for their frail, plaintive sound and the moods of loneliness and sadness they evoked.

40   The refrain from a popular children's ditty of the Meiji period.

41   This is mentioned to indicate that the house belongs to someone of means. In the early years of the Meiji period, glass windows inset in *shōji* panels were expensive and still relatively rare.

42   The widow of Azechi no Dainagon is the grandmother of Murasaki, who becomes the very favorite of the hero of *Genji Monogatari*. It is the Azechi widow (now a nun) with whom young Murasaki lives when Genji discovers her in chapter 5, "Wakamurasaki," on a night when the nun is at her prayers. As soon as he spies Murasaki, Genji knows that the child will grow up to be the woman of his dreams, and, indeed, she already resembles Fujitsubo, who has heretofore obsessed him (and who turns out to be the young girl's aunt). The equation of Midori with the young Murasaki, and the passing Nobu with the traveling Genji, is an obvious hint on Ichiyō's part at the blossoming, inarticulate love between Nobu and Midori. In addition, the young Murasaki, "at such an uncomfortable age, not quite a child and still without the discernment of an adult" (Seidensticker, *Genji*, p. 103) sounds like the very model for Midori. Both young girls haven't a clue to what the future will bring.

43   Literally, "Over his *yukata* he wore a *tōzan* kimono" (Yukata o kasaneshi tōzan no kimono ni). *Tōzan* was a finely woven, lustrous cotton, usually with a pattern of vertical stripes. It was an expensive fabric favored by men of taste for their visits to the quarter.

44   See note 5 above. Otori days were not consecutive. The number depended on how many days in November fell under the *otori*, or bird, sign of the zodiac.

45   A popular song of the *yakkaibushi* variety.

46   The *shimada* was the fashionable hair style for young, unmarried women and for courtesans. There were many variations, but essentially the larger the chignon, the more youthful or ostentatious. The hairdo, then, is a clear sign that Midori is no longer considered to be a child. The fact that it is a large (here translated as "glorious") shimada suggests Midori's affinity with the demimonde. The style first became popular in the Edo period, in the 1680s, after it was introduced by the women at a teahouse in Shimada, the twenty-fourth station on the Tōkaidō, and it remained a favorite coiffure through the Taishō period (1912–26). Today the shimada is a style reserved for the geisha house and for weddings and other festive occasions.

Separate Ways

1   Narrow sleeves (*tsutsu-sode*), the better to work in.

2   Persimmon tannin was used to treat umbrellas.

3   A kind of carnival game in which arrows were blown through a bamboo tube, with a prize for hitting the target.

4   Literally, "Instead of a carriage, it will probably be a cart of fire that comes." Ichiyō plays with the meaning of "hi no kuruma" to pun on "basha." The fiery cart has two meanings: (1) the carriage that drives sinners through hell, and (2) straitened circumstances. A similar pun may be found in chapter 4 of "Child's Play." (See note 24 to that story.)

5   "Nishiki no mamori-bukuro": paper charms with a child's name written on them were placed inside a brocade bag and carried by the child for good luck and protection. The little charm-bags thus became a means of identification.

6   A song from a game that children played, forming a ring around one of their number and chanting, in part:

Mawari no mawari no kobotoke,
Naze sei ga hikui na?
Oya no hi ni aka no mama kutte toto kutte,
Sore ga sei ga hikui na!

Round and round we go, around the little monk.
Why are you so short?
You ate fish and red rice on the day you should
   have fasted in memory of your parents.
That's why you're so short!

7   An allusion to the puppet play *Katsuragawa Renri no Shigarami* (The River Katsura and the Floodgate of Eternal Love, 1858) by Suga Sensuke. In the play, Chōemon, the head of a draper's shop, is a middle-aged man charged with watching after a fourteen-year-old girl, Ohan, when her father dies; in one scene he carries her across the Katsura River. Here, in an analogy to Kichizō's dependence on Okyō, the roles are reversed: Chōemon rides to safety on Ohan's back.

8   The saying was that great, gawky trees would never make good pillars. Ichiyō alludes to the proverb, "Udo no taiboku hashira ni naranu."

9   This too is based on a proverb: "Sanshō wa kotsubu de mo piriri to karai" (A grain of pepper may be small, but it is very hot).

10 "Koyubi no mamushi," so called because the first joint of the finger would bend, but not the second.

11 Literally, "Honey comes to him who waits" (Mateba kanro).

Bibliography

Several *zenshū*, or complete editions, of the writings of Higuchi Ichiyō have been published since the appearance in 1912 of the two-volume Hakubunkan edition of the collected works, the first true zenshū, which included the first publication of Ichiyō's diaries. I have used the two most recent zenshū: the 1954–56 edition in seven volumes from Chikuma Shobō and the current edition, in five volumes, which began to appear in 1974 and is now nearing completion, also from Chikuma Shobō. In the fall of 1979 yet another complete edition was launched, this one by Shōgakkan, but it has come too late to be of use in this study. The following bibliography consists of a catalog of first editions of Ichiyō's completed stories, a listing of those stories previously available in translation, and a selected bibliography of works consulted.

First Editions

"Yamizakura"
   23 March 1892. *Musashino*, no. 1. Three chapters, seven pages. (Pagination according to 1974 Chikuma Shobō zenshū.)
"Wakarejimo"
   Early April–18 April 1892. *Kaishin Shinbun*. Fifteen chapters, thirty-five pages.
"Tamadasuki"
   17 April 1892. *Musashino*, no. 2. Five chapters, thirteen pages.
"Samidare"
   23 July 1892. *Musashino*, no. 3. Six chapters, sixteen pages.
"Kyōtsukue"
   Seven installments: 18–25 October 1892. *Kōyō Shinpō*. Six chapters, twelve pages.
"Umoregi"
   Three installments: 20 November, 4 December, 18 December 1892. *Miyako no Hana*, nos. 95–97. Ten chapters, twenty-nine pages.
"Aketsukiyo"
   19 February 1893. *Miyako no Hana*, no. 101. Six chapters, twenty-two pages.
"Yuki no Hi"
   31 March 1893. *Bungakkai*, no. 3. Five pages.
"Koto no Ne"
   30 December 1893. *Bungakkai*, no. 12. Two chapters, five pages.
"Hanagomori"
   Two installments: 28 February, 30 April 1894. *Bungakkai*, nos. 14, 16. Seven chapters, twenty pages.

"Yamiyo"
    Three installments: 30 July, 30 September, 30 November 1894. *Bungakkai*, nos. 19,
    21, 23. Twelve chapters, thirty-five pages.
"Ōtsugomori"
    30 December 1894. *Bungakkai*, no. 24. Two chapters, fifteen pages.
"Takekurabe"
    Seven installments: 30 January, 28 February, 30 March, 30 August, 30 November, 30
    December 1895; 30 January 1896. *Bungakkai*, nos. 25, 26, 27, 32, 35, 36, 37. Sixteen
    chapters, forty-five pages.
"Noki Moru Tsuki"
    Two installments: 3, 5 April 1895. *Mainichi Shinbun*. Five pages.
"Yukugumo"
    5 May 1895. *Taiyō*, no. 5. Three chapters, fourteen pages.
"Utsusemi"
    Five installments: 27–31 August 1895. *Yomiuri Shinbun*. Five chapters, thirteen
    pages.
"Nigorie"
    20 September 1895. *Bungei Kurabu*, no. 9. Eight chapters, thirty-one pages.
"Jūsan'ya"
    10 December 1895. *Bungei Kurabu*, no. 12 (special issue on women writers, which
    also included a republication of "Yamiyo"). Three chapters, nineteen pages.
"Kono Ko"
    1 January 1896. *Nihon no Katei*, no. 2. Nine pages.
"Wakare-Michi"
    4 January 1896. *Kokumin no Tomo*, no. 18. Three chapters, ten pages.
"Ware-Kara"
    10 May 1896. *Bungei Kurabu*, no. 6. Thirteen chapters, thirty-six pages.

                              Previous Translations

"Jūsan'ya" (The Thirteenth Night)
    "The Thirteenth Night." Trans. Hisako Tanaka. *Monumenta Nipponica* 16
        (1960–61): 157–74.
    "La tredicesima notte." Trans. Atsuko Ricca Suga. *Narratori Giapponesi Moderni*.
        Milan: Bompiani, 1965.
"Nigorie" (Troubled Waters)
    "Palude mortifera." Trans. Harukichi Shimoi. *Sakura* 5–6 (1920): 123–26.
    "Borongo felhok." Trans. Thein Alfréd. *Mai Japán Dekameron*. Budapest: Nyugat,
        1935.
    "Muddy Bay." Trans. Hisako Tanaka. *Monumenta Nipponica* 14 (1958): 173–204.
    "In the Gutter." Trans. Seizo Nobunaga. *Takekurabe*. Tokyo: Information Publica-
        tions, 1960.
    "V kalném proudu." Trans. Miriam Jelínková. *5 Japonských Novel*. Praha, Czecho-
        slovakia: Odeon, 1969.
    "Trübe Wasser." Trans. Jürgen Berndt. *Träume aus zehn Nächten*. Berlin: Aufbau
        Verlag, 1975.
"Ōtsugomori" (On the Last Day of the Year)

"The Last Day of the Year." Trans. Tei Fujiu. *Hanakatsura.* Tokyo: Ikuseikai, 1903.
"Takekurabe" (Child's Play)
"They Compare Heights." Trans. W. M. Bickerton. *Transactions of the Asiatic Society of Japan* 7 (1930): 131–37.
"Growing Up." Trans. Edward Seidensticker. *Modern Japanese Literature,* edited by Donald Keene. New York: Grove Press, 1956.
"Teenagers Vying for Tops." Trans. Seizo Nobunaga. *Takekurabe.* Tokyo: Information Publications, 1960.
"Die Liebe der kleinen Midori." Trans. Oscar Benl. *Der Kirschblütenzweig.* Munich: Nymphenburger, 1965.
"Wakare-Michi" (Separate Ways)
"The Parting of the Ways." Trans. W. M. Bickerton. *Transactions of the Asiatic Society of Japan* 7 (1930): 120–30.
"Yamizakura" (Flowers at Dusk)
"Kirschblüte in der Dämmerung." Trans. Shigeko Matsuno. *Das Junge Japan* 2 (1925): 73–75, 99–103.

Selected Sources

Aoki, Kazuo. *"Takekurabe" Kenkyū.* Tokyo: Kyōiku Shuppan Sentā, 1973.
Asō, Isoji; Itasaka, Gen; and Tsutsumi, Seiji, eds. *Saikaku Shū,* vol. 1, in Nihon Koten Bungaku Taikei series. Tokyo: Iwanami Shoten, 1959.
Awashima, Kangetsu. "Zatsu." *Waseda Bungaku* (December 1906), pp. 73–76.
Baba, Kochō. *Meiji Bundan no Hitobito.* Tokyo: Mita Bungaku Shuppanbu, 1942.
———. *Meiji no Tokyo.* Tokyo: Marunouchi Shuppan, 1974.
Ebara, Taizō; Teruoka, Yasutaka; and Noma, Kōshin, eds. *Teihon Saikaku Zenshū,* vols. 2, 7, 11. Tokyo: Chūō Kōronsha, 1949–76.
Higuchi, Etsu, ed. *Ichiyō ni Ataeta Tegami.* Tokyo: Konnichi no Mondaisha, 1943.
Imai, Kuniko. *Higuchi Ichiyō.* Tokyo: Manrikaku, 1940.
Ishihara, Setsuko. "Higuchi Ichiyō no Sakuhin ni Arawareta Josei." *Shukutoku Kokubun* (June 1966), pp. 90–115.
Ishimaru, Hisashi. "Higuchi Ichiyō—Meiji no Buntai." *Kokubungaku: Kaishaku to Kanshō* (January 1969), pp. 73–78.
———. "Higuchi Ichiyō to Saikaku." *Kokubungaku: Kaishaku to Kanshō* (March 1973), pp. 122–25.
Ishiyama, Tetsurō. *Higuchi Ichiyō.* Tokyo: Nihon Hyōronsha, 1941.
Itagaki, Naoko. *Meiji, Taishō, Shōwa no Joryū Bungaku.* Tokyo: Ōfūsha, 1967.
Itō, Sei. *Nihon Bundan Shi,* vol. 4. Tokyo: Kōdansha, 1964.
Jimbō, Kazuya. *Tamenaga Shunsui no Kenkyū.* Tokyo: Hakujitsusha, 1964.
Kaishaku Gakkai, ed. *Higuchi Ichiyō no Bungaku.* Tokyo: Kyōiku Shuppan Sentā, 1976.
Keene, Donald. "The Comic Tradition in Renga." In *Japan in the Muromachi Age,* edited by John Whitney Hall and Toyoda Takeshi. Berkeley: University of California Press, 1977.
Kimura, Masayuki. "Ichiyō Bungaku ni Arawareta Joseizō: Toku ni 'Nigorie' ni okeru Kindaiteki Jiga no Mondai." *Kokugo Kokubun Kenkyū* (February 1967), pp. 50–62.

————. "Ichiyō Bungaku ni okeru Kindaiteki Jiga no Mondai: 'Nigorie,' 'Jūsan'ya' o Chūshin ni." *Sapporo Daigaku Kiyō Kyōyōbu Ronshū—Kaigaku Kinen Gō* (March 1968), pp. 191–218.

————. *Ichiyō Bungaku Seiritsu no Haikei.* Tokyo: Ōfūsha, 1976.

Kōda, Rohan. "'Takekurabe.'" *Chūō Kōron* (June 1907), pp. 44–47.

Konishi, Jin'ichi. *Sōgi.* Tokyo: Chikuma Shobō, 1971.

Lane, Richard Douglas. "Saikaku: Novelist of the Japanese Renaissance." Ph.D. dissertation, Columbia University, 1957.

Leutner, Robert, trans. "Saikaku's Parting Gift." *Monumenta Nipponica* 30 (1975): 357–91.

Maeda, Ai. "'Nigorie' no Oriki." *Kokubungaku* (October 1969), pp. 142–43.

Masamune, Hakuchō. "Ichiyō to Rohan." In *Bundan Jinbutsu Hyōron.* Tokyo: Chūō Kōronsha, 1932.

Matsuzaka, Toshio. *Higuchi Ichiyō Kenkyū.* Tokyo: Kyōiku Shuppan Sentā, 1976.

Mori, Ōgai; Kōda, Rohan; and Saitō, Ryokuu. "Sannin Jōgo." *Mezamashigusa* (April 1896), pp. 35–49.

Munemasa, Isoo. *Saikaku no Kenkyū.* Tokyo: Miraisha, 1969.

Munemasa, Isoo; Matsuda, Osamu; and Teruoka, Yasutaka, eds. *Ihara Saikaku Shū,* vol. 2, in Nihon Koten Bungaku Zenshū series. Tokyo: Shōgakkan, 1973.

Muramatsu, Teikō. *Hyōden Higuchi Ichiyō, Sakuhin to Sakka Kenkyū.* Tokyo: Jitsugyō no Nihonsha, 1967.

Nagai, Kafū. "Sato no Konjaku." In *Fuyu no Hae, Kafū Zenshū,* vol. 17. Tokyo: Iwanami Shoten, 1964.

Nakamura, Yukihiko. *Gesaku Ron.* Tokyo: Kadokawa Shoten, 1966.

————. *Kinsei Shōsetsushi no Kenkyū.* Tokyo: Ōfūsha, 1973.

————, ed. *Shunshoku Umegoyomi,* in Nihon Koten Bungaku Taikei series. Tokyo: Iwanami Shoten, 1962.

Nakarai, Tōsui. "Ichiyō Joshi." *Chūō Kōron* (June 1907), pp. 36–41.

Nishida, Taketoshi. *Meiji Jidai no Shinbun to Zasshi.* Tokyo: Shibundō, 1961.

Nishio, Yoshihito. *Zenshaku Ichiyō Nikki,* vol. 1. Tokyo: Hakuteisha, 1973.

————. *Zenshaku Ichiyō Nikki,* vols. 2–3. Tokyo: Ōfūsha, 1976.

Noda, Hisao. *Kinsei Shōsetsushi Ronkō.* Tokyo: Hanawa Shobō, 1961.

Noma, Kōshin. *Saikaku Ronsō.* Tokyo: Chūō Kōronsha, 1975.

————, ed. *Saikaku Shū,* vol. 2, in Nihon Koten Bungaku Taikei series. Tokyo: Iwanami Shoten, 1960.

Oka, Yasuo. "Saikaku to Meiji Ni-jū Nendai no Bungaku—Kōyō, Rohan, Ichiyō Nado o Chūshin ni." *Kokubungaku* (May 1965), pp. 43–48.

Okano, Takao. *Shuppan Bunkashi.* Tokyo: Muromachi Shobō, 1954.

Okitsu, Kaname. *Meiji Kaikaki Bungaku no Kenkyū.* Tokyo: Ōfūsha, 1968.

————. *Saigo no Edo Gesakushatachi.* Tokyo: Jitsugyō no Nihonsha, 1976.

————. *Tenkanki no Bungaku: Edo kara Meiji e.* Tokyo: Waseda Daigaku Shuppanbu, 1960.

Saitō, Ryokuu. "Kongōso." *Mezamashigusa* (January 1896), pp. 1–12.

Sargent, G. W., trans. *The Japanese Family Storehouse.* Cambridge: Cambridge University Press, 1959.

Sasabuchi, Tomoichi. *Bungakkai to Sono Jidai,* vols. 1–2. Tokyo: Meiji Shoin, 1959–60.

Seki, Ryōichi. "Higuchi Ichiyō." *Kokubungaku* (February 1969), pp. 86–87.

———. *Higuchi Ichiyō: Kōshō to Shiron*. Tokyo: Yūseidō, 1974.
———. "Ichiyō Nikki no Himitsu." *Kokubungaku* (August 1964), pp. 20-27.
———. "'Takekurabe' no Shukō," part 1. *Kaishaku* (May 1970), pp. 83-89.
———. "'Takekurabe' no Shukō," part 2. *Kaishaku* (July 1970), pp. 48-54.
Shimazaki, Tōson. "Ichiyō Joshi ni Tsuite." *Chūō Kōron* (June 1907), pp. 43-44.
Shioda, Ryōhei. *Higuchi Ichiyō*. Tokyo: Yoshikawa Kōbunkan, 1972.
———. *Higuchi Ichiyō Kenkyū*. Tokyo: Chūō Kōronsha, 1975.
———. *Meiji Joryū Sakka Ron*. Tokyo: Neiraku Shobō, 1965.
Shioda, Ryōhei, and Wada, Yoshie, eds. *Ichiyō Zenshū*, vols. 1-7. Tokyo: Chikuma Shobō, 1954-56.
Shioda, Ryōhei; Wada, Yoshie; and Higuchi, Etsu, eds. *Higuchi Ichiyō Zenshū*, vols. 1-5. Vol. 4 (poetry, letters) and vol. 5 (bibliography), forthcoming. Tokyo: Chikuma Shobō, 1974-.
Sōma, Gyofū; Wada, Yoshie; and Seki, Ryōichi, eds. *Higuchi Ichiyō, Meiji Joryū Bungaku, Izumi Kyōka Shū*, in Gendai Nihon Bungaku Taikei series. Tokyo: Chikuma Shobō, 1974.
Takada, Mitsuho et al. "Higuchi Ichiyō." *Kokubungaku: Kaishaku to Kanshō*, special issue (November 1974).
Takahashi, Toshio. *Saikaku Ronkō*. Tokyo: Kasama Shoin, 1971.
Takita, Teiji. *Saikaku no Shoshigakuteki Kenkyū*. Tokyo: Hakuteisha, 1965.
Tanabe, Natsuko. *Ichiyō no Omoide*. Tokyo: Chōmeikai, 1950.
Taniwaki, Masachika; Jimbō, Kazuya; and Teruoka, Yasutaka, eds. *Ihara Saikaku Shū*, vol. 3, in Nihon Koten Bungaku Zenshū series. Tokyo: Shōgakkan, 1972.
Teruoka, Yasutaka, and Gunji, Masakatsu. *Edo Shimin Bungaku no Kaika*, in Nihon no Bungaku series. Tokyo: Shibundō, 1967.
Teruoka, Yasutaka, and Higashi, Akimasa, eds. *Ihara Saikaku Shū*, vol. 1, in Nihon Koten Bungaku Zenshū series. Tokyo: Shōgakkan, 1971.
Tsukada, Mitsue. *Gokai to Henken: Higuchi Ichiyō no Bungaku*. Tokyo: Sōbunsha, 1967.
———. "Ichiyō to Sono Chichi." *Joshidai Kokubun* (November 1967), pp. 83-94.
Ueshima, Kintarō. *Higuchi Ichiyō to Sono Shūhen*. Tokyo: Kasama Shoin, 1969.
Wada, Yoshie. *Higuchi Ichiyō*. Tokyo: Jūjiya Shoten, 1941.
———. *Higuchi Ichiyō*. Tokyo: Kōdansha, 1974.
———. "Higuchi Ichiyō no Bungaku." *Kokubungaku* (December 1965), pp. 67-71.
———. *Higuchi Ichiyō no Hito to Sakuhin*. Tokyo: Gakushū Kenkyūsha, 1964.
———. *Higuchi Ichiyō no Nikki*. Tokyo: Kigansha, 1943.
———. *Higuchi Ichiyō Shū*, in Nihon Kindai Bungaku Taikei series. Tokyo: Kadokawa Shoten, 1970.
———. *Ichiyō no Nikki*. Tokyo: Chikuma Shobō, 1956.
———. *Ichiyō Tanjō*. Tokyo: Gendai Shokan, 1969.
Yamamoto, Fumio. *Nihon Shinbunshi*. Tokyo: Kokusai Shuppan, 1948.
Yamane, Kenkichi. *Higuchi Ichiyō no Bungaku*. Tokyo: Ōfūsha, 1976.
Yoshida, Seiichi. *Higuchi Ichiyō Kenkyū*. Tokyo: Shinchōsha, 1956.
Yoshida, Seiichi et al. "Rōmanshugi Bungaku no Sōgō Tankyū." *Kokubungaku*, special issue (August 1958).
Yoshie, Hisaya. *Saikaku Bungaku Kenkyū*. Tokyo: Kasama Shoin, 1974.
Yuchi, Takashi. *Higuchi Ichiyō Ron*. Tokyo: Shibundō, 1926.

Index